THIS REMOTE PART *of the* WORLD

The Carolina Lowcountry and the Atlantic World

Sponsored by the Lowcountry and Atlantic Studies Program
of the College of Charleston

Money, Trade, and Power
Edited by Jack P. Greene, Rosemary Brana-Shute, and Randy J. Sparks

The Impact of the Haitian Revolution in the Atlantic World
Edited by David P. Geggus

London Booksellers and American Customers
James Raven

Memory and Identity
Edited by Bertrand Van Ruymbeke and Randy J. Sparks

This Remote Part of the World
Bradford J. Wood

The Final Victims
James A. McMillin

THIS REMOTE PART *of the* WORLD

Regional Formation in Lower Cape Fear, North Carolina, 1725–1775

BRADFORD J. WOOD

University of South Carolina Press

Published in Columbia, South Carolina, by the
University of South Carolina Press

Manufactured in the United States of America

08 07 06 05 04 5 4 3 2 1

Library of Congress Cataloging-in-Publication Data

Wood, Bradford J., 1970–
This remote part of the world : regional formation in Lower Cape Fear, North Carolina, 1725–1775 / Bradford J. Wood.
p. cm. — (The Carolina lowcountry and the Atlantic world)
Includes bibliographical references and index.
ISBN 1-57003-540-7 (cloth : alk. paper)
1. Fear, Cape, Region (N.C.)—History—18th century. 2. Fear, Cape, Region (N.C.)—Social conditions—18th century. 3. Frontier and pioneer life—North Carolina—Fear, Cape, Region. 4. Regionalism—North Carolina—Fear, Cape, Region—History—18th century. 5. Land settlement—North Carolina—Fear, Cape, Region—History—18th century. 6. Human geography—North Carolina—Fear, Cape, Region—History—18th century. I. Title. II. Series.
F262.B9W66 2004
975.6'29—dc22

2004000832

To Susan, to my mother,
and to the memory of my father

CONTENTS

ILLUSTRATIONS

Figures

Tables

ACKNOWLEDGMENTS

Like most scholarly projects, this book was made possible by other people who provided constant support and encouragement. My first and foremost scholarly debt is to Jack P. Greene. Jack has always given me wise advice and loyal support, and he was especially giving of his time between 1996 and 1999 when he supervised my doctoral dissertation. He also continues to offer other historians an inspiring model through his own exemplary scholarship. Michael P. Johnson also provided great insight and encouragement while I was working on my dissertation. I feel truly fortunate to have worked with both Jack and Mike. Christine M. Daniels gave me a rigorous and thought-provoking introduction to early American history during my Master's program at Michigan State. The collective members of the Colonial British American History Research Seminar at Johns Hopkins also offered many useful suggestions and provided me with a wonderful group of peers and friends.

I received financial support from The Johns Hopkins University throughout my doctoral research on this project. My funding from Hopkins took the form of research and teaching fellowships, a summer Southern history research grant, and a Carrie M. Kurrelmeyer Award. I also received an Archie K. Davis Fellowship from the North Caroliniana Society, research travel money from Knox College, a Jacob M. Price Fellowship from the William L. Clements Library at the University of Michigan, and various forms of financial and professional support from Eastern Kentucky University.

While conducting research for this project, I relied on the assistance of many archivists and librarians. I thank the Eisenhower Library at Johns Hopkins, the Michigan State University Library, the Seymour Library at Knox College, the Crabbe Library at Eastern Kentucky University, the Library of Congress, the Southern Historical and the North Carolina Collections at the University of North Carolina, the Perkins Library at Duke University, the Massachusetts Historical Society, the Clements Library at the University of Michigan, the South Carolina State Archives, and the South Carolina Historical Society. The North Carolina State Archives put forth an especially courteous and professional effort to help meet my persistent requests for assistance.

Countless others generously shared their ideas. At the 1998 Charles M. Andrews Symposium at Johns Hopkins, I was able to reconsider some important points because I received thoughtful and constructive feedback from a number of scholars. Two weeks at the Harvard International Seminar in the History of the Atlantic World during the summer of 2002 provided me with a remarkably stimulating intellectual environment to help me consider the context of this project. Opportunities to present papers to the North Carolina Research

Triangle Early American History Seminar and the Historical Society of North Carolina proved helpful for working out various ideas. Other aspects of this project have been presented to the annual conferences of the Omohundro Institute of Early American History and Culture and the American Society for Eighteenth-Century Studies. The Kentucky-Area Early American History Seminar has also provided me with a forum for my work on two occasions.

Other scholars helped me in various ways since I began this project. A handful of generous and helpful individuals read part or all of the entire manuscript at one stage or another. Robert Olwell, Don Higginbotham, Bob Calhoon, Jeff Crow, Alan D. Watson, and Peter Onuf read parts of the manuscript and offered especially helpful comments. A. J. R. Russell-Wood and John Marshall supervised graduate school fields that proved valuable in a variety of ways. Robert Cain, Ken Robinson, and H. G. Jones, made some useful suggestions regarding North Carolina history.

Graduate school friends also did much to make my work easier. Ellen Pearson read drafts of every chapter, and, with Mike Pearson, behaved with characteristic kindness on many occasions as I rented a room in their house for several months. Jeff McClurken offered his friendly company many times when we were both bleary-eyed from reading. Michelle Lemaster contributed quiet encouragement and a steady stream of e-mail. Other helpful peers, relatives, and friends who assisted me in various ways over the years include Amy Hay, Dave Burke, Paul Hronec, Jerry and Terry Wellman, John and Norma Wood, and Bruce Wood.

Eastern Kentucky University provided me with a welcoming and collegial environment for the last few years of work on this book. A special thanks goes to Thomas H. Appleton, who lent his keen proofreading eye to every chapter and still found kind things to say. Other members of the History Department faculty and staff encouraged and aided this project in various ways. As department chair, Ron Huch tried to make it as easy as possible for me to be both a teacher and a scholar.

I also want to express my gratitude to those who have made the actual publication of this book possible. The Program in the Carolina Lowcountry and the Atlantic World at the College of Charleston gave me a Hines Publication Prize, and Randy Sparks gave me advice about handling the publication process. Alex Moore at the University of South Carolina Press has been an invaluable resource. Several anonymous readers gave constructive feedback. The *North Carolina Historical Review* gave permission to use material in Chapter Five that they had already published, and the Johns Hopkins University Press also allowed me to include parts of Chapters Two, Three, and Four that will be in a forthcoming collection of essays. Assistance and permission for the use of illustrations and other copyrighted material came from the North Carolina Collection at the University of North Carolina Chapel Hill, the University of North Carolina

Press, the South Caroliniana Library, the North Carolina State Department of Archives and History, the Massachusetts Historical Society, the British Museum Library, and the British Public Records Office.

Anything that I have accomplished has been made possible by family members. My wife's parents, Bill and Donna Kroeg, have helped both of us through this project in a variety of ways. Stephanie Mullen and Chris Wood, along with their spouses Patrick Mullen and Karen Wood, have helped me in innumerable ways through the years. My parents, Roger and Jane Wood, did seemingly everything conceivable for their children, and, without their inspiration, I doubt that I could have ever imagined receiving a doctoral degree and pursuing an academic career. I regret that my father did not live to see this book published, but his influence and support is evident to me on every page.

My final and greatest thanks goes to Susan Kroeg. When I met Susan almost ten years ago, I scarcely knew where the Cape Fear River was. Only I can fully appreciate how much she has contributed to this book and to my own happiness, but I hope readers will understand that this is partly her book too.

A NOTE ON METHODOLOGY

This book relies on an unusual approach to its sources. Most of the empirical basis for this study derives from two computer databases. Because more traditional textual sources were scarce, records from various kinds of local records were linked together in databases to create detailed profiles of the inhabitants of the colonial Lower Cape Fear. After this step had been completed, an effort was made to integrate and compare the findings from this record linkage with the extant contemporary writings and, in doing so, to construct a fuller history of the region.

First of all the data was entered into a computer database. Separate fields were created to store all the pertinent information, such as date, type of activity, or descriptive phrases, from various sources, and the entries were organized to correspond with references to individuals in the records. These references exceeded 29,000 entries and included the following: over 5,000 appearances in county court minutes, over 250 wills, over 2,700 real estate conveyances, over 1,400 land patents, over 1,300 names in port records, six complete and one partial tax list, lists of officeholders, over 1,700 civil suits in county court dockets, church records, over 800 appearances in the Wilmington town records, two militia lists, sheriff's bonds, safety committee minutes, and miscellaneous sources. Almost all references to individuals in these sources were included in the database with the significant exception of those who witnessed documents. Witnesses were excluded because their presence revealed little about the transaction and their inclusion would have required a substantially greater investment of time and resources. A more detailed listing of primary sources can be found in the bibliography and, where appropriate, within the notes.

Once the data had been entered, the computer sorted the references alphabetically by names, consolidating the data for each individual. Then a second database was set up incorporating all the references into biographical files for every individual mentioned. Over 5,000 names were identified. In some cases it was difficult to differentiate between individuals with the same name and such individuals were probably conflated in some places, but the data usually provided enough information to make a reliable decision. The data in this biographical database was then utilized to produce much of the information used in the text and in the many tables in this book.

This methodology requires a slightly unorthodox method of citation as well. The scope and complexity of information derived from the databases makes references to individual sources and page numbers wholly impractical. As a consequence, when data comes from the databases, citations refer merely to "Lower Cape Fear computer biographical files." When information has been derived from the databases in an unusual or potentially confusing manner, every effort has been made to explain those procedures in the text or in notes.

The Lower Cape Fear computer biographical files, like all sources used by historians, have their strengths and weaknesses. The strengths of this methodology should be evident in the following pages, as database files make it possible to describe and understand eighteenth-century Lower Cape Fear society and culture more fully than would be possible in any other way. Some readers might feel that at times numbers are allowed to do too much of the talking, but they provide a welcome alternative approach for studying the lives of thousands of people who have been otherwise silenced. A few words of caution should still be offered about the limitations of the Lower Cape Fear computer biographical files. Because these files have been constructed from surviving local records, they share the same biases as those records. Some elite individuals appear in the records over two hundred times, many people appear only once, and most slaves and women make no appearance in the records at all. By describing those who do appear in the surviving records, it becomes possible to learn more about the roles of everyone in the Lower Cape Fear, but obvious gaps remain.

Other limitations also exist because the kinds of records that survive are not as complete or representative as one would like. Consequently, readers should be aware that while this study often makes use of numbers, a certain amount of imprecision is still inevitable. It is impossible to know how many settlers had the same name, how many mistakes county clerks made in their records, or how many important documents were destroyed by over two centuries of accidents. The surviving colonial records of New Hanover and Brunswick counties appear surprisingly complete for eighteenth-century North Carolina and provide enough evidence to carry much of the interpretive weight of this study. At the same time, because of the limitations of surviving records, I have generally refrained from using more advanced techniques of statistical analysis that depend upon a more carefully controlled selection of data. In other words, I have only used quantitative approaches that I believed would work reasonably well with the source materials. In many cases the numbers reveal important general trends while some interesting details remain vague or elusive. While constructing databases and tables and throughout my work on this book, I have tried to maintain a careful negotiation between the Lower Cape Fear that exists now in records for historians to study, read, and analyze, and the Lower Cape Fear that existed once but can now only be imagined.

THIS REMOTE PART *of the* WORLD

INTRODUCTION

"This Remote Part of the World"; or, Life inside the Boundary House

In 1774, government authorities in London sent Hugh Finlay to tour the British colonies in North America and assess the status of roads and other routes used for postal deliveries. Finlay's journey took him to many obscure locales and across much rugged, sparsely populated terrain on the margins of the colonial American world, and he recorded his travails in a journal.[1] As Finlay traveled north from Charles Town, South Carolina, he stopped at the Boundary House, which received its name because "the line dividing South [Carolina] from North Carolina runs thro' the middle of it, one half of the hall in one Province and the other half in another."[2] Few eighteenth-century writers mentioned this halfway point between the two Carolinas, but it gradually became noteworthy, not only as a marker of the boundary between two colonies, but also as a stop on the post road.[3] In 1767, North Carolina's governor, William Tryon, who diligently tried to improve the province's postal system, told an official in Charles Town that he had "obtained a promise from several persons settled on the post road to convey the general post to and from Suffolk in Virginia and the Boundary House between the two Carolinas."[4] The forty-two–mile journey from the second-to-last postal stop in North Carolina, at the port town of Brunswick, to the Boundary House must have been a grueling one for many eighteenth-century travelers.[5]

Finlay was the only visitor to explain fully the meaning of the name Boundary House, but he was not the only one to mention the place in his writings. Not surprisingly, the first known record of the Boundary House relates to the surveying of the boundary between the two colonies. The official map of the boundary clearly marks "The little Boundary House."[6] Anglican missionary John Barnett referred to the Boundary House in one of his many reports to his superiors in London: "Nine times in the year I preach at the Boundary House situated on the line between the two Carolinas." As Barnett related, a large congregation met at the Boundary House. When he first preached there, "they were so unacquainted with the Liturgy that I was obliged to make every response myself, but I for many Sundays afterwards spent about half an hour before divine service in explaining every part of the Liturgy." By the time of his letter, in 1767, he had "the pleasure of seeing it as well performed as in most Country Churches."[7] With Barnett's hard work and the growth of the region, the

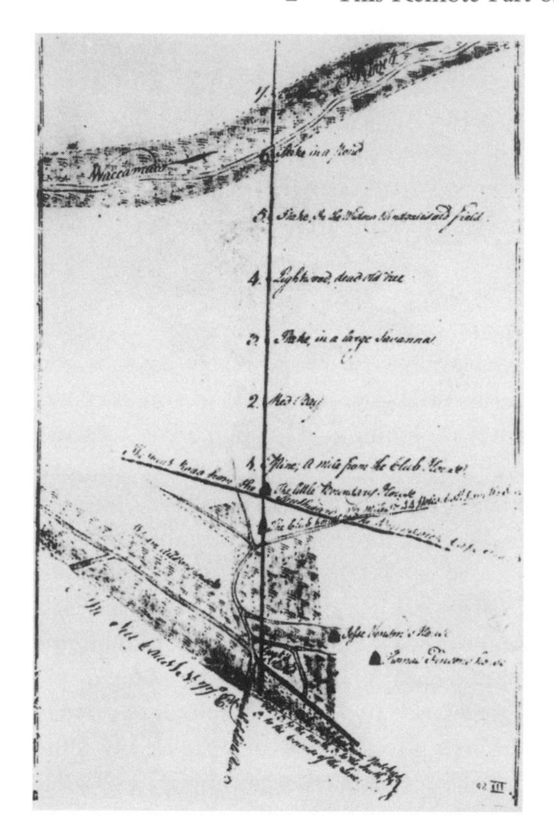

This drawing of the North Carolina–South Carolina boundary marks the location of "The Little Boundary House" near the "Great Road" running from Brunswick into South Carolina. From "A Map of the Division Line between the Province of North and South Carolina containing thirty miles along the Sea Coast from the Mouth of Cape Fear River, and from thence continued on a NW Course for Sixty two miles and one Quarter." Image courtesy of the North Carolina Collection, University of North Carolina Library at Chapel Hill; original in the British National Archives, reference TNA(PRO) CO 700/North Carolina No. 8.

Boundary House, seemingly the most marginal of places, had become a religious center for many people. In 1775, Nicholas Christian, one of Barnett's successors, wrote that he performed religious services at five locations, including "between the North and the South province . . . near thirty miles from the Town of Brunswick where I reside."[8]

The American Revolution brought the Boundary House into surviving records a few more times. In May 1775, news of the Battle of Lexington and Concord spread along the post road through the Carolinas. Cornelius Harnett asked fellow Whig Richard Quince to instruct "the bearer of this news" to "proceed as far as the Boundary House" before forwarding the news to the south "with the greatest possible dispatch."[9] More than a year later, William Hooper, one of North Carolina's delegates to the Continental Congress, mentioned that troops had been stationed at "the Boundary House on the little River" so that they would be conveniently positioned to await British invasions in either North Carolina or South Carolina.[10] Over time, people began to depend on the Boundary House. In 1791, as preparations were being made for President George Washington's tour through North Carolina, no "public house" could be found near the North Carolina–South Carolina border. An official observed that "A Mr. Dupree lives near this, a very obliging hospitable man, but who lived in a very small house when I was last there." There was hope that Dupree might still prove helpful, though, because "he did live at the Boundary House, which . . . [was] a pretty good [public house]." The writer thought Dupree intended to return to the Boundary House, but he remained uncertain.[11] By this time, the Boundary House may have begun to fade into memory and had perhaps finally become noteworthy only as a marker of the political boundary that gave it its name.

Those who experienced life inside the Boundary House undoubtedly crossed back and forth between the two Carolina colonies many times a day, and it is difficult to know how much consequence they attached to the imaginary line. The very fact that Finlay and others took note of the Boundary House's unusual position suggests that he and other contemporaries paid attention to the North Carolina–South Carolina boundary. At the same time, the Boundary House example also shows that in eighteenth-century America boundaries did not function in the same way that they do now. For people in the Boundary House, political boundaries could be important, but not necessarily in the ways that they have become important to more-modern sensibilities.

The Boundary House represents an attempt to fix boundaries in an eighteenth-century world in which clear demarcations and definitions of geographic space could be elusive.[12] As European historian Peter Sahlins noted, modern notions of territorial sovereignty were still emerging during this period.[13] When the first section of the North Carolina–South Carolina boundary began to be surveyed in 1737, Gabriel Johnston, the North Carolina governor, reported to the Board of Trade in London that "the running of this Line is farr from being compleated. The Commissioners were put to great charges and endured vast Fatigue."[14] More than thirty years later, authorities still at work on the western limits of this boundary recognized the difficulty and artificiality of imposing jurisdictional boundaries on functional geographic space, writing that "if the line is to be marked thro' the Woods the lands of many private people will be cut in two, part will lye in one province and the house in another." This would be inconvenient for the collection of taxes and quitrents and for land matters that could be avoided with a more "natural Boundary."[15] In 1762, Governor Arthur Dobbs complained, along similar lines, of "the great confusion occasioned in those Tracts adjoining to the Boundary Line" because of uncertainty about legal and political jurisdictions.[16] A few years before the first surveying of the North Carolina–South Carolina boundary, William Byrd's work on the Virginia–North Carolina boundary inspired him to write some of the most creative and self-consciously-crafted American prose of the eighteenth century in his *Histories of the Dividing Line betwixt Virginia and North Carolina*. Byrd's writings draw a sharp rhetorical contrast between the Virginia and North Carolina sides of the boundary, but ultimately underscore the practical problems with such boundaries by noting the division of farms and communities, the challenges of accurate surveying, and the impenetrability of the Dismal Swamp between the two colonies.[17]

Byrd and other colonists wrestled with the realization that all boundaries, political or otherwise, are historical constructs.[18] They fulfill the needs of those who create them and, because people's needs change, are never completely fixed. Those inside the Boundary House drew lines through their lives in various places, sometimes observing the importance of political jurisdictions and sometimes concerning themselves with other matters. If historians want to understand life in the Boundary House, they would be wise to look for different kinds of boundaries. In other words, the Boundary House not only problematizes political boundaries, but also shows something deeper. It shows that the spatial organization of life in colonial British America followed its own logic. Far from being arbitrary, boundaries drawn in the lives of settlers fit into patterns, like Barnett's repeated trips to the Boundary House.

Boundaries matter, whether they be real or metaphorical, political or social, because they structure people's lives. In order to be meaningful, boundaries have to mark an important limit that gives not only shape and definition but also context. Eighteenth-century surveyors could sometimes give shape and definition to colonial jurisdictions, but the boundaries they drew held meaning only in certain contexts, as demonstrated by the existence of the Boundary House.

A sense of remoteness provided one important context for many who passed through the Boundary House. Most of those who left written references to the Boundary House lived on the northern side of the building and consequently were under the political jurisdiction of North Carolina, a colony that must have seemed one of the most marginal places in the English-speaking world. Perhaps because of its reputation as poor and unsettled or because of the relative isolation caused by the colony's dangerous coastline, North Carolina settlers often described their location as "remote." In 1730, when settlers had been moving into the most southern parts of North Carolina for only a few years, the vestry of a newly formed parish along the Cape Fear River expressed their sense of geographic distance in poignant terms, describing their new home as "this Remote Part of the World."[19] A few years later, James Murray, a recently arrived settler, wrote a relative in Scotland that he appreciated his correspondence because he feared he would be forgotten "in this remote corner of the world."[20] In 1740, missionary James Moir described traveling to "the remotest Parts" of his mission.[21] Even decades later, in 1763, when Wilmington, along the lower reaches of the Cape Fear, had grown into the most important town in North Carolina, an Anglican clergyman noted that "Wilmington is not at all central, but a remote part of the Province."[22] No matter how boundaries were drawn, a feeling of remoteness and marginalization characterized colonial life, and it probably seemed particularly acute in some of the spaces just north of the Boundary

House. Moreover, geographic space must have assumed great significance to settlers who found themselves positioned in a "Remote Part of the World."

Frenetic movement and dispersion provided another important context for those who tried to impose a spatial order on the eighteenth-century American world. Enormous expansion characterized colonial British America between the beginning of the eighteenth century and the start of the American Revolution. To borrow Richard Hofstadter's apt statement, "it was growth—growth consistently sustained and eagerly welcomed, growth as a source of grand imperial hopes and calculating private speculation—which was the outstandingly visible fact of mid-eighteenth-century life in the American colonies."[23] Several decades of peace with European rivals, repeated waves of transatlantic immigration, increasing prosperity, and colonial populations that were increasingly well adapted, stable, and healthy all made substantial contributions to this impressive and seemingly omnipresent growth.[24]

As the British colonies in America flourished, they also dispersed. The availability of land provided one of the most important attractions to life in the American colonies, and the opportunity for colonies to expand into larger geographic spaces made growth possible. In 1700, the settlement of eastern North America had reached only a preliminary stage. Settlers spreading out from the Chesapeake Bay colonies and from Virginia covered two large areas. In the north, a number of other settlement centers were still taking form, most notably around New York City and Philadelphia but also at other sites along the Connecticut, Hudson, and Delaware Rivers. South of Virginia, settlement remained even more dispersed, the most significant areas of settlement being in the Albemarle section in northern North Carolina and around Charles Town and Port Royal in South Carolina. Remarkably, by the American Revolution the empty spaces had been filled in and there was a continuous band of settlement from Maine to Georgia. In the same period, the population of colonial British America increased tenfold.[25]

This geographic expansion had important implications, partly because new settlements did not develop arbitrarily. As colonists settled new areas, they simultaneously attempted to impose their own cultural standards on the new societies they created and continually reassessed those standards in accordance with their own experiences. Both of these processes required settlers to consider the character of the new places they occupied and to develop a new understanding of their relationship to geographic spaces. An absence of unsettled areas between settlements enabled the broader expression of local cultures, but as settlers differentiated themselves from their neighbors, as well as from the wilderness, it also became imperative to create different kinds of boundaries. Inevitably, newly settled areas often became distinct and separate regions, socially, economically, politically, and culturally.

Between 1700 and 1775, no colony in British America experienced more impressive growth or exhibited a clearer pattern of regionalization than North Carolina. In 1700, a small, poor, and notoriously disorderly settlement clung to the coastline around Albemarle Sound, receiving the scorn of neighboring colonies. By 1775, North Carolina had become the fifth-largest colony in population in British mainland America. New areas of settlement had opened up along the length of the Cape Fear River, near New Bern on the coast, across the entire North Carolina Piedmont, and into the edges of the Blue Ridge Mountains as colonists left very little land open anywhere in the eastern two-thirds of present-day North Carolina. Colonial North Carolinians also developed a notably well-articulated sense of regional identity. Over the course of the century, contemporaries recognized regional geographic designations that included Albemarle, Bath, the Granville District, the Upper Cape Fear, the Lower Cape Fear, the Backcountry, and the Piedmont. These regions did not come into being as part of any larger system or plan of settlement but grew out of the processes of expansion and immigration. Precise models of colonization and elaborate promotional efforts therefore have little applicability for the history of these new regions. The whole province of North Carolina evolved, not as one colony, but as a series of separate colonies of colonies.[26]

The Lower Cape Fear region, in southeastern North Carolina, presents a particularly interesting case of regional development. Between 1700 and 1725, the Lower Cape Fear region remained completely unoccupied by colonists. In 1725 it became one of the last significant mainland coastal enclaves to be settled by British colonists, but, remarkably, by 1775 it was the wealthiest and arguably the most important region in North Carolina. As with the other regions of North Carolina, the Lower Cape Fear, because of the contingencies and circumstances of settlement, developed into a distinct region gradually. Because of its importance within North Carolina and the southern colonies, scholars have tried to locate the Lower Cape Fear within broader geographic entities, ignoring the importance of its distinct regional character.

This study strives to recapture the regional character of settlement and development in the Lower Cape Fear before the American Revolution. It does so not only to draw attention to the key elements of Lower Cape Fear society that made it distinctive, but, even more important, to open a window into the broader processes of regional development, into the forces that shaped life for settlers expanding into the many new regional societies of early- and mid-eighteenth-century America. A close look at the Lower Cape Fear region makes it possible to discern the boundaries of everyday life, to comprehend the experience of living in "this Remote Part of the World," and to see patterns of growth and development.

While the colonial Lower Cape Fear can accurately be described as a regional society, the concept of the region requires some explanation. The word *region* is used often by scholars partly because of its flexibility, and it derives much of its meaning from the contexts and ways in which it is used. No matter in what way they are discussed or conceptualized however, regions tend to share some defining characteristics. First, regions are defined by geographic spaces of some kind or another and, as such, shed light on the geographic organization of societies. Usually the term *region* is reserved for spaces smaller than a nation-state but larger than a local neighborhood or community. Second, regions occupy bounded spaces, though, as with other kinds of boundaries in the early modern world, their boundaries are often fluid, imprecise, and permeable. Third, regions have important internal characteristics or consistencies that separate them from the world external to the region.[27] Because the meaning and importance of those internal characteristics and consistencies depends on one's perspective, regions are constructed and functional entities, rather than static and absolute geographic locations. In other words, regions, like boundaries, derive their significance and meaning from the roles they play in people's lives. This makes regions far too complex and varied to be reduced to any single defining characteristic.[28]

Historians of late-eighteenth- and early-nineteenth-century America often use the concept of the region to discuss areas much larger than the Lower Cape Fear. Partly because of the devastating consequences of the American Civil War, differences between the northern and southern parts of the United States have become inextricably linked with the historical development of the nation-state. As Peter Onuf has noted, in the early republic both nationalist and sectionalist tendencies "represented imaginative efforts to conceive and promote collective, translocal interests."[29] But the development of both of these tendencies flourished after the American Revolution.[30] The formation of the vast geographic identities related to nation-states, so vividly described by Benedict Anderson as "imagined communities," required improvements in communication, the centralization of political authority, a more widely dispersed print culture, and other changes that came after 1776.[31] Consequently, these large-scale regional frameworks have little relevance for scholars wishing to understand the experience of settlers during the colonial period. The Lower Cape Fear would come to be identified as part of "the South," but the conception of the South as a distinct and coherent region would not be constructed until after the colonial period and would become important only in the nineteenth century.

Historians of colonial British America have also attached considerable significance to the political boundaries between colonies. On some level, this emphasis is both desirable and unavoidable. For scholars who focus on elite politics, the boundaries between colonial governments provide important markers, and political authority can even have a considerable degree of influence on topics traditionally associated with social history. But, as the existence of the Boundary House suggests, historians should not let political boundaries determine the limits of their perspective. In recent decades, social historians and other scholars have begun to move the study of colonial America away from political boundaries. Expressing concern for a different range of issues that transcended earlier preoccupations with government, these scholars have proposed several alternative rationales for drawing boundaries in historical study.

Perhaps most important, scholars have used the geographer's concept of the cultural hearth, or core area, as a useful tool for describing differences or boundaries between places in colonial America.[32] These scholars have carefully drawn a framework to explain the development of early American cultures in terms of the duplication and fusion of traits from a number of especially influential core areas of settlement. The concept of the cultural hearth has exerted considerable influence over broader understandings of colonial American history. It correlates heavily with a five-part regional model that has gained widespread acceptance since the 1980s.[33] In this regional schema, colonial British America can readily be broken down into New England, the Middle Colonies, the Chesapeake Bay area, the Lower South, and the West Indies. Each of these areas could be described as spheres of influence for separate cultural hearths. Along similar lines, scholars have suggested that staple production and labor regimes help to describe important geographic continuities and discontinuities within colonial British America.[34] All of these distinctions have gained acceptance because they do reflect notable differences between places.

At the same time, neither this five-part regional model nor any other framework currently used by early American historians sufficiently explains the geographic organization of colonial British America in the eighteenth century. For one thing, almost all of these extralocal geographic designations are too large to capture the diversity, variation, and separate experiences of this period. They tell us much about the places designated as cores, but less about areas on the margins, where spheres of influence from different hearths or areas compete and collide. As the leading authority on the application of cultural hearths to early America has commented, "the duplication process tends to break down in the sphere zone, the area of contacts between different cultural traditions."[35] Hearths remain relevant in such places, but the development of colonial British America proves far too complex to be captured in a handful of regional categorizations. As the following pages will make clear, before 1776 the experience of settlers in the Lower Cape Fear cannot be readily subsumed into an anachronistic United States or South; a generalized Lower South or North Carolina; an extended Carolina cultural hearth; or a rice-production zone.

Scholars of colonial British America have been attentive to local variations and experiences in other ways, however. Indeed, since the late 1960s local case studies have exerted a profound influence on the historiography of early America, and at times scholars have been overwhelmed with these self-described "community studies." These studies have provided valuable insight into the localized patterns of interaction and geographic organization that characterized a number of seventeenth-century settlements, though they sometimes seem far more relevant for New England towns than for other places. The idea of a closely knit settlement is conveyed by the use of the intensely loaded and contested word *community,* though at this point in scholarly discussions of early America it often confuses far more than it clarifies. When the community-studies model is applied to eighteenth-century settlements, however, it becomes even more problematic. Improvements in transportation and communication reduced the level of isolation that characterized seventeenth-century life and, by the eighteenth century, colonists were far more integrated into the Atlantic world. While some sense of community may have lingered on between various groups of settlers, the processes of geographic organization and social interaction gradually moved from relatively contained neighborhoods to noticeably larger regions.

The Lower Cape Fear and other eighteenth-century regions like it thus provide the logical geographic framework for studying the period between the earliest colonial settlements and the construction of the American nation-state. These regions mattered because they performed functions in the lives of those who created and occupied them, and the Lower Cape Fear region formed out of the experiences of settlement, growth, and development. While regions such as the Lower Cape Fear served as the most important functional area of interaction for many eighteenth-century Americans, their role was transitional and would ultimately be superseded by the influences of larger regions and of the nation-state. Consequently, the strong emotional reactions associated with nationalism and southern regionalism in the nineteenth century did not develop in the colonial Lower Cape Fear. But if self-conscious and clearly defined loyalties to the Lower Cape Fear region remained limited, settlers lived in a profoundly regional system of interaction and experience.[36] Because, as Hugh Finlay, William Byrd, and others discovered, eighteenth-century boundaries proved fluid and complicated, it remains difficult to define the limits of the Lower Cape Fear without some necessary oversimplification. Still, the Lower Cape Fear Region's settlement gave birth to a separate North Carolina county, New Hanover, so in many ways the boundaries of the region and county overlapped. In the 1760s, part of New Hanover County was split from the original county to create Brunswick County; hence, for the purposes of this book, the Lower Cape Fear region will be defined as the area encompassed by New Hanover and Brunswick Counties before 1776.[37]

Choosing the colonial Lower Cape Fear for a case study leads to both promising opportunities and significant methodological challenges. Because North Carolina, unlike South Carolina, set up and maintained a county-based system of government, the lives of residents of the Lower Cape Fear can be traced through far more local records than those of most colonists in the area that is

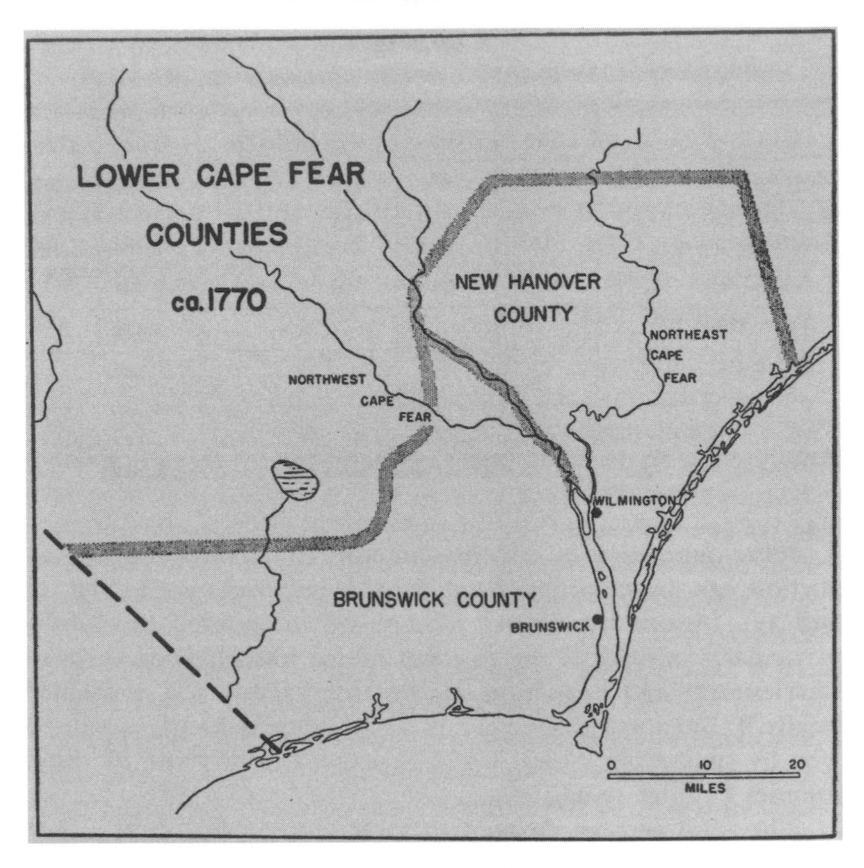

The Lower Cape Fear region began as part of New Hanover County and was divided into the two counties of New Hanover and Brunswick during the 1760s. From Harry Roy Merrens, *Colonial North Carolina in the Eighteenth Century: A Study in Historical Geography*. Copyright © 1964 by the University of North Carolina Press. Used by permission of the publisher.

broadly categorized as the Lower South. Several surviving tax lists make it possible to reconstruct significant portions of the region's population; court dockets provide important clues about legal matters; and land records reveal much about land and property. Many of these Lower Cape Fear records are more complete than even those for other parts of North Carolina, and in general the sources for the Lower Cape Fear are as good as or better than those for any comparable area in the British mainland colonies south of Virginia. Consequently, this study probably rests on a more complete empirical foundation than any comparable study of a locality in the eighteenth-century Lower South. At the same time, scholars who are familiar with source materials from after the American Revolution or from many places in the northern colonies will quickly notice the relative paucity of surviving documents from this time and place. Most discouraging, few residents of the Lower Cape Fear made a conscious effort to record their thoughts or feelings, so these matters often have to be inferred from surviving public records and other sources of information about their lives. It must also be acknowledged that there is much more evidence about the lives of the region's more privileged and powerful than about those who were marginalized. But, while some voices are partly lost to historians, every effort has been made to consider a full range of perspectives while reconstructing the broad and varied contours of experience within the region. Sometimes these matters can be addressed by scrutinizing quantitative patterns. Along these lines, approximately twenty-nine thousand different references have been recorded in a computer database (this database is described more fully in the Note on Methodology). At other times, the most promising approach depends on devoting careful attention to some of the few surviving personal writings that are available. In the end, it is possible to get a meaningful and sometimes surprisingly vivid glimpse of life in the Lower Cape Fear region.

Even though it has never before received serious scrutiny from social historians or been fully considered as part of the broader processes that characterized eighteenth-century settlement, scholars have long noted the distinct character and separate development of the Lower Cape Fear Region. Two scholars in particular have provided a valuable foundation for any work on the Lower Cape Fear. In 1965, E. Lawrence Lee published *The Lower Cape Fear in Colonial Days,* the culmination of more than a decade of research on the region's history. Lee's book, while it, belongs to a time before the rise of social history and shows little interest in placing the history of the Lower Cape Fear in broader debates about early America, provides the only full-length, twentieth-century historical study of the colonial Lower Cape Fear.[38] The year before the publication of Lee's work, in 1964, H. R. Merrens, one of the most talented of a cohort of historical geographers especially interested in Colonial British America, published *Colonial North Carolina in the Eighteenth Century: A Study in Historical Geography*. Merrens's book, in many ways still the most valuable socioeconomic portrait of colonial North Carolina, suggests the broad regional patterns of geographic organization that characterized the province, noting some of the most distinctive characteristics of the Lower Cape Fear.[39] Unfortunately, despite his training as a geographer, Merrens did not pursue a detailed analysis or case study of the process of regionalization. Merrens and Lee also both continued a tradition of scholarship that has found it difficult to categorize the Lower Cape Fear. They recognized, correctly, that the Lower Cape Fear differed substantially from the rest of North Carolina However, like many other scholars, they pointed out that in some ways the Lower Cape Fear functioned as an extension of the South Carolina lowcountry, and this oversimplifies the region's complicated history.

Comparisons with other parts of the Carolinas inevitably make the Lower Cape Fear seem very different. It was a distinctive place and cannot readily be pushed into models based on the characteristics of other places. But all places are in a sense distinctive. The significance of the Lower Cape Fear is that its differences reflect important processes. It became a separate region between 1725 and 1775 in ways that do not fit into current scholarly categorizations, but it shares much with other regions formed in early- to mid-eighteenth-century America. To give two notable examples, historical geographers James Lemon and Robert D. Mitchell have constructed detailed descriptions of settlement in two other eighteenth-century American regions, southeastern Pennsylvania and the Shenandoah Valley of Virginia.[40] While neither Lemon nor Mitchell engaged extensively with the concept of the region, their work is broadly suggestive of the regional character of eighteenth-century America. As settlers moved into new areas, they formed new regions that shed the controlling influence of earlier cultural hearths, labor patterns, staple regimes, and political structures. Such regions should not be treated as representative or unrepresentative so much as they should be treated as part of a different paradigm, as part of the regionalization of early America.

Early American regions formed in a multiplicity of different circumstances during the eighteenth century, but this study illustrates at least four different patterns, or forms of behavior, that contributed to the formation of one such region, the Lower Cape Fear. These four patterns are *differentiation, common experience, network formation,* and *centralization.* The seven chapters of this book illustrate and explore these and other aspects of the regionalization of early America as they played out in the Lower Cape Fear. Chapter 1 considers the expectations, background, and characteristics of settlement and immigration in the Lower Cape Fear beginning in 1725. Chapter 2 describes the occupation, acquisition, and use of land in the Colonial Lower Cape Fear. Chapter 3 explores the role of family in kinship in the region. Chapter 4 provides a portrait of social interaction, structure, and networks in the Lower Cape Fear. Chapter 5 places the history of the region in the context of colonial politics, law, and constructions of authority. Chapter 6 analyzes the Lower Cape Fear's distinctive plantation system and economy. Finally, Chapter 7 details the development and role of Wilmington and Brunswick, the Lower Cape Fear's two port towns.

Settlers differentiated themselves from those in other regions as they recognized the distinctive characteristics of their own way of life. This process operated with particular power for the residents of the Lower Cape Fear because countless factors differentiated them from settlers in the Upper Cape Fear, Albemarle, and the South Carolina lowcountry. To give two examples, chapter 2 illustrates patterns of land use that characterized and distinguished the Lower Cape Fear from its neighbors, and chapter 6 describes the elaborate and distinctive export economy based on forest industries that made the Lower Cape Fear unlike any other region in colonial British America. As they became aware of these differences, settlers were reminded of all they had in common with other residents of the Lower Cape Fear. Distinctive geographic areas did not necessarily develop into separate regions because geographic patterns depended on the needs of settlers, but the significant degree of local variation in places such as colonial North Carolina created a powerful precondition for regionalization.

Common experiences also contribute to the formation of powerful bonds. In the Lower Cape Fear, early years of political turbulence, late settlement, and disputed land claims, among other things, gave settlers a common past to underscore additional differences with those outside of the region. Chapter 1 recounts some of the experiences of those who constructed and peopled the Cape Fear settlement, for example, and chapter 5 describes the shared regional political culture and perspective that unified Lower Cape Fear leaders in power struggles with those from other areas of North Carolina. The more the region developed, the more important shared experiences became for settlers. In this sense, the many localities of eighteenth-century America had many separate histories as a consequence of the many settlement schemes and movements of people associated with rapid expansion.

Network formation made the Lower Cape Fear into a distinct social universe. As settlers' social and kinship connections grew within the Lower Cape Fear, the region came to dominate a greater and greater proportion of social interaction. Even during the first generation of settlement, few settlers often went beyond the Lower Cape Fear. Chapter 3 considers the strong kinship networks and family bonds that tied settlers to the region, and chapter 4 explores the regional character of social interaction and networks within the Lower Cape Fear. With so many ties within the Lower Cape Fear, settlers inevitably began to see the region as a distinct place. In an eighteenth-century world in which most interaction occurred face to face but settlers increasingly moved beyond local neighborhoods, regional networks proved central to life in colonial British America.

Centralization also contributed to the formation of the Lower Cape Fear. As central-place theorists have pointed out, central places develop strong interconnections with their hinterlands. By the late colonial period, these ties had developed between the Lower Cape Fear and its ports, as settlers in the region all looked to Wilmington or Brunswick to meet important needs. This in turn distanced them from other individuals who might have looked toward New Bern, Georgetown, or Charles Town. Chapter 7 focuses on these port towns. With the growth of both colonial British America and the Atlantic world, even seemingly remote parts of the world began to form their own identities and to be organized in relation to their own geographic centers.

By 1775, the imaginary boundaries of the Lower Cape Fear region transcended and often took precedence over similar boundaries between neighborhoods, parishes, counties, and colonies. But, like all these other constructions, the Lower Cape Fear region remained rooted in a historical moment. Fifty years before, early settlers would have had great difficulty envisioning the Lower Cape Fear as a region, and they probably clung closely to the few scattered neighborhoods in the area. After 1775, larger political and geographic entities would become increasingly important. In a few short years, Lower Cape Fear residents would participate in military combat under the authority of the Continental Congress and contribute to the formation of a national government. Within less than a hundred years, people from the same place would fight to preserve the political boundaries and status of North Carolina and other states like it. But, in 1775, it would have been very difficult to see beyond the Lower Cape Fear and envision all these changes.

Chapter 1

ENTRIES AND EXPECTATIONS

In 1725, Maurice Moore acquired a 320-acre piece of land about fifteen miles from the mouth of the Cape Fear River, divided it into lots, and began selling parcels as part of a town to be called Brunswick. Maurice's younger brother Roger contributed an additional piece to the town, and Maurice allotted parts of the town for various purposes. He included lots for a courthouse, a church, a cemetery, markets, and common areas for the public. Moore chose a site for the town that would prevent large oceangoing vessels from being blocked by a shoal several miles upriver. The brothers also began using their connections to try to get the new town made an official port of entry by British authorities. Even the name of the town represented a calculated political move, intended to gain the favor of the new British king, George I, of the house of Brunswick-Hanover. All these measures were necessary because Brunswick had been laid out in a virtually uninhabited region, and the Moores knew that they had to provide the proper incentives and trappings of civility to draw new settlers. The Moores hoped to fill this region with colonists and make Brunswick the center of a thriving society.[1]

The Moores had chosen contested terrain. The region in question, which became known as the Lower Cape Fear, occupied a position between the settlements of North and South Carolina. These two groups of settlements had begun as part of the same proprietary, but had long since separated in a variety of ways, officially and unofficially. South Carolina profited enormously from slaves laboring to produce rice and other commodities, while North Carolina languished under relative poverty and a notorious level of political factionalism. They left the area between them a wilderness and made little effort to explore and draw their shared boundary. For more than a generation, Native American tribes had inhabited the area between the two colonies and offered a further deterrent to settlement. Equally important, the Lord Proprietors, in an attempt to prevent land speculation and mismanagement by colonists, had forbidden the colonial land office to give settlers ownership of new lands in the southernmost parts of North Carolina by restricting land patents.

The Moores saw little reason to be deterred by these obstacles, however. Maurice and Roger Moore were powerful men, coming from one of South Carolina's most prominent families. Maurice's father, James Moore, who had come to South Carolina from Barbados in the 1670s, served as governor of South Carolina between 1700 and 1703 and became a member of the influential and

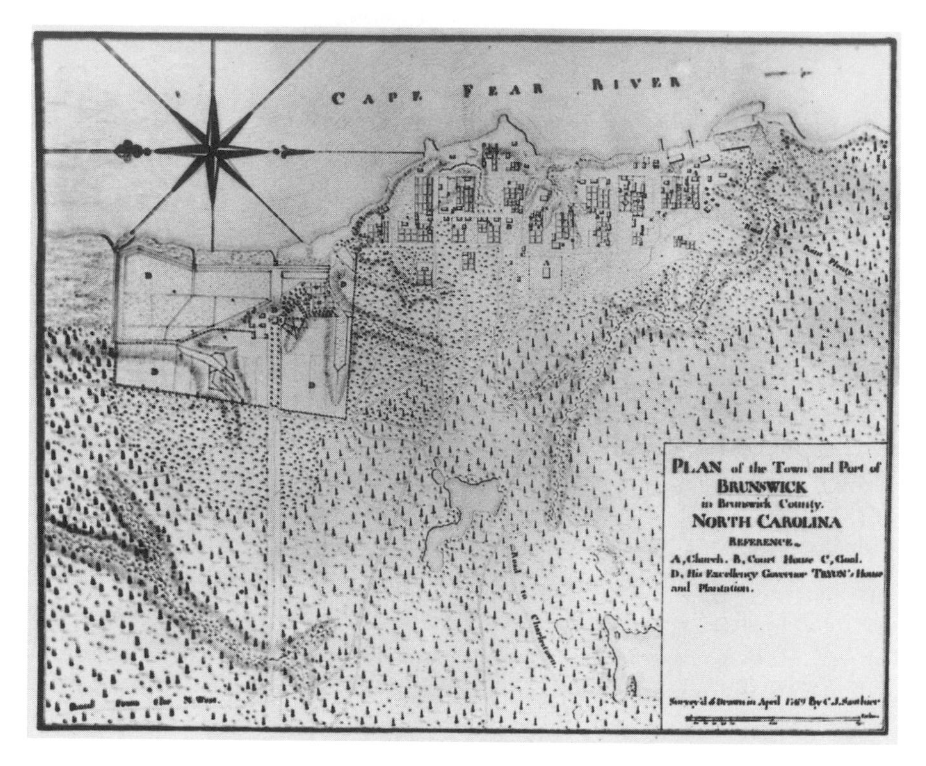

This 1769 map by C. J. Sauthier shows Maurice Moore's plan for the town of Brunswick. By permission of the British Library.

contentious South Carolina political faction associated with the area around Goose Creek in Berkeley County. James married a stepdaughter of wealthy Barbadian Sir John Yeamans and had ten children, among them Maurice and Roger.[2] These connections insured that Maurice and Roger would be wealthy and influential planters and slave owners. But, in the early eighteenth century, South Carolina's elite demonstrated its character in a variety of ways that distinguished it from those in the other British mainland colonies to the north. South Carolinians amassed more wealth, owned more slaves, and achieved as great a degree of political consensus as any group of British colonists outside the West Indies.[3] Indeed, they shared enough traits and connections with West Indian planters that several historians have described the South Carolina lowcountry as part of a larger "Barbadian cultural hearth."[4] The Moores and their South Carolinian allies began settlement in the Lower Cape Fear with a common vision formed out of their experiences in the South Carolina lowcountry. When Maurice and Roger Moore entered the Lower Cape Fear, they were also exhibiting the expansiveness and dynamism of colonial South Carolina society.

Yet the 1725 movement into the Cape Fear could not have taken place without certain circumstances that were beyond the control of the Moores. Maurice Moore must have recognized this because he had been aware of the possibilities of the Cape Fear region for ten years. He arrived in North Carolina in 1712 as an officer among South Carolina troops sent to assist North Carolina during the Tuscarora War. When the others returned, Moore decided to stay in North Carolina, where he married the sister of Edward Moseley, one of the colony's most prominent landholders, lawyers, and politicians. In 1715, he became a colonel and was made the head of North Carolina troops to aid South Carolina in the Yamasee War. In the Cape Fear region, Moore and his troops averted an ambush and defeated the Waccamaw and Cape Fear groups. Not only did this encounter introduce Moore to the region, it also reduced the threat of a hostile Native American presence in the region and made it much more promising for colonial settlement. Even after this decisive change, neither Moore nor anyone else moved immediately into the Lower Cape Fear.[5] Perhaps Native Americans continued to discourage potential settlers: local legend recounts the story of a band of Native Americans who raided Roger Moore's plantation. Swift retaliation eliminated this group from the Lower Cape Fear region, removing one more impediment to the plans of the Moores.[6] As early as 1720, settlers who had difficulty getting land in South Carolina resolved to "view Cape Fear" and found that they "like[d] it pretty well."[7]

In order to overcome the proprietors' ban on land grants in the area, Moore needed support from North Carolinians with political authority. He participated in political affairs in tandem with Edward Moseley, his brother-in-law, and no doubt forged other alliances with important leaders in the Albemarle section of North Carolina. But the crucial event for Moore came in 1724 with the appointment of George Burrington as governor of North Carolina. In Burrington, Moore found a governor who not only was willing to overlook the proprietary prohibition but also would share his own ambition and determined interest in the Lower Cape Fear. Perhaps for this reason, the Moores and Burrington sparked rumors that they hoped to form a separate province that would be independent of both North and South Carolina.[8] Some South Carolinians, at least, considered this a serious possibility, remarking that debtors hoped to make the Cape Fear settlement "a Government independent from this or No[rth] Carolina."[9] At the same time, because North Carolina, under Burrington's leadership, supported Moore's endeavor, the new settlement became associated with the colony without regard to the unresolved contention that the Lower Cape Fear was within the boundaries of South Carolina. The Moores and Burrington thus helped set into motion the creation of the Lower Cape Fear region. The Moores' South Carolina perspective separated it from North Carolina regions, and Burrington's imposition of North Carolina authority separated it from South Carolina regions. Despite its ties to both colonies, the

Lower Cape Fear began as a discrete entity, and the common experience of life in the new settlement played an important role in the development of the Lower Cape Fear as a separate region.

With Burrington's support, Maurice Moore began to promote and encourage settlement in earnest. Also, in the next several years, a number of Moore's wealthy relatives and connections came to the Lower Cape Fear. Some of the most important of these newcomers were related to Moore either by blood or through the myriad marital connections between prominent eighteenth-century families in North and South Carolina. Because of these connections, in the coming years the Moores and their supporters would become known in the Lower Cape Fear as "The Family." Some Lower Cape Fear arrivals in this Family, such as Edward Moseley, the Swanns, and the Ashes, represented the most prominent planters and leaders of the Albemarle region of North Carolina.

Historians have devoted much more attention to the conspicuous South Carolina contingent that accompanied Maurice Moore.[10] Foremost among these were his brothers Roger and Nathaniel, and others included Eleazer Allen, Edward Hyrne, Nathaniel Rice, William Dry, Job Howe, and Richard Eagles. Historians have cited a number of reasons for emphasizing the South Carolina migrants. First of all, they played a disproportionately important role in the economic development of the region. Many of them brought large accumulations of capital, slaves, and other resources to the region. Also, because of the maneuvering of Maurice Moore and Governor Burrington, many of them managed to acquire enormous amounts of land.[11] Roger Moore owned more slaves and acquired more land in the Lower Cape Fear than any other individual in the region before the American Revolution.[12] The eight former South Carolina residents who patented land in the region before 1730 eventually expanded their patents to include more than ninety-one thousand acres.[13] Many of the new arrivals undoubtedly expected to acquire landholdings for the same lucrative rice-producing regime that had already engulfed the lowcountry areas to the south. Equally important, by emphasizing the South Carolina connections behind the Moores and the settlement of the Lower Cape Fear, it is deceptively easy to explain the notable differences that distinguished the Lower Cape Fear from the rest of North Carolina during the colonial era.

Unfortunately, it is impossible to determine what portion of the earliest settlers in the Lower Cape Fear region came from South Carolina. Early people moving into this region left no journals, lists of passengers, or other detailed accounts of their travels. Nonetheless, existing data sheds some light on the subject. It is possible to trace the origins of a significant sample of individuals who settled in the lower Cape Fear during the colonial period. Out of 340 instances in which Lower Cape Fear residents can be traced to other locales, the trail leads to South Carolina only 47 times.[14] While one might expect South Carolina connections to appear more prominently in the earliest years of settlement, they represent a mere 24 of the 130 traceable ties during the first fifteen years of settlement. Of course, this data is strongly biased toward prominent individuals, such as landholders, and it remains possible that, if the leaders of the Lower Cape Fear were not overwhelmingly from South Carolina lowcountry society the Lower Cape Fear did attract large numbers of South Carolinians of more modest means.

The most suggestive piece of information regarding the size of the South Carolina contingent in the Lower Cape Fear comes from a petition signed by nine Cape Fear inhabitants in the fall of 1731. In a heated debate between immigrants and George Burrington, the petition was intended to defend the Moores and other local leaders from charges of land fraud. The petition closes by remarking that "tho we are about 1200 persons in our familys," they had not acquired as much land as some of the crown's officers in North Carolina. Given the sparse population of the Lower Cape Fear at this early date, this document suggests that The Family, the Moore clan, constituted a large presence indeed. On the other hand, a majority of these twelve hundred people were probably slaves, and the petitioners may well have exaggerated to strengthen their case. Equally important, at least three of the nine signatories were Maurice Moore's kin from the Albemarle section of North Carolina and not from South Carolina.[15] The document does indicate that prominent South Carolina immigrants like the Moores brought large slaveholdings to the Lower Cape Fear and also encouraged relatives to take advantage of the region's opportunity, and this in itself probably insured an important and enduring South Carolina influence.[16]

There are also other contemporary comments to suggest that South Carolinians may have arrived in the Lower Cape Fear with large numbers of slaves and family members. According to South Carolinians, many people took their families to the Lower Cape Fear to escape the taxation and authority of the South Carolina government. At the time, South Carolina faced a crushing depression, and taxes were particularly onerous. By going to the Lower Cape Fear, people would be too far away to be governed from Charles Town and, when given a choice, they readily grasped an opportunity to be governed by the far weaker and less centralized government of North Carolina. As a South Carolina Assembly report described the situation in 1757, "it happened that sundry Persons who were settled near Charles Town removed from thence with their Families and Slaves and sat down upon the South Banks of Cape Fear River near the sea."[17] Another South Carolina official made reference to "sundry persons with their families [who] removed up to the South banks of Cape Fear River."[18] South Carolinians also complained that the Cape Fear provided a refuge for debtors attempting to defraud their creditors.[19] There are no reliable figures on the size of slaveholdings before the 1750s and 1760s, but records indicate that those linked to South Carolinians tended to own more slaves than those tied to other prominent places.[20] In any case, it seems plausible that many

Table 1.1 **Number of Lower Cape Fear Residents Who Can Be Linked to Residences in Other Regions, by Decade**

Location	*Total*	*1725–29*	*1730–39*	*1740–49*	*1750–59*	*1760–69*	*1770–75*
Upper Cape Fear	63	2	9	18	19	12	3
England	56	3	17	8	13	14	2
South Carolina	47	8	16	9	5	7	2
Northeastern North Carolina	36	10	12	6	4	4	0
Middle colonies	35	1	13	5	9	6	1
Scotland	33	0	11	7	10	4	1
Ireland	19	2	5	2	8	2	0
New England	16	1	6	1	2	6	0
Island colonies	15	0	5	0	3	6	1
North Carolina backcountry	8	0	2	1	2	3	0
Other southern colonies	8	2	3	1	2	0	0
Continental Europe	4	0	2	2	0	0	0

South Carolinians might have considered moving to the Lower Cape Fear and imagined some of the same possibilities that had driven Maurice Moore to plan Brunswick.[21] South Carolinians, then, played a very significant role in the settlement of the Lower Cape Fear. The South Carolina lowcountry provided the Lower Cape Fear region with initiative, capital, resources, settlers, and, perhaps most important, an example of how to create a prosperous and stable colonial society. In other words, the Lower Cape Fear, like many other settlements in colonial British America, began because of the efforts of a relatively unified charter group.

But other groups of settlers in the Lower Cape Fear clearly rivaled the numbers and influence of the South Carolinians. These other groups also made significant contributions to the new Lower Cape Fear settlement and, while they never quite seem to have equaled the influence of the Moores during the early decades of settlement, they offered the region alternative expectations and visions of success. The Moores arrived first, but their perspectives never dominated as fully as those of charter groups in some other colonial settlements. Consequently, because it could not readily be subsumed into either North or South Carolina, the region became more distinct. It also developed independently of nearby societies, contributing to the formation of the Lower Cape Fear as a separate region by unifying different perspectives through the shared experiences of the new settlement.

The older North Carolina settlement in the Albemarle region to the north would also have an important influence on the Lower Cape Fear's development. The earliest immigrants to North Carolina came south from Virginia into the Albemarle region and brought many of the same traits that characterized the Chesapeake Bay colonies. Unfortunately, Albemarle lacked the economic possibilities of Virginia and Maryland because the treacherous North Carolina coast prevented significant overseas exportation of tobacco and other staple crops. Without these economic advantages, northern North Carolina also did not draw enough resources to develop an established local elite that could govern with any kind of stable authority. Just as South Carolinians later complained that the relative wilderness of the Cape Fear provided a refuge for debtors and lawless individuals, Albemarle quickly acquired an unusual reputation for harboring the less desirable elements from Virginia and other British American colonies. Thomas Lowndes expressed a widely held sentiment in 1729 when he wrote a letter to the Board of Trade referring to "North Carolina which (ever since t'was a separate Government) has only been a Receptacle for Pyrates Thieves and Vagabonds of all sorts."[22]

The travails of the Albemarle settlement seemed designed to make immigrants from northern North Carolina every bit as anxious and insecure as the Moores were self-confident and assertive. The Carolina proprietors showed far less interest in Albemarle than in the settlement centered around Charles Town.

Perhaps partly as a consequence, the early decades of government in what would become known as North Carolina seemed like an endless succession of failed governors and revolts against authority, including two full-fledged attempts to overthrow the government, known as Culpepper's Rebellion and Cary's Rebellion. Throughout their existence, the early North Carolina settlements remained vulnerable to attack from hostile Native Americans, and without help from South Carolina the colony might not have survived the Tuscarora War in the early eighteenth century. Research indicates that early North Carolina colonists challenged legal authority and gender norms with surprising frequency and brazenness. Even in the 1720s, pirates and smugglers hid along the North Carolina coast, and William Byrd's *Histories of the Dividing Line* made North Carolinians a target for stinging mockery. In short, early-eighteenth-century northern North Carolina may have been as poor and fractious a society as any in British America.[23]

Such a place did not offer men of talent and influence the wealth or the prestige required to move into the highest circles of Anglo-American society. No matter how much they cultivated civility, North Carolinians could not escape the stigma of being from an uncivilized and disreputable borderland.[24] Some of Albemarle's leaders may have handled these constraints better than others, but it seems likely that they would have weighed heavily on Edward Moseley.

It would be difficult to exaggerate the prominence of Moseley in early-eighteenth-century North Carolina politics. Unlike Maurice Moore, however, Moseley had not been born to wealth, security, and power. His origins are obscure. At age fifteen, he was apprenticed as an orphan from Christ's Church Hospital in London. According to William Byrd II, Moseley "had been bred in Christ's Hospital and had a Tongue as Smooth as the Commissary, and he was altogether as well qualify'd to be of the Society of Jesus."[25] Whether because of this smooth tongue or some other attributes, Moseley showed an extraordinary resilience in North Carolina politics. He involved himself in repeated controversies, was accused of engineering Cary's Rebellion, and after one particularly heated struggle with Governor Charles Eden was prohibited from holding public office for three years. Yet Moseley continued to emerge from these activities at least as powerful as his opponents. Moseley served in an enormous variety of positions: justice of the peace, vestryman, council member, assemblyman, speaker of the assembly, surveyor general, treasurer, judge of the vice-admiralty, chief justice of the General Court, member of the Virginia boundary commission, and baron of the Exchequer. He demonstrated his intelligence and talent as a surveyor, mapmaker, attorney, political leader, planter, and book collector. At his death in 1749, Moseley possessed more than thirty thousand acres, in three counties, and owned close to a hundred slaves.[26] Yet all of these achievements and experiences must have given him an acute sense of the limitations placed on North Carolina's elites.

The Lower Cape Fear offered Moseley and other Albemarle leaders like him an opportunity to escape the economic and political problems that had plagued North Carolina since its inception. William Hilton and many other visitors to the Lower Cape Fear reported that the region might be able to produce valuable staples. The recent rice boom across the disputed South Carolina border suggested only the most obvious and promising possibility for getting rich in the unsettled lands south of Albemarle. It was also common knowledge that the Cape Fear River provided the only port in North Carolina that could enable access to oceangoing vessels of a significant size and thereby open a lucrative direct trade with Great Britain or the British West Indies. Perhaps most important, the enormous undeveloped area of the Lower Cape Fear allowed the colonists' imaginations to construct social and cultural possibilities that were clearly impossible in the more ossified Albemarle region.

Moseley seized the opportunity. Shortly after Maurice Moore's land acquisition in 1725, Moseley began obtaining land in the Lower Cape Fear, and he continued to accumulate holdings steadily for the next decade. In 1735, Moseley moved from his residence in Chowan County, at the northern end of the colony, to Rocky Point, the most highly regarded section of the Lower Cape Fear. He also married Ann Sampson, who had ties to the region, and politically aligned himself, with the Moores, as strongly in favor of the development of the Lower Cape Fear. Moseley continued in his new residence and maintained his support of the region until his death in 1749.[27]

Other Albemarle residents followed similar courses of action. Several of the most important men in Albemarle purchased land and moved to the Lower Cape Fear soon after the region was opened for settlement. Most notably, these included John and Samuel Swann, John Baptista Ashe, and Alexander Lillington. A total of thirty-six Cape Fear residents can be traced to northern North Carolina.[28] A substantial majority of these appeared in the Lower Cape Fear records before 1740 and, as a group, they patented almost as much land in the Lower Cape Fear as those with ties to South Carolina.[29] While the limited slaveholdings in the Albemarle region indicate that they probably did not bring nearly as many slaves as the South Carolinians, men like Moseley and John Baptista Ashe clearly had the means of obtaining enslaved labor.[30] Like Moore and other South Carolinians, Edward Moseley and other immigrants from the Albemarle region carved out an important economic and social niche along the Cape Fear River. Indeed, material aspirations probably played an important role in the alliance between Lower Cape Fear settlers from various locales such as Albemarle and the South Carolina lowcountry.

There is considerably less contemporary and historical comment on the migration of North Carolinians into the Lower Cape Fear, but this silence undoubtedly conceals an important and complicated process in the development of the region. For one thing, while North Carolinians by no means dominate the relatively elite sample of migrants that can be traced by existing records, proximity dictates that they were far more likely to make up a large portion of the colony's poorer newcomers. Lower-class families from other colonies or from Europe would have found it much more difficult to obtain the resources to get to the Lower Cape Fear than families from farther up the North Carolina coast.[31] Indeed, the lack of comment on the influx of North Carolina residents can probably be attributed to the fact that most contemporaries would have taken this process for granted. Two sources provide evidence that most of the region's settlers immigrated from nearby settlements. Hugh Meredith wrote that the early inhabitants of the Lower Cape Fear were "mostly such as were born or have lived in the neighboring Colonies." Similarly, when Governor Burrington commented that "a great number of people have come into this Country to Settle lately," he added, "I hear of more that are coming from the Neighboring Colonies."[32] So, in the absence of definitive evidence, it must be assumed that North Carolinians and South Carolinians made up the largest share of free lower-class immigrants to the Lower Cape Fear during the colonial period.[33]

Perhaps even more important, during the early and middle eighteenth century the entire colony of North Carolina was involved in an enormous population movement into the southern backcountry. Between 1730 and 1770 the population of the colony leaped from about 35,000 to 175,000 or 185,000 inhabitants, according to conservative estimates. Contemporary accounts present compelling evidence that a large portion of this population could be attributed to immigration into the colony's backcountry.[34] Many of these immigrants settled in the upper reaches of the Cape Fear River and formed another society distinct from that of the Lower Cape Fear. Still others moved southward from Pennsylvania and other colonies into the North Carolina Piedmont and mountains. Inevitably, some representatives of these two groups of new settlers spent some time in the Lower Cape Fear. Fully sixty-three Cape Fear residents also resided in the Upper Cape Fear counties of North Carolina at some time.[35] While many of these individuals may not have resided in the Lower Cape Fear for long, before moving upriver to more open land and other opportunities, as a group they must have made a significant impact while they were in the region. Indeed, the sample suggests that some settlers probably shifted from previous residences up and down the Cape Fear River throughout the period.[36] Similarly, eight other Lower Cape Fear residents could be tied to backcountry counties beyond the Cape Fear River.[37]

Considerable evidence demonstrates then, that the settlement of the Lower Cape Fear can be seen not only as an episode in the expansion of South Carolina led by Maurice Moore and his relatives, but also as an episode in the transformation of North Carolina led, at least in part, by elite North Carolinians like Edward Moseley. Indeed, of the 340 Cape Fear residents who left evidence of residence elsewhere, fully 107 can be traced to locales within North Carolina, while only 47 can be traced to South Carolina. As these numbers also indicate, however, focusing on these two migrations to the Lower Cape Fear still leaves out a sizable portion of the picture.

But North Carolina immigrants to the Lower Cape Fear may have had the most to gain by seeing this new region as distinct from its neighbors. The colony as a whole had a poor reputation that bore many negative implications. By constructing a different and better identity for the Lower Cape Fear, North Carolinians could restore confidence in their way of life. Still, perspectives shaped by experiences in other parts of North Carolina continued to influence life in the Lower Cape Fear, even while the creation and development of the Lower Cape Fear settlement encouraged the negotiation of a new set of shared goals and perspectives within the region.

Wealthy leaders from the South Carolina lowcountry and Albemarle region of North Carolina played only the most conspicuous role in the construction of the Lower Cape Fear region; thousands of other immigrants helped to shape this process. Local records and contemporary accounts tell us much about the movements and activities of settlers in the early Lower Cape Fear, but they reveal little about their thoughts and motivations for immigrating. One immigrant, however, has left a record of his reasons for going to the Lower Cape Fear and, indeed, a relatively thorough account of his feelings and thoughts about life in the region during several decades of residence.

James Murray grew up in Unthank in Scotland's valley of the Ewes. Before making plans to establish himself in North Carolina, he served as an apprentice to a London merchant engaged in the West Indian trade.[38] In May 1735, several months before his departure from Scotland, Murray wrote to a relative and explained his reasons for leaving. Murray felt discouraged by the limited opportunities available to him in Scotland. The depressed economic conditions of early-eighteenth-century Scotland, which are evident in countless historical accounts, echo through Murray's letter: "The small encouragement that I have to stay here and not so much as the prospect of doing better has determined me to accept of the first good opportunity to push my fortune in any other part of the world." Murray expressed these concerns to a friend, who suggested he go to North Carolina, "where there is a fine navigable river lying in a convenient place for trade call'd Cape Fare River."

While Murray's letter indicates that he planned to go to North Carolina for a variety of reasons, he clearly found the economic reasons most compelling. Much of this no doubt reflected the difficult times in Scotland, and Murray could be confident that in the Lower Cape Fear "it is cheaper living there than anywhere in Scotland." At the same time, he thought the region offered unusual opportunities. He planned to obtain land that "will in all probability double the value every year, the place growing daily more populous as the Land Lower

James Murray emigrated from Scotland to the Lower Cape Fear and became one of the region's most prominent planters and merchants. The only surviving portrait of Murray was made from an original painted by John Singleton Copley. Courtesy of the North Carolina Collection, University of North Carolina at Chapel Hill.

down in that River has already done." He also took comfort in the region's safety from foreign enemies and in information indicating that the Lower Cape Fear climate was "as healthy as England."

Murray recognized that the opportunities available to him in the Lower Cape Fear depended partly on his elite status and were not available to everyone. He assured his kinsman: "My own fortune is sufficient both to buy a handsome plantation and carry on as large a trade as I have occasion for." Perhaps even more important, Murray had well-placed connections. His most important ally was clearly the newly-appointed North Carolina governor, Gabriel Johnston. Johnston himself was Scottish, and over the coming years he used his position as governor simultaneously to encourage immigration from Scotland and to develop the Cape Fear. It was significant that Murray could write, "I am sure of the Governor's interest to support me."[39] Murray could also rely on valuable trading connections with men in England and the West Indies, as well as Scotland, that would make his business in the Lower Cape Fear more lucrative. Before his departure, Murray consulted with his friend Henry McCulloh about various commodities, expenses, prices, and business opportunities in the Cape Fear.[40] Given all of these motivating factors, it is not surprising that, when

Murray asked advice, "All the merchants that I have talked to that have any knowledge of these parts say it is the best thing that I can do."[41]

If Murray gives the best account of an individual's motivations for moving to the Lower Cape Fear, he was not a typical Lower Cape Fear immigrant. Indeed, he would serve on the Governor's Council, own a large plantation, and ultimately, when he moved to New England in 1765, become perhaps the region's most important absentee landowner.[42] Murray's letter does, however, carry a significance that transcends its atypicality. In it, Murray expresses some of the themes that characterized the last key component of immigration to the colonial Lower Cape Fear. This third pattern of migration, like Murray's journey from Scotland, proved to be transatlantic. Settlers who shared Murray's transatlantic perspective cared less about the Lower Cape Fear's place within the Carolina colonies, but they recognized that the region offered a distinct set of opportunities compared with other parts of early America, and, because of this, began to differentiate it in their own way.

Of course, like many immigrants coming to the New World both before and after, not all of Murray's information could be relied on, and not all of his expectations would be borne out. The ebb and flow of Murray's experiences in the Lower Cape Fear can be traced through his letters, which constitute far and away the largest surviving body of private writings from the colonial Lower Cape Fear. These letters, which necessarily make Murray a necessarily central figure for any scholarly study of life in the region, also provide a window into the ways that Murray and his correspondents viewed the prospects for a successful life in his new home.

Murray's letters indicate that the initial period of settlement in the Lower Cape Fear region led to a variety of promotional schemes as people sought to take advantage of the region's economic potential. Henry McCulloh, one of Murray's most frequent correspondents, paid special attention to immigration to the region because of his involvement in large-scale land speculation schemes in North Carolina. In 1736, Murray told McCulloh that he expected some families from Ireland to settle in the Lower Cape Fear, and he wrote Andrew Bennet that "a great number of Irish expected next year will raise our Country in a hurry."[43] A group of Swiss settlers also considered immigrating to the region, visited Lower Cape Fear lands, signed contracts with promoters, and negotiated for land with Governor Johnston.[44] Neither of these groups ever arrived in large enough numbers to leave much information in surviving records or to make a substantial impact on the development of the region. Perhaps they shared the experience of a group of Dutch settlers that Murray met when he arrived in Charles Town on his way to the Cape Fear. These settlers were "deterr'd from proceeding by misrepresentations" of the Lower Cape Fear region. Indeed, the region was held in such low repute in the South Carolina lowcountry that Murray confessed he was "almost in doubt my self whether to come here from the strange stories they told me."[45] Immigration to new settlements often depended as much on rumors and reputations as on real opportunities, and the Lower Cape Fear clearly had both supporters and detractors. The region probably did not have a sufficiently positive reputation or sufficiently promising opportunities to encourage large numbers of immigrants from such geographically and culturally different places as the Netherlands or Switzerland, even though the Lower Cape Fear seems to have been well suited to the aspirations and interests of James Murray and many other settlers.

The British Isles proved to be the dominant source of transatlantic migration to the Lower Cape Fear, primarily because of the kinds of connections and opportunities that were available within the British Empire and that helped to make Murray's new home so hospitable. Murray's communication with David Tullideph, another Scottish merchant interested in the possibilities of the Lower Cape Fear, shows how these ties could be put to use. Before Murray crossed the Atlantic, he had agreed to investigate some of the possibilities available to Tullideph in the new settlement.[46] When Murray arrived, he hesitated to give any advice on the region, waiting to consult with Governor Johnston before he chose a specific location for his home or for Tullideph's investment. Tullideph, anxious to start making profits, indicated to Murray that he planned to send slaves for a plantation in the Lower Cape Fear, but Murray dissuaded him. Murray wanted to wait for more information and expressed concern about Tullideph's plan to invest in the region as an absentee owner of a plantation.[47] As a new settler himself, Murray was still trying to assess the potential of the region and had begun to realize that transatlantic ties, while they could be helpful, had limitations that could be overcome only with personal supervision. Eventually, Murray came to the conclusion that the region would not be as profitable as he hoped until more settlers arrived; under those circumstances, he said, the province would "soon be one of the best in America." In the meantime, however, Tullideph invested his resources elsewhere.[48]

Murray continued to invest in the Lower Cape Fear until the 1760s, and while he sometimes expressed frustration with the Lower Cape Fear and never obtained vast wealth, he clearly improved his economic status. For those like Tullideph who could consider a variety of economic opportunities, the Lower Cape Fear sometimes was not enticing enough, but for those like Murray who faced the kind of economic desperation that characterized early eighteenth-century Scotland, the Cape Fear offered a relatively promising future.

Scottish immigration to North Carolina in the eighteenth century has given rise to considerable contemporary and scholarly comment. The magnitude and concentration of this movement makes it possible to say, with only a little exaggeration, that the Upper Cape Fear region around Cumberland County, North Carolina, was practically a separate Scottish Highland colony. While numbers are imprecise, the use of Gaelic in the region provides one indicator of the prominence of Scots. Most of these Scottish refugees came through the Lower Cape Fear ports on their way upriver. The characteristics of this Scottish migration are fairly well known. Most of the immigrants came from the Scottish Highlands, which underwent several wrenching and tension-filled transitions in the early eighteenth century that ultimately led to out-migration and panicked anxieties about depopulation. The three most important of these transitions were the destruction of the Scottish clan system, the rise of rackrenting, and population pressure on the region's resources. Poorer migrants went overland to the Lowlands or northern England. Those who had or could obtain the necessary resources frequently moved their whole family to North America, and the most popular destination was North Carolina. The migration got under way in the 1730s, picked up during the late 1740s, and grew considerably in the years after 1770.[49] In 1773, a pamphlet writer using the name Scotus Americanus painted North Carolina in glowing terms for prospective Scottish migrants, reflecting that "migrations to America from many parts of Britain particularly to the province of North Carolina, have, of late, become very frequent and numerous, and are likely to continue to do so."[50]

It has never been maintained that this Scottish presence played a comparable role in the development of the Lower Cape Fear, but it has often been assumed that some of this migration spilled over into the adjacent Lower Cape Fear counties. A total of thirty-three Lower Cape Fear residents can be traced to Scotland. Not only is this figure lower than might be expected, it also does not correspond well with what scholars already know about the Scottish migration to the Upper Cape Fear. For one thing, the arrivals in the Lower Cape Fear reached their highpoint in the 1730s and trailed off to only one arrival during the 1770s, when the migration to the backcountry was at its peak. Even more significant, a relatively high proportion of those in the Lower Cape Fear with ties to Scotland were engaged in some form of commerce, while the preponderance of backcountry immigrants pursued agrarian activities.[51] This information suggests that Murray's motives may, indeed, have been reasonably typical of the more prominent Scottish migrants to the Lower Cape Fear, who were probably motivated by economic opportunities and saw a chance to take advantage of transatlantic trading patterns. They recognized that Scottish immigrants populating the Lower Cape Fear's hinterland would require a commercial entrepot down the river. A number of these men did, in fact, become prominent in the trade of the region.[52] The different pattern of Scottish migration to the Lower Cape Fear also suggest a divide between Scottish highlanders, who tended to go upriver, and Scottish lowlanders, who seemed to stay in the Lower Cape Fear more frequently. The slightly more significant numbers of arrivals in the 1730s probably also corresponds to the influence of Governor Johnston. In contrast,

TABLE 1.2 **Lower Cape Fear Residents Who Emigrated Directly and Indirectly from Residences in the British Isles**

	Total	*Resided in Other Colonies*	*% Resided in Other Colonies*
From England	56	17	30
From Scotland	33	5	15
From Ireland	19	8	42
Total	108	30	28

most of the Scottish migrants to the rest of North Carolina appear to have been influenced more by the push of hardship and insecurity in Scotland than by the pull of a promising investment.[53]

A look at those with other transatlantic ties, in tables 1.2, 1.3, and 1.4, supports the conclusion that many immigrants to the Lower Cape Fear arrived with hopes of bettering their economic status with involvement in trade. Significantly, more Lower Cape Fear residents can be traced to England than to any other locale except for the adjacent and easily accessible Upper Cape Fear region. Out of the sample of 340 connections, 56, or about 16 percent, can be linked to England.[54] Some of the English immigrants were prominent, and the group had a distinctly commercial orientation.[55] This data corresponds with the dominant trend of eighteenth-century English migration, in which those traveling over long distances more often tended to be elite individuals, such as merchants.[56] Evidence also indicates that, unlike the shiploads of Scottish travelers to the backcountry, eighteenth-century English arrivals in North America tended to arrive more gradually, aboard ships with small groups.[57] Along similar lines, nineteen individuals can be traced to Ireland; nine of them described themselves as merchants.[58] A number of those with links to England and Ireland had also lived elsewhere in the British American colonies before moving to the Cape Fear, indicating that the region attracted individuals who moved around in the English-speaking world and had far-reaching connections.[59] An analysis of the contingent of fifteen Lower Cape Fear residents with ties to the British West Indies and other island colonies reinforces this assertion. This group lived in a variety of places, including Jamaica, Barbados, St. Kitts, Antigua, Nevis, the Bahamas, and Bermuda. They almost all pursued either commercial or maritime occupations. Of the fifteen, four described themselves as merchants, four considered themselves to be "mariners," and at least five owned ships. In contrast to the West Indian immigrants of an earlier generation who settled the South Carolina lowcountry in an effort to expand their agricultural endeavors and grow provisions for the islands, these islanders came in small numbers, and few of them considered themselves to be planters or mentioned any agricultural occupation.[60] Evidently the opening of an oceangoing port in the Lower Cape

TABLE 1.3 **Some Characteristics of Lower Cape Fear Residents Who Can Be Linked to Residences in Other Regions**

Location	*Total*	*Merchant*	*Planter*	*Patenting Land*	*Acres Patented*	*Out-migrants*
Upper Cape Fear	63	10	21	19	21,651	15
England	56	26	9	23	53,999	1
South Carolina	47	16	12	26	114,483	0
Northeastern North Carolina	36	9	14	25	92,500	4
Middle colonies	35	10	6	13	23,447	3
Scotland	33	14	6	11	18,169	0
Ireland	19	9	4	9	19,460	0
New England	16	8	6	6	10,401	1
Island colonies	15	4	2	2	3,160	3
North Carolina backcountry	8	1	2	1	520	2
Other southern colonies	8	3	3	0	0	1
Continental Europe	4	1	0	0	0	0
Total	340	111	85	137	357,970	30

Note: The number of individuals patenting land and the total number of acres patented includes patents taken out by individuals who do not appear to have resided in the Lower Cape Fear and are excluded from the other numbers but who can clearly be linked to the location in question. These figures also do not include land outside of the Lower Cape Fear counties of New Hanover and Brunswick.

TABLE 1.4 **Some Characteristics of Lower Cape Fear Residents Who Can Be Linked to Residences in Other Locations, by Percentages and Averages**

Location	*% Merchants*	*% Planters*	*% Patenting Land*	*Average Acres Patented*	*% Out-migrants*
Upper Cape Fear	16	33	30	344	24
England	46	16	41	964	2
South Carolina	34	26	55	2,436	0
Northeastern North Carolina	25	39	69	2,569	11
Middle colonies	26	17	47	670	8
Scotland	42	18	33	551	0
Ireland	47	21	47	1,024	0
New England	50	38	38	650	6
Island colonies	27	0	13	211	20
North Carolina backcountry	13	25	38	65	25
Other southern colonies	38	38	0	0	13
Continental Europe	25	0	0	0	0
Total	32	25	40	1,053	9

Note: Average acres patented refers to the total number of acres patented by all individuals who patented land and who could be linked to the region, divided by all the individuals linked to that region who became residents of the Lower Cape Fear.

Fear inspired many important merchants in the Atlantic world to resettle where they could take better advantage of the promising opportunities.

Some Lower Cape Fear residents had also lived in other British mainland colonies other than North and South Carolina. Most of these can be linked to the northern nonplantation colonies. Thirty-five lived in the Middle Colonies; sixteen lived in New England. Merchants were prominent in both groups, and these were probably representative of the important mercantile interests and communities of Philadelphia and Boston.

In Pennsylvania, at least, there is evidence that the Lower Cape Fear attracted the attention of a broader range of people. In 1731, Benjamin Franklin published in the *Pennsylvania Gazette* "An Account of the Cape Fear Country, 1731," by Hugh Meredith, his former business partner. He saw fit to publish this item because, for the last three or four years, the Cape Fear region had "been the Subject of much Discourse, especially among Country People; and great numbers resorting thither continually from this and the neighboring Provinces." Apparently not all of those were departing to resettle, because some went "merely to view the Place and learn the Nature of the Country, that they may be capable of judging . . . if they should remove and settle there."[61] Many of these travelers were probably Welsh.

Somewhat more surprisingly, there were only six individuals with ties to Virginia and Maryland, and only two linked to Georgia. While these colonies shared slave-owning and plantation-oriented interests with the early settlers of the Lower Cape Fear, these similarities did not outweigh more practical considerations. Such settlers often had land available to them closer by, and this and the costs of relocating to the Cape Fear must have dissuaded many.

Thus the early development of the Lower Cape Fear involved negotiation between individuals with diverse backgrounds, expectations, and desires. But even as these people struggled to impose their own visions, hard realities intruded on the process of settlement and frustrated some of their hopes. Many entertained hopes of profiting on rice, like planters in the South Carolina lowcountry, but the land of the Lower Cape Fear could not profitably produce large quantities of rice; indeed, by the end of the colonial period, rice proved to be marginal to the region's export profits. Others probably hoped to see an end to the social and political turmoil in colonial North Carolina by setting up a new regime in the Lower Cape Fear, but the settling of the region resulted in decades of polarizing political controversy. And no matter how much the region developed, socially and culturally, it would remain for the colonial period what many considered to be a "Remote Part of the World."[62] Even James Murray, who began his journey to the Lower Cape Fear with such high hopes, ultimately left the province, frustrated with the economy and concerned for his health because of the climate. For many, the new regional identity of the Lower Cape Fear was not entirely positive.

Still, the sheer presence of so many newcomers reveals some comparatively positive perceptions of the Lower Cape Fear. Immigrants in the early modern British Atlantic world could choose from a wide range of choices in selecting their new homes. The Lower Cape Fear was not the most popular destination for immigrants, but it drew thousands of settlers into a relatively unknown and remote place in the space of a few decades. Many of these settlers, at least, must have made conscious choices based on their hopes and expectations about the region. Consequently, population data provides some of the most reliable information on immigration to the Lower Cape Fear. In the absence of detailed records, it is possible to discern that many people migrated to the region, and this aggregate data reflects numerous individual choices. Of course, it tells us little about why they came. Presumably many responded to some of the same motives as James Murray, Maurice Moore, or Edward Moseley.

The data remains imperfect in other ways. To begin with, there are no reliable numbers from which to derive any kind of population estimates before the 1750s. In addition, the numbers that do exist do not necessarily correspond to voluntary immigration. The vast majority of the people in the colonial Lower Cape Fear had no such choice. Slaves and other dependents came to the Lower Cape Fear against their will, and their large numbers skew any attempt to judge perceptions about the Lower Cape Fear from population estimates.

Fortunately, existing records at least make it possible to estimate the relative size of the European American and African American population of the Lower Cape Fear region in the late colonial period. Because slave owners were taxed for adult males in their households and for their slaves, lists of the number of taxables in each county provide a guide to the size of both populations in different parts of North Carolina.[63] At the same time, significant problems with these sources prevent anything more than a crude estimate. It is sometimes difficult to ascertain the ratio of taxables to the number of nontaxable residents such as Euro-American women and children.[64] More importantly, the extant lists of taxables for each county come from different sources, and consequently some numbers contradict each other. One set of numbers comes from the county tax lists, which include breakdowns of the taxables in each household.[65] Other data derives from estimates reported to the secretary of the province and included in the governor's letters to the Board of Trade in the *Colonial Records of North Carolina*.[66]

Despite the limitations of these sources, they do reveal some important characteristics of the population of the colonial Lower Cape Fear, as is evident in tables 1.5, 1.6, 1.7, 1.8, 1.9, and 1.10.[67] To begin with, they make it clear that a significant majority of the colonial Lower Cape Fear's population consisted of African American slaves. None of the figures for either county indicate that African Americans made up fewer than 55 percent of the population at any time. At one point in the 1760s, slaves appear to have comprised more than 70

TABLE 1.5 **The Population of the Lower Cape Fear as Estimated from County Tax Lists, 1755–63**

Year	*White Taxables*	*Estimated White Population*	*Black Taxables*	*Estimated Black Population*	*Black % of the Population*	*Estimated Total Population*
1755	397	1,628	1,441	2,723	63	4351
1762	574	2,353	2,053	3,880	62	6233
1763	579	2,374	2,129	4,024	63	6398

TABLE 1.6 **The Population of New Hanover and Brunswick Counties as Estimated Separately from Tax Lists, 1767–72**

County	*Year*	*White Taxables*	*Estimated White Population*	*Black Taxables*	*Black Population*	*Estimated of the Population*	*Black % Estimated Total Population*
N.H.	1767	503	2,062	1,451	2,742	57	4,804
Bruns.	1769	249	1,021	1,172	2,215	68	3,236
Bruns.	1772	231	947	1,087	2,054	68	3,001

Table 1.7 **The Population of the Lower Cape Fear as Estimated from *Colonial Records*, 1754–67**

Year	*White Taxables*	*Estimated White Population*	*Black Taxables*	*Estimated Black Population*	*Black % of the Population*	*Estimated Total Population*
1754	362	1,484	1,374	2,597	64	4,081
1755	362	1,484	1,374	2,597	64	4,081
1756	396	1,624	1,420	2,684	62	4,308
1763	509	2,087	2,161	4,084	66	6,171
1765	738	3,026	2,582	4,880	62	7,906
1766	736	3,018	2,708	5,119	63	8,137
1767	735	3,013	2,577	4,870	62	7,884

Table 1.8 **The Population of New Hanover County Estimated from *Colonial Records*, 1765–67**

Year	*White Taxables*	*Estimated White Population*	*Black Taxables*	*Estimated Black Population*	*Black % of the Population*	*Estimated Total Population*
1765	529	2,169	1,476	2,790	56	4,959
1766	507	2,079	1,531	2,894	58	4,973
1767	511	2,095	1,492	2,820	57	4,915

TABLE 1.9 **The Population of Brunswick County Estimated from *Colonial Records*, 1765–67**

Year	*White Taxables*	*Estimated White Population*	*Black Taxables*	*Estimated Black Population*	*Black % of the Population*	*Estimated Total Population*
1766	209	857	1,106	2,090	71	2,947
1765	229	939	1,177	2,225	70	3,164
1767	224	918	1,085	2,051	69	2,969

TABLE 1.10 **Averages of Population Estimates Using Both Sources**

Counties	*Year*	*Average Estimated White Population*	*Average Estimated Black Population*	*Average Black % of the Population*	*Average Estimated Total Population*
Both	1755	1,556	2,660	59	4,216
Both	1763	2,230	4,054	55	6,284
N.H.	1767	2,079	2,781	57	4,860

percent of the population of Brunswick County.[68] Thus, slaves undoubtedly played an important part in the development of the Lower Cape Fear, despite their relative silence. While cementing bonds with South Carolina's more slave-oriented societies, they also distinguished the Lower Cape Fear from other North Carolina regions, where slaves continued to be much scarcer.

The coerced arrival of thousands of slaves therefore dramatically influenced the development of the new Cape Fear settlement, offering a stark counterpoint to the hopeful plans of free immigrants like the Moores, Edward Moseley, and James Murray. Traditionally, historians have assumed that slaves were brought into North Carolina almost exclusively overland, because the slaves shipped into the colony left little record. Recently scholars have unearthed more evidence that indicates that the sea-borne slave trade to North Carolina may have been more substantial than it was once thought, though still far smaller than the trade to Virginia or South Carolina.[69] In any case, it remains clear that the origins and experiences of slaves brought into the colonial Lower Cape Fear Region remained diverse, complicated, and difficult to trace.

Because North Carolina markets lacked the wealth necessary to entice transatlantic slave traders, few slaves came directly from Africa to the Lower Cape Fear. Elite North Carolinians regularly complained about the lack of shipments of slaves from Africa. In 1733, Governor Burrington noted the difficulty of obtaining slaves in North Carolina because of the lack of a slave trade with Africa.[70] Similarly, James Murray wrote to fellow merchant Richard Oswald that slaves were especially expensive in the Lower Cape Fear, where there was no supply "but from the West Indies or the Neighbouring Colonies."[71] Recent research reveals, however, that at least six sizeable shipments of slaves from Africa appear to have arrived in North Carolina between 1756 and 1768.[72] Unfortunately, it is impossible to determine precisely how many slaves arrived on each of these shipments or where in North Carolina they disembarked. The characteristics of North Carolina's ports make it likely that these vessels went to the Cape Fear, and the size of the ships suggest that as many as one thousand Africans may have arrived in the region on these voyages, but the numbers might also be considerably lower.

The coastal trade between British colonies also brought many enslaved people to the Lower Cape Fear region. Fragmentary surviving port records reveal that more than three hundred slaves came to the Lower Cape Fear between 1771 and 1775, in a combination of ships predominantly from Jamaica, but also including some from other British West Indian colonies and from Charles Town, South Carolina.[73] These records probably reveal a pattern of slave importation that had persisted for some years. Between 1749 and 1767, more than eight hundred other slaves arrived in the colony from shipping voyages to unspecified ports in North Carolina, and it seems likely that a high percentage of these disembarked in the Lower Cape Fear.[74] In the years leading up to the American

Revolution, the Wilmington Safety Committee also noted small importations of slaves by Lower Cape Fear settlers Harold Blackmore, Arthur Mabson, Cornelius Harnett, and others.[75] The coastal slave trade into the Lower Cape Fear proved too small to maintain regular voyages devoted to the trade, so slaves arrived haphazardly, in small numbers, on voyages focused on other trading activities. While the slaves arrived in small or even solitary groups, hundreds of slaves were gradually added to the region's population in this manner. The marginal character of this trade also probably gave Cape Fear slave buyers little leverage in markets and forced them to purchase an eclectic mix of slaves perhaps deemed less desirable by owners and traders in other colonies.[76]

The bulk of the Lower Cape Fear region's slaves must have come into the region either overland or on coastal voyages during the early years of settlement, most frequently from the South Carolina lowcountry. Indeed, it is hard to imagine that South Carolina planters such as the Moores would have migrated without taking at least some of their slaves. Slave ownership played such a large role in the growth of South Carolina lowcountry society that many Cape Fear settlers saw it as a prerequisite for economic success. Large numbers of slaves lived in the Lower Cape Fear shortly after the settlement started, and the enslaved population of the region probably continued to grow because of some natural increase and small-scale importations. Once settlers arrived in the Lower Cape Fear, the proximity and scale of slave markets in the South Carolina lowcountry would have enticed those who wished to purchase labor. In 1734, at least 110 slaves arrived in North Carolina from ships leaving Charles Town, and in all likelihood these slaves were bought by those in the new Lower Cape Fear settlement.[77]

John Dalrymple tried to import slaves from South Carolina to the Lower Cape Fear on at least two occasions. In 1737, a group of slaves that Dalrymple brought from Charles Town had to be quarantined because of a potentially contagious illness.[78] By fall 1739, Dalrymple was purchasing slaves again, as the importer of 1 adult slave who had accompanied 176 other survivors of the middle passage from the Gambia to Charles Town.[79] James Murray also came to rely on South Carolina connections to purchase slaves after Lower Cape Fear efforts to establish a direct slave trade from Africa failed. Murray's letters reveal attempts to purchase South Carolina slaves over several decades and from different merchants.[80]

The regular slave trade from South Carolina and other locales to the Lower Cape Fear wrenched apart some slave families and presented a daunting challenge for those who tried to participate in slave communities. No doubt many slaves resisted this difficult transition, and occasional advertisements for runaway slaves in the colonial newspapers of North and South Carolina reveal that flight from one colony to the other often seemed to be a response to sale and forced migration.[81] Even slaves who did not have strong ties to the South Carolina lowcountry or other stops on the slave trade to the Lower Cape Fear would have been forced to adapt to a variety of different circumstances that would influence their lives in the Lower Cape Fear. Entry into the Lower Cape Fear Region combined with the characteristics of slavery and the region itself to shape the experiences of thousands of enslaved people.

Various sources also give some indication of the magnitude of the total population of the Lower Cape Fear from the mid-1750s to the 1770s. In 1755, little more than four thousand people lived in the region. By the American Revolution, the combined population of the two Lower Cape Fear counties probably exceeded eight thousand inhabitants, with a larger share in New Hanover County. This made them less populous than most North Carolina counties, and Brunswick was one of the least populous in the colony. Indeed, only about 5 percent of North Carolina's population resided in the Lower Cape Fear in the late 1760s.[82]

Population estimates also give a sense of the growth of the Lower Cape Fear settlements. Prior to the 1750s, there is little data on the number of inhabitants in the region. Nonetheless, it is clear that the population grew quite rapidly in the ten years after the region opened up. In 1732, George Burrington wrote, while commenting on the growth of the Cape Fear, "I beleive the number of people are doubled since I was there last year."[83] About the same time, a group of settlers petitioned the Society for the Propagation of the Gospel because they were "upwards of 1500 Souls and are daily increasing and have no Minister."[84] By 1736, James Murray complained that provisions were scarce and inadequate for the numerous new arrivals.[85] As more settlers arrived and claimed resources, the influx gradually slowed, but the population of the Lower Cape Fear continued to grow steadily throughout the colonial period. In 1742, one Anglican missionary wrote that in the Lower Cape Fear "we have about 3000 Inhabitants, two thirds whereof are Negroes."[86] According to the recorded numbers of taxables, the population of the region certainly showed significant growth between 1754 and 1772. Of course, population growth was a common feature of colonial American societies in the eighteenth century. Moreover, the increase in the Lower Cape Fear seems slight when compared with rates for counties in the North Carolina backcountry. On the other hand, population in the Lower Cape Fear grew much more quickly than in the older Albemarle counties, and such significant levels of growth must be partly attributed to immigration.[87] Thus, fifty years after Maurice Moore laid out his plan for Brunswick, the Lower Cape Fear continued to beckon newcomers.

If the Lower Cape Fear did not continue to attract as many settlers as the Carolina backcountry, it did become an important and distinctive region in North Carolina. Those who followed Moore not only filled the Lower Cape Fear with people, they also stimulated growth in a variety of ways: they developed the land; formed families and networks; instilled forms of legal and political order;

wrestled with the problems and contradictions of plantation slavery; sought prosperity; and attempted to impose their own ideas of civility and authority. As they participated in these activities, the inhabitants of the Lower Cape Fear behaved in ways that subtly differentiated them from the inhabitants of nearby regions of colonial British America. Conversely, colonists elsewhere simultaneously recognized their own differences from settlers in the Lower Cape Fear and other places, as regional cultures burgeoned and became rooted in geographic space.

Chapter 2

LAND AND REGION

In 1761, twenty-two-year-old William Bartram arrived in the Cape Fear River, where he planned to go into business. While his father, John Bartram, had already achieved some renown as a botanist, few who encountered William in North Carolina would have imagined that he would later become one of the most famous Americans of the eighteenth century because of his travel writings, drawings, studies, and observations about nature. At this time, Bartram's vocation remained uncertain, and, at his father's urging, he had agreed to test his aptitude for trade. Surviving letters and documents do not fully explain why he chose to begin his career as a merchant along the Cape Fear River, but the decision was probably made with careful deliberation after considering a variety of factors. No doubt many of the expectations that drew James Murray and other merchants to the Lower Cape Fear region helped to lure Bartram. William Bartram himself had never been to North Carolina before, but he would have been aware that the Bartram family also had important ties to this area.[1]

In any case, when William Bartram considered the Cape Fear as the site for his new trading enterprise, he did so as part of the personal process of interpreting and imagining a new place. By 1761 this new place had come to mean something to William Bartram, even if its precise meaning to him eludes historians. For all Anglo-American settlers, but perhaps for a naturalist more than for most, the meaning of a place depended partly on one's perception of its physical environment.

William had no doubt heard of North Carolina when he was a child: his grandfather died there and one of his uncles lived along the Cape Fear River. His grandfather settled on Bogue Sound in 1709, but died fighting Native Americans in the Tuscarora War two years later. John Bartram, William's father, had been left in Philadelphia, but William's uncle, also named William Bartram, stayed in North Carolina.[2] Colonel William Bartram, as the brother who remained in North Carolina would become known, migrated to the new Cape Fear settlement in 1726, bought a plantation, called Ashwood, on the fringes of the Lower Cape Fear region, and became a man of some prominence in local affairs.[3] The name Ashwood came from a member of the Ashe family, who had owned it before Colonel Bartram, but by the time the naturalist William Bartram wrote about his visit to Ashwood in his famous *Travels,* he had begun to think of it as "the ancient seat" of Colonel William Bartram.[4] Previous experiences and impressions of the Lower Cape Fear settlement no doubt influenced many new settlers' perspectives on the land of the region, and young William Bartram's long-standing family connection to the area, as well as the possibility of assistance and advice from his Uncle William, encouraged the young merchant to migrate to the Cape Fear.

Despite his later devotion to science, William Bartram in 1761 focused on the Lower Cape Fear environment as a potential source of profit. His first encounter with the region proved to be discouraging: he arrived "to a bad Market, [during] a wrong season of the Year" as "the excessive rains . . . [had] almost destroyed the Country" after they "continued Incessantly for 7 or 8 days and kept me in Idleness." The rains were so bad that his uncle had "been a Greate Sufferer by this Inundation," while the "banks of the River being overflowed spread over the Low Lands to a greate distance" and "many People . . . [were driven] from their Dwellings & forced to seek shelter in the Woods & Sandhills."[5] Despite already having scientific interests, Bartram assessed the rains in terms of their human consequences, unaware that the Lower Cape Fear region's increasingly wet weather during the early 1760s reinitiated a cycle of alternating thirty-year periods of wetness and dryness that characterized the region for a more than a millennium before European settlement and that have continued until the present.[6]

Bartram's reaction typified the response of many immigrants to the region, who sought pattern and meaning in self-interest and local perspectives. Young William Bartram's uncle, for example, described "the Largest fresh in our River that Ever was Known Since the C[o]untry was Set[t]led" as having "Don[e] Many Thousands of Pounds of Damage," remarking that he expected to "Loos Neer two Hundred Pounds worth."[7] Years later, when William Bartram the naturalist composed his *Travels,* he would still note the agricultural potential of lands along the Cape Fear River.[8] By about a year after his arrival in the Lower Cape Fear, William had expanded his trading activities to include shipments of Lower Cape Fear turpentine to Philadelphia, but his business in the region ultimately did not last, and it apparently yielded few profits. In 1765, William ended his residence in North Carolina and joined his father, the newly appointed "king's chief botanist" on an expedition to Florida.[9]

William Bartram did spend enough time in the Lower Cape Fear region to indulge his scientific curiosity, occasionally wandering through the wilderness and recording information about various plants in the manner that later in the century would establish his international reputation. As he went, Bartram observed, described, and categorized the particular and distinctive botanical world of each place he visited. One peculiar discovery made his temporary place of residence along the Cape Fear River very important and distinctive to botanists. By 1759, the North Carolina governor, Arthur Dobbs, noted a carnivorous plant near his residence at Brunswick and wrote Peter Collinson in London to inform the scientific community of what would become known as the Venus flytrap. As soon as William Bartram arrived in the Lower Cape Fear, John Bartram eagerly encouraged his son to learn more about Dobbs's intriguing discovery. He noted that, if such a plant existed, "it will be A fine curiousity & furnish matter for phylosofical contemplation." The elder Bartram also correctly realized that the Venus flytrap grew near Brunswick for specific ecological reasons and that it would not be found near Ashwood or elsewhere. John advised his son that "ye moors near Bruinswick knowed it well: if it leith in thy way to speak with Moris More [Maurice Moore]: ask him about it."[10] The distinctive plant can be found in the wild only within the pine barrens and swamps of the Lower Cape Fear region and a few places adjacent to the region across the South Carolina border. From the perspective of botanists like John and William Bartram, this obscure and anomalous plant marked off the Lower Cape Fear region as a distinctive place, just as other settlers would find yet other local details and characteristics that would enable them to connect places and meaning.

William Bartram never resided in the Lower Cape Fear region again after 1765. He would write voluminously about other places and other natural environments in the decades after his departure, but his experiences in North Carolina would remain important to him for the rest of his life. In his *Travels,* he described Ashwood's location "on the high banks of the river, near seventy feet in height," where it "commands a magnificent prospect of the low lands opposite, when in their native state, presenting to the view grand forests and expansive Cane meadows."[11] By this time, a visit to Ashwood must have been bittersweet for the naturalist: Colonel William Bartram and his son Billy, the naturalist's cousin, had both died. In his fifties, William Bartram again wrote about Ashwood in a letter to his cousin Mary Bartram Robeson. He assured her that "Time, vicicitudes of Fortune, tribulation; I may say indeed the decrepitude of old age, are not sufficient to erace from my hand those impressions which it received during my residence in my Unkles family in No. Carolina." After many years, the "delightful country" of Ashwood and its "striking scenes of past transactions" returned to William Bartram in "Dreams by Night, or serious reveres by day." As Bartram recognized, his perspective on Ashwood depended on his imagination: he had not visited North Carolina for decades, and he did not bother to ponder how it might have changed in his absence.[12] In less than five years, William Bartram ran the gamut of settlers' approaches to the land along the Cape Fear River, treating it as an economic resource, contemplating it as a distinctive environment, and finally reifying it as part of personal memory and experience.

As William Bartram's experience indicates, a variety of factors motivated Anglo-American settlers to go to the Lower Cape Fear in the early eighteenth century, but matters related to land certainly played a key role for many and continued to structure the experience of settlers once they entered the region. To some extent, this observation holds true for settlers in all British American colonies, but in the Lower Cape Fear, land matters took a distinctive direction. Settlers such as William Bartram who entered the Lower Cape Fear region made their own choices, and neither the broader contemporary patterns that they fit into nor the categories later imposed by historians predetermined the formation and character of specific regions. As with all places, the Lower Cape Fear proved more suited to some uses than to others, and settlers both shaped and were shaped by the geography of the region they created.

The process of land acquisition differentiated the colonial Lower Cape Fear from other areas of the British American southern colonies in significant ways. Perhaps most important, the process of land distribution in the region resulted in an incredible degree of confusion and contestation.[13] Partly as a result of this situation, landholdings became unusually stratified and remained that way until after the Revolution. At the same time, Lower Cape Fear settlers chose to use land in rather unconventional ways. A heavy emphasis on forest industries, such as naval stores and lumbering, meant that entrepreneurs required large amounts of land and had unusually little incentive to develop the land they possessed. Finally, settlers within the Lower Cape Fear, like those in other regions of British America, occupied the land in different ways because of the varying exigencies of their localities and because of their differing circumstances.

Some geographic factors strongly encouraged settlers to consider the Lower Cape Fear to be a separate region. To begin with, the Cape Fear River itself proved crucial. Settlement throughout early America clustered around rivers and waterways, major rivers playing an enormous role in the spatial organization of early America. Because the Cape Fear was one of the largest and most conveniently located rivers in the Carolinas, it made sense that a bond would form among settlers who lived near enough to rely on it in various ways. The Cape Fear River directed trade, enabled communication, defined neighborhoods, and structured travel. Those beyond the river valley, or reliant on other river systems, became outsiders.

The geographic characteristics of North Carolina's Outer Coastal Plain also contributed to the Lower Cape Fear's regional identity. This flat, poorly drained area of low elevations, known to contemporaries by many labels, including tidewater, flatwood, or lowcountry, differentiated life in the Lower Cape Fear from life up the river in the more elevated and drier Inner Coastal Plain. While the Outer Coastal Plain exhibited a variety of different kinds of land, including sand dunes, tidal marshes, bottomlands, savannahs, and pine barrens, a preponderance of wetlands made the area ill-suited for agriculture, compared with more inland parts of North Carolina. Long-leaf pine trees dominated the landscape of the Outer Coastal Plain.[14]

The Lower Cape Fear region also differed from other parts of North Carolina because of its climate. The Cape Fear River marked the northernmost reaches of the climate zone that included most of South Carolina and Georgia. The more tropical crops that could be grown in South Carolina could also be grown along the Lower Cape Fear, but less effectively and in a shorter growing season.[15] Unlike the rest of North Carolina, however, the warmer, coastal weather patterns made the Lower Cape Fear seem part of a more exotic and semitropical plantation world.

No aspect of geography played a larger role in the history of the Lower Cape Fear region than the coast. The Cape Fear coast was a mixed blessing. As is indicated by the name Cape Fear, North Carolina's coastline presented numerous hazards to eighteenth-century seamen, and it acquired a notorious reputation even before the arrival of colonists in the area. But the mouth of the Cape Fear itself was something of an exception. While it remained comparatively dangerous, the Cape Fear provided a navigable port for early-modern oceangoing vessels. This port differentiated it from the rest of North Carolina, which remained far less accessible and more isolated. The coast did not make a thriving port possible, but it offered comparatively good opportunities for shipping.

The settlers who arrived in the Lower Cape Fear between 1725 and 1775 altered and reconceived these geographic conditions according to their own agendas, but they were far from the first to do so. Like most of the North American continent, the land of the Lower Cape Fear had been occupied and shaped by Native American inhabitants long before the arrival of the first European Americans.[16] In 1521, a Spanish expedition claimed the area for Spain and dubbed it Chicora.[17] As early as 1524, French explorers had also entered the region, when Giovanni da Verrazano and his crew visited the mouth of the Cape Fear River.[18]

Yet neither the Spanish nor the French ever seriously attempted to found permanent settlements in North Carolina. During the 1660s, however, the new Carolina proprietary charter inspired two Anglo-American efforts to plant colonies on the Cape Fear. Both were influenced by the explorations of William Hilton, who visited the region in 1663 and "found as good tracts of land, dry, well wooded, pleasant and delightful as we have seen any where in the world."[19] The first group of settlers came from the Massachusetts Bay Company, the second from Barbados. In both cases, some settlers did actually move to the Cape Fear, but, for reasons that have escaped posterity, neither settlement lasted very long. The second settlement appears to have been substantial: one promotional pamphlet claimed it had a population of about eight hundred.[20] By 1667, however, once again "the plantations at Cape Feare are deserted."[21] The primary cause for these failures appears to have been the hostility of local tribes, limited resources, and a lack support from England.[22] While Hilton had imagined and expressed great promise for the region, these two failed expeditions ruined the reputation of the region for decades, and until the Moores and their allies moved northward in the 1720s, the land was again left solely to the Native Americans.

Thus, geography and perspectives on the region's land helped to differentiate the Lower Cape Fear from other colonial regions. While acquiring, conceptualizing, and developing the natural environment of the Lower Cape Fear, settlers recognized regional characteristics and ultimately came to identify those characteristics with their own way of life. At the same time, because land ownership played a central role in social and economic relationships, land matters contributed to the growth and elaboration of Lower Cape Fear society.

From the beginnings of British settlement in North America, the lure of easily obtained land drew many settlers from Europe. As the colonies developed and the boundaries of settlement shifted, promoters heralded one place after another as the best opportunity for industrious newcomers to better their station or even to obtain riches. Contemporaries interested in promoting or participating in new settlements gradually constructed different identities for geographic spaces. These constructions of spaces then played a continually important role in the development of local and regional identities after settlement. The vast, unsettled regions of North Carolina, including the Lower Cape Fear, fit into this pattern in the early eighteenth century, and it was in this tradition that Scotus American described North Carolina as "Upon the whole, . . . the best country in the world for a poor man to go to, and do well."[23]

The dynamics of colonial promotion and settlement encouraged such high expectations. In some cases these hopes were realized. But settling in the Lower Cape Fear, as in most places, usually involved risk and sometimes led to disappointment. Often, the degree of progress achieved by settling in a place like the Lower Cape Fear depended on one's perspective. In 1745, Pennsylvanian William Logan traveled through the Lower Cape Fear and encountered a ferrykeeper whom he named as John Malsby. According to Logan, Malsby "lived formerly at the Middle Ferry on Skulylkill, but left it & came to this Wilderness Country in hope of getting an Estate, by the purchase of Lands." As an educated and urbane Quaker merchant, Logan looked on the Lower Cape Fear and Malsby's endeavors with contempt. On Malsby's expectations of wealth, Logan wrote that he was "much mistaken or I am," and he went on to complain about the uncomfortable accommodations at Malsby's house.[24]

From the perspective of Logan and no doubt many others, land schemes and new settlements like those on the Lower Cape Fear enticed naive and desperate people to abandon more settled and civilized homes in the pursuit of illusory riches. But it is easy to imagine that Malsby saw the matter differently and that he may not have regretted his choice. Indeed, there is evidence to suggest that Malsby did well by migrating to the Lower Cape Fear. He appears a number of times in the local records of the region, with his surname more often spelled as Maultsby. Maultsby, like Logan, was a Pennsylvania Quaker. To Logan it appeared that Maultsby came to the Lower Cape Fear merely to reprise his career as a ferrykeeper, but before his death in 1758, the records would also describe him as a planter. Maultsby also succeeded in obtaining land, eventually more than a thousand acres. The Maultsby family "estate" also extended beyond mere land. In 1755, his son paid taxes on four slaves, who presumably worked the land.[25] Logan might have remained skeptical, but, depending on what resources he brought with him, Maultsby may have done quite well for himself in the Lower Cape Fear.

Whether their expectations were realistic or not, eighteenth-century British colonists repeatedly attempted to assess the prospects for settlement in the Lower Cape Fear in economic terms. Most frequently, they did so by considering the products that could be produced from the region's land. Hugh Meredith speculated that some areas "might make tolerable good Rice-Ground, as is done with the like in South Carolina," and exulted of another piece of land: "Here I saw the finest Crop of Indian Corn I ever have seen; the stalks of which measured 18 foot long."[26] Upon visiting the Lower Cape Fear in 1765, Lord Adam Gordon commented along the same lines that the region's lands, "when properly cleared and Cultivated, will produce all manner of Grain in plenty and perfection." But he also observed that the land did not produce rice comparable with that in South Carolina and that the present settlers devoted more resources to naval stores and lumber than to crops.[27] In the 1740s, George Minot attempted to sell his plantation in the Lower Cape Fear by boasting that "the soil is peculiar for Indigo which is now made in that Neighborhood to great Proffitt."[28] In newly settled places like the Lower Cape Fear, the relative ease of obtaining land created a more varied range of economic options and shifted emphasis to the land's ability to produce valuable commodities.

Cultural imperatives also reinforced the economic emphasis on land ownership. Anglo-American culture celebrated land ownership as a vehicle to economic and political independence and as an indicator of status. Land meant independence, and independence was, in the words of Scotus Americanus, "a great sweetener of life and every blessing, and makes up for many superfluous refinements in what is called polite society."[29] Consequently, while many Lower Cape Fear residents described themselves as merchants and profited in trade, they also often aspired to the lifestyle of the planter. James Murray, for example, lived in Brunswick and devoted himself primarily to trade only long enough to find and purchase a country plantation. By 1751, he declared, "I see nothing yet to tempt [me] to dip any more in the Trade of this River. I imagine I can live more contentedly as a Planter and be of some use both to my family and the Publick."[30] For men like Murray, the status and relative security of plantation life proved more comfortable than the potential profits of commercial activity. Owning a plantation and participating in commerce also enabled elite men like Murray to choose between alternative economic activities, seeking either greater security or more opportunistic gains according to their own preferences. For people without the resources to engage in transatlantic trade like Murray, land ownership not only meant more security, it also offered them a chance to elevate their status.

Whether attempting to duplicate the large rice plantations of the South Carolina lowcountry, striving to live like country gentlemen, or scrabbling to obtain subsistence and property for their families, Lower Cape Fear landowners had to adjust to the character and limitations of the region's land. Contemporary accounts indicate no consensus about the quality of land in the region, perhaps in part because tracts could vary a great deal. In any case, the possibilities for cultivation were clearly limited. The climate and riverine characteristics of the region encouraged many who hoped to cultivate rice, but little rice was, in fact, produced in the Lower Cape Fear.[31] Some could grow rice profitably, but the Lower Cape Fear would never be a region of rice planters. Meredith, after praising the region in a number of ways, still commented that the region would be filled much more quickly if it were "less barren" and warned prospective settlers that the Lower Cape Fear could not provide sufficient land for as many people as resided in Bucks County, Pennsylvania. Similarly, in 1735 George Burrington told the Board of Trade that "all the plantable Land Upon Navigable Streams" had been claimed before he left for England. If Burrington could make this claim so early, there must have been large amounts of uncultivable land in the Lower Cape Fear. Continual complaints about grain shortages underscore these agricultural problems. As early as 1753, John Rutherford reported to the assembly that "the Inhabitants there were really in Distress for want of Grain." On several occasions, the legislature placed prohibitions on the exportation of grain from the region.

Lower Cape Fear crops were constrained not only by a shortage of good land for rice cultivation but also by a preponderance of pine barren lands. As one contemporary said, "The pine barren is worst, being almost all sand." Yet, if pine barrens were useless for agriculture, they offered other opportunities. The pine barren "bears the pine tree . . . naturally yielding good profit in pitch, tar, and turpentine." These commodities generally derived from the long-leaf pine. Grouped under the name "naval stores" because of their usefulness to the Royal Navy, they would prove to be the most important source of profits for the inhabitants of the Lower Cape Fear. If early settlers were dismayed by the poor farm land, most seem to have adapted and taken advantage of this important and comparatively plentiful Cape Fear resource.[32] If, then, the Lower Cape Fear quickly acquired a reputation for poor farm land, it also redeemed itself for many as an excellent region for the production of forest products.

The close relationship between expectations for the region and hopes for economic success made the distribution of land ownership particularly important for the development of the Lower Cape Fear. Theoretically, the system of land acquisition in North Carolina should have allowed for an equitable and relatively uncomplicated distribution of land. Like many colonies, North Carolina operated on a headright system, whereby new householders could obtain a certain number of acres for themselves and additional acres for each servant, slave, or other person, or "head," they brought into the colony. Land patents could also be purchased from the Lords Proprietors, and ownership of a patent could be transferred. Both the proprietors and later the royal government attempted to limit the size of landholdings in North Carolina and ordered that no patent should exceed 640 acres without special permission from London. Equally important, depending on how the land had been acquired, many landholders were obligated to pay quitrents, a form of land tax. Thus, the authorities planned to institute a land system that would prevent large concentrations of land, provide the government with revenue, and, most important, encourage settlement with abundant and easily obtained land.[33]

In fact, during the settlement of the Lower Cape Fear, the system proved far more complicated, divisive, and chaotic than officials ever could have imagined. Some settlers acquired tens of thousands of acres, while others left the province because of their frustration at trying to obtain land. The government collected few quitrents in the region for the first fifteen years of settlement, and even then collection required compromise after a long and hotly contested political struggle. To assess fully the influence that land problems had on prospective settlers is impossible, but in many cases land ownership and boundaries remained uncertain for years and fueled acrimonious disputes. Officials in London revealed their total inability to enforce directives related to land. This scrabble for land in the Lower Cape Fear would continue to shape the region for the rest of the colonial period.

It had always been hard for officials to place constraints on the expansion of colonial settlements, but before the appointment of Governor George Burrington, North Carolina's proprietors appeared to have been relatively successful. Settlers obtained land primarily through headrights. North Carolina had as many small landholders and fewer large concentrations of land than virtually any other British southern colony, and no hard evidence exists that settlers had moved into the Lower Cape Fear against the proprietors' wishes.[34]

Much of this transition could be attributed to the character of Burrington himself and to his desire to capitalize on the settlement plans of the Moores in the Lower Cape Fear. Burrington was an enormously strong-willed and often violent man who showed little concern for instructions from his superiors. During his years as proprietary governor from 1724 to 1725 and royal governor from 1730 to 1734, various North Carolinians accused Burrington of many violent and illegal acts: threatening to kill people, stealing horses, perpetrating land fraud in a variety of ways, using the government for his own personal interests and vendettas, physically assaulting opponents, and smashing furniture to disrupt official proceedings. Perhaps most astounding of all was the allegation that he had attempted to blow up with gunpowder the house of the chief justice of North Carolina. As one critic put it, Burrington had "since his arrival here last been guilty of almost every crime saving that of murther."[35] During

Burrington's first term as governor he divided the colony's leaders into two hostile camps, but in his second term he united them all in opposition to his administration and, ultimately, claimed that they had conspired to overthrow and assassinate him.[36] In this political climate, it is easy to see why land might have been distributed to settlers haphazardly.

Burrington alone, however, could not have caused all of the land problems in the Lower Cape Fear. The Moores, Edward Moseley, and many other North Carolinians blatantly opposed the proprietors' land policies, and Burrington's unruly and contentious administration merely gave them a chance to disregard those policies. Indeed, evidence suggests that settlers left Burrington little choice in the matter. Burrington claimed that some people were already moving to the Cape Fear in 1724 when he started issuing land patents. If so, it would have been almost impossible to have enforced the proprietors' instructions and, by not patenting the land being settled, the government would have lost the opportunity for any quitrent revenue on the illegally settled lands. Moreover, settlers might even have been able to obtain rights to land from the government of South Carolina. Burrington's story is corroborated by a mysterious reference in the 1724 North Carolina General Court records to crimes against "one peter pedro of Cape Fair in South Carolina lately barbarously murther[e]d."[37] After the area had been settled against the proprietors' wishes, the colonial assembly praised Burrington's "Indefatiguable Industry and the Hardships he underwent in carrying on the Settlement at Cape Fear [which] deserves our thankful Remembrance."[38] The settling of the Cape Fear pleased many local leaders enough that they seemed willing to overlook Burrington's other glaring indiscretions. Nonetheless, Burrington's enemies secured his removal, and his first term as governor ended in 1725.

The pressure to settle the Lower Cape Fear lands was intense enough that Burrington's temporary successor as governor, Richard Everard, initially opposed Burrington's measures but ended up conceding at least as much land to prospective settlers as had Burrington. Everard also managed to continue Burrington's legacy of violence and disregard for instructions. The council complained to the king that Everard imprisoned people for criticizing his family, assaulted a respected man, and distributed land unlawfully. When the Crown purchased North Carolina from the proprietors, it replaced him with Burrington, who reclaimed his former office in 1731.[39]

Once Burrington and other colonial leaders had agreed on the importance of opening the Cape Fear to settlement and acted accordingly, the issue of land patents in the region became a central weapon in the colony's political disputes. Burrington and his many enemies simultaneously charged each other with illegal land transactions, speculation, greed, and deceit. Ironically, after having begun the patenting of Cape Fear lands, Burrington now charged Moseley, the Moores, and a number of other leaders with obtaining land through inappropriate means, while he himself held in excess of ten thousand acres of land in the region. Everard also received a share of the criticism, and other land seekers also fought each other over boundaries and ownership. All of these groups sought to shift blame, because the British authorities were bound to view these land policies with displeasure. Through the decade of the 1730s, the lands of the Lower Cape Fear continued to be a source of controversy, primarily because of four main issues: the alleged existence of "blank patents"; the shift to royal government; speculation; and quitrents.

Accusations that settlers in the Lower Cape Fear had obtained "blank patents" caused great concern in North Carolina and London. Supposedly, Everard had been persuaded to sign and give out patents without all of the appropriate information so that the bearers could fill in the amount and location of the land at their pleasure. According to a number of people, Edward Moseley and the Moore family held some of these blank patents. Murray, the Scottish immigrant, went so far as to dub them, derisively, "ye blank patent gentry."[40] Yet Governor Burrington and members of the Moore family denied these allegations. It had been customary for decades to leave some information off patents until the land had been surveyed, making more information available, and competing sides differed in their descriptions of just how incomplete the patents were. Governor Johnston insisted that he had seen the blank patents, that more existed, and that they were being sold. Others claimed that they had never existed.

It is impossible to tell exactly what occurred with these allegedly blank patents, but in any case, the controversy probably reflected a number of related problems with the patent system that may or may not have resulted from the use of incomplete patents. First of all, the size of patents in the early years of settlement along the Cape Fear definitely exceeded the 640–acre limit the proprietors imposed and that the Crown subsequently supported. Indeed, extant patents in the Lower Cape Fear issued before 1740 averaged more than 800 acres each.[41] The purchase of most of these early patents also contributed to a more concentrated and less equitable distribution of land than had prevailed under the headright system.[42] Further, many of the patented lands were surveyed and documented haphazardly, if at all, leading to overlapping claims and countless disputed boundaries. Many settlers also took out warrants for land, probably for speculative purposes, and waited long periods of time before applying for patents. Finally, many tracts of land were probably changing hands or being settled before the patent process took place. Burrington might have contributed to these problems by issuing many warrants but no patents during his term as royal governor from 1731 to 1734.[43] At the same time, self-interested settlers no doubt preferred to delay the patent process so that they could avoid paying quitrents, while speculators could took advantage of the inconsistent land documentation.

Given all these difficulties, when Governor Johnston took office a few incomplete land patents may have been the least of his problems. Johnston, however, chose to make them a central part of his case against Moseley, Moore, and other powerful individuals who held large amounts of land in the Lower Cape Fear. Johnston added considerable anxiety and animosity to the situation by proposing that all patents issued after 1725 be invalidated.[44]

The land situation was further complicated by the transition from proprietary to royal government. When the Crown purchased the colony from the proprietors, the rush for land in the Lower Cape Fear was in full force. In fact, the transition did little to disrupt the day-to-day function of political and legal authority in North Carolina, but colonists did not know exactly what to expect. Some speculators and settlers, anticipating tighter restrictions on land policies, moved to obtain as much land as they could before royal authority had the chance to assert itself. For one Lower Cape Fear leader, this rush for land raised the possibility that "before his Majesty's commissions can take place amongst us most of the Land will be disposed of under a sham proprietary title."[45]

In response to these concerns, Burrington's instructions as royal governor required him to inquire about land patented under the established proprietary system and expressed concerns about their legitimacy.[46] Others worried that they should wait until the beginnings of royal government before patenting land. In 1731, Meredith wrote that the official patenting process was "generally disapprov'd and seldom practis'd, the Title not being thought so good." He said that those looking to obtain land "daily expect Persons with Power from the King to sell Lands on more easy and certain terms."[47] So, while the North Carolina government moved easily into the Crown's control, even seemingly distant and subtle changes in political structure added confusion and panic to the precarious conditions of land ownership in the Lower Cape Fear.

At the same time that settlers were moving into the Lower Cape Fear and the proprietors' were relinquishing their control of North Carolina, quitrents became another source of disputes related to land. These events were interrelated. Quitrents, or taxes paid to the Crown for patented land, promised to be an increasingly important source of revenue since even large amounts of land were patented along the Cape Fear River. Equally important, the new royal government sought to put itself on a firmer financial base by doubling the previous quitrents and refusing to accept payment in locally produced commodities. Unfortunately for the Crown, no one had ever been able to collect quitrents reliably in North Carolina, and the changed circumstances only intensified resistance. On one level, this resistance could be attributed to the difficulty faced by all early-modern polities in trying to enforce unpopular directives. As Governor Johnston wrote, when his receiver-general met with problems collecting quitrents, "habitations are so scattered and lye at such a distance from one another that it is impossible [that] the Receiver could go about among them."[48] At the same time, the new leaders and principal landholders of the Lower Cape Fear made every effort to mobilize popular opposition to the payment of quitrents. Moseley, the colony's treasurer, but not the collector of quitrents, set a conspicuous example by flatly refusing to pay his own quitrents. Others were confident that nonpayment would be treated with clemency because "they are assured by Mr Moseley and the Family of the Moores that the Quitt Rents are too high for the poor people."[49] Many also avoided quitrents by not applying for patents on land they occupied, warranted, and used. No doubt partly for these reasons, Burrington apparently made little effort to collect quitrents and saw the increased rates as ill-advised. Under greater pressure from London, however, Governor Johnston placed more emphasis on resolving the quitrent problems, but he had little success.[50] As late as 1751, James Murray accepted the job of collecting quitrents and "attempted to go through with it without Success but not without Danger."[51]

Widespread speculation created additional difficulties. Burrington repeatedly accused Moseley, whom he described as "the great Land Jobber of this Country," of profiting from land sales.[52] According to these allegations, Moseley and the Family monopolized all the available land and profited heavily by selling to prospective settlers. Murray's advice regarding land in the Lower Cape Fear suggests a more complicated situation. Murray wrote that, if a person looking for fifty acres could locate land, he could "have 10 times that quantity." However, finding land was the challenge: "[only] people that are acquaint[ed] with ye country know where ye vacant land is." Once the inhabitants selected land themselves, it was difficult to purchase because "they get a warrant survey & patents & then screw as much as they can from a stranger for it, who in turn serves others the same way."[53]

Land speculation was not limited to those who resided in the Cape Fear. The most ambitious land speculation schemes in colonial North Carolina were orchestrated by Henry McCulloh, a British official. McCulloh managed to obtain a patent for seventy-two thousand acres in the Lower Cape Fear by using his influence with London. He was also involved in other promotional and speculative land schemes with British businessmen, including Arthur Dobbs. McCulloh's plans led to decades of dispute about his land ownership, obligations, and intentions. Ultimately, he lost his lands in the region because he failed to recruit settlers, but not before infusing even more turmoil into the politics of land in the Lower Cape Fear.[54] As noted earlier, David Tullideph, a Scottish connection of James Murray's, also investigated landowning opportunities in the Lower Cape Fear, but then opted not to settle in North Carolina. A steady stream of letters from Murray to the British Isles provided Tullideph with advice about land opportunities, but both Murray and Governor Johnston eventually decided to discourage Tullideph from the challenges of absentee land ownership in the new settlement.[55]

Many Lower Cape Fear residents probably also acquired land for speculative purposes. It is impossible to determine precisely the motivations behind the patenting of land, but the enormous amounts of land patented in the early years of settlement greatly exceeded the needs of the region's still quite small population. Undoubtedly, many hoped to sell this land at higher prices to later settlers. Rampant speculation, therefore, sometimes made good land much less accessible and delayed the productive use of a considerable portion of the Lower Cape Fear's land. But land speculation offered a rather narrow avenue to wealth in the Lower Cape Fear, because after the many problems with land ownership finally died down, only a comparatively small portion of the land patented in the region changed hands. Moreover, while Burrington accused Moseley of speculating in Lower Cape Fear land, few other contemporaries attributed much importance to profits from the resale of patented lands in the region. Whether on Henry McCulloh's scale or on a more modest level, attempts at land speculation amounted to relatively little in the Lower Cape Fear, but they added to other difficulties related to the acquisition of land.

The combination of these problems made the land situation in the Lower Cape Fear uncertain, to say the least. Because few held title to their land unequivocally, landed property itself became insecure. In a more established region, this situation could produce a crisis; in the Lower Cape Fear, it led to chaos and hindered settlement. Circumstances discouraged newcomers from acquiring land when, as Burrington aptly put it, "land is not wanting for men in Carolina, but men for land." To advance the settlement of a new region, land had to be an easily accessible incentive.[56] The political situation also suffered, as indicated by Governor Johnston's statement, "I am sorry there is nothing done with regard to the Blank Patents, it being impossible to go on with Publick Business here till their fate is determined one way or the other." Indeed, some leading landholders refused to pass legislation until their patents had been confirmed.[57] Disputes over land extended to the distant backcountry, where Moravian Bishop Augustus Spangenburg wrote, "Land matters in North Carolina are also in unbelievable confusion, . . . [officials] cannot now give a Patent without fearing that when the tract is settled another man will come and say 'That is my land.'"[58] According to Murray, even those most deeply involved in the settlement of the Lower Cape Fear began to recoil from the region over land matters. In 1735 he wrote "ye Governor is pretty warm with ye assembly about ye quitrents & it is report'd Mr Roger Moore intends to remove with his family to Virginia."[59]

Fortunately for the Moores, conditions improved before they felt compelled to give up their investment in the Lower Cape Fear. Governor Johnston realized that he would have to compromise somewhere. In 1739, he came to an agreement with local leaders and prepared an appropriate bill. According to this legislation, all the disputed patents would remain valid, but the quitrent system would be improved and more thoroughly enforced. The bill passed the North Carolina assembly, only to have London officials strike it down under the influence of Henry McCulloch. McCulloch feared that some of the disputed patents would infringe on his own land schemes. Yet even though the compromise never became law, it did defuse most of the antagonisms between Johnston's royal government and Lower Cape Fear landholders. For one thing, Johnston decided to let all the patents in the region stand unquestioned. Whatever Johnston's motives, this decision was surely a prudent one. By 1740, most of the land in question had been occupied for years, and many settlers had invested heavily in the improvement of their land. More important, the abuses were not likely to continue: there simply was not enough good land remaining in the region to justify such schemes. By 1740, North Carolinians had patented more than 425,000 acres in the Lower Cape Fear. Over the next thirty-five years, they patented fewer than 300,000 more, and the average patent was significantly less than the official maximum of 640 acres.[60] Johnston's own administration contributed to a massive rush to patent lands between 1735 and 1740, when the governor tried to invalidate warrants that had not been turned into patents within a certain amount of time. Because early settlers had more land from which to choose, the land patented in the early years also tended to be the more valuable.

The disorganization of the patent system continued to plague North Carolina officials, but after 1740 it was a much more important issue in the backcountry, where settlers were still taking up land at a rapid pace. Johnston did renew his attempts to obtain better quitrent legislation, but his stance on the patents sufficiently mollified the Lower Cape Fear leadership that they were willing to yield on this point. The quitrent problem would not be resolved so easily, however. When the Lower Cape Fear assented, politicians in Albemarle made their own stand against Johnston. The quitrents system never did meet the expectations of London officials, who ultimately gave up and found more effective ways to provide crucial revenue to the colony's government.[61] Like the many other disputes that had marked the acquisition of land in the Lower Cape Fear since the 1720s, the quitrent crisis faded, as colonists compromised over their different interests.

Land records, displayed quantitatively in tables 2.1 and 2.2, clearly demonstrate that the land situation in the Lower Cape Fear differed substantially after 1740, when the two sides had agreed to compromise. Enormous amounts of land were patented before 1730, and especially between 1735 and 1740. During the early 1730s, few patents were issued because of Burrington's moratorium on patents, but Burrington issued many warrants, many of which probably became patents during Johnston's administration after 1735. After 1740, governors issued fewer and smaller patents, and fewer individuals received patents. If the smaller patent size can be attributed to closer regulation under Johnston, the other figures strongly suggest declining interest in Lower Cape Fear lands. The demand for patents seems to have reached a low point in the late 1750s, but it recovered and grew steadily until just before the Revolution.[62]

Sale of land in the Lower Cape Fear reflected a similar trend. Land conveyances grew from 1730 to 1740, apparently uninfluenced by the lack of new patents in the early 1730s, but dropped sharply in the early 1740s. The number of sales remained low and somewhat sporadic for the next few decades, but also showed undeniable signs of recovery and increased sales before the Revolution.[63] Clearly, opportunities to acquire land were rarer for those arriving after 1740. Landowners who first appeared in the Lower Cape Fear records before 1740 averaged about twice as much land as those arriving during any later decade during the colonial period. In fact, those arriving before 1730 on average accumulated almost four times as much land as those arriving in the 1730s. At the same time, newcomers continued to acquire new land, even if in smaller quantities. Almost three-quarters of the identifiable landholders in the colonial Lower Cape Fear did not arrive until after 1740.[64]

While the political tension over land matters subsided in the 1740s, the land disputes of the preceding fifteen years continued to influence life in the Lower Cape Fear for the rest of the colonial period. For one thing, many individual animosities persisted because of contested land matters. On one occasion, James Murray claimed land and then discovered that it had already been settled, and he also wrote letters describing land disputes that embroiled several of his friends in the Lower Cape Fear.[65] As late as 1767, Murray sold some of his land in the region partly in response to another planter's illegal activity and intimidation.[66] William Farris encountered even greater frustration when he was provided with a plat and patent for land, only to discover that "no such Land could be found." Farris believed that a surveyor perpetrated this fraud "only to amuse [himself] and deceive" Farris.[67] Many other Lower Cape Fear settlers met with similar difficulties.[68]

Perhaps even more important, the distribution of land had become intensely stratified.[69] Land patents in the Lower Cape Fear before 1740 proved significantly larger than those in all of North Carolina under the propriety government or those in any single county of South Carolina before 1722.[70] Not only had more land been patented before 1740, the magnitude of land conveyed in the remaining decades of the colonial period suggests that a significant portion of this land was not redistributed through purchases. Further, as late as 1780, landholdings in the Lower Cape Fear counties of New Hanover and Brunswick were characterized by much greater average sizes than in any other North Carolina counties, and holdings in New Hanover were particularly concentrated. At the same time, a relatively high proportion of Lower Cape

TABLE 2.1 **Land Patents in the Lower Cape Fear, by Five-year Intervals**

Years	*Number of Patents*	*Recipients*	*Acres*	*Average Patent Size in Acres*	*Average Acres per Recipient*
1725–29	118	35	104,992	890	3,000
1730–34	33	20	40,363	1,223	2,018
1735–39	348	200	282,405	811	1,412
1740–44	157	113	64,466	411	570
1745–49	145	117	40,800	281	349
1750–54	102	78	24,116	236	309
1755–59	93	78	19,439	209	249
1760–64	117	88	31,962	273	363
1765–69	205	140	56,602	276	376
1770–75	172	105	43,672	254	416

Note: The following tables and information about the acquisition of land in the Lower Cape Fear counties derive largely from land-patent records and not warrants and quitrents, because the land-patent records appear to be more complete. Patents are also a more accurate indication of ownership and settlement than warrants and more reliable than fragmentary quitrent lists. On this point, see also note 11, chapter 1. Information from the land patents has been compared with the quitrent lists that exist for 1750 and 1751 to establish a significant degree of consistency. More than 73 percent of the tracts of land in the quitrent rolls were consistent with patent and conveyance records, and the remaining tracts could readily be explained by unrecorded transfers of land through inheritance and other methods; see Quitrent Records of North Carolina, July 11, 1750, May 13, 1751, Secretary of State Papers, North Carolina Department of Archives and History, Raleigh; William S. Price Jr., "'Men of Good Estates': Wealth among North Carolina's Royal Councillors," *North Carolina Historical Review* 49 (1972): 75–77. Also note that the patents for the years 1735–39 include the massive patent for seventy-two thousand acres granted to Henry McCulloch by London authorities. These figures exclude land outside the Lower Cape Fear counties that was owned by Lower Cape Fear residents.

TABLE 2.2 **Land Conveyances in the Lower Cape Fear, by Five-year Intervals**

Years	*Number*	*Acres*	*Average Acres per Conveyance*
1725–29	14	1,642	117
1730–34	60	18,236	304
1735–39	303	51,311	169
1740–44	155	25,893	167
1745–49	214	33,351	169
1750–54	169	45,713	270
1755–59	215	40,549	189
1760–64	298	58,405	196
1765–69	292	54,715	187
1770–75	366	54,961	150

Note: These figures exclude land outside the Lower Cape Fear counties owned by Lower Cape Fear residents.

Fear householders owned some land, as demonstrated by tables 2.3 and 2.4. A comparison with other North Carolina counties around 1780 indicates that land ownership was more common in New Hanover than in a number of older northern counties, though still less common than in more recently settled back-country counties.[71] Less data exists for Brunswick County, but landownership was rarer in Brunswick. A much lower percentage of householders in Brunswick owned land than in New Hanover or perhaps anywhere else in North Carolina.[72]

Although the reasons for this difference remain obscure, two possible explanations suggest themselves. First, land in Brunswick may have attracted the Moores and other early settlers because of more inland swamps for rice cultivation or because of other characteristics of the land. Once these lands had been patented, they might have continued to remain in the hands of a relatively small number of men. Equally important, large inland areas of the county near Waccamaw remained unsettled at the end of the colonial period. It is possible that in the late colonial period, these open areas attracted some poorer settlers who could not afford to obtain their own land.[73] In either case, the configuration of land ownership in the counties of New Hanover and especially Brunswick proved markedly different from that elsewhere in colonial North Carolina.

Wealthy planters not only held a high proportion of the region's land, as shown in tables 2.5 and 2.6, they held better land that could yield greater profits. Of

TABLE 2.3 **Landownership among Heads of Households, 1755–72**

Year	*County*	*Heads of Households*	*Landowners*	*% Owning Land*	*Average Acres per Landowner*
1755	Both	261	162	62	1,400
1762	Both	437	246	56	1,128
1763	Both	407	255	63	1,098
1767	N.H.	338	210	62	846
1769	Bruns.	196	82	42	1,355
1772	Bruns.	196	80	41	1,122

Note: Lower Cape Fear computer biographical files. Heads of households were identified by their appearance on tax lists for the appropriate years; landownership was determined by extant patents and conveyances. These figures are, however, certainly understated: they do not consider inherited lands and at least some patents and conveyances have probably not survived.

course, early settlers were quick to occupy areas that were well suited to rice planting and other forms of agriculture. Often these promising tracts of land clustered together. Along the same lines, they also seized land on the waterways.[74] That some Lower Cape Fear planters had, in the words of Scotus Americanus, "a river at their door, and easy conveyance for their commodities to market," was important. The Cape Fear River and countless other streams and tributaries in the region made this situation possible. But land on these waters was more difficult to find after the first couple of decades of settlement. Later land patents were far more likely to border other plantations or even roads, and were far less likely to be on major waterways.

These concentrated landholdings had far-reaching implications. Because existing records privilege the elite perspectives of large landholders like the Moores, it is difficult to ascertain how many other individuals failed in attempts to acquire land or how they felt about the circumstances. A petition to the governor and council reveals one response to the stratification of land ownership in the Lower Cape Fear. In February 1735, George Gibbs petitioned regarding a disagreement with Roger Moore over land. Gibbs described himself in terms suggestive of the kind of settler that London authorities wanted and that had already occupied much of North Carolina. He had migrated overland, from "the Jerseys," obtained a warrant for land in 1728, and arduously moved his family to

TABLE 2.4 **Percentage of Landowners in North Carolina Counties circa 1780**

County	*Heads of Household*	*Landowners*	*Percentage*
Tyrrell	540	426	79
Randolph	573	443	77
Montgomery	455	348	77
Caswell	1,225	910	74
Nash	674	496	74
Gates	578	422	73
Camden	601	429	71
Hertford	621	443	71
Cumberland	812	579	71
New Hanover	359	255	71
Orange	1,179	831	71
Pasquotank	643	451	70
Halifax	1,174	808	69
Surry	1,802	1,231	68
Granville	1,225	325	67
Carteret	452	301	67
Rutherford	487	311	64
Chowan	467	263	56

Note: This table has been adapted from data in Francis Grave Morris and Phyllis Mary Morris, "Economic Conditions in North Carolina about 1780; Part 1, Landholdings," *North Carolina Historical Review* 16, no. 2 (1939): 107–33. Conflicts between data in this table and table 2.3 can be attributed to more complete land records after the Revolution. At the same time, the Revolution itself may in some cases have caused changes in the distribution of landed property as loyalists departed, men were killed in battle, and property was damaged.

TABLE 2.5 **Average Size of Landholdings in North Carolina Counties circa 1780**

County	*Landowners*	*Average Acres per Landowner*
New Hanover	253	934
Brunswick	172	804
Granville	825	571
Johnston	531	565
Beaufort	412	551
Nash	496	512
Bladen	955	509
Warren	525	484
Halifax	808	464
Jones	253	463
Carteret	299	444
Cumberland	577	434
Caswell	907	420
Surry	1,205	311
Orange	826	380
Wilkes	603	379
Chowan	262	359
Hertford	434	355
Montgomery	348	319
Gates	412	311
Randolph	395	286
Rutherford	311	284
Tyrrell	426	277
Perquimans	388	230
Camden	429	170
Pasquotank	451	166

Note: See note 77, chapter 5.

TABLE 2.6 **Characteristics of Lower Cape Fear Landowners, by Decade of First Appearance in Local Records**

Decade	*Number*	*Average Acres Patented*	*Average Acres Purchase*	*Average Gross Acres*	*Average Net Acres*
1720s	32	5,175	1,365	6,540	3,980
1730s	204	1,171	475	1,646	1,193
1740s	239	289	310	600	312
1750s	179	213	283	496	349
1760s	202	174	283	458	271
1770s	40	33	115	148	139
Total	896	609	364	973	639

Note: Lower Cape Fear computer biographical files. Landowners have been identified by patents and conveyances. Land obtained through inheritance could not be traced reliably. The years refer to the earliest date the individual appeared in any of the sources used for the database, whether the reference related to land ownership or not. *Gross Acres* refers to the sum of the acres they patented and purchased. *Net Acres* refers to their gross acres minus the sum of the acres they sold.

the Lower Cape Fear. Next, he cleared some land and paid quitrents. Gibbs intended to use the land "raising . . . Bread for . . . [his] family." He also had three sons and aspired to leave "a Tract of Land for each of them . . . [with] One hundred Acres of Good Land in each tract." After occupying this one piece of land for seven years, Gibbs felt that "now I have brought myself in a way that I could live comfortably," and he even owned a few slaves.

But Gibbs then discovered that Roger Moore claimed to have a warrant for his land, which he had secured from Governor Burrington "long after" Gibbs had obtained his warrant. Gibbs protested that "Mr. Roger Moores Covetous Eye" had focused on his land. Moore had decided "he must and will have the Land," regardless of Gibbs's claim to it. Gibbs was clearly embittered that a man of Moore's wealth and means would, to swell his enormous landholdings, threaten the Gibbs's family livelihood. To make matters worse, Gibbs knew he had fewer headrights with which to obtain land because his large family remained vastly outnumbered by Moore's slaves. Gibbs worried about having enough land to leave his sons, but "Mr. Moore is pleased to have so many Tracts for each of his Sons which he pretends to hold by the rights of his Negro's." Gibbs added, with savage irony, "I suppose he'l give none of the Land to his Negro's."[75] Gibbs must have spoken for many less-wealthy settlers in the Lower Cape Fear who felt abused and threatened by imperious behavior of "King Roger" Moore and others like him. The distribution of land in such a lopsided and controversial manner must have intensified these animosities. Gibbs's story was not unique. Other Lower Cape Fear residents complained about Roger Moore seizing tracts unlawfully and using land that belonged to others.[76]

On the surface, it may be difficult to comprehend why Roger Moore even wanted Gibbs's land. He already had access to tens of thousands of acres in a region that supposedly had little cultivable land. Of the unsettled lands in eastern colonial North Carolina, Burrington wrote that "not an hundredth part of the grounds are Plantable"; specifically, "the barren Pine lands will never be cultivated; [and] the several sorts of wet lands . . . cannot be cleared and drained, without great charge, and labour, therefore not hitherto attempted."[77] That Gibbs had found such fertile and highly valued land that Moore felt compelled to cultivate it instead of some of his other lands seems unlikely. Had Moore patented the land, he would have been pressured, if not required, to clear a portion and pay quitrents for it. Moore might have pursued Gibbs's land in the hopes of selling it at a profit, but the glutted land market in the Lower Cape Fear would have discouraged such an investment.

In fact, Moore's behavior is much more comprehensible when considered in conjunction with the unusual characteristics of land use in the Lower Cape Fear. Land in the Lower Cape Fear was not valued for cultivation purposes so much as for its forest resources. The two primary sources of profit in the region were naval stores and lumber, not crops. Both naval stores and lumber required considerable amounts of land, but, unlike most forms of agriculture, they did not require particularly intensive use of land: except for the trees, the land had little utility. This situation had at least two important consequences. First of all, large naval stores producers needed access to large amounts of land. Also, they had little commitment to the long-term improvement of much of this land. At the same time, imperatives that led planters to acquire as much land as possible as part of their aspirations for an improved social and economic status undoubtedly reinforced these circumstances.

Residents of the Lower Cape Fear were quick to recognize the need for large amounts of land, but they sometimes had a difficult time convincing metropolitan authorities that they were not simply trying to horde large amounts of land out of greed. For example, in 1731 Cornelius Harnett petitioned for more land than allowed by the normal headright system in order to build and make full use of a sawmill. Governor Burrington and the council recognized the economic benefits of such a project and believed it reasonable to grant the additional land, but they hesitated because they did not want to violate the Crown's instructions. Similarly, metropolitan authorities also required that landholders clear a certain portion of their lands to maintain their title. In England, land left unsuitable for cultivation could be considered only a sign of indolence or apathy. But for the lumber industry, clearing more land would be unproductive, and the regulations had to be changed to make establishment of a sawmill sufficient substitute for clearing the requisite number of acres. Burrington did admit to giving some extra land on another occasion, "upon application from some men who imploy their slaves chiefly in makeing Tar and Pitch." They claimed "that less quantitys would be made and their business cramped, if they were not permitted to take up more then fivety Acres, for each Person in their Familys," as the headright system dictated. Burrington quickly qualified his action to the Board of Trade by adding that "the land was barren and unfit for cultivation." Others, like James Murray, remained unconvinced. He blamed North Carolina's "Poverty, idleness, & uselessness to our Mother Country" on the ability to hold large amounts of land at low rents without cultivating it.[78] Perhaps North Carolina would have been better off if settlers had adhered more closely to metropolitan models of land use, but no crop brought profits comparable with those from the naval stores and lumber industries in the Lower Cape Fear.

Because of the opportunities for profit in the naval stores industry, producers showed few scruples in fulfilling their insatiable need for land. Throughout the colonial Lower Cape Fear, officials complained that residents were "boxing" and "burning" on unclaimed land. The terms *boxing* and *burning* referred to inserting boxes in trees to gather turpentine and burning lightwood to produce tar and pitch. Once a tract of land had been used for this purpose, it often had little value; hence, it was more profitable to avoid officially obtaining possession of the land. Magistrates prosecuted some for the offense, but it continued. In other cases, individuals simply used trees on lands that belonged to neighbors. In one instance, Nathaniel Moore and his brother-in-law James Grange even set up two tar kilns on a tract of land occupied and cultivated by another farmer.[79] In the Lower Cape Fear, even land suitable for agriculture became another opportunity for the expansion of the forest industry.

Settlers also realized that lands intended for use in forest industries had to be treated differently. Some settlers believed that different kinds of land produced better pine trees for tar production, as William Bartram's father, John, learned when he visited North Carolina in 1765. He was "informed that ye deep sandy land that hath not A clay bottom doth not produce near so much tar as to ye quantity of woods as ye trees that grows where ye clay is near ye surface." Local experts estimated that a "kiln that will yeald 170 barrels in clay ground will not yeald above 150 in deep sandy ground."[80] Murray recognized the specific concerns associated with the Lower Cape Fear's forest industries when he relocated to New England in the 1760s and gave explicit directions for the use of resources on his plantation. Writing from Boston in 1767, he cautioned his nephew Thomas Clark not to let anyone "make waste of the Mill timber by making turpentine within its bounds."[81] Murray, when Clark responded in a manner that dissatisfied him, wrote even more emphatically and clearly to John Ancrum regarding the use of land near his sawmill. Ancrum had allowed another planter to dam the mouth of a creek near Murray's land, threatening to "backwater" Murray's mill. He also disapproved of using wood on his land for "making shingles, because I know what wanton waste will be made of the timber," but he agreed to permit it as long as it was done to his specifications and with appropriate supervision.[82] A regional economy based so heavily on forest industries could, after all, exhaust thousands of acres of pine land within a matter of years, and those who wished to prosper in the Lower Cape Fear had to pay attention to these concerns.[83] By the 1760s, because they believed that decades of experience and attempts at improving the land gave those within the region special expertise, Murray and other Lower Cape Fear landowners adhered to regional conventions and assumptions about the use of their land.

Lower Cape Fear residents adapted to the characteristics of the land in other ways. The same swampy, well-watered lands that proved useful for rice cultivation also turned out to be the ideal breeding grounds for malaria-carrying mosquitoes.[84] Because the threat from disease-carrying mosquitoes was seasonal, one relatively effective response to this situation was to move away from swampy lands during the worst months of the summer and early autumn. Residents of the Lower Cape Fear found that drier land along the coast provided a refuge from infected mosquitoes. The area around New Topsail Sound became a popular summer vacationing spot for wealthier inhabitants fleeing disease. In

1758, James Murray's wife and daughter took ill, but they "went to the Sound near the Sea In October, & they recovered so fast that . . . [Mrs. Murray] was impatient to be home."[85] Similarly, Janet Schaw commented that her brother, Lower Cape Fear planter Robert Schaw, bought land on the sound for his children to live on, because, she claimed, rice planting "renders the air perfectly putrid." Other prominent men in the region who owned second homes on the sound included Benjamin Heron, Robert Howe, James Hasell, Caleb Grainger, Caleb Mason, William Hooper, Cornelius Harnett, Alexander Lillington, Archibald MacLaine, and Governor Gabriel Johnston.[86]

No matter how much Anglo-Americans adapted to the environment or developed better ways of using their land, the Lower Cape Fear remained distinctive in eastern North Carolina for its sparse population (see tables 2.7 and 2.8). The best indication of the region's population distribution was provided by Anglican missionaries sent by the Society for the Propagation of the Gospel (SPG); they had to travel throughout the area to fulfill their obligations to Anglican settlers. In 1728, the Reverend John LaPierre described the settlers in the region as "a poor dispersed multitude of people residing up and down Cape Fear."[87] James Moir complained that, in his Lower Cape Fear parish, "the inhabitants are very much scattered, and most of them live at a great distance from one another which makes it impossible for me to serve them as I could wish." He would have preferred to serve in northern North Carolina, where "there is ten times the number of white people to what we have at cape fear."[88] Similarly, John MacDowell related that "people's houses where we are obliged to attend are more than 30 some of them 40 miles distant . . . and often we have to ride 15 or 20 miles without seeing a house to flee to for shelter from a thunder shower."[89]

To find that the region was at first sparsely populated is not surprising, but such comments continued throughout the colonial period. For example, as late as 1774, an SPG minister discovered a group of settlers in the more remote parts of Brunswick County who lived where "common prayer had never before been read nor the gospel preached." He traveled more than forty miles and crossed over twelve swamps to get to this "remote wild place," where he found "above thirty families, but very scattered."[90] Visitors to the region also frequently commented on the dispersed population and on the distance between residences.[91] Concerns about sparse population no doubt influenced those seeking land, because few settlers relished the thought of living far from opportunities for interaction. James Murray, for example cautioned David Tullideph about acquiring land far up the northeast branch of the Cape Fear River because he was "afraid you will get none to live in such an out of ye way place as it will be for some time." Instead, Murray offered advice on how Tullideph might acquire "a plantation within ye settlements."[92] Decades later, Murray believed the continuing "thinness" of the Lower Cape Fear settlement hindered economic development.[93]

TABLE 2.7 **Estimated Population Density in the Lower Cape Fear, 1755 and 1763**

Year	*Total Population Estimate*	*White Population Density per Square Mile*	*Black Population Density per Square Mile*	*Total Population Density per Square Mile*
1755	4,216	0.71	1.34	2.12
1763	6,284	1.12	2.04	3.16

Note: Estimates of population density have been determined by dividing the Lower Cape Fear population estimates from table 1.10 by the regional land areas given in Marvin M. Kay and Lorin L. Cary, *Slavery in North Carolina, 1748–1775* (Chapel Hill: University of North Carolina Press, 1995), 229.

TABLE 2.8 **Estimated Total Population Density in Other North Carolina Regions, 1755 and 1767**

Region	*1755*	*1767*
Northern North Carolina	3.86	5.43
Upper Cape Fear	0.64	1.45
Backcountry	1.42	3.51

Note: Estimates of population density for these regions have been adapted from data given in Kay and Cary, *Slavery in North Carolina,* 221–29. I have also simplified some of their regional classifications, combining the Albemarle and Neuse-Pamlico into "Northern North Carolina" and creating a broad category for "Backcountry." For Kay and Cary's regional typology, see ibid., 221–22.

A variety of factors prevented a more concentrated arrangement of the region's settlers. Of course, the existence of two towns, Brunswick and Wilmington, strongly indicates some need for centralization. As tables 2.9 and 2.10 reveal, about one-quarter of all land conveyances in the Lower Cape Fear involved town lots, and both Brunswick and Wilmington both played an important role in settlement and land acquisition.[94] But even with some population concentrated in these towns, the region still had comparatively few settlers per square mile. Indeed, the urban functions performed by these locales probably lessened the imperatives for closely knit settlements in the countryside. Gabriel Johnston no doubt identified another key cause when he pointed out that, because naval stores could be produced easily on undeveloped and unpatented land, "in many parts of the Country the lands are waste & not a house [is] to be seen in travelling a great many miles together."[95] Even lawful landholdings in the region tended to be concentrated, encouraging settlers to disperse their actual homes if not their land claims. Having been settled later than the rest of

Table 2.9 **Conveyances of Lots in the Town of Brunswick, by Five-year Intervals**

Year	*Conveyances*	*% of All Lower Cape Fear Conveyances*	*Quarter-acre Lots Conveyed*
1725–29	2	14	6
1730–34	16	27	38
1735–39	14	5	30
1740–44	5	3	9
1745–49	5	2	11
1750–54	3	2	10
1755–59	7	3	12
1760–64	6	2	20
1765–69	14	5	22
1770–75	9	2	12
Total	81	4	172

Note: Lower Cape Fear computer biographical files. The town was for the most part divided into quarter-acre lots.

Table 2.10 **Conveyances of Lots in the Town of Wilmington, by Five-year Intervals**

Year	*Conveyances*	*% of All Lower Cape Fear Conveyances*	*Quarter-acre Lots Conveyed*
1730–34	7	12	15
1735–39	89	29	413
1740–44	45	29	84
1745–49	46	21	64
1750–54	54	32	88
1755–59	53	25	77
1760–64	38	13	41
1765–69	38	13	58
1770–75	64	17	88
Total	434	21	928

Note: Lower Cape Fear computer biographical files. The town was for the most part divided into quarter-acre lots. Unlike Brunswick, Wilmington did not exist until the early 1730s.

eastern North Carolina, the Lower Cape Fear was predisposed to accumulating fewer settlers in the colonial period.

Even given this consideration, the Lower Cape Fear clearly did not attract many settlers in comparison with the Carolina backcountry. Indeed, a comparison of population density in the Lower Cape Fear and in the North Carolina backcountry is instructive. Historians have long cited sparse population as a defining characteristic of the southern backcountry, while differentiating the backcountry and lowcountry societies of the Carolinas.[96] But by 1767, the North Carolina backcountry was more densely settled than the Lower Cape Fear.[97] Moreover, a much higher percentage of the Lower Cape Fear's population was enslaved, exacerbating the limits placed on social interaction and communication by a sparser settler population. Prospective settlers considered many motives, especially matters related to land. Settlers were probably aware that, in the Lower Cape Fear, land was hard to obtain, had been taken up in vast quantities early on, could only be very profitable through the production of unfamiliar commodities, and often remained a contested matter even after it had been patented and occupied. Those who, for whatever reason, remained undeterred by these considerations found themselves living in a scattered countryside, and this development had important implications for the region's social and institutional development. Distance between residences necessarily made it more difficult to maintain social networks and to keep settlers within the reach of authority and differentiated the Lower Cape Fear from older, more densely populated regions of North Carolina.

Patterns of settlement in the Lower Cape Fear region varied considerably from place to place. Settlers chose their new homes based on the availability of land, proximity to kin, transportation, economic circumstances, and countless other factors that were far from uniform throughout the region. Some settlers opened distant tracts of land surrounded by wilderness, but most settled nearer groups of others and formed themselves into geographic "neighborhoods" that could provide forms of social and economic support for their new lives. A closer look at several of these eighteenth-century neighborhoods, the data for which are partly summarized in tables 2.11 and 2.12, reveals much about the process of land acquisition in the colonial Lower Cape Fear. This study will illustrate some of the continuities and differences in the development and settlement of three Lower Cape Fear neighborhoods: Rocky Point, Lockwoods Folly, and Old Town Creek.

Perhaps no part of the Lower Cape Fear region attracted as much attention from early settlers as Rocky Point, on the Northeast Branch of the Cape Fear River. The area received its name from early explorers who noticed an uncharacteristic collection of rocks and stones along the banks of the Cape Fear.[98] A 1734 visitor described Rocky Point as "the finest place in all Cape Fear."[99] Maurice Moore, Edward Moseley, and a number of the Lower Cape Fear's

TABLE 2.11 **Land Ownership in Three Lower Cape Fear Neighborhoods**

	Rocky Point	*Lockwoods Folly*	*Old Town Creek*
Identifiable residents or landowners	62	64	61
Number patenting land in neighborhood	16	36	31
Number patenting land in the Lower Cape Fear	40	47	44
Average acres patented in neighborhood	1,505	409	768
Total acres patented in neighborhood	24,080	15,761	23,690
Percentage of groups' Lower Cape Fear Patents located in neighborhood	11	58	46
Number who first obtained land in the neighborhood by purchase	11	10	11
Number who purchased land in the neighborhood	15	16	17
Total acres purchased	15,565	8,230	14,912
Average acres per purchaser	1,038	514	877

Note: Lower Cape Fear computer biographical files.

TABLE 2.12 **Slave Ownership in Three Lower Cape Fear Neighborhoods**

	Rocky Point	*Lockwoods Folly*	*Old Town Creek*
Residents appearing on tax lists	34	37	25
Number owning slaves	33	22	22
Average slaves per slaveowner	22	8	19

Note: Lower Cape Fear computer biographical files.

wealthiest men lived in the vicinity of Rocky Point. Some of these included Samuel Swann, John Ashe, Alexander Lillington, George Moore, John Swann, John Porter, Frederick Jones, and Thomas Merrick. Sixty-two different landowners and residents of the Rocky Point neighborhood can be identified from various records. All but nine of these individuals owned land near Rocky Point (a fact that reflects the property-oriented biases of the source material) and the rest appear to have been heads of households.[100]

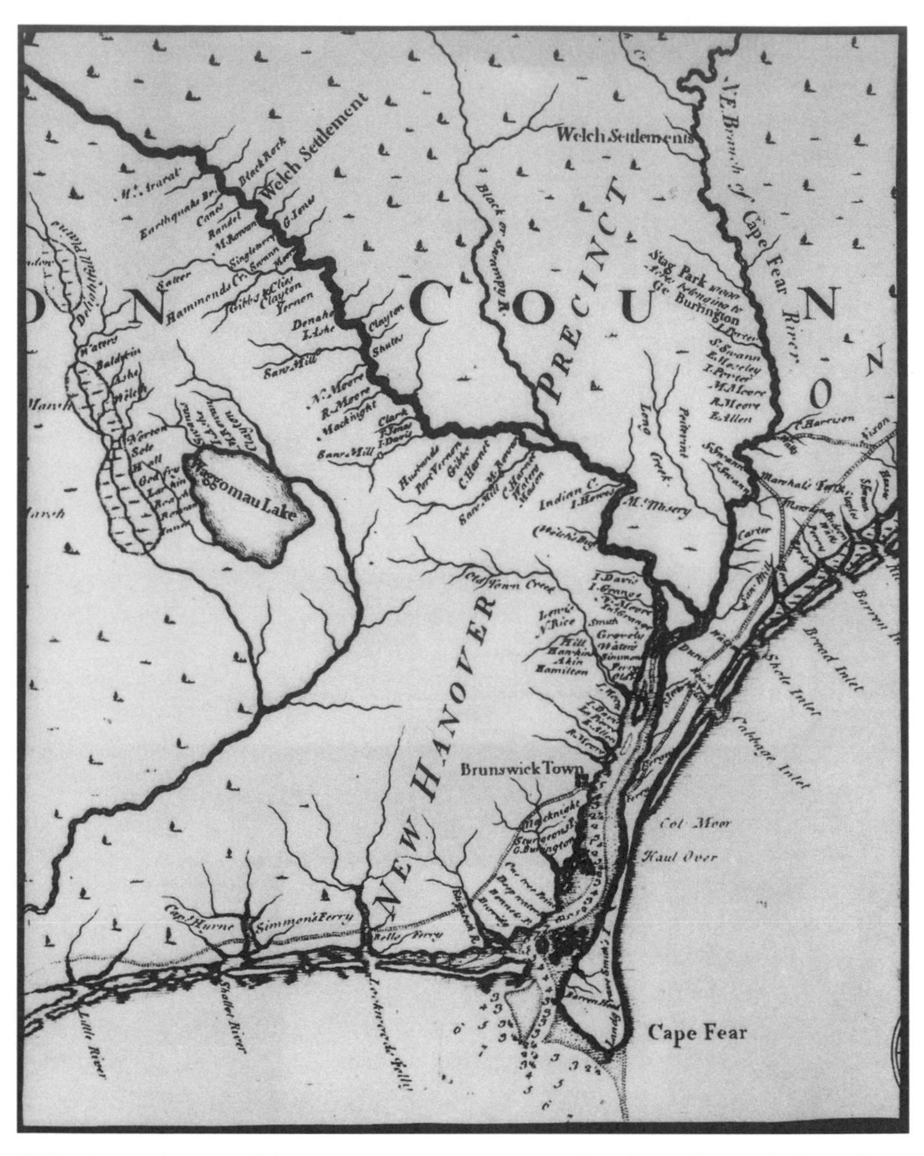

Following settlement of the Lower Cape Fear region, Edward Moseley made the earliest surviving map (1733) of North Carolina. Lockwoods Folly is visible just west of the mouth of the Cape Fear River, and Old Town Creek can be found due north of Brunswick Town. Rocky Point is not labeled, but the cluster of plantation names on the Northeast Cape Fear River south of Stag Park reveals its location. Photograph courtesy of the North Carolina Collection, University of North Carolina at Chapel Hill; original used by permission of the South Caroliniana Library, University of South Carolina.

James Wimble's 1738 map of North Carolina included Rocky Point at the epicenter of the lines emanating from Pelham Precinct. No such precinct was ever created, but Wimble apparently anticipated its existence during the early years of rapid growth in the region. Lockwoods Folly and Old Town are also visible on this map.

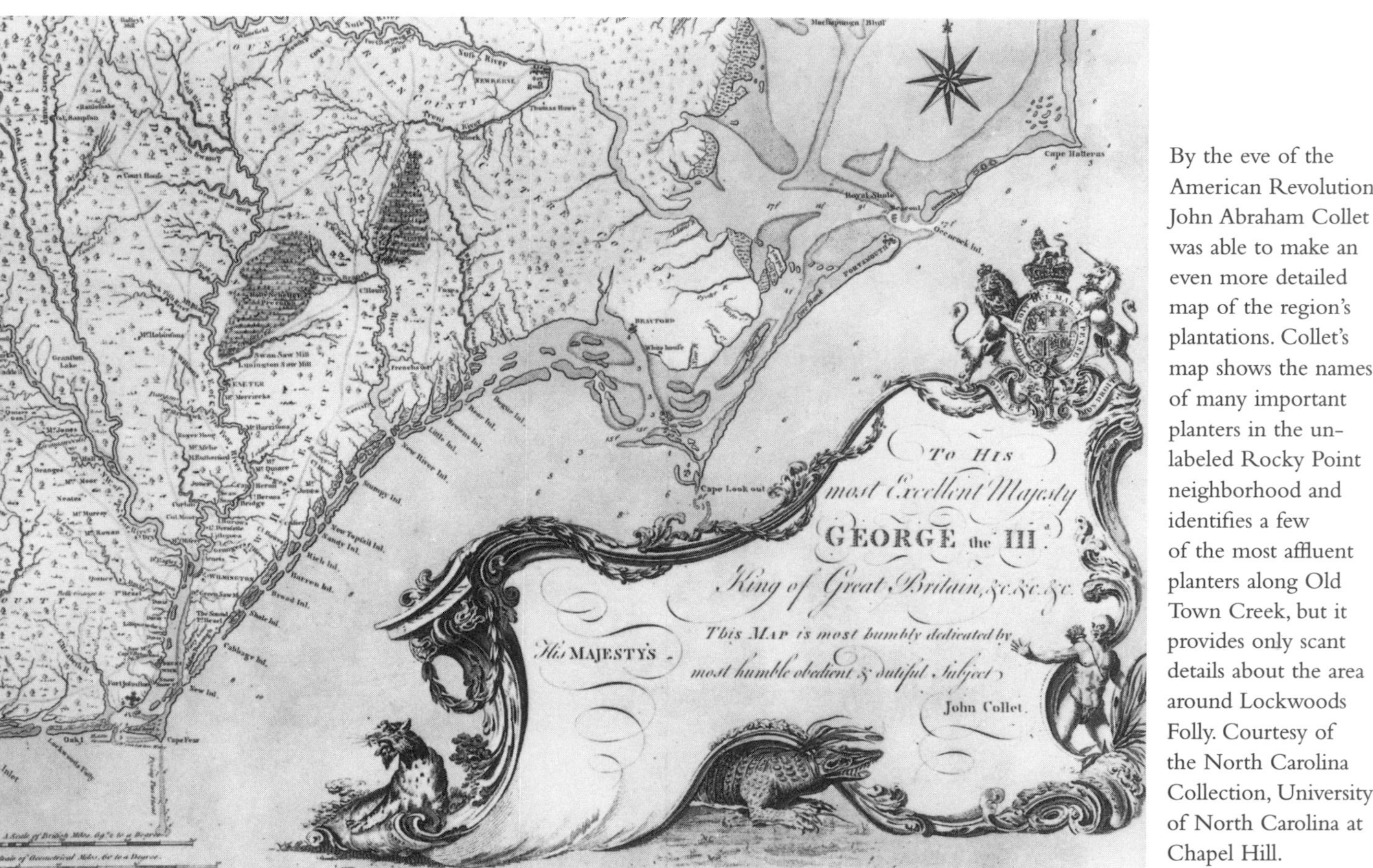

By the eve of the American Revolution, John Abraham Collet was able to make an even more detailed map of the region's plantations. Collet's map shows the names of many important planters in the unlabeled Rocky Point neighborhood and identifies a few of the most affluent planters along Old Town Creek, but it provides only scant details about the area around Lockwoods Folly. Courtesy of the North Carolina Collection, University of North Carolina at Chapel Hill.

Tax lists make the wealth of these residents of Rocky Point evident. Of the thirty-four who appeared on tax lists, thirty-three owned slaves, and the slave owners averaged more than twenty slaves each. Much of the area's wealth can be attributed to the Moores and other important planters who patented large amounts of land in the 1720s. The sixteen landowners who patented land near Rocky Point also owned large amounts of land elsewhere in the Lower Cape Fear. Indeed, the land they patented at Rocky Point made up only 11 percent of their total patented lands.[101] A few of these wealthy landowners, like Roger Moore, lived on other plantations in the Lower Cape Fear, but the great majority appear to have lived on their Rocky Point lands at least some of the year. Interestingly, no surviving evidence indicates why so many important planters should have preferred to live in this particular place. Nothing suggests that the lands at Rocky Point promised significantly greater profits. After Maurice Moore made his residence at Rocky Point in the 1720s, relatively good land, coupled with the opportunity for more refined company, probably attracted many.

Land patents provide the best evidence of settlement patterns near Rocky Point and the two other neighborhoods, as shown in tables 2.13, 2.14, and 2.15. Most strikingly, of the thirty patents in the Rocky Point area, twenty-seven were located on waterways, twenty-six of them having access to the Cape Fear River itself. Settlers clearly placed a premium on water transportation. Also, more than two-thirds of the patents near Rocky Point derived from the first five years of settlement, and all but two from the first twenty-five years of settlement. Lands at Rocky Point were obviously in great demand. Patents also indicate that settlers valued neighbors. More than two-thirds of patented land was adjacent to at least one other settler's land. The only exceptions to this tendency occurred in the first twenty-five years of settlement, and almost all occurred in the first five years, when a sparser population made isolation less avoidable.[102] These records indicate that Lower Cape Fear settlers acquired land in neighborhoods that helped them to consolidate economic connections, foster social networks, and utilize water transportation and other geographic features of the region.

Even though most of the occupied land at Rocky Point had been obtained through patents, a significant percentage of landowners gained their holdings by purchasing land that had already been patented. Also, while the wealthiest arrivals settled before 1730 or 1735, the sixty-two identifiable Cape Fear residents arrived more gradually, reaching a low point of three by the 1740s, but growing to sixteen between 1770 and 1775.[103] Rocky Point had about a dozen men of extraordinary wealth, but most of the landowners in the area exhibited holdings that were more typical for the Lower Cape Fear. Still, by 1773, an advertiser in the *Cape Fear Mercury* could expect his audience to be familiar with "the well known valuable lands of Rockey Point."[104] As the neighborhood

TABLE 2.13 **Characteristics of Land Patents near Rocky Point**

	Patents	*On Water*	*On Cape Fear River*	*No Adjacent Patentees*	*One Adjacent Patentee*	*Two or More Adjacent Patentees*
1720s	21	19	18	6	9	6
1730s	5	5	5	2	2	1
1740s	2	2	2	1	1	0
1750s	1	1	1	0	0	1
1760s	1	0	0	0	0	1
1770s	0	0	0	0	0	0
Total	30	27	26	9	12	9

Note: Lower Cape Fear computer biographical files.

TABLE 2.14 **Characteristics of Land Patents near Lockwoods Folly**

	Patents	*On Water*	*On Cape Fear River*	*No Adjacent Patentees*	*One Adjacent Patentee*	*Two or More Adjacent Patentees*
1720s	3	3	2	2	1	0
1730s	12	11	0	5	4	3
1740s	6	6	0	2	1	3
1750s	11	11	1	7	1	3
1760s	5	5	0	5	0	0
1770s	10	9	0	4	3	2
Total	47	45	3	25	10	11

Note: Lower Cape Fear computer biographical files.

TABLE 2.15 **Characteristics of Land Patents near Town Creek**

	Patents	*On Water*	*On Cape Fear River*	*No Adjacent Patentees*	*One Adjacent Patentee*	*Two or More Adjacent Patentees*
1720s	7	7	4	3	4	0
1730s	28	28	0	9	14	5
1740s	2	2	0	0	0	2
1750s	1	1	0	0	0	2
1760s	6	6	0	4	2	0
1770s	1	1	0	0	0	1
Total	45	45	4	16	20	9

Note: Lower Cape Fear computer biographical files.

continued to grow in the decades after the first settlers arrived, it evolved to meet the needs and perceptions of different landowners, acquiring a reputation for prosperity, and, as the name implies, a distinct geographic identity.

In contrast to the famous prosperity and status of Rocky Point, the neighborhood surrounding Lockwoods Folly River and Lockwoods Folly Inlet became a home for somewhat humbler people. The origins of the name Lockwoods Folly cannot be reliably traced, but two different interpretations suggest the dual identity of the neighborhood. On the one hand, several contemporaries tell the story of a Barbadian settler named Lockwood who tried to settle there in the seventeenth century, but who made some foolish blunders that led to the temporary abandonment of the place.[105] This construction of Lockwoods Folly underscores the fluid manner in which the geographic characteristics of the Lower Cape Fear region were interpreted and reinterpreted, especially before the arrival of permanent settlers provided more persistent and fully developed identities for places.

This interpretation of the name probably would also have suited those who emphasized the neighborhood's shortcomings compared with Rocky Point and other places. The Reverend John MacDowell conveyed this impression of Lockwoods Folly when he described families of poor dissenting fisherman who lived there.[106] Compared with Rocky Point, at least, the area did seem poor. Virtually no contemporary maps show important plantations near Lockwoods Folly, whereas some show as many as a dozen near Rocky Point.[107] Both patents and land purchases averaged less than half the number of acres in Rocky Point. Fewer individuals owned slaves, and they averaged only slightly more than one-third as many as slave owners in Rocky Point. Only three patents before 1730 mentioned Lockwoods Folly, and the area exhibited no rapid movement to patent lands during the colonial period. Not many Lockwoods Folly landowners patented as much land elsewhere in the Lower Cape Fear, and at least a few of those who did, like Maurice Moore and John Porter of Rocky Point, never lived on their Lockwoods Folly lands. Very few Lockwoods Folly residents had access to the all-important Cape Fear River, and they were also more isolated. Fewer than half of those who patented land in the area had neighbors living on adjacent tracts.[108] In this context, Lockwoods Folly seems to have begun as a relatively poor and isolated neighborhood in a remote and unsettled region.

On the other hand, another interpretation of the name Lockwoods Folly emphasizes the place's positive aspects. In the seventeenth century, the English-speaking people sometimes used the French word *folie* to describe a pleasant place or favorite residence.[109] In this sense, Lockwoods Folly could be seen as a promising location where newcomers obtained land and bettered their prospectsthough not as much as others did at Rocky Point. Although settlers took out smaller patents in Lockwoods Folly, they acquired more than twice as many patents as did settlers at Rocky Point. Landed wealth was less stratified at Lockwoods Folly. Real estate conveyances indicate a similar trend. Perhaps these facts explain Janet Schaw's comment that Brunswick County lacked poor residents, especially near the sea.[110]

If there was no land rush in Lockwoods Folly, settlers did move in. By the end of the colonial period, slightly more landowners can be identified there than in Rocky Point.[111] The relative isolation of land patents might be considered a disadvantage, but it might also be considered a luxury unobtainable in other places, like Rocky Point, where there was more competition for open lands. Also, the lack of access to the Cape Fear River could have been compensated for by access to Lockwoods Folly River. Lockwoods Folly River, while by no means comparable to the Cape Fear, was navigable by small vessels, and practically all those who patented land in the area had access to this river or to another major waterway.[112] During the colonial period, Lockwoods Folly had several ferries in operation, a site for holding Anglican religious services, at least one grist mill, and a road commission.[113] Shortly after the Revolution, when the town of Brunswick remained practically abandoned, Lockwoods Folly became the county seat of Brunswick County. The differences between Rocky Point and Lockwoods Folly thus could easily be overstated.

A third Lower Cape Fear locale, Old Town Creek, or simply Town Creek, combined some of the differing characteristics of Rocky Point and Lockwoods Folly. Some of the wealthiest and most important men in the Lower Cape Fear made their home along Old Town Creek, which enters the Cape Fear just south of Wilmington and just below the shallow "Flats" that make the Cape Fear impassable for large oceangoing vessels. These included Eleazer Allen, Nathaniel Rice, James Hassell, and John Baptista Ashe. But Old Town Creek never approached the status of Rocky Point. Landholding along Town Creek was less stratified than in Rocky Point, and residents patented less land throughout the Lower Cape Fear. Patents and purchases of land were also considerably larger than in Lockwoods Folly, however. Slave ownership was almost as widespread and large in scale as in Rocky Point. Town Creek settlers also patented land adjacent to other settlers about as frequently as those at Rocky Point. As with Rocky Point and Lockwoods Folly, virtually all the patents indicate access to major waterways, though more frequently this access was to Town Creek itself and not to the Cape Fear.

In one respect, Old Town Creek distinguished itself from the other two neighborhoods. More than half of Town Creek land patents and the arrival of almost half of its identifiable residents can be traced to the decade of the 1730s.[114] Town Creek evidently became the object of a land rush after the first wave of settlers seized the very best Lower Cape Fear lands. This finding reinforces other indications that Old Town Creek offered some of the most sought-after lands in the Lower Cape Fear, though not lands comparable with those at Rocky Point and perhaps some other locations. As the Lower Cape Fear marked a midpoint between the wealthy rice planters of South Carolina and the small farmers of Albemarle, Town Creek marked a midpoint between the Moores at Rocky Point and poor fisherman at Lockwoods Folly.

Aside from these obvious variations in economic status, the process of land acquisition bore important similarities in all three neighborhoods. The most obvious is that all three neighborhoods depended on the location of waterways, indicating the powerful influence of the Cape Fear River system on the spatial organization of settlement and social development throughout the region.[115] All three neighborhoods continued to attract newcomers throughout the colonial period, though in Rocky Point and especially in Town Creek the pull in the earlier years of settlement was much more evident. In all three locales, settlers obtained most of their land through patents, though in all three cases more than half as much land was then resold. Settlers in the three neighborhoods appear to have had a preference for patenting land adjacent to other settlers, though this preference was considerably less pronounced in the more sparsely populated locale of Lockwoods Folly.[116] However, notwithstanding these similarities, Rocky Point, Lockwoods Folly, and Town Creek demonstrate how the interaction of settlers and the land itself led to different outcomes because of local variations. At the same time, these neighborhoods provided a way of organizing the geography of the Lower Cape Fear and thereby enabled distant and different areas of settlement to be integrated into the larger region.[117]

All three of these neighborhoods began shortly after Maurice Moore opened the Lower Cape Fear to settlement in the 1720s, but the elaboration and development of neighborhoods in the Lower Cape Fear constituted only one of several aspects of the settlers' continual adaptation of and to the natural environment. By the late colonial period, the inhabitants of the Lower Cape Fear had remade the region. Travelers could find transportation by boat, ferry, a growing network of roads, and even a drawbridge.[118] When Janet Schaw visited the Lower Cape Fear on the eve of the Revolution, she remarked on how the residents powered mills with the "vast command they have of water." Schaw also expressed wonder at some of the plantations on the Lower Cape Fear, but she praised them somewhat grudgingly because they failed to accord fully with her metropolitan standards.[119] Scotus Americanus, on the other hand, offered clear praise for some increasingly refined Lower Cape Fear residences: "Merchants in this town, and considerable planters in the country, are now beginning to have a taste for living, and some gay equipages may be seen. . . . Their houses are elegant, their tables always plentifully covered and their entertainment sumptous."[120] Perhaps nothing demonstrated the growth of the Lower Cape Fear more convincingly than the increasing importance of its own urban centers of Wilmington and Brunswick, where residents could find trade, services, local leadership, and social interaction.[121] Summer cottages on the sound, while providing relative safety from deadly diseases, also reinforced the appearance of more comfortable and refined living in the Lower Cape Fear. Finally, as fathers passed away and left land to their children, the division of estates lessened the stratification of landholding.[122]

All of these factors suggest that the residents of the Lower Cape Fear interacted with their natural environment quite effectively. At the end of the colonial period, the Lower Cape Fear still had a sparsely settled population, a very unequal distribution of land, an unusual and seemingly wasteful attitude toward land use, a legacy of disputes over land tenure, and a considerable degree of local variation. But if the inhabitants of the Lower Cape Fear may have differed from some other colonists in these ways, they succeeded in making the land they lived on less of a wilderness and far more of a British American place. Equally important, the land they had settled had taken on a more specific spatial identity that differentiated it from other British American places. The Lower Cape Fear had become a place associated with a specific kind of land, and its settlers had developed their own relationship with that land.

Chapter 3

FAMILIES

Sarah Allen was born in South Carolina in 1697 and came to the Lower Cape Fear with her husband, Eleazer Allen, in 1734. Eleazer quickly became one of the most important men in the colony of North Carolina, and few men did more to influence the early development of the new Cape Fear settlement. In 1735, the commission to draw the boundary between North and South Carolina began its work by meeting at the Allens's home in southern New Hanover County, not far from the Boundary House.[1] While the Allens joined the Moores and the rest of the South Carolina contingent who moved into the Lower Cape Fear after 1725, they maintained strong ties to South Carolina society for a time. On several occasions North Carolina political leaders who may have found themselves at odds with Eleazer Allen questioned his eligibility for important political positions in their colony by suggesting that the Allens resided in South Carolina. It is unclear whether these references were inspired by the location of the Allen residence, close to the still ill-defined boundary between the colonies, or by regular and extended trips to the Allens's former home.[2] Either explanation underscores the importance of the perhaps promising but no doubt difficult transition the Allens must have experienced when they moved into the Lower Cape Fear region.

The Allens's move into the Lower Cape Fear enabled Eleazer to build one of the largest and most profitable plantations in the region, which he named Lilliput. The choice of the name—an obvious reference to Jonathan Swift's famed satire *Gulliver's Travels*—suggests some of the ways that the couple may have perceived their new home. The act of naming plantations helped plantation owners to redefine their surroundings and, in a sense, by calling this new place Lilliput, the Allens claimed ownership of it. The choice of a literary name reveals not only a desire for ownership but also for refinement, as Eleazer placed his plantation within a transatlantic world of letters and ideas that marked his elite status and cultural identity. There is no way of knowing what other meanings this name might have held, but it is interesting to speculate on whether Eleazer also chose the name because his wealth and elite background made him feel like Gulliver, towering over the seemingly less significant and therefore Lilliputian-like individuals in the new settlement along the Cape Fear.

Gradually, Eleazer's political and economic maneuvering began to cause problems that might have been a source of anxiety for both members of the Allen household. North Carolina's collector of quitrents during the turbulent disputes over Lower Cape Fear land ownership and quitrents, Eleazer found himself accused of fraud for abusing his office.[3] He was also forced to take out a rather large mortgage, which threatened to cost him most of his estate.[4] It is unclear what role Sarah may have played in her husband's decisions or actions. Indeed, eighteenth-century wives often had a very limited range of choices, but during their life together, after 1734 Sarah's hopes and fortunes must have been inextricably bound to Eleazer's place in Lower Cape Fear society.

In 1750, Eleazer passed away and made Sarah a widow. She inherited his entire estate, including Lilliput, and, while Eleazer suggested that Sarah make certain gifts to relatives with his property, he left everything to her unconditionally.[5] Records indicate that, years later, Sarah still owned as many as fifty-five slaves.[6] It could be argued that Sarah Allen had achieved the ultimate opportunity for female autonomy in the Lower Cape Fear. She had enormous wealth, personally owned a diversified and profitable plantation, and could impose her authority on a large number of slaves. But all of these connections may not have been meaningful to a fifty-year-old woman in Sarah's position. She had left her childhood home, her husband had died, she had no children, she lived on a large plantation in a relatively isolated portion of the Anglo-American world, and she bore the added burden of managing a sophisticated set of business concerns in an uncertain economy. Under these circumstances, women of Sarah's background and cultural expectations might have found any autonomy afforded by the profits from Lilliput's crops and naval stores operation to be of limited value.

These circumstances compelled Sarah to build a new life for herself, using the connections and experiences available to her from her sixteen years of life in the Lower Cape Fear. A few years after Eleazer's death, she successfully petitioned North Carolina's council about a mistake in one of her husband's land patents.[7] Sarah might also have found considerable solace in religion, and she clearly maintained strong ties with the Anglican Church, writing letters in behalf of Anglican missionary John MacDowell. These letters convey both her support for the Anglican Church, most evident in her desire to prevent him from leaving the parish, and an aristocratic contempt for less elite settlers, befitting the widow of Eleazer Allen, expressed most powerfully in her disdain for "the caprices & inconstancy of the Low minded penurious herd." She also tried to utilize her remaining ties to South Carolina lowcountry society, but found that after her departure for the Lower Cape Fear she had lost a significant number of friends to "death & removals."[8]

By 1756, Sarah Allen clearly had had enough of plantation management. Henry Laurens wrote to one of her relatives that "Mrs. Allen makes no great hand of her Plantation at Cape Fear. She seems determin'd to go for London this Spring to finish her days with your Lady."[9] Sarah relied on her husband's male friends in the Lower Cape Fear for assistance with business matters. James Murray's assistance to Sarah Allen proved extensive. He pursued legal matters for her, arranged for the auction of some of her property, hired overseers for her slaves, and supervised various aspects of her plantation. Consequently, when she lost much of the profits from her indigo crop because a ship was taken by pirates, Murray felt personally responsible for not having provided her with sufficient insurance. Yet his letters to Sarah Allen reveal that she maintained an active interest in her estate, as Murray not only provided accounts for the sale of her corn and tar but also kept Allen informed about the lives of her slaves and promised to be guided by her directions for her crops.[10]

Sarah Allen went to London as Laurens predicted, but she finished her days in the Lower Cape Fear in 1761. Despite Eleazer's death and the urbane pleasures of London, Sarah had developed strong ties to her adopted home in North Carolina. In one letter, Murray advised her to consult two Lower Cape Fear women, a Mrs. Dry and Mrs. DeRosset, who could satisfy her desire for updated news about her acquaintances in the region.[11] Sarah's will also reveals much about her life in the Lower Cape Fear. It mentions nineteen different individuals, but no immediate family members or even intimate friends. As a wealthy and important widow with kinship and social ties in the region, she felt compelled to recognize many of those ties with minor bequests; despite the Allens's widespread connections, fully eleven of the people mentioned resided in the Lower Cape Fear. Her close ties to her niece Sarah Frankland's family in England and Eleazer's long-standing property interests in South Carolina easily account for the eight exceptions to this pattern.

Even though Sarah Allen, unlike most women in her world, died childless, her will reveals that she had formed two powerful sets of family connections that gave shape to and reinforced her attachment to the Lower Cape Fear. Her marriage to Eleazer constituted her primary and most important family connection, and her will underscores the significance of that relationship even though Sarah outlived Eleazer by eleven years. Sarah wanted to be buried in the Lower Cape Fear, "as near the Remains of my late Husband as may be, so as not to hurt the foundation of his Tomb." She also stipulated that one acre of land from Lilliput be reserved as a cemetery for the two of them after the rest of the plantation was sold. Sarah also requested "that my Letters and Mr. Allens, of which there are several bundles, be kept sacred from the Eyes of" all but two close friends, who were instructed that "the fire will be the properest Repository for them." Along the same lines, Sarah's wedding ring was her first specific bequest. She gave it to her niece Sarah Frankland "as a memento of my Conjugal happiness, not doubting hers is equal, and may it be as lasting."

Sarah Allen's will also reveals that she had formed a fairly elaborate extended kinship network, with especially strong bonds to female kin in the Lower Cape Fear. Most of the women mentioned in her will were either nieces or grandnieces, and virtually all of them received personal bequests intended to convey affection rather than economic resources. Mrs. Mary Jane Dry got a gold watch "to be worn in rememberance of her affectionate Aunt, who living or dying wishes her happiness." Sarah left her grandniece Miss Rebecca Dry "a Dozen tea Spoons and Strainer, in a black Shagreen case, almost new, designed to accompany an eight-sided silver coffee pot." Rebecca Dry's gift served to remind her that Sarah gave the coffee pot to Rebecca when Sarah journeyed to England five years earlier and as "a small Instance" of Sarah's affection. Sarah also gave Rebecca "a Shagreen writing stand quite new to encourage her in that part of her Education, in which she seems to be making great progress within these late months." The choices in Sarah's will suggest both her notions of feminine refinement and her close ties to younger women in her extended family. Mary Jane and Rebecca Dry, and others like them, may have provided Allen with comfort and companionship in her later years as she learned to function in Lower Cape Fear society without her powerful husband. Women's kinship networks also intertwined with other familial relationships, and William Dry also figured prominently in Sarah Allen's will by being named an executor and receiving "a mourning Ring in Testimony of my Sense of his invarrying goodness to me."[12] Over three decades, family connections carried Sarah Allen to the Lower Cape Fear and provided her with valuable relationships in her new home until her last days.

Settlers in the Lower Cape Fear attempted to follow Anglo-American cultural norms by organizing themselves into families. Many first immigrated to the region with family members, as Sarah Allen did; others came because they had relatives who lived in the region or recommended it to them, and still others sought to start families after they had arrived and established themselves. Not surprisingly, Lower Cape Fear residents valued their families deeply.[13] On many levels, Lower Cape Fear European American families appear to have been typical of eighteenth-century families in the southern colonies, reenacting the familiar script of patriarchal authority, increasingly affectionate nuclear families, and extensive relationships of dependence and obligation.[14] Indeed, all of these attributes were important to many families in the colonial Lower Cape Fear. At the same time, however, a variety of regionally distinctive factors influenced family life in the region and complicated obvious similarities to other Anglo-American families.

Just as families bound colonists together, they also connected them to geographic spaces and regional identities. In the Lower Cape Fear, ties to nearby family members reinforced the regional character of kinship networks. Over time, families who immigrated to the region became linked through marriage to one another, forming new households and kinship networks with common Lower Cape Fear roots. Immigrant families rapidly became Lower Cape Fear families.

Appropriately enough, then, a group of people known as The Family dominated the Lower Cape Fear during the first decades after settlement. The exact origins of this nickname, given to Maurice Moore, his brothers, and their many allies, cannot be traced, but the name conveys obvious meanings. The most important existing document relating to the name The Family comes from a 1735 letter to the Board of Trade regarding the blank patent controversy. In this letter, the authors asserted their importance to the region and cited the large size of their families—"about 1200 persons"—to explain their need for large amounts of land.[15] Perhaps this emphasis on families led the opponents of these elite landowners to dub them with this derisive name.

Whatever its origins, the name suggests several important historical realities about the eighteenth-century Lower Cape Fear. On one level, it suggests how closely allied Moore and many of the other principal landowners in the region were. The name clearly conveyed the political unity of the Moores and their supporters. Also, in an eighteenth-century Anglo-American context, the term *family* conveyed the sense of a particular power structure. The name suggested that Maurice Moore functioned as a powerful patriarch: for the Moores and their allies to refer in their 1735 letter to "our familys" and to "those und[e]r our care [who] consist of near twelve hundred souls" was entirely appropriate.[16] Families in eighteenth-century British America provided the most common place for the exercise of power over dependents: it was the ideal model of government. All of these kinds of family played an important role in the development of the eighteenth-century Lower Cape Fear.

Perhaps most important, The Family reflected the importance of kinship ties in uniting the settlers of the Lower Cape Fear. It indicated that some of the region's principal leaders shared many kinship ties, primarily as a result of intermarriage. The Family eventually included prominent leaders from the Moore, Ashe, Swann, Moseley, Porter, Davis, Jones, and Lillington clans, all of whom were related to the Moores, and to one another, in various ways. These ties not only influenced the recruitment of leaders and settlers for the region, they also became increasingly elaborate, uniting the Lower Cape Fear elite and differentiating it from elites in other locales.

The Moores provide an instructive if exceptional example. As the most powerful family in the region, they articulated an elite model of behavior that many other families no doubt emulated. A close look at the Moores' family relationships also illustrates that contemporaries were correct about them in at least one respect:[17] the Moores, like many other early settlers, clearly developed impressive and complex kinship ties in the Lower Cape Fear.

James Moore, the South Carolina governor, and his wife Margaret Berringer Moore had ten children, including Maurice and Roger. Despite the prominence of the Moores in South Carolina, almost one whole generation of them participated in the migration to the Lower Cape Fear. Four of the ten children never moved to the Lower Cape Fear; however, three of these, Jehu, Anne, and Margaret, died before settlement in the region was fully under way. Only James

Moore Jr. lived in South Carolina for many years after Maurice founded Brunswick, probably because, as the eldest male heir, he could expect to inherit more land in South Carolina than would any of his siblings. Perhaps not surprisingly, brothers Maurice, Roger, Nathaniel, and John all moved northward, together. More striking, however, sisters Mary and Rebecca and their husbands did the same. Mary, in fact, married into two of the region's most prominent immigrant families, the Howes and the Cliffords. Mary died in 1735. Rebecca Moore married wealthy South Carolina merchant William Dry I, and they both moved to the Cape Fear in the 1730s, where William became one of the more important merchants in North Carolina. Rebecca's story may also reflect a more personal aspect of family relations. Moore family records claim that Rebecca and Roger Moore were twins, perhaps explaining some of the motivation for the migration of the Drys. In any case, kinship played an undeniably powerful role in the movement to the Lower Cape Fear of this generation of Moores.

Once families had relocated to the Lower Cape Fear they began to identify with their new homes and develop new networks of interaction, and the Moores were no exception. Marriage provided the most important means of cementing intraregional ties. Even though the Moores had much stronger ties to South Carolina than did more typical immigrant families, from the first generation they intermarried more with Lower Cape Fear residents than with outsiders. Governor James Moore had eighteen grandchildren who probably reached marriageable age after their parents moved to the Lower Cape Fear, and at least ten of them married other Lower Cape Fear residents. Four others appear to have died unmarried, and, even though they were all born in South Carolina and most of them had two parents from South Carolina, only four married South Carolinians. Not only did this pattern assure that later generations of Moores would be even more deeply rooted in the new region, it also tied the Moores to numerous other prominent Lower Cape Fear families—such as the Ashes, the Granges, the Porters, the Davises, the Drys, the Lillingtons, and the Howes.

James Murray's correspondence also confirms the importance of marital unions and the complex role that matrimony played in the development and definition of the Lower Cape Fear elite. As Murray consulted with other single men, he discussed the importance of marriage as a means of social and economic advancement. While he visited with relatives in Scotland, where he found a wife, Murray wrote back to friends in the Lower Cape Fear to keep track of whether an "old flame" still remained "undisposed of."[18] He also recognized the widespread desire to marry into the region's elite, cannily advising a friend considering settlement in the Lower Cape Fear that he should "bring out a Wife with you . . . [in case] . . . all the Ladies that would be agreeable to you here should be pre-engaged."[19] He also expressed his pleasure when his close friend John Rutherford married "a very agreeable Lady with an Opulent fortune for this Country," and he regularly congratulated friends and acquaintances on successful marriage matches.[20] Perhaps even more important, Murray paid close attention to marriage choices both within his own family and within Lower Cape Fear society, recognizing marriage as a process that profoundly shaped kinship ties and social relations. Sometimes Murray's perspective on marriages conveyed his satisfaction at a valuable alliance that might make both partners happy, such as when his sisters married Thomas Campbell and Thomas Clark.[21] At other times, the Scottish settler gossiped about the consequences of marriages within the region, noting in one letter that "the Matchmakers have laid out Widow Moseley for Mr Ross but others think her a woman too much after the Col[onel]s own heart to yeild to an attack from that Quarter."[22] On a few occasions, Murray emphasized the dangers of poorly chosen marriage matches and expressed grave disdain of those who failed to choose spouses according to appropriate criteria. In 1758 he sought to influence his daughter Dolly by relating a cautionary tale about an unfortunate young female acquaintance in Virginia who "married a young spend thrift against the will of all her Relations."[23] Along similar lines, Murray repeatedly criticized a relative's marriage to future revolutionary leader William Hooper. Still, while Murray thought little of Hooper, he understood that sometimes "love impelled."[24] Over several decades, Murray's letters provide reminders of the importance of marriage choices in the establishment and structuring of Lower Cape society.

Clear patterns can be discerned by examining the marriage choices of elite Lower Cape Fear families. Rankings of resident ownership of land patents and slaves provide a useful guide to elite intermarriage. Land patents tend to reveal the wealthiest individuals who arrived during the region's land rush between 1725 and 1740. The ten individuals who patented the most acres in the Lower Cape Fear included Roger and Maurice Moore, and they both had already taken wives when they took their families to the Cape Fear.[25] Of the remaining eight, six married into other prominent Lower Cape Fear families. One, George Burrington, did not have a wife while in the Lower Cape Fear. Robert Halton, the remaining exception, proves the rule—because he had a wife in England when he arrived in North Carolina, never remarried, but had an openly avowed illegitimate son by a woman from the Lower Cape Fear. With or without a formally acknowledged marriage ceremony in the Lower Cape Fear, most of these men had developed strong emotional ties to the region from an early date. Because of the profound emphasis on familial ties in the early modern Anglo-American world, marriage and the formation of new families within the Lower Cape Fear intensified the importance of the new settlement for many people.

Slave ownership rankings depend on tax lists from between 1755 and 1773 and tell more about the region's wealthiest individuals during the last decades before the American Revolution. By this time, the process of kinship network formation had progressed considerably in the Lower Cape Fear. Among the top ten slave owners in the Lower Cape Fear, eight married into other elite Lower Cape Fear families, and one remained unmarried.[26] The one leading slave owner who took a bride who was not from the Lower Cape Fear, William Dry II, married Mary Jane Rhett of South Carolina, and this was partly because of his Moore family ties as the son of Rebecca Moore. Evidently, by this time, the rest of the Lower Cape Fear elite intermarried with one another as much and probably more than with the Moores. Also, the region's elite had entered into another generation by the late colonial period, and a number of the largest property owners in these years had been born in the Lower Cape Fear, reinforcing regional identities even more.

By the late colonial period, marriage also served to integrate wealthy individuals into the Lower Cape Fear elite. While six of the top ten slave owners had some kind of kin relationship to the Moores, the remaining four indicate an interesting trend. All four of them apparently came from families who did not participate in the original migration from South Carolina and Albemarle and drew on transatlantic sources of wealth and influence. Frederick Gregg came from Ireland, and the Quinces and Eagles both came from England, though Richard Eagles Sr. had lived in South Carolina for a time. William Ross Sr.—of unknown origin, though his name strongly suggests a Scottish background—not only married into the Lower Cape Fear elite (he married the widow of Edward Moseley and John Sampson) but also probably acquired most of his slaves and other property by doing so. Thus marriage simultaneously enabled the elaboration of kinship networks, integrated newcomers into preformed networks, and opened another avenue for economic mobility to males. Appropriately, then, those who wished to succeed in the region found the process of family formation to be a valuable step forward.

At the same time, the use of the nickname The Family reveals a seemingly contradictory aspect of life in the Lower Cape Fear. To distinguish a faction by the term *family* may suggest that it was unusual for a group of local leaders to be so much like a family.[27] If the leadership of the Lower Cape Fear had been no more than a "tangled cousinry," as some have claimed of other elites in the southern colonies, there would have been no need for the name. Family connections would have been obvious and typical. In this sense, the kin-based political connections of the Moores stand in juxtaposition to the relatively tenuous and fragile nature of family life in the Lower Cape Fear. No matter how well developed Lower Cape Fear kinship networks might have been, circumstances prevented the maintenance of predictable and secure familial relationships.

Nothing interfered with the establishment of kinship connections in the Lower Cape Fear so powerfully as high mortality. Deadly epidemic diseases such as malaria, yellow fever, and smallpox played a prominent and tragic role in the settlement of the southern colonies. Subtropical climate conditions, plenty of standing water for disease-carrying mosquitoes, a variety of pathogens drawn from three continents, and living conditions that did little to prevent contagion all contributed to the comparatively early death of colonial southerners. Frequent deaths disrupted customary kinship relations, orphaned children, reduced the size of families, and left relatives mourning the loss of their loved ones. Unlike many other places in colonial British America, the Lower Cape Fear left no parish registers listing births and deaths, no census, and not even a significant list of residents' ages by which to gauge the region's demographic structure.[28] Consequently, to calculate mortality rates and compare them closely with findings for other colonial American locales is impossible.

Nonetheless, contemporary perceptions are also an important indicator of health conditions, and extant writing about the Lower Cape Fear makes it clear that the region experienced a relatively high rate of mortality. In a telling 1763 letter to the Society for the Propagation of the Gospel, Anglican missionary John MacDowell described his own severe illness and went on to remark that "this has been a fatal year to us Europeans here." MacDowell explained that poor health seemed omnipresent and that there were many he had "seen since I have been here, hearty & Gay & Brisk one week & the next attended to their grave." He sought permission to leave his parish in the Lower Cape Fear because "this is a dismal climate & when one gets sickly here, I have hardly ever known an instance of his recovering."[29] In a similar vein, shortly after her arrival in the Lower Cape Fear, Janet Schaw remarked on the unhealthy appearance of the region's inhabitants, which was "in every respect the reverse of that which gives the idea of strength and vigor." She went on to describe people with "short waists and long limbs, sallow complexions and languid eyes." She thought their unhealthy appearance was undoubtedly linked to "the constant slow fevers that wear down their constitutions, relax their nerves and infeeble the whole frame."[30] Hugh Henry Meredith pointed out that the Lower Cape Fear would attract more settlers if the area was "but tolerably healthful, (which it is far from)."[31] In fact, nearly every visitor who wrote about travels in the Lower Cape Fear, including the anonymous authors of "A New Voyage to Georgia," *American Husbandry,* and "Journal of A French Traveller," as well as Hugh Finlay, Johann David Schoepf, and Robert Hunter, remarked on the poor health in the region or on some form of illness.[32]

Compared with most of the English countryside and the northern British colonies, poor health characterized all of the plantation colonies. But the virulence of pathogens could vary enormously, depending on local conditions. At least four sets of preconditions influenced the danger from severe epidemic diseases in colonial localities. First, some of the deadliest diseases came from West Africa and thrived in tropical or subtropical climate conditions. The Lower Cape Fear's temperatures were generally warmer than those anywhere else in either North Carolina or the Chesapeake; they were closer to those in the South

Carolina lowcountry.[33] Second, the two most important potentially fatal diseases in the southern colonies, malaria and yellow fever, spread through mosquitoes and proved to be much more common in poorly drained, swampy areas that provided standing water where mosquitoes could breed. Both Janet Schaw and the author of "A New Voyage to Georgia" commented on the impressive numbers of mosquitoes in the Lower Cape Fear.[34] In this respect, the Lower Cape Fear bore a strong resemblance to the South Carolina lowcountry. The same swamps that encouraged would-be rice planters in both places also magnified the frequency of deadly diseases.

Third, contagious diseases appeared more often and spread more quickly in urban areas, and especially ports, where travelers could introduce pathogens from other parts of the world. No place in the southern colonies provided an arena of contagion comparable with Charles Town, but Wilmington and Brunswick certainly made the Lower Cape Fear the most important Atlantic trade entrepot in North Carolina. Contemporaries noted the epidemic conditions that periodically afflicted these two towns. By 1740, some North Carolinians complained that "it is notorious that Brunswick is the most sickly unhealthy place in the whole Colony," a situation they attributed to "the unwholesome Water and Pernicious Vapours rising from the Ponds and Marshes with which it is almost Surrounded." Brunswick probably also received more contagious newcomers because most vessels had to clear customs there, where deeper water could handle larger ships.[35] After another epidemic in 1742, James Murray wrote that "the people are almost Dead . . . [in] Brunswick."[36] But if Wilmington was the healthier of the two towns, it also suffered from epidemics. Moravians who came from the backcountry to trade with the Lower Cape Fear reported "a sickness which is epidemic at Wilmington," where the "patients die in four or five days." Four years later, they commented again on "the unhealthy air of Wilmington."[37]

Finally, and perhaps most important, mortality rates varied depending on the level of immunity in the affected population. People who survived exposure to malaria or yellow fever could acquire a significant degree of immunity. This acquisition meant, first of all, that, because malaria and yellow fever were common in West Africa, the diseases proved less deadly for Africans than for Europeans. It also meant that adults who had been born in the malarial regions of North America could withstand these diseases more effectively than those who immigrated from Europe or the northern colonies. Consequently, the differing origins of settlers in the Lower Cape Fear made levels of mortality different from those in other regions. Those from South Carolina and many from Albemarle would have had some immunity, while those from the British Isles and the northern colonies would have been much more severely afflicted. Along these lines, Governor Gabriel Johnston eagerly recommended North Carolina native Christopher Bevis as an SPG missionary partly because his "Constitution is enur'd to the Climate."[38] Indeed, because most parts of the colonial south were occupied by Creole populations in the late colonial period, transatlantic migrants to the Lower Cape Fear might have experienced high mortality rates even for the southern colonies.

To sum up, contemporary perceptions strongly suggest that European American mortality rates in the Lower Cape Fear had a devastating effect on families and may have approached rates in the South Carolina lowcountry. Yet the relatively isolated, cooler, and drier conditions in the Lower Cape Fear probably prevented diseases from having as severe an impact as they did closer to Charles Town. At least one Lower Cape Fear resident, James Murray, acknowledged that health conditions were worse in South Carolina by advising Henry McCulloh to send his wife to the Cape Fear rather "than to trust her self this summer in so sickly and Mortal a place as So[uth] Carolina."[39] As Murray recognized, local circumstances contributed to various demographic outcomes, and the Lower Cape Fear's struggles with disease differed from those in surrounding areas in both North and South Carolina.

If the comparative scale of deadly diseases in the Lower Cape Fear remains somewhat uncertain, the influence of high mortality on Lower Cape Fear families is undeniable. Murray provides the best account of the way that tropical diseases could disrupt families. In October 1757, Murray returned from a trip to the sound, where his pregnant wife and his daughter had gone to recover from illness. Shortly after arriving at her home, however, Mrs. Murray "relapsed into her intermittent fevers, attended with Swellings." Another return to the sound in November failed to have the desired effect. In February 1758, Mrs. Murray gave birth, then died two days later. The newborn child, a daughter, lived only another two weeks. Within three more weeks, Murray's other daughter, Jeany, also died. Murray wrote that he "did not imagine any thing in this world or the Loss of all of it would have to sit so heavy on my Spirits." If he had not lost all of his world, he had lost most of his family, in a mere month and a half.[40]

Rather than continue in lonely grief, Murray remarried, and at age forty-eight began to build a new family. Once again, however, his family was disrupted by "an epidemical fever, which prevailed and was often mortal in this Town and neighborhood." Not only was Murray's second wife in danger, but "my youngest Son . . . the most engaging of all our Children was next seized, and died 17th October." This death caused the family "inexpressible Grief, from which we were roused by the dangerous attack upon our third Daughter Betsy." Betsy struggled not only against the fever but also against a lameness that remained in one leg, while her sister Nancy suffered from a mere sore throat. Murray added that, as he wrote, "some gloom still remains," because his wife's health continued to be in jeopardy. Four years later, Murray took the surviving portion of his family and moved to New England, at least in part to be in a healthier environment.[41] Murray's decision to depart may have been unusual in the Lower Cape Fear, but the diseases that ravaged his family were not unusual there.

Demographic disruption made it difficult for Lower Cape Fear residents to establish the normative nuclear family pattern dictated by Anglo-American cultural expectations. Surviving wills provide the best evidence about the structure of European American families in colonial Lower Cape Fear. Testators normally made reference to all of their immediate family members in their wills.[42] An analysis of 258 extant wills for New Hanover and Brunswick counties before 1776 reveals a pattern of demographic disruption. Only slightly more than one-half of the testators had a spouse, almost two-thirds were childless, and almost one-quarter lacked a male child to serve as a traditional patrilineal heir. Considerably more than half of all testators did not have a nuclear family when they wrote their will. Parents averaged a mere 3.3 surviving children.[43] This data bears a striking similarity to data on family structures in wills from colonial South Carolina.[44] In both places, deadly diseases took their toll on families.

The frequent disruption of family structures in the Lower Cape Fear could be particularly hard on children. Murray's letters reveal anxiety about the difficulties of raising children in the region. In 1750, he remarked that his daughter Dolly alone survived, but consoled himself with the knowledge that she was "a thumping Girl," and Murray derived pleasure from other healthy births in the family.[45] But a constant awareness of health risks did not alleviate and probably exacerbated the more commonplace challenges of child rearing. On several occasions, Murray reflected on the limits placed on children growing up in the new Lower Cape Fear settlement: if he had sons survive to adulthood, he hoped to "make Lairds in Carolina," but the region offered Dolly and other daughters only "an uncultivated indolent set of Men to match them with." Murray wrote that he planned to send Dolly to live with "her Aunt at Boston for better breeding than this place could afford."[46] He hoped that both Lower Cape Fear society and the region's marriageable men would be "much Improv'd by the time" his daughters "came to market."[47] Regardless of such uncertain outcomes, Murray made it clear that he considered raising children "one of the most valuable purposes of life," and when his wife died he assured Dolly that as a single parent he would be "as good a father to you as you can desire."[48] Murray and other settlers in the Lower Cape Fear quickly recognized health problems and obstacles to forming families and caring for children in the newly settled region, but they still approached these tasks with considerable determination.

Like elsewhere in the southern colonies, residents of the Lower Cape Fear made special provisions to deal with the plight of orphaned children.[49] North Carolina legislators passed laws to place orphans under the care and jurisdiction of county and superior courts.[50] County courts had to hold a separate orphan court once every year. This response to the problem followed the pattern of strong, locally active systems of county courts first established in the Chesapeake Bay colonies and carried to North Carolina by the settlers of the Albemarle region. Generally, courts assigned guardians to orphans who had significant estates, while they bound out less fortunate orphans as apprentices. Justices also attempted to make sure that guardians and masters did not take advantage of orphans. They gave careful consideration to the interests of the children and sought to provide them with suitable homes, guardians, masters, and at least some education.[51]

In practice, however, the courts could never have realized all of these goals. First of all, the administrative demands of such a system made it impractical. There were far too few orphans in each county to justify convening a separate orphans' court once a year. In New Hanover, and in some other North Carolina counties, business related to orphans was integrated into the other business of the county court at its quarterly sessions. Also, because justices often needed to confer with prospective guardians and others before making an appointment, the appointment of guardians and masters had to be timed to coincide with local networks of travel and communication.[52]

Equally important, the relatively large and sparsely populated size of the county court's jurisdiction made it hard for justices to insure that orphans received proper care. To determine how frequently Lower Cape Fear orphans were mistreated in their new homes is difficult; however, compared with records in other North Carolina counties, New Hanover's court minutes provide unusually detailed complaints from several apprenticed orphans.[53] In June 1741, for example, the county court in New Hanover heard a complaint against Mary Gallant for "inordinately beating and abusing an orphan child, her apprentice." What might have constituted inordinate beating for an early-eighteenth-century North Carolina court is unclear, but the child remained under Mary's care and authority after she posted bond for her good behavior in the future.[54]

Some orphans brought complaints of a less-violent nature. William Martindale complained that his master, Michael Dyer, had refused to teach him the trade of shipwright in accordance with his apprenticeship. The justices gave careful consideration to the appropriate course of legal action before ordering Dyer to pay bond for the orphan's instruction, but both Dyer and the orphan agreed to end the indenture.[55] Dyer and Martindale apparently negotiated a more satisfactory arrangement without the intervention of the court. The experience of Margaret Clark also underscored the limits of the courts' ability to supervise the care of orphans. She had been apprenticed to Jennet Cowan, a Wilmington widow, but in 1768 complained that her "mistress has failed to clothe and educate her." Even more disconcerting than Margaret's lack of clothing, given eighteenth-century gender expectations, Cowan had hired her out to Jacob Hook "without allowing her necessary apparel." Perhaps the court might have left Clarke in Cowan's care after the payment of a bond, but in this case

TABLE 3.1 **Orphans Apprenticed or Assigned Guardians in Various North Carolina Counties**

County	*Years*	*Total Orphans*	*Orphans per Year*
Pasquotank	1755–62, 1769–72, 1775	223	17.2
Edgecombe	1758–75	280	15.6
Chowan	1755–75	323	15.4
Rowan	1754–75	190	8.6
Tryon	1769–75	48	6.9
Cumberland	1755–65, 1772–75	90	6.0
Onslow	1754–75	93	4.2
New Hanover	1759–61, 1764–75	63	4.2

Note: The data in this table has been adapted from table 1 in Alan D. Watson, "Public Poor Relief in Colonial North Carolina," *North Carolina Historical Review* 54, no. 4 (1977): 364.

the court did not have such an option. Cowan had moved out of Wilmington and resettled up the Cape Fear River in Cumberland County, leaving her hired out and poorly clad apprentice behind. The justices placed Clarke in the care of Hannah Nevin, another Wilmington widow, who they presumably considered more trustworthy.[56]

If the county courts faced difficult obstacles in supervising the care of orphans placed under their care, it seems likely that many orphans received no help at all from the court system. A study of the treatment of orphans by colonial North Carolina courts (see table 3.1) reveals that the New Hanover County Court handled the affairs of only about four orphans per year, as few as in any other county studied. Given that health conditions in New Hanover probably led to significantly higher mortality than in the other North Carolina counties, this discrepancy is difficult to explain. The population of New Hanover was less than that of some of the other counties, but surely there were more than four orphans a year in a county with more than two thousand white inhabitants. It seems clear that many orphans simply did not come before the courts.

There are several reasons why the county court did not assign guardians or apprenticeships to a large number of New Hanover County orphans. First, some testators named guardians for their children in their wills, and the courts normally did not interfere with the deceased's wishes in such matters: the provisions of the deceased might make the court's involvement superfluous. But such provisions were not made frequently enough to account for the large number of orphans that must have been omitted from the New Hanover court's proceedings.[57] There does not appear to have been any formal mechanism for notifying the county court that orphans were in need of supervision. If the deceased father had a widow, she would continue to care for the children, if she possessed the means, without court action. If the children lacked both parents, the executor or administrator of the estate generally functioned as guardian for the orphans. In some cases, other family members or friends may have taken care of the children on their own initiative. Thus, in a more recently settled and sparsely populated county with high mortality, such as New Hanover, informal and kinship networks probably provided as efficient a means of helping orphans as did the county courts in Albemarle and the Chesapeake region, where courts played a larger role.[58]

The frequent disruption of nuclear families placed additional pressure on local extended kinship relations.[59] When a spouse or a sibling died, relatives might seek emotional support or assistance from other kin.[60] At the same time, other factors made it difficult for Lower Cape Fear residents to rely extensively on extended kinship networks. For one thing, extended kin networks could themselves be affected by high mortality. Perhaps even more important, because settlement in the Lower Cape Fear did not begin until relatively late in the colonial period, a high percentage of the region's residents were immigrants whose extended kin may have been too far away to be of much help. Assistance often had to come from individuals who were within the Lower Cape Fear region.

The choices of Lower Cape Fear testators demonstrated these limitations on extended kin networks (tables 3.2 and 3.3 show these choices). Testators were far more likely to choose non-kin as the executors of their estates.[61] Because executors bore the important burden of protecting the family's interests and insuring that the testators' wishes were respected, the selection of executors took on paramount importance for those writing wills. Ideally, most testators would have chosen widows or adult sons to be executors, but this was not always an option. The greater frequency of non-kin testators suggests that many Lower Cape Fear residents could not rely on extended kin to provide even the most important kinds of assistance. At the same time, the importance of kinship ties depended on circumstances, and it should not be assumed that extended kin relationships were unimportant for settlers in the Lower Cape Fear. Indeed, except for the selection of executors, testators seemed to have placed greater emphasis on extended kin relationships than on non-kin relationships. More wills mentioned extended kin, and extended kin accounted for greater total numbers.[62]

Lower Cape Fear residents probably alternated in their emphasis on extended kin and non-kin ties for several reasons. First, many Lower Cape Fear residents probably could not rely on extended kin in the region because they simply were not present. More than one-half of all Lower Cape Fear testators made no reference at all in their wills to extended kin.[63] Most Cape Fear residents left their

TABLE 3.2 **A Comparison of the Significance of Extended Kin and Non-kin in Lower Cape Fear Wills**

	Extended Kin	*Non-Kin*
Named Executors	89	289
Number of wills mentioning extended kin and non-kin	133	104
Total mentions	404	267

Note: Lower Cape Fear computer biographical files.

TABLE 3.3 **Relationships of Lower Cape Fear Executors**

	Number	*Percent of Possible Executors in Category*
Widow	100	65
Sons	74	25
Daughters	3	1
Other Kin	87	NA
Non-kin	289	NA
Total	553	NA

Note: Lower Cape Fear computer biographical files. *Percent of Possible Executors in Category* refers to the maximum number of individuals mentioned in the will that could be appointed as an executor. For example, if a testator had four sons and named two of them as executors, the percent of possible executors would equal fifty for that testator.

extended kin behind when they migrated to the region, and extended kin in the Lower Cape Fear might succumb to the region's deadly diseases. Executors had to be nearby and actively involved in the handling of an estate, so if kin were far away or in poor health, testators wisely chose trustworthy friends, neighbors, or other non-kin. Extended kin ties probably remained important to Lower Cape Fear residents regardless of distance. Indeed, the absence of extended kin in the Lower Cape Fear may have made settlers fonder of relatives in their old homes. They indicated as much by referring to extended kin in their wills and often making them bequests of at least symbolic value. Settlement in a new region simply required that new networks be formed within the region, whether based on kinship or other criteria, to complement more distant sources of support and assistance.

In contrast, an examination of Lower Cape Fear wills shows far less emphasis on neighborhood connections. In the three neighborhoods of Rocky Point, Lockwoods Folly, and Old Town Creek, the wills of forty-one colonial residents have survived. Of the 313 names mentioned in the wills from these three neighborhoods, however, only 57 can be identified as neighbors. These numbers can be misleading, of course, because most of those mentioned in wills were nuclear family members who would not have been identified as separate heads of households or residents in any of the three neighborhoods. Still, neighbors made up less than one-third of the individuals mentioned who were part of the testators' immediate families. On the other hand, of the relatively small minority of people who were mentioned in wills but who had no identifiable kinship relation to the testator, most can be identified as neighbors.

These findings show that neighborhood connections probably did have considerable significance, but, for the purposes of inheritance at least, those connections were still much less important than kinship connections. This emphasis on kinship in wills is particularly impressive for a region that provided substantial obstacles to the maintenance of kinship networks. These patterns do not reveal a great deal of variation between neighborhoods, either, though limited data suggest that there might be some relationship between the emphasis on kinship and the prosperity of the neighborhood, perhaps because settlers in places like Rocky Point had greater resources with which to encourage the formation of elaborate kin ties. Ideally, testators probably preferred to leave bequests to individuals who participated in both kinship and neighborhood networks. Of the 57 neighbors who did make it into wills, 36, a significant majority, were also somehow related to the testator. Failing this, testators most often overlooked distance and turned to relatives, but location and distance still proved to be important. It was highly unusual for Lower Cape Fear testators to mention in their wills anyone who resided beyond the Lower Cape Fear region itself.

If circumstances could alter the relative importance of distant kin and unrelated friends, there is no question that Lower Cape Fear residents, like colonists throughout British America, experienced even more important relationships within their households. But in the colonial plantation societies, at least, the household was not always conterminous with the nuclear family.[64] Lower Cape Fear patriarchs exercised power over slaves as well as over dependent members of their own families.[65] As a magisterial recent work on slavery in two other regions of the colonial south has aptly expressed it, "The dominant social ethos and cultural metaphor of seventeenth- and early-eighteenth-century Anglo-America, patriarchalism, embodied the ideal of an organic social hierarchy."[66] In spite of the intense brutality of plantation slavery, slave owners were able to construct a worldview that simultaneously emphasized discipline and protection and that conceptualized slaves as subordinate family members.[67]

Given this context, the relatively large numbers of slaves in the Lower Cape Fear differentiated households in the region from those in the rest of North Carolina. Data shown in tables 3.4 and 3.5 and derived from tax lists reveal that Lower Cape Fear householders were consistently more likely to own slaves than were householders in any other county of North Carolina.[68] Perhaps even more important, slaves made up a significantly higher portion of households in the

TABLE 3.4 **Slaves as a Percentage of the Total Estimated Population in Various Regions of North Carolina, 1767**

Region	*Estimated Total Population*	*% Slaves*
Lower Cape Fear	4,216	63
Northeastern North Carolina	37,284	24
Upper Cape Fear	2,040	29
Backcountry	40,313	15

Note: For Lower Cape Fear population estimates, see chapter 1. All other data in this table has been adapted from Marvin M. Kay and Lorin L. Cary, *Slavery in North Carolina, 1748–1775* (Chapel Hill: University of North Carolina Press, 1995), 226–27.

TABLE 3.5 **Distribution of Slaves among Households in Selected North Carolina Counties**

County	*Year*	*Households*	*% with Slaves*
New Hanover	1755	265	55
Perquinians	1772	361	53
Chowan	1772	488	52
New Hanover	1763	410	52
New Hanover	1767	347	50
Brunswick	1769	197	46
Brunswick	1772	195	45
Beaufort	1764	306	37
Onslow	1771	511	32
Cumberland	1767	579	23
Anson	1763	302	10
Orange	1755	753	7

Note: Data in this table has been adapted from Alan D. Watson, "Household Size and Composition in Pre-Revolutionary North Carolina," *Mississippi Quarterly* 31, no. 4 (1978): 551–69; Merrens, *Colonial North Carolina,* 74–81.

Lower Cape Fear than in the rest of the province. Indeed, the Lower Cape Fear region was the only part of North Carolina in which slaves made up most of the population, as they did in the South Carolina lowcountry.[69]

Moreover, the scale of slave ownership in the Lower Cape Fear reinforced patriarchal attitudes and drew a sharp contrast with the predominantly all-white households in the rest of the province. Those settlers with considerable slaveholdings found it much easier to envision themselves within a long-standing British tradition of patriarchalism that imagined heads of households as omnipotent father figures.[70] At the same time, slaveholdings in the Lower Cape Fear could seem insignificant compared with some in South Carolina.[71] Lower Cape Fear residents owned many slaves for a region in North Carolina, but few compared with other slave societies in the early-modern Atlantic World. Indeed, the close proximity of the South Carolina lowcountry made some Lower Cape Fear patriarchs acutely aware that they were still "masters of small worlds."[72]

The slaves themselves constantly contested the assertion of slave-owner authority, whether based on patriarchial ideology or some other rationalization, and strove to form and maintain their own relatively autonomous families. They faced significant challenges. Isolation from other slaves often made the formation of close relationships difficult, and the imposition of physical distance frequently disrupted families once they were formed. Moreover, these differing units of production and the specific attitudes of slave owners could lead to widely differing opportunities for the development of kinship connections between slaves.

Plantation size had more influence on the formation of slave families than any other measurable variable in the Lower Cape Fear and elsewhere in colonial British America. Consequently, the Lower Cape Fear's relatively large concentrations of slave labor proved favorable to family-building aspirations among those in bondage.[73] More than 73 percent of all slaves in the Lower Cape Fear lived on plantations with twenty or more slaves, and more than 87 percent lived on plantations with ten or more slaves. Also, the Lower Cape Fear region had the most balanced sex ratio among slaves in North Carolina, and a clear majority of Lower Cape Fear slaves at least conceivably could have taken a partner of the opposite sex on their own plantations. Scotus Americanus remarked upon these family units of slaves, writing that they "have small houses or huts, like peasants, thatched to which they have little gardens, and live in families separated from each other."[74] Kay and Cary estimate that about 64 percent of slaves in the Lower Cape Fear estate inventories could have been grouped in dual-headed families, while a mere 18 percent could not have been grouped into families at all. Compared with those on the larger rice plantations of South Carolina, the sizes of completed slave families on the few Lower Cape Fear plantations that have left records were not as large, but they appeared to be at least as large as those on most plantations in the Chesapeake Bay area. Slaves who could not form families on their own plantation may have found some consolation by traveling to nearby plantations, the Lower Cape Fear having by far the highest slave-population density in colonial North Carolina.[75]

Of course, even if slaves formed families, those families could be torn apart with alarming ease. Slaves faced the possibility that a family member would be sold away, as well as the shared dangers of demographic disruption and other obstacles that they, like free families, faced. Schoepf's account of his visit to Wilmington provides a vivid picture of the emotional turmoil slave sales could cause. Describing an enslaved father up for auction, Schoepf writes, "His anxiety lest his son fall to another purchaser and be separated from him was more painful than his fear of getting into the hands of a hard master." During the auction, this father continually cried out that whoever purchased him must also purchase his son. In this case, "it happened as he desired," but, as Schoepf realized, slaves could not always exert such influence: "Often the husband is snatched from his wife, the children from their mother . . . and no heed is given the doleful prayers with which they seek to prevent a separation."[76] Elkanah Watson witnessed a slave family at an auction in Wilmington who were "driven in from the country, like swine for market." This time, "a poor wench clung to a little daughter, and implored, with the most agonizing supplication, they must not be separated. But alas, either the master or circumstances were inexorable."[77]

While slave families remained together, they usually managed to maintain a significant degree of autonomy over their relationships despite the controlling impulses of slave owners. Slave owners often found it in their interest to encourage the formation of slave families because it generally led to the birth of more slaves. In some cases, this situation might have made matters easier for slave families. Along these lines, John Brickell wrote that, in colonial North Carolina, fruitful slave women were "very much valued by the Planters, and a numerous Issue esteemed the greatest Riches in this Country."[78] Based on scattered evidence from some large plantations, it appears that slave women in North Carolina had children at a relatively young age. But other evidence suggests that slaves made their own choices about reproductive matters. Unusually long intervals between the birth of slave children reveal that slaves may have continued African sexual taboos and practices of birth control, in direct opposition to the slave owners' wishes and interests.[79]

Brickell's account of slave marriages in North Carolina also reveals that slaves practiced their own family rituals. He described a courtship practice that appears to be a form of the West African custom of bride wealth. According to Brickell, "the Man makes the Woman a Present, such as a Brass Ring or some other Toy, which if she accepts of, becomes his Wife." This practice of gift giving bears a strong resemblance to West African practices, but, in Brickell's account, some adaptation had also taken place. Unlike in West Africa, "if ever they part from each other, which frequently happens . . . she returns his Present." Perhaps because of the distinct possibility of separation, enslaved couples reconceptualized their marriage practices in accordance with the conditions of their life.[80]

Sources do not permit a more rigorous examination of slave-family relationships, but population data indicates that by the late colonial period there was a relatively healthy pattern of natural increase among slaves in the Lower Cape Fear. The clearly limited importation of slaves into the Lower Cape Fear after 1750 could scarcely account for an increase in the slave population of within the region of almost 5 percent between 1755 and 1767.[81] A population capable of producing a significant degree of natural increase must have been healthy enough to promote the formation of many families, even though the slaves experienced arduous, coerced labor and confronted a deadly disease environment.

Lower Cape Fear settlers demonstrated patriarchal attitudes not only through the treatment of their slaves but also through inheritance practices that were influenced by regional concerns (see tables 3.6, 3.7 and 3.8).[82] If wills indicate that the relative importance of extended kin and non-kin depended on circumstances, they also leave no doubt that the nuclear family provided Lower Cape Fear residents with their strongest ties. Almost 60 percent of all individuals mentioned in wills were members of the testator's immediate family, and the percentage would no doubt be much higher if not for demographic disruptions and individuals immigrating without families.[83] Like other Anglo-American testators, those in the Lower Cape Fear favored sons in their wills and showed a concern for passing on significant amounts of property to their male heirs, as well as for preserving the economic security of their widows and other children.

Sons were more likely to receive any property, whether it were land, slaves, or livestock. Daughters often inherited significant property, too, but usually only after sons had been provided for. Widows generally inherited substantial portions of estates, but often their shares were intended for the maintenance of children as well; some widows lost some of their inheritance if they remarried, and most were prevented from passing on all of their inheritance in their own wills.[84] The power that testators could exercise was perhaps most evident in the wills of such Lower Cape Fear testators as David Brown, who left his "undutiful" widow, Ann Brown, only one shilling, citing "her Misbehavior to me during our Cohabitation together & since."[85] Moreover, Anglo-American law gave unusual freedom to testators. In North Carolina, widows could disregard their deceased husband's wills and receive one-third of their husband's real estate, but, beyond this one stipulation, Lower Cape Fear testators could bequeath their property any way they wished.[86]

Within this patriarchal tradition of inheritance, however, most Lower Cape Fear residents proved to be surprisingly liberal in their provisions. A very low proportion of testators clearly practiced the patriarchal tradition of primogeniture, which gave all the family's land to the eldest male child. In many cases, this practice may have been a consequence of a lack of male heirs, but, even with this qualification, primogeniture was still strikingly rare.[87] Equally important, an even lower percentage entailed property to prevent heirs from transferring their property. Less than 2 percent of Lower Cape Fear wills included entail provisions.[88] Further, the late settlement of the Lower Cape Fear also made it unlikely that significant amounts of property were encumbered by entail, as they were

TABLE 3.6 **Relationships Mentioned in Lower Cape Fear Wills**

Relationship	*Mentioned*	*Mentioned per Will*
All	1,656	5.96
Spouse	154	0.55
Sons	299	1.07
Daughters	243	0.87
Unborn children	5	0.02
Immediate family	978	3.52
Other kin	384	1.45
Non-kin	267	0.96

Note: Lower Cape Fear computer biographical files.

TABLE 3.7 **Provisions for Widows**

Terms of Will	*Percentage*
All of bequest given forever	49
All of bequest given at least for life	21
Some of bequest given for widowhood or other limited term	30

TABLE 3.8 **Disposition of Different Kinds of Property in Wills, by Relationship of Recipients**

Relationship	*% of Possible Land Bequests*	*% of Possible Slave Bequests*	*% of Possible Livestock Bequests*
Widows	67	53	41
Sons	90	75	73
Daughters	38	62	61
Other kin	35	39	43
Non-kin	41	39	44

Note: Lower Cape Fear computer biographical files. *% of Possible Bequests* refers to the percentage of possible times that an individual received a specific bequest in the appropriate category. For example, in 90 percent of the wills in which the testator had at least one son and left specific bequests of land, some of the land went to a son.

in Virginia during the colonial period.[89] Some testators were probably influenced by the legal preclusion of entails in nearby South Carolina. If Lower Cape Fear residents did not push to make entails illegal in their colony, they at least made the practice irrelevant through disuse.

Lower Cape Fear testators also broke with patriarchal inheritance customs in other important ways. For one thing, not only younger sons, but even daughters, often received land, the most gender-linked form of property. Widows also received unusually liberal provisions. Almost one-half of Lower Cape Fear widows inherited all of their property to own unconditionally, rather than with the usual restrictions to use of property in their lifetime or during their widowhood. Almost one-quarter more received property for their lifetime. These provisions were clearly more beneficial to widows than were those made in the colonial Chesapeake or in England, though they were not comparable with those made in South Carolina.[90] A small percentage of widows received less than dower because of the wills of their husbands, and more received their husbands' entire estate.[91] Finally, widows were named as executors 65 percent of the time, indicating that husbands felt their wives could manage the family's estate effectively.[92]

Because of the combined consequences of high mortality and recent immigration, Lower Cape Fear patriarchs felt compelled to rely more on their wives and daughters. If a husband died young and left young children, naturally a woman assumed her spouse's responsibilities. In some cases, this assumption meant that women controlled more property and fulfilled different roles than would have been socially acceptable if a male were present to direct the household. In other situations, women who lacked nearby kin assumed a greater degree of autonomy to maintain their security. Indeed, elite Lower Cape Fear widows often acquired impressive estates. At least eight women in the Lower Cape Fear owned more than a thousand acres, and at least forty owned more than five hundred acres from patents and purchases alone.[93] One Lower Cape Fear widow, Margaret Haynes, even referred to herself as a "planter," suggesting that she engaged in a traditionally male occupation.[94] By the end of the colonial period, about thirty Lower Cape Fear women headed their own households, and virtually all of them owned slaves. Women without spouses appear to have owned more valuable property in slaves than in land, perhaps because landownership was culturally linked to masculinity and independence.[95] As William Tryon observed of Cape Fear dowry practices, "When a man marries his Daughters he never talks of the fortune in Money but 20 30 or 40 Slaves is her Portion."[96] To cite one example, Anne Moore, a widow, somehow acquired forty-seven slaves of her own, whether through her powerful relatives in the Moore family or from her two marriages to Peter Taylor and the wealthy John Swann.[97] While women without spouses never made up much more than 5 percent of Lower Cape Fear householders or landowners, they appear to have been disproportionately wealthy.[98] About one-half this number conducted business by running an ordinary or inn.[99] Murray underscored the economic importance of Lower Cape Fear widows when he advised Archibald Douglas that he should attempt to become the fourth husband of a Mrs. Hamilton, "a Rich Widow for you." Clearly, Murray was not the only one who paid attention to such material considerations because he warned Douglas that she was unlikely to be available by the time he arrived in town.[100]

Women attempted to protect their property, even from spouses. Like women in other parts of British America, a number of elite women obtained marriage settlements to maintain some control over their belongings after they married. These agreements were rare, usually involved widows, and varied considerably, depending on the wife's circumstances.[101] In another instance, Ephraim and Ann Vernon separated, and Ann received property that included two plantations and some slaves.[102] Widows commonly remarried, which usually meant that they legally forfeited control over their estates to their new husbands.[103] As long as Lower Cape Fear widows remained single, however, they evidently had economic opportunities that were unusual for women in colonial British America, and there must have been a significant number of widows in the Lower Cape Fear region. Indeed, evidence about testator patterns, cited above, makes it reasonable to postulate that distinctive attitudes toward the relationship of gender and property existed in the Lower Cape Fear, giving some women more security and autonomy than in other healthier and more settled parts of North Carolina.

Still, if demographics and settlement exigencies gave Lower Cape Fear women opportunities for unusual autonomy, some women may have been ambivalent about availing themselves of those opportunities. Women in the Lower Cape Fear, like Sarah Allen, may have had more promising material opportunities, but they also used those opportunities within the constraints of Anglo-American gender expectations.[104] For one thing, like male heads of households, they placed great importance on the security of their family, and this emphasis often meant that they chose to perpetuate patrilineal inheritance practices. Daughters might marry and lose control of their property, but sons could continue to provide support for other family members. Consequently, Lower Cape Fear widows who left wills seldom departed from the practices of male testators. In fact, one widow, Anne Ross, proved to be one of the few Lower Cape Fear testators to follow the conservative and highly patriarchal inheritance practice of primogeniture. As one of the wealthiest widows in the region and the owner of about thirty slaves, Ross gave all of her land and slaves to one son, even though she had five other sons and a daughter. She also made her sons executors of her estate.[105] Ross, like self-defined "planter" Margaret Haynes, presents an exceptional case; most women probably fitted between these two positions. In the Lower Cape Fear, it was common and acceptable for women to engage in a variety of traditionally male tasks in the place of their husbands or brothers. In some cases, this development probably gave women more autonomy. But it did not constitute a serious departure from the domestic sphere, and there is no indication that women behaved in ways that dramatically challenged the social order of the Lower Cape Fear.[106]

The dilemma of Justina Davis illustrates some of the choices and challenges that life in the colonial Lower Cape Fear presented to women. Davis apparently caught the eye of Arthur Dobbs, the North Carolina governor, and Dobbs's courtship efforts became a source of mockery for the unidentified author of one surviving letter from the region. The author characterized the aging Dobbs as "Our Old Silenus of the Envigorated age of Seventy Eight who still Damns this Province with his Baneful Influence." Perhaps the author disagreed with Dobbs's political decisions, but the governor's most grievous fault appears to be that he "grew stupidly Enamored with Miss Davis, a Lovely Lady of sprightly fifteen of a good Family and some Fortune."

Despite having reservations, Davis submitted to her parents' wishes and agreed to marry Dobbs, but the situation was complicated because she "loved and was beloved by Dear Eighteen Y—g M—r Q—n-ce." According to the letter writer, the treacherous Dobbs, described as "old in every human characteristic but sense," tried to deprive his new bride of much of his estate by conveying it to other relatives before the wedding. When a sympathetic source revealed Dobbs's plans to Davis, her friends sent for her "Pensive & Dejected Lover [Y—g M—r Q—n-ce]," encouraging the couple to "consummate" a marriage. Whether Davis and her young partner ever married in any sense or merely provided a subject for gossip and satire remains a matter of conjecture, but Dobbs's fondness for Davis continued. Davis ultimately married the governor, in 1762. The correspondent implies that Dobbs discovered the union, vented his anger, and behaved in such a way that "no pen can describe the Rage and Ridicule." Either way, Justina Davis, who seems to have had a very limited range of choices and been subject to substantial pressure from various quarters, apparently accepted the role of Dobbs's wife for the remaining years of his life. Perhaps because she came to appreciate the value of a powerful husband, she would later marry Abner Nash, another future governor of North Carolina.[107]

Davis's difficulties were no doubt exacerbated by the contrast between the relative newness and insecurity of Lower Cape Fear families and the metropolitan and transatlantic prominence of Arthur Dobbs. Moreover, new settlements had to establish clear gender and family mores just as they had to establish new political and social institutions. The difficulties of starting a new settlement, immigration, demographic disruption, the cultural heterogeneity of plantation colonies, and a sense of remoteness could all challenge the stability of domestic and social hierarchies.[108] Dobbs's courtship of Davis, and the anonymous letter writer's response to it, underscore the powerful consequences of such tensions in the Lower Cape Fear.

Thus, even assumptions about Anglo-American family life could be shaped by regional circumstances. While colonists attempted to meet metropolitan standards in their family life, these standards were often filtered through local expectations, opportunities, and experiences. South Carolinians, for example, generally emulated the elite families of Charles Town society. In the Lower Cape Fear, however, settlers lacked such a unified influence and adopted a variety of perspectives for their families. London, Edinburgh, Charles Town, Boston, Philadelphia, the nearby North Carolina towns of New Bern and Edenton, and other locales each provided relevant models of behavior for some Lower Cape Fear families.

Yet Anglo-American settlers from each of these places agreed on the importance of a certain degree of civility in their family lives along the Cape Fear River. No one in the Lower Cape Fear articulated this emphasis on civility more thoroughly than did Janet Schaw. Schaw was, in fact, quite impressed with the women of the region, "many of whom would make a figure in any part of the world." She found them to be "amiable" and "agreeable" company, but she lacked such flattering adjectives to describe Lower Cape Fear men, who knew "no such nice distinctions." A local man offered her an explanation for this disparity between the genders. In his account, women passed on the appropriate mores from generation to generation after the first settlements, but men lost such social graces because of the physical labor required by their new home. While not all Lower Cape Fear men still lived such lives of toil, and "tho' necessity no longer prescribed these severe occupations, custom has established it as still necessary for the men to spend their time abroad in the fields."[109] William Tryon's wife must have shared the desire for refined appearances that Schaw admired in the women of the Lower Cape Fear. After Tryon and his wife arrived in the Cape Fear, he wrote his uncle that "as you are acquainted with Mrs Tryons Neatness you will not wonder that we have been pestered with scouring of Chambers White Washing of Cielings, Plaisters Work, and Painting the House inside and out."[110] But both Schaw and Tryon ultimately viewed the North Carolinians as rebels and irredeemably uncivil colonists.

Even those who were more attached to the Lower Cape Fear might have experienced some anxiety about family life in the region, however. When settlers moved so far away from the centers of culture, they sometimes abandoned appropriate rules of conduct. James Murray continually expressed these concerns during the decades he lived in the Lower Cape Fear. Shortly after his arrival, he wrote a relative and thanked him for his correspondence because he feared he would be forgotten "in this remote corner of the world." He wished he could write equally satisfying letters in return, "but alas it is not to be expected from a new country such as this where you know nobody."[111] This remoteness led not only to a lack of attention to metropolitan standards, which caused Janet Schaw to find a ball that was given in the Lower Cape Fear to be "laughable" and prompted Murray to remark that "people here both men and women are very careless about their dress having few opportunitys to appear in publick and these among themselves."[112] It sometimes also led to the separation of families, as Lower Cape Fear residents participated in social and kinship networks across the Atlantic world. As he eagerly awaited the return of his wife from Boston, James Murray wrote, "I discover . . . by this Separation that so much of my Happiness depends upon my Dear B- that I shall be very averse to such another parting while it pleases God to continue us in life."[113]

Most Cape Fear settlers must have anticipated these differences when they went to the region. As Scotus Americanus commented, in a rare moment of candor, "It is not pretended, that they, all at once, can enjoy life in the same taste and elegance as they do in Scotland." Rather, he maintained that such refinements had to be temporarily sacrificed for the sake of independence and prosperity, but that they would come to newly settled regions in time.[114] Many probably availed themselves of this independence in ways that seemed scandalous by more refined and metropolitan-oriented standards. The Reverend John LaPierre claimed that the inhabitants of his parish practiced "incest or polygamy."[115] Indeed, LaPierre's status as a religious leader declined among his parishioners when he spoke openly against such practices by "a great man." Decades later, another missionary, John MacDowell, complained that one of his parishioners was "a person who committed incest, with his own uncles widow & has a child by her which he owns publicly."[116]

Contemporaries expressed particular outrage at interracial liaisons, but the large size of the enslaved population of the Lower Cape Fear made it inevitable that there would be some such alliances. Many of the orphans brought before the New Hanover County Court were illegitimate children, and a significant portion were the products of interracial mixtures, such as "a mulatto girl named Barbara Baker, who was born of a white woman."[117] The most prominent families in the Lower Cape Fear certainly participated in such transgressions. During his trip through the region, Francisco de Miranda met the family of renowned revolutionary General Robert Howe. Howe was a notorious womanizer, and, according to Miranda, his wife had "the manner of a divorcee," while Howe "amuses himself in dissipation elsewhere." But Miranda's sensibilities received an even greater affront from "one lovely daughter, eighteen years old, [who] has just had two sons by one of the Negro slaves."[118]

Neither the cultivation of civility nor domestic indiscretions distinguished the Lower Cape Fear from the rest of colonial British America, of course. In Charles Town and Philadelphia, colonists probably worked at least as hard to imitate English families.[119] In the North and South Carolina backcountry, settlers violated social taboos at least as frequently and probably with even greater impunity. In this respect, Lower Cape Fear families differed from many other British American families in their liminal position between these two sets of expectations.[120] Residents of the Lower Cape Fear found themselves simultaneously trying to reconcile the demands of elite identity formation and the necessities of settling a remote and sparsely populated wilderness.[121] These tensions inevitably impinged on the domestic lives and the settlers' perceptions in the

Lower Cape Fear. Ultimately, conflicting ideologies about family life, along with extended kin networks, the treatment of orphans, interracial households, the formation of slave families, and inheritance practices, reinforced the distinctive character of the Lower Cape Fear and integrated most individuals into a regional conception of family life. Settlers recognized that these aspects of family life had been shaped by conditions in the Lower Cape Fear region, and Lower Cape Fear families became part of the identity of the place itself.

Chapter 4

NEIGHBORS AND NETWORKS

Peter Dubois spent the late winter and early spring of 1757 in the port town of Wilmington, North Carolina. The Huguenot traveler was evidently visiting this region of North Carolina for the first time, but he had acquaintances elsewhere in the colony. Dubois wrote several detailed letters about his visit to his friend Samuel Johnston, a prominent lawyer and political leader in the older settlements near Albemarle Sound. Dubois's letters to Johnson record various reactions to Wilmington and its inhabitants. Initially, at least, Dubois expressed pleasant surprise. He told Johnston that "my Entertainment at this Place Exceeds my Expectations" and "from what I Have yet Seen it has greatly the preference in My Esteem to New Bern." From Dubois's perspective, which had undoubtedly been influenced by his own travels and by the normative assumptions of eighteenth-century Anglo-America, "the Regularity of the Streets" in Wilmington "Equal[led] to those of Philadelphia and the Buildings in General [were] very Good." He found that "Many [of the buildings were] of Brick two & three Stores High with double Piazzas w[hi]ch Make a good appearance."

Still, while Dubois remained in Wilmington at least another few months and continued to acknowledge the ways in which the town's inhabitants upheld eighteenth-century Anglo-American standards of civility, he remained dissatisfied with his visit. As a newcomer to Wilmington, he lacked a network of social connections to make his stay more enjoyable, and as a consequence he expressed his discontent to Johnston in no uncertain terms. In February, after praising Wilmington's streets and buildings, he told Johnston somewhat playfully that "I Cannot yet find a Social Co. who will Drink Claret & Smoke Tobacco till four in the Morning. I Hope However to Make Some proselytes Soon . . . In which I don[']t doubt but [that I] Shall have the Best wishes of All Lovers of Society." Less than a month later, he expressed himself more bluntly: "I Live Very Much Retired for want of a Social Set."

Dubois recognized that Wilmington presented some social opportunities, admitting that the gentlemen of the town might provide him with the "Social Set" he desired, but he found them "Intollerable" because "Gaming Prevails in all Companies." Dubois considered gaming "the Bane of Society." Instead of making connections with "the Devotees of Cards," he decided to "Pass My hours Chiefly at Home with my Pipe and Some agreeable Author." But Dubois clearly did not relish this solitude, and he admitted to Johnston that "I have often'd Longed for ye Co." He felt isolated from Johnston and other familiar acquaintances while he was on the banks of the Cape Fear, and he "Wish'd the distance to Edenton Might be Rode in an hour or two." Because he knew that he could not readily travel from Wilmington to Edenton, he hoped that Johnston would make him feel better by writing as frequently as possible.

Dubois's letters illustrate the importance of social networks in colonial British America. Few early European Americans would have been content to do without either a "Social Set" or the other forms of satisfaction and support that colonists derived from kinship, local networks, and other common bonds. As Dubois's letters also reveal, social interaction often depended on complicated considerations. His assessment of the gentlemen of Wilmington and their proclivity toward gambling depended heavily on his own assumptions about acceptable and enjoyable companionship. Many other early European Americans might have been more tolerant of gambling, but powerful and broader cultural constructions related to concepts such as civility, status, race, ethnicity, gender, and religion played a large role in determining patterns of interaction everywhere in colonial British America. Similarly, many early Americans maintained meaningful relationships over considerable distances, just as Dubois relied on his friendship with Samuel Johnston. Correspondence undoubtedly offered the most frequent and practical opportunity for long-distance communication, though the possibility of riding "an hour or two" or even farther might have been a tempting way to overcome shorter but still significant distances.[1]

At the same time, Dubois often "Longed" for Johnston's company, and anyone reading his letters is left with a sense of his isolation. Travel to Wilmington proved to be a significant social obstacle for Dubois, and few factors played as important a role in the construction of early American social networks as distance. In this sense, Dubois's experience seems atypical. As an elite, white male, Dubois was far more likely to travel longer distances and exceed the geographic limitations of his regular social networks than were poorer whites, bound laborers, and women. But geographic circumstances influenced patterns of interaction for everyone in early America. As Darret Rutman and others have powerfully reminded us, social interaction in early America usually meant face-to-face interaction.

During the early years of settlement, Lower Cape Fear residents established various local social relationships. Over time, these relationships developed into much more elaborate networks of friendship, cooperation, and interdependence. By the end of the colonial period, the Lower Cape Fear contained a complex mosaic of associations between colonists. The region's inhabitants regularly filled roles as diverse as master, slave, patriarch, dependent, patron, client, friend, enemy, competitor, partner, neighbor, stranger, imperialist, and colonist. By doing so, they continually attempted to comprehend social relationships within their own intellectual frameworks and asserted the multivalent and subjective character of identity.

In eighteenth-century America, both identities and intellectual frameworks were necessarily deeply rooted in local experience and interaction. Early-modern technology placed clear limits on communication and transportation, preventing all but the most elite individuals from frequently interacting in more distant social networks. Following the logic of network analysis advocated by Rutman, considerable evidence illustrates the importance and configuration of local social relationships in the colonial Lower Cape Fear.[2] The local nature of these networks insured that Lower Cape Fear society would be firmly connected with place. Because social contacts were almost always confined to the Lower Cape Fear region, settlers created a distinct regional society and identity.[3]

It would be a serious mistake, however, to confuse localism with stagnation or total isolation. On some levels, Lower Cape Fear inhabitants participated in worlds far beyond the Lower Cape Fear region itself and shared cultural values with other individuals across the Atlantic world. The gradual spread of print culture, expanding networks of trade through the ports of Wilmington and Brunswick and overland to other regions, and increasing awareness and concern relating to the British Empire all had powerful influences on life and society in the Lower Cape Fear.

Moreover, regional patterns of social interaction and broader cultural influences from other parts of the Atlantic world were neither mutually exclusive nor in tension. Indeed, the two tendencies could reinforce each other. Neighborhoods and local experiences gave individuals a social language of responses and understandings that could be applied to interactions beyond the Lower Cape Fear. Interactions beyond the Lower Cape Fear enabled individuals to refine their conceptions of themselves and their neighbors by contrasting them with others and placing them into broader conceptualizations. But, given the obstacles imposed by early-modern life, these external contacts and associations could never fully transcend the continuing, concrete, and far more frequent experiences of social interaction within the Lower Cape Fear itself.

Neither a widely dispersed population, demographic disruption, nor the settlers' individualist ethos created a social vacuum in the Lower Cape Fear. Residents of the region vigorously sought out opportunities for social interaction. Often, because distance made social contacts more difficult, hosts attempted to make the most of visits and demonstrated an emphasis on hospitality that has since become a key component of modern southern stereotypes. Scotus Americanus wrote that prosperous individuals in the Lower Cape Fear were "polite, humane, and hospitable; and never tired of rendering strangers all the service in their power."[4] When William Tryon, the future North Carolina governor, first toured the Lower Cape Fear, he wrote that his journey "was accomplished with more ease and better accommodations than I could possibly have expected to have experienced, and I found the Gentlemen very ready in giving the hospitality their Plantat[ions] afforded."[5] Josiah Quincy Jr., a prominent visitor from

Massachusetts, asserted that the home of eminent Lower Cape Fear merchant William Dry was "justly called the house of universal hospitality." Quincy added that "his servants excell in cookery—and his sensible lady exceeds (at least I think equals) Sister Q[uincy] in the pastry and nick-nack way."[6] An anonymous visitor to the Lower Cape Fear in 1735 went from plantation to plantation and repeatedly found the residents gracious and helpful. This visitor was especially impressed by the kindness of "Mr. Roger More."[7]

These reports of enthusiastic hospitality underscore two characteristics of social life in the Lower Cape Fear. The first is that people clearly valued social occasions and enjoyed the company of others. The second is that opportunities for social interaction had significant limits and could not be taken for granted. Society in Wilmington and Brunswick, for example, did not offer the same refined gatherings as Charles Town and some other larger cities. Governor Dobbs lamented the consequences of this underdeveloped high society when he complained to the Board of Trade about the lack of adequate naval protection in the area: Royal Navy sailors should have been stationed in the Lower Cape Fear, and they did "look into Cape Fear and stay some days"; unfortunately, they were little help, because "finding no balls or entertainments there, they sail away & spend the winter in Charles Town, under pretence that they can't clean at Cape Fear altho' they may have all conveniences for it."[8]

It also might not have been easy for many settlers to find kindred spirits. James Murray never seemed to have derived much satisfaction from his social connections near his Point Repose plantation. Yet Murray was aware that he had foregone other chances to bond with local residents, and he wrote shortly before leaving North Carolina that the people of the Lower Cape Fear were "neither better or worse in gross than those of other Countries: that I have not been a great favourite with them is more my own fault than theirs."[9]

Geographic distance placed the most important constraints on the social lives of most Anglo-American Lower Cape Fear inhabitants. These constraints had at least two very important consequences for the development of social networks in the Lower Cape Fear. First, they imposed limits on the extension of networks. Beyond a certain distance it was simply not feasible for most people to maintain frequent contact. By necessity, networks seldom extended beyond the Lower Cape Fear region into South Carolina or other North Carolina counties. The regional nature of these networks, therefore, served as a powerful force encouraging settlers to identify primarily with the Lower Cape Fear. Second, they gave social interaction a decidedly local character. The importance of ties between neighbors illustrates the local nature of Lower Cape Fear networks.

In the decades after settlement, Lower Cape Fear residents repeatedly demonstrated their recognition of and involvement in local neighborhoods. By providing personal and institutional units of identification and by allowing settlers to rely on those who lived nearby for assistance and companionship, these neighborhoods served several important functions at once. As Scotus Americanus wrote, Lower Cape Fear residents were "fond of company, living very sociable and neighbourly, visiting one another often."[10] In the 1740s, George Minot attempted to increase the saleability of his Lower Cape Fear plantation by pointing out that it was in Rocky Point, which was "allowed to be the best Neighbourhood in the whole place." He also tried to promote his piece of land by describing the respectable neighbors, "all [of] which are Persons of Fashion & Education & [who] Live in a General manner & most of [th]Em has had University Education." These pleasant neighbors even kept "3 Packs of Dogs among [th]Em for Deer hunting And very often have matches of Horse Raceing in the Neighberhood, which they much delight in & are all Liveing within 3 miles of my House there."[11] Minot recognized that the human environment around his land might be as important to a prospective buyer as the quality of the land itself. Neighborhoods also provided a logical framework for more local institutional functions such as road repairs and slave patrols that required too much direct attention to be handled by the county court or the parish vestry. Consequently, the courts appointed committees to attend to business in geographic areas roughly conterminous with neighborhoods.[12] By 1776, some neighborhoods were beginning to define themselves in opposition to other neighborhoods. The Wilmington Safety Committee received a request for gunpowder from the inhabitants of the neighborhoods of Lockwoods Folly and Shallotte because of "their apprehensions of danger from the people of Waggaman." Their sense of danger was no doubt deeply rooted in their awareness that many of the "people of Waggaman" may have identified with tory ideologies, but they still chose to express their differences and concerns in terms of small, nearby localities.[13]

It is difficult, of course, for historians to recapture the range of social interactions available to settlers in neighborhoods of the Lower Cape Fear or anywhere else in colonial America. Innumerable conversations must have occurred every day, influenced the thoughts of the participants, and not been recorded in any retrievable way. However, many interactions can be found in the surviving records of the Lower Cape Fear and, while it is difficult to assess the meanings of these interactions for contemporaries, it is possible to discern some very important and suggestive patterns. These interactions can best be culled from wills, powers of attorney, kinship connections, conveyances, legal actions, and various other pieces of information.

To render analysis more manageable and comprehensible, this study focuses especially on patterns of interactions for individuals living in the three Lower Cape Fear neighborhoods identified and described in chapter 2: Rocky Point, Lockwoods Folly, and Town Creek. Evidence from all three of these neighborhoods powerfully demonstrates that distance played a determinative role in the development of Lower Cape Fear social networks. Settlers linked to any of the

TABLE 4.1 **Lockwoods Folly Ties**

	No. of Personal Ties	*% of Personal Ties*	*No. of Economic Ties*	*% of Economic Ties*
with Lockwoods Folly	27	75	77	67
with Town Creek	8	22	23	20
with Rocky Point	1	3	15	13
Total	36	100	115	100

Note: Two other important qualifications apply to the data used in this and the following tables regarding interactions between neighborhoods. First, the numbers included refer only to the minority of recorded transactions in which both participants could be traced to one of the three neighborhoods. Obviously, most parties participated in many other recorded transactions, but it was not feasible to trace the distances of transactions throughout the region. Still, transactions across the three neighborhoods should provide a reasonably representative indication of the influence of distance on social networks. Second, some individuals had multiple potential places of residences in the three neighborhoods; as a result, their neighborhood location could not be treated as static. Instead, they were assessed on a case-by-case basis. A person owning plantations in Town Creek and Lockwoods Folly was treated as resident of Lockwoods Folly when interacting with others owning land in Lockwoods Folly and as resident of Town Creek when interacting with those owning land in Town Creek. A person interacting with residents of Rocky Point would have been treated as a resident of Town Creek because Town Creek was closer and the more likely place to have been traveled from. This technique is obviously imprecise and probably inflates continuity between neighborhoods. On the other hand, it is fairly consistent with the logic of network analysis, and many of these difficulties only prove relevant to a small minority of individuals in the study. This technique also partly explains why the numbers of interactions between neighborhoods do not always yield reciprocal totals.

three neighborhoods were far more likely to interact with those in their own neighborhoods than in neighborhoods elsewhere.

Lockwoods Folly (see table 4.1) was the most isolated of the three locales. Lockwoods Folly not only lacked direct access to the Cape Fear River, it was surrounded by less-populous land and had fewer roads nearby. These factors might explain why three-quarters of all Lockwoods Folly personal interactions within the three neighborhoods were with others linked to Lockwoods Folly.[14] Almost all the rest were with those linked to the closer Town Creek, rather than with the more distant Rocky Point. Landed conveyances and other economic interactions reflect a similar pattern, though in this case Lockwoods Folly residents were more likely to transcend the distance to Rocky Point—a result, no doubt, of Rocky Point's more impressive property resources.[15] Because of their somewhat lower socioeconomic status, Lockwoods Folly residents left a more limited trail of references and, consequently, fewer interactions.

TABLE 4.2 **Town Creek Ties**

	No. of Personal Ties	*% of Personal Ties*	*No. of Economic Ties*	*% of Economic Ties*
with Lockwoods Folly	14	15	34	20
with Town Creek	49	54	99	58
with Rocky Point	28	31	37	22
Total	91	100	170	100

Town Creek (see table 4.2) was the most centrally located of the three neighborhoods. Residents not only tended to reside on the waters of Town Creek itself, they could easily enter the Lower Cape Fear. Town Creek's position rested not only between Rocky Point and Lockwoods Folly, but also between the region's two towns, Wilmington and Brunswick. Consequently, its patterns of interaction proved to be less insular. Nonetheless, most Town Creek ties within the three neighborhoods occurred with other Town Creek neighbors. Interactions with the other two neighborhoods were fairly equally distributed, though there were more personal ties with Rocky Point. This could be due to Rocky Point's slightly closer and more accessible location or to the greater likelihood of wealthier Rocky Point residents appearing in the records.

Rocky Point residents (see table 4.3) experienced more recorded interactions than those in the other two neighborhoods, but their interactions reaffirm the findings for the other three neighborhoods. A clear majority of ties occurred within Rocky Point. A significant minority of Rocky Point ties were with those from relatively nearby and downriver Town Creek, and a small number took place with those from Lockwoods Folly. In other words, those in Rocky Point, as well as those in Lockwoods Folly and in Town Creek, participated more frequently in the three neighborhoods' networks. Indeed, distances (see table 4.4) proved to be a determinative factor in the development of social networks. Statistical analysis based on the data in table 4.5 confirms that, when both participants can be traced to one of the three places, a strong negative correlation existed between distance and interaction.[16]

These patterns of interaction in Lockwoods Folly, Town Creek, and Rocky Point fit well with what scholars already know about social relationships in other regions of early colonial America. That most social networks were spatially restricted, as table 4.4 indicates, is no surprise. A number of scholars have demonstrated persuasively, for example, that most people in the seventeenth-century Chesapeake Bay region seldom interacted with individuals who resided more than five miles away.[17] As one leading authority has discovered for St. Clement's manor in Charles County, Maryland, "All the repeated and ordinary contacts of

Table 4.3 **Rocky Point Ties**

	No. of Personal Ties	*% of Personal Ties*	*No. of Economic Ties*	*% of Economic Ties*
with Lockwoods Folly	4	3	40	19
with Town Creek	43	36	53	26
with Rocky Point	72	61	115	55
Total	119	100	208	100

Table 4.4 **Distances and Ties between Lower Cape Fear Neighborhoods**

Neighborhood	*Estimated Distance in Miles*	*Ties*
Lockwoods Folly to Rocky Point	42	23
Lockwoods Folly to Town Creek	31	31
Town Creek to Rocky Point	23	69
Town Creek to Lockwoods Folly	31	50
Rocky Point to Lockwoods Folly	42	89
Rocky Point to Town Creek	23	99
Within Lockwoods Folly	5	104
Within Rocky Point	5	185
Within Town Creek	5	172

Note: Information in this table derives from the sources described for tables 4.1, 4.2, and 4.3. These distance estimates have been made by the author using a variety of atlases and maps of the region.

Table 4.5 **Ties between Neighborhoods and Towns**

Neighborhood or Town	*Estimated Distances in Miles*	*Personal Ties*	*Economic Ties*	*Legal Ties*
Lockwoods Folly to Wilmington	25	30	78	33
Town Creek to Wilmington	5	62	111	38
Rocky Point to Wilmington	15	105	257	112
Lockwoods Folly to Brunswick	15	24	72	8
Town Creek to Brunswick	10	43	87	8
Rocky Point to Brunswick	40	37	112	5

male residents involved other households lying within an approximate five-mile radius of the home, a journey of an hour or two."[18] The limits of these local networks did not differ dramatically from those in some areas of early-modern England.[19] The geographic area encompassed by contemporary definitions of Lockwoods Folly, Town Creek, and Rocky Point probably did not exceed ten miles, and settlement patterns may have made them functionally even smaller so that these three areas may well have resembled the spatially limited neighborhoods of the seventeenth-century Chesapeake. At the same time, while neighborhood interactions appear to have been predominant in both places, contacts beyond neighborhoods were clearly less exceptional in the Lower Cape Fear.

Equally important, seventeenth-century Chesapeake models present an inappropriate and far too simplistic basis for explaining interaction between settlers in the colonial Lower Cape Fear. Social networks in the Lower Cape Fear developed in relation to a very different set of circumstances. First, social networks could be altered significantly by the distribution of the population. Colonists who lived in more sparsely settled areas, like many parts of the Lower Cape Fear, no doubt felt compelled to maintain some social relationships over greater distance. While population densities were not constant throughout the Chesapeake region, late-seventeenth-century St. Mary's County, for example, averaged about three times as many people per square mile as the Lower Cape Fear in 1755, and about two times as many people as the Lower Cape Fear in 1763. Both the Chesapeake and the Lower Cape Fear were also far-less-densely populated than comparable areas of early-modern England.[20]

Second, geographic and transportation conditions inevitably differ across space and time. Travel was probably significantly easier in the Lower Cape Fear because, by the eighteenth century, there were somewhat greater needs and better resources for travel in the colonies. But it could still be extraordinarily difficult by modern standards. Third, social networks tend to be configured around locations, or "nodal points," that perform meaningful functions and depend on a society's needs. In both the Chesapeake and Lower Cape Fear, county courts and parish churches provided important meeting places. But in the Lower Cape Fear neither of these sites played as crucial a role in social networks as in the two port towns. Ordinaries and leisure activities also facilitated social interaction in the region. Fourth, geographic similarities do not incorporate cultural values, such as hierarchy and race, that can dramatically influence and circumscribe social networks. To give only the most obvious example, Lower Cape Fear slaves had to construct networks in a much different way than Anglo-American settlers, regardless of similar geographic circumstances.[21] Fifth, and finally, a number of factors insured that colonists in the Lower Cape Fear, and in British America in general, would be far less isolated than colonists in the Chesapeake a century before. Lower Cape Fear residents were increasingly involved in the larger Atlantic world.

To give one example of the ways that social network formation depended on local circumstances: if Lower Cape Fear settlement patterns led to even sparser populations than elsewhere in colonial America, residents had to rely more often on transportation resources to maintain their connections. The various means of travel available in colonial North Carolina left much to be desired, but, in the Lower Cape Fear, at least, many settlers worked hard to improve matters. A variety of formal and informal mechanisms improved both overland and water transportation.

Contemporary travelers complained bitterly about the difficulty of traveling on roads through the Lower Cape Fear and its environs.[22] Hugh Finlay, surveyor of the post roads in colonial America, wrote in his journal that, "on the whole, the road from Charles Town to Wilmington is certainly the most tedious and disagreeable of any on the Continent of North America." He lamented the difficulty of passing "through a poor, sandy, barren, gloomy country without accommodations" and concluded that there were few people on the road because "neither man nor beast can stand a long journey thro' so bad a country."[23] Similarly, Robert Hunter, who wrote of his travels through much of America shortly after the Revolution, characterized his trip from South Carolina to Wilmington as "the most tiresome and disagreeable journey I ever in my life experienced (not even excepting the Green Mountains in Massachusetts)."[24]

Clearly, road conditions south of Wilmington must have been wretched, and there is little reason to think that they would have been significantly better anywhere else in the Lower Cape Fear, but it would be misleading to attribute this to indifference. A combination of swamps, sandy soils, and water barriers conspired against settlers' efforts to improve roads in the Lower Cape Fear. Also, as Elizabeth Catherine DeRosset complained in a 1775 letter, frequent storms in the region could make roads impassable from flooding and debris.[25] Moreover, road conditions were apt to be much poorer in a newly settled and sparsely populated region, no matter what the terrain was like.[26]

While North Carolina's assembly passed some pieces of legislation regarding transportation matters, the upkeep of roads generally fell to more local administrative units.[27] In the earliest years of settlement before New Hanover became a county, provincial authorities felt compelled to act on these matters. In 1727, the General Court of North Carolina ordered early settler Cornelius Harnett to keep a ferry near Brunswick because "it is highly necessary that a Ferry should be settled over the Cape Fear River," and it forbade anyone within a ten-mile area from competing with his ferry business.[28] In 1734, shortly after the creation of New Hanover County, legislation set up a new system for administrating roads in the southern parts of North Carolina. In each area, the county court appointed road commissioners, who had been given considerable independent authority in matters relating to transportation. In sparsely populated areas, this new system was probably much more efficient than regulation by the county courts, and New Hanover continued to use the system until 1773, after every other North Carolina county had placed these matters under the control of the county court.[29] Countless other pieces of legislation and county court action also contributed to the road system, often in response to local petitions complaining about poor road conditions. Obviously, not all of these laws and orders could be enforced. Road commissions depended on the labor of the taxables in their districts and, at times, neither commissioners nor laborers were willing to cooperate with the system. Further, as Marvin Michael Kay and William S. Price Jr. have shown in great detail, road labor requirements in North Carolina were an unusual and often very onerous form of taxation.[30]

Nonetheless, by the end of the colonial period, overland transportation had become considerably easier in North Carolina. In 1775, Janet Schaw described the "great road" that ran through the Lower Cape Fear. As Schaw wrote, this road began at Wilmington and went "clear across the country to Virginia on one side and South Carolina on the other."[31] This major road had been established by 1733, shortly after the settlement of the Cape Fear made it practical to traverse the whole colony of North Carolina, and it was part of a developing road network that, while still limited, had expanded considerably since the region was opened up for settlement. Even more impressive to Schaw, and perhaps even more indicative of the progress Cape Fear residents had shown in overcoming transportation barriers, the road crossed the Cape Fear River with a bridge, "which tho' built of timber is truly a noble one, broader than that over the Tay at Perth. It opens at the middle to both sides and rises by pullies, so as to suffer Ships to pass under it." This drawbridge, constructed over the Northeast Cape Fear River by Benjamin Heron, appears to have been unprecedented in colonial British America. Heron built the bridge with the authorization of the assembly to replace a ferry at the same spot, intending it to enable the passage of watercraft on the river.[32] Colonists also implemented other facilities that made travel through the Lower Cape Fear more bearable. Local leaders encouraged ordinaries that provided accommodations for travelers.[33] Even more important, by the end of the colonial period, the region had a system of ferries that should have been adequate to surmount any significant water barriers.[34]

On the other hand, Heron's bridge symbolized more than just an improving overland travel system. The Lower Cape Fear residents' extensive utilization of inland waterways made the bridge necessary and noteworthy. The relative ease of water passage and the difficulty of poor roads combined to make boats, rafts, perriaugers, and other watercraft as important in the Lower Cape Fear as in any part of colonial British America.[35] Of course, waterways, like land routes, could sometimes become impassable or inconvenient, but contemporaries clearly found them reliable enough to use with great frequency.[36] Murray insisted that watercraft were absolutely necessary for trade in the Lower Cape Fear.[37] Schaw described a sort of water-borne funeral procession. As a funeral service was about to start, the arrival of some guests, "above a hundred of whom (of both sexes) arrived in canoes," interrupted the clergyman. After the ceremony, "they got into their canoes, and I saw them row thro' the creeks." She supposed that "they have little spots of ground up the woods, which afford them corn and pork, and that on such occasions they flock down like crows to a carrion."[38] If Schaw expressed disdain for these canoe passengers, use of water transportation was not limited to only one class. She also noted that her friend, prominent Cape Fear merchant John Rutherford, possessed "a very fine boat with an awning to prevent the heat, and six stout Negroes in neat uniforms to row her down."[39] Thus, inland waterways probably did as much as roads to structure transportation routes and spatial relationships in the Lower Cape.

Improving means of transportation contributed to the extension of local networks, but geographic barriers also continued to reinforce the regional boundaries of the Lower Cape Fear. Poor road conditions clearly continued to discourage travel overland to Albemarle, the Neuse-Pamlico area, or South Carolina. The Cape Fear River and its tributaries proved to be the main route out into the countryside. But most of the creeks and inlets along the Cape Fear provided little access to the areas beyond New Hanover and Brunswick Counties. The Cape Fear fostered connections with settlers in the Upper Cape Fear region, but it also underscored the differences between the regions. The flow of the Cape Fear at once made the Lower Cape Fear an entrepot and social center and the Upper Cape Fear a hinterland and western frontier. Finally, the difficulty of inland transportation and social connections placed greater emphasis on the maritime aspect of the Lower Cape Fear, encouraging some settlers to cast their social nets outward across the Atlantic.

Even with their limitations and shortcomings, transportation routes enabled Lower Cape Fear settlers to transcend neighborhood social networks and to interact with more distant Lower Cape Fear residents. But interactions outside of neighborhoods were far from anomalous instances of extended travel. Even in highly dispersed populations like those in newly settled areas of colonial America, people quickly established common meeting places to serve various institutional, cultural, and social functions. More important, while the colonies south of Virginia were famous for their lack of urbanization, the Lower Cape Fear had two important towns: Wilmington and Brunswick. Any systematic look at social interaction in the Lower Cape Fear must consider the activities in these towns as a necessary complement to more localized neighborhood interactions.[40] Indeed, if these towns appear small when compared with colonial Charles Town or Philadelphia, it would be difficult to exaggerate their importance for social interaction in the Lower Cape Fear.

Rutman's work on Middlesex County, Virginia, indicates that county courthouses and parish churches were two of the most important kinds of meeting places for colonial Chesapeake society. Settlers frequently demonstrated a willingness to travel to the church or courthouse to fulfill their religious, legal, or social needs.[41] Lower Cape Fear residents surely would have made the same effort to visit both of these locales. Religion played an important part in the identities and lifestyles of many early Americans, and both churches and services played a central part in their experience. Even more important, county courts performed an array of useful functions that maintained order and assisted in the development of local social relations. Of course, these functions included criminal and civil actions, which helped to resolve disputes, stabilize property relations, and maintain public order. But North Carolina county courts, like those in the Chesapeake, also took responsibility for probating estates and keeping records; formalizing sales and deeds; supervising the treatment of orphans, apprentices, servants, and slaves; and administering public buildings, roads, county finance, and commerce.[42] All of these important matters could encourage Lower Cape Fear residents to participate in county court activities beyond their own neighborhoods.

Quantitative records of interaction in Lockwoods Folly, Rocky Point, and Town Creek also demonstrate that settlers' participation in county legal actions transcended the distance between neighborhoods. By tallying participation in legal actions brought in the New Hanover County Court from court minutes and dockets, it becomes evident that there was no significant correlation relating distance between neighborhoods to litigation.[43] There does appear to have been a comparatively large amount of litigation involving residents in Rocky Point, but this is most likely a consequence of the neighborhood's considerable and interrelated property interests, rather than the result of proximity. Indeed, county court actions were so frequently related to debt and other property matters in eighteenth-century British America that these numbers suggest that business networks also transcended local neighborhoods. After all, to bring suit against someone outside the neighborhood, a litigant had both to attend the county court and to have interacted outside neighborhood networks in some context that caused a grievance against the defendant. While large land conveyances did have a localized character, smaller exchanges inevitably occurred over larger distances.

At the same time, to apply Rutman's structure rigidly to the Lower Cape Fear and posit that churches, county courts, and markets provided common points of interaction for settlers is to overlook the obvious. In the Lower Cape Fear region, unlike in Virginia or many other places in the southern British colonies, these interactions did not occur separately or distinctly. They overlapped and reinforced each other in towns. Virtually all of the obvious functions requiring interaction and travel in the Lower Cape Fear were performed in either Wilmington or Brunswick. The New Hanover and Brunswick county courthouses were located in the towns. The Anglican parishes were roughly conterminous with the two counties, and churches were also built in the two towns. Lower Cape Fear economic exchanges normally took place in the stores of Wilmington and Brunswick, where town merchants could import and export goods across the Atlantic and up and down the Cape Fear River. Official warehouse sites were also set up in the towns, where laws required the inspection of all major export commodities.[44]

Moreover, both Brunswick and Wilmington also served as locations for specifically social gatherings. Wilmington had the first known coffee house in North Carolina and was one of two towns with still houses for the distillation of alcoholic beverages.[45] When Francisco de Miranda visited the town shortly after the Revolution, he encountered a billiard house and commented on its popularity in the Lower Cape Fear.[46] Janet Schaw attended a ball in Wilmington during her visit, and in 1775 the Wilmington Safety Committee admonished some Wilmington residents who planned a "Public Ball."[47] There were about a half-dozen ordinaries in Wilmington, some of which acquired a reputation for their quality and accommodations. The county court and legislation regulated ordinaries, or taverns. Some ordinary keepers lost their license for keeping a disorderly house.[48] These locales no doubt accommodated a variety of consumer desires and, in some cases, they probably transgressed against laws and community standards of morality. For example, two Wilmington women, Mrs. Lettice Blackmore and Mrs. Elizabeth Saunders, lost their ordinary license because they were harboring sailors.[49]

At the same time, ordinaries and other social gatherings were not always confined to towns. Ordinaries frequently served to accommodate travelers at ferries or remote locales along Lower Cape Fear roads. For individuals crossing long distances, these could be welcome places of rest and lodging. Evidence indicates, however, that ordinaries outside of towns usually offered less satisfactory conditions. At least one visitor to an ordinary at Lockwoods Folly in 1745 was quite unimpressed.[50] Some Lower Cape Fear residents found entertainment outside of town. Hunting proved to be a favorite pastime among the upper classes.[51] Lower Cape Fear residents were so fond of horse racing that they continued the sport in violation of the orders of the Wilmington Safety Committee.[52] But even if these activities could not be carried on in towns, it also seems unlikely that they were confined to neighborhoods.

Thus, neighborhood networks played an important role in the Lower Cape Fear, but social networks also extended well beyond these neighborhoods and were ultimately shaped by interactions in the Lower Cape Fear's towns. As table 4.5 illustrates, in every category, residents were more likely to have connections with those who either owned land or lived in Wilmington than even with other members of their own neighborhoods. Brunswick, although it never achieved the size of Wilmington, also played an important role in social connections. Furthermore, the number of ties to the two towns showed no significant relationship to distance. It is a commonplace among historians to discuss the importance of towns in economic and political development, but this data strongly suggests that they played a very important role in the formation of social networks as well. Wilmington and Brunswick were, as many scholars have reminded us, not especially large urban centers. Yet, even in this relatively rural and sparsely populated region, the presence of towns did much to shape the way settlers experienced interactions with one another.

Thus, town and neighborhood networks combined to structure the bulk of social interactions in the Lower Cape Fear. But the development of both types of spatial identification enhanced awareness of extraregional differences. Whether settlers found themselves more connected to Lockwoods Folly, Wilmington, or another locale, their social world remained defined by networks within the Lower Cape Fear region.

Colonists in the Lower Cape Fear, like Anglo-American settlers elsewhere, evaluated themselves and others according to preconceived standards and expectations. So, if Lower Cape Fear society shaped the views and social worlds of the region's residents, they also simultaneously shaped the larger society. Social understandings of identity and otherness had to be continually constructed from local experiences, but they could also draw on a fully developed set of Anglo-American cultural norms. In this sense, social interaction in the Lower Cape Fear transcended technological factors, distances, and other questions of spatial organizations. In other words, residents often chose with whom to interact in ways that had little to do with location. It is often difficult, however, to discern precisely what characteristics influenced the development of social networks. Colonists drew upon a wide and infinitely complex range of variables in choosing friends and acquaintances. Moreover, little direct testimony from contemporaries in the Lower Cape Fear elucidates this process.

At the same time, some obviously important factors suggest themselves. Categories such as religion, ethnicity, social status, gender, and race clearly played important roles in the lives of early Lower Cape Fear residents. Again, all of these categorical constructs defy simple explication, but the remainder of this chapter will use existing evidence to consider some of the ways that the specific environs of the Lower Cape Fear influenced them. First, this chapter will discuss the social role of the Anglican Church in the Lower Cape Fear. Second, it will devote attention to social networks among the region's most conspicuous ethnic minority, the Scots. Third, it will present and interpret evidence relating to social status. Fourth, it will give specific consideration to one group with clearly circumscribed possibilities for social interaction, enslaved people of African descent.

Scholars have long acknowledged that religious identities played an important role in early modern societies, yet, at the same time, religious institutions in the southern British colonies were notoriously weak and ineffectual. Churches and clergymen in the Lower Cape Fear certainly did not demonstrate a very impressive degree of authority. Indeed, with the notable exception of the officially established Anglican Church, little evidence remains regarding religious practices in the region during the colonial period.

Yet Anglican Church records, mostly consisting of letters from missionaries to religious authorities, do reveal much about religion in the region. To begin with, they illustrate the enormous difficulties of performing even the most basic and important Anglican religious rituals. It even proved difficult to have a clergyman nearby. Missionaries had to be sent from England; they were often underpaid and not satisfied enough with their new homes to continue; and they frequently fell prey to the region's deadly disease environment. No one in North Carolina did more to support the Anglican Church than Governor Arthur Dobbs, yet when Dobbs died in the Lower Cape Fear, he had to be buried by a justice of the peace because there was no clergyman within more than a hundred miles of his home.[53] Even when missionaries were available, the size of parishes made it virtually impossible for them to satisfy the religious needs of their parishioners. Clergy often complained that they lacked a fixed location where they could perform services; and at least one was forced to preach regularly in six different places.[54] The Reverend James Moir decided that the Lower Cape Fear had a greater need for missionaries than did any other place in America.[55]

The people of the Lower Cape Fear clearly showed limited support for the Anglican Church, and the region's clergy often blamed this condition for their difficulties. After one session of North Carolina's assembly failed to pass desired legislation, Moir complained that "nothing was to be done for the proper encouragement of an established ministry."[56] Financial matters proved to be a particularly sore spot for the clergy. The first clergyman in the region seldom received a salary, had to sell his house and land, worked in the fields to support himself, and lived "no better than a mendicant."[57] Moreover, depending on one's perspective, the residents of the Lower Cape Fear could be immoral, disputatious, unfamiliar with religious doctrines, intolerant, and indifferent to religion.[58] James Murray found the region's lapses in piety to be so notable that he wrote evangelical preacher George Whitefield pleading that there was no place in America "where your preaching is so Much wanted as in this."[59]

These complaints did not fully reflect the range of religious attitudes in the Lower Cape Fear. There is evidence of considerable concern for the Anglican Church. Shortly after his arrival in Brunswick, Murray also wrote a friend that "people in the Country are not void of Religion." He pointed out that, to secure financial support for their clergyman, the residents "wrote a letter to the B(isho)p of London to get the Societys mission for him."[60] On several occasions, the Reverend John MacDowell described preaching to enormous groups of people in the southern reaches of his parish.[61] While some missionaries wrestled with problems that might be attributed to the church's limited resources in North Carolina, the Reverend Richard Marsden found fewer problems by employing his own resources. Marsden, who had obtained a prosperous living through other means, preached at his own house, asked for no fees or salaries, and even gave his congregation food. Perhaps not surprisingly, Marsden gained a relatively impressive following.[62] Further, repeated and important legislation from the colony and generous bequests from Lower Cape Fear residents show that the Anglican Church did play a significant role in many lives in the region.[63]

Anglican missionaries also complained repeatedly about dissenters in the Lower Cape Fear. Indeed, the presence of large numbers of dissenters has often been cited as evidence of the limited advantages of the established church in North and South Carolina. Significant numbers of nonconforming Protestants certainly resided in the colonial Lower Cape Fear. As early as 1742, James Moir estimated "one half of the whites" were "Dissenters of various denominations." Some dissenters probably played prominent roles in the region. Moir also claimed, in the same letter, that the majority of the parish vestry in Wilmington were "professed Dissenters." Thus, because vestries were popularly elected by the parish population, dissenters could serve on them and control aspects of the Anglican Church.[64] In 1759, some Lower Cape Fear Anglicans complained that "Enthusiastic anabaptists" were "numerous" and "daily increasing in this parish."[65] Several years later, another contemporary wrote that "New Light baptists are very numerous in the southern parts of this parish."[66]

Contemporaries explained the presence of religious dissent in a variety of ways. Most frequently they argued, as did John Brickell in his *Natural History of North Carolina,* that the absence of Anglican clergy provided opportunities for dissenting clergymen.[67] A more obvious explanation suggests itself, however. Lower Cape Fear settlers came from a variety of religious and ethnic backgrounds, and there was no reason for non-Anglicans to change denominations simply because of their location. Some evidence on dissenting congregations confirms a relationship between settlers who came from less orthodox Anglican locations and religious dissent. The best-documented group of dissenters in the early Lower Cape Fear were Presbyterians, who were visited by the Reverend Hugh McAden, a dissenting clergyman, in 1742 and 1743. McAden found the greatest interest for his ministry in the area known as the Welsh Tract. While details are scant, it is likely that McAden appealed to dissenters of Welsh descent in the area, many of whom had probably migrated from religiously tolerant Pennsylvania.[68] Along similar lines, in 1762 the Reverend John MacDowell asserted that the only dissenters in his parish were poor fishermen who had come from Cape May in New Jersey.[69] Scottish and Ulster Scottish immigrants must have swelled the numbers of dissenters in the Lower Cape Fear, and even neighboring regions that supplied newcomers also had significant dissenting contingents.[70]

Thus, given the lack of available missionaries and resources and the diverse backgrounds of the region's inhabitants, it would be unreasonable to assess the

The walls of St. Philip's Church still stand in their original location at Brunswick as a reminder that Lower Cape Fear settlers built one of eighteenth-century North Carolina's most impressive churches. Courtesy of the North Carolina Office of Archives and History, Raleigh, North Carolina.

importance of Anglicanism in the Lower Cape Fear in terms of the institutional presence and popularity of the established church. It is, after all, impossible to discover the colonists' religious beliefs. Surviving records attest only to the social role of the Anglican Church, and, even with the missionaries' dissatisfaction and the presence of significant numbers of dissenters, it appears to have been quite an important role. Indeed, the Anglican Church ultimately functioned as a social institution in ways that clearly transcended its spiritual significance.

Lower Cape Fear residents struggled for several decades to build established churches in Brunswick and Wilmington, and their success, late in the colonial period, demonstrated the growing social dominance of the Anglican Church. These church-building efforts began as the machinations of one religious faction and evolved into a common aspiration of the Lower Cape Fear's elite. Before 1750, Anglicans bemoaned the lack of a church, and dissenters rejected the established church so thoroughly that Anglicans could not use the New Hanover county courthouse as a place of worship.[71] By the 1750s, Anglicans began work on churches, and the assembly passed legislation to encourage and fund the buildings. Support for the churches does not appear to have been widespread, however; progress was slow, and residents resisted paying for the churches.[72] Two other tactics, however, proved much more useful in raising funds for the church. First, legislation made provisions to use profits from a public lottery for the churches. Second, and perhaps more important, officials sold pews in the new churches. In Wilmington, at least, the sale of the pews gave many Wilmingtonians a personal stake in the building of the church.[73] St. James's Church in Wilmington proved to be more of an indicator of social status than of zeal for Anglicanism. A plan of the first pew occupants in the St. James church included the most prominent individuals in the Lower Cape Fear and quite a few unlikely Anglicans. Revolutionary leader Cornelius Harnett, for example, owned a pew, even though his tombstone epitaph in the nearby cemetery later testified to his deistic convictions: "Slave to no sect he took no private road / But looked through nature up to nature's God."[74] Some pew owners, including John Rutherford, James Murray, and Robert Hogg, were from predominantly Presbyterian Scotland, and others, including James Moran, Archibald MacLaine, and Mathew Rowan, were from Ireland. At least two came from Pennsylvania Quaker families, and several others had French Huguenot connections.[75] The foremost pews belonged to the governor and the council, with the Moores, Howes, Quinces, Drys, Ashes, and Swanns not far behind.

There are two feasible explanations for this heterogeneous collection of St. James's pew owners. First, it is possible that the Anglican Church had drawn converts from the upper ranks of various cultural groups in the Lower Cape Fear. But there is no obvious reason for such a movement toward the Anglican Church during the colonial period, and the letters of the Society for the Propagation of the Gospel missionaries hardly suggest an upsurge of piety in the region. On the other hand, it is possible that the Anglican Church was providing these "converts" with more secular services. For one thing, an established Anglican Church could reinforce hierarchy. This must have given it a certain amount of appeal for the region's elite. Little is known about the membership of St. Philip's Church, in Brunswick, but contemporaries considered the church building the most impressive in colonial North Carolina. Such an edifice could well be considered a tribute to the stature of the Lower Cape Fear elite, Anglican or not.[76] Moreover, many dissenters had ties to the Anglican Church that went beyond owning pews. While missionaries lamented the presence of dissenters on vestries because of its religious implications, the same presence showed non-Anglican concern for the established parish government. Indeed, the nonecclesiastical responsibilities of the parish made such participation distinctly in the interests of dissenters.[77] One Anglican missionary juxtaposed the established Anglican order with the behavior of increasingly numerous and socially marginal dissenters. The Reverend John Barnett wrote, of the region's "New Light Baptists," that the "most illiterate among them" were "their Teachers," with "even Negroes speak[ing] in their Meetings." Such religious practices no doubt made the Anglican Church seem necessary to the Lower Cape Fear elite.[78]

Whether Lower Cape Fear residents gravitated toward the trappings of Anglicanism for secular or pious reasons, the church clearly played an important role in the region. In the earliest years of settlement, social networks probably grew along religious lines since few groups were comfortable enough to cross cultural and denominational boundaries. But within a relatively short period of time, colonists at the top of Lower Cape Fear society were willing to overlook very different religious backgrounds and sit near one another in Anglican pews. Religion provided one category that assisted Lower Cape Fear colonists in defining and articulating their social relationships, but it was a category that, with time, could be subsumed to other regional considerations.

Eighteenth-century British America also attracted diverse ethnic groups. Increasingly ethnic colonial populations forced many colonists to reconsider their identities. Many saw their origins in a new light as they moved from more homogeneous surroundings and encountered cultural others for the first time. At the same time, while immigration encouraged the articulation of ethnic identities, ethnic identities were in flux even in Britain, as English, Scottish, and Irish subjects experienced changes in their relationships to one another.[79]

Consequently, like other regions settled in the early eighteenth century and like neighboring Albemarle and South Carolina, the Lower Cape Fear developed into an ethnically diverse society. Most European American newcomers to the region were of English descent, but of the ethnic minority groups, Scottish colonists became far more important than any other in the Lower Cape Fear. Not only does evidence indicate that the Scottish were more numerous than other ethnic minorities, several Scottish merchants in Wilmington played important roles in the area's trade, and there were many ties between settlers in the Lower Cape Fear and the much larger Scottish community up the Cape Fear River. In the Lower Cape Fear, therefore, the Scottish had more opportunities than any other group of non-English settlers to develop networks with those from a similar cultural background.

Two of the most detailed accounts of life in the colonial Lower Cape Fear come from Scottish writers. Murray's letters reveal much about the role of Scottishness in his social interactions. As mentioned in chapter 1, Murray's decision to migrate to the Lower Cape Fear had been influenced by political and economic ties to the region. Governor Gabriel Johnston's regime probably brought quite a few Scottish immigrants to the Cape Fear and gave them a unifying set of political interests. Murray's letters contain no prolonged reflections on Scottish culture and identity, but Murray's ties to Scotland did not entirely fade after he left the British Isles. For one thing, Murray returned to Scotland several times and stayed there for a period of five years, between 1744 and 1749. During those years, he married a distant Scottish relative, Barbara Bennet, and ultimately took her to his Point Repose plantation. Murray's ties to a broader Scottish community also flourished in his correspondence. His most frequent epistles went to Scottish friends and relatives, including Henry McCulloh, James Innes, James Moir, Archibald Douglas, and various members of the Scottish Rutherford, Murray, Clark, Hooper, and Bennet families. Murray's letters often make it clear that he held distant Scottish friends dearer than many of his closest acquaintances in the Lower Cape Fear.[80] As communication across the Atlantic world improved in the eighteenth century, correspondence made it easier for many elites like Murray to maintain contact with their cultural roots.

Janet Schaw's visit to the Lower Cape Fear lasted only a matter of months, but she, too, wrote in ways that showed her ties to Scotland and Scottish culture. As an elite Scottish woman, Schaw, not surprisingly, considered the most scrupulous agricultural methods in the Lower Cape Fear inferior to those of a typical East Lothian farmer.[81] For her, Scotland remained the standard of comparison in agriculture and in virtually everything else. Even more so than in Murray's case, the primary figures in her social world were Scottish, including John Rutherfurd, Robert Schaw and his family, Thomas Cobham, Robert Hogg, and others. She had little time to develop her own social networks in the New World so she used her Scottish kinship and social connections. In the years immediately after their arrival, many Scottish immigrants probably did the same. Yet, even Schaw's writings about the Lower Cape Fear do not explicitly address the subject of Scottish identity. Indeed, Schaw seldom uses the words *Scotland* or *Scottish,* instead using *Britain* and *British* when referring to her homeland and its culture. The fundamental dichotomy for her was not between things English and Scottish, but between Old World and New.

The timing of Schaw's visit, at the beginning of the American Revolution, makes it only logical that she should emphasize the rift between the British Crown and its increasingly different American subjects. The shift of allegiance precipitated by the imperial crisis also had powerful implications for the Lower Cape Fear's Scottish minority. People from Scottish backgrounds found it far more difficult to support the politics of colonial protest than they had found it to integrate into the society, economy, and more localized political concerns of the Lower Cape Fear. Many of them resisted the American Revolution and, combined with the large Scottish population upriver, formed one of the largest Loyalist networks in North America. By the time of the defeat by revolutionary forces of a band of primarily Scottish and armed Loyalists at Moore's Creek Bridge in early 1776, circumstances had made most Scots in the Lower Cape Fear far more aware of their different political and cultural backgrounds.[82]

At the same time, it would be easy to overemphasize the importance of the Scots in the Lower Cape Fear. The Scottish population of the Lower Cape Fear never approached the proportions of the Upper Cape Fear, and overall, more immigrants certainly came from North Carolina, South Carolina, and perhaps

TABLE 4.6 **Ties between Scots**

Type of Ties	*No. with Other Scots*	*% with Other Scots*
Personal	57	36.7
Economic	29	21.8
Legal	5	4.8
Total	91	23.2

even other areas of the British Isles; so, however important connections to other Scots must have been qualitatively, they were necessarily and greatly outnumbered by connections with the region's non-Scottish inhabitants. An analysis of recorded connections among identifiable Scottish residents of the Lower Cape Fear (see table 4.6) confirms both the significance and the limitations on Scottish networks in the region.[83]

In personal matters such as wills, Scots relied much more heavily on one another, and more than one-third of those they interacted with in that capacity were among the group of identifiable Scottish residents, even though that group made up fewer than 3 percent of the references in the database.[84] In economic interactions, other Scots were considerably less important, appearing only slightly more than one-fifth of the time. Yet, given the small sample, this still suggests a tendency to favor Scots. In legal actions, however, the proportion between Scots appears to be insignificant.

Clearly, Scots placed priority on interactions with those who shared their ethnic identity, but those interactions probably never made up close to a majority of their social connections and, in some areas of their lives, played no determinative role in the formation of networks. If this was true for Scots in the Lower Cape Fear, it was probably even more starkly true for the smaller Welsh, Irish, and French Huguenot minorities in the region. Thus, ethnicity played a role in the development of Lower Cape Fear social networks, but the preponderance of people of English descent forced all of the ethnic groups in the region to participate in Anglo-American dominated networks and social milieus. Ethnicity, like religion, remained an important category of difference for many, but its importance was shaped by the distinctive circumstances of regional development.

A consideration of the influence of religion and ethnicity on social networks reveals an important characteristic of social development in the Lower Cape Fear. As in all societies, social connections in the Lower Cape Fear were arranged according to hierarchical relations, and to a large extent these relations governed patterns of interaction. A common understanding of hierarchy pervaded early-modern Anglo-American societies, even if this understanding could change and take varying forms according to local conditions. Hierarchical ideologies distinguished between those who were independent because of their status as property-owning, European American males and all those others whom contemporaries considered "dependents," including slaves, children, wives, servants, and propertyless males. Within this larger pair of distinctions, other factors could still make an enormous difference in social standing. Moreover, the population and economy of a region could alter the configuration of these secondary hierarchical characteristics. In the Lower Cape Fear, the large percentage of the population of African descent made race a very important category that overlapped with, reinforced, and complicated ideas of dependency.

As mentioned above, the role of the established church and the dominant position of English culture in the Lower Cape Fear enabled religion and ethnicity to impinge on social status in the region. Some other variables remain imperceptible in historical sources. Appearances, mannerisms, and a variety of other verbal and nonverbal gestures could serve as indicators of civility and refinement in early America.[85] Because of the complexity and variety of factors that played a role in the cultivation of civility, it is difficult to provide tangible measures or precise definitions in these matters, but they clearly played an important role in the lives of Lower Cape Fear settlers. For example, the status of individuals could be heavily influenced by their access to a world of material goods. In this vein, James Murray's sister wanted to "be sure to have her goods of the Newest fashion as well as of the best kinds."[86] For the Murrays and others, wealth and material possessions no doubt derived much of their cultural meaning from the performance of conspicuous consumption.

Throughout colonial America, material position and property ownership played a crucial role in determining social status. Because material possessions were viewed in the context of early-modern economic culture, it would be misleading to impose modern and anachronistic conceptions of economic class on colonial Lower Cape Fear property distinctions.[87] Nonetheless, wealth did serve as an important, though not monolithic, indicator of social status. Not surprisingly, scholars studying colonial British America have devoted much attention to the distribution of wealth.[88] Unfortunately, research on colonial North Carolina fits poorly into the existing historiography on colonial wealth. Probate records for colonial North Carolina did not normally include valuations of estates, the most fruitful source for scholars of early American wealth.[89] Consequently, it is impossible to compare or assess information on wealth in the Lower Cape Fear in the sophisticated terms used in a wider context.

At the same time, a significant amount of data exists relating to the distribution of the two most socially and economically important forms of wealth among free people in the Lower Cape Fear—land and slaves. This data, shown in tables 4.7 and 4.8, demonstrates that early-modern expressions of hierarchical social order often described actual economic conditions. Both landownership, as indicated by land patents, and slave ownership, as indicated by tax lists, were clearly stratified. In both cases, the top one-half of the property owners

TABLE 4.7 **Distribution of Wealth, from Acres Patented**

Rank	*Percentage of Acres Patented*
Top 1%	19.90%
Top 5%	41.90%
Top 25%	73.50%
Top 50%	89.00%
Bottom 50%	10.90%
Bottom 25%	3.30%

Note: Other data on landownership, from conveyances and quitrent lists, is too incomplete to provide any estimates of property distribution. Also, land in the Lower Cape Fear varied wildly in quality and value, making acreage a very crude indicator of landed wealth.

TABLE 4.8 **Distribution of Wealth, from Slave Ownership**

Rank	*Amount of Average Slaveholdings*
Top 1%	9.60%
Top 5%	33.00%
Top 25%	76.20%
Top 50%	91.50%
Bottom 50%	8.50%
Bottom 25%	2.50%

Note: Slave ownership in this table refers to each individual's average slaveholdings from all of the extant Lower Cape Fear tax lists, rather than from any one year.

controlled around nine-tenths of the property.[90] Moreover, both of these forms of property conveyed more than merely pecuniary meaning. Land ownership suggested independence and economic competence, while slave ownership suggested mastery over social inferiors.

However, it remains difficult to determine how these two patterns of wealth-holding compare to those in other areas of colonial America because so many other forms of wealth are excluded and because so much of the population is left out of the data. For example, other evidence suggests that at least minimal levels of both landownership and slave ownership were relatively widespread in the Lower Cape Fear.[91] Also, evidence on wealth in early America indicates that wealth in slaves tended to be more stratified than wealth in general, and the relationship between slave headrights and North Carolina land patents makes a similar pattern for landholdings likely.[92] Following this logic, however, it can be safely assumed that total wealth in the Lower Cape Fear was less stratified, and we can draw some limited conclusions. To begin with, wealth in the Lower Cape Fear was certainly less stratified than in Bertie County, in the Albemarle region, and probably no more stratified than in Orange County, in the North Carolina backcountry.[93] Perhaps even less surprisingly, wealth in the Lower Cape Fear also does not appear to have been as stratified as in most of the South Carolina low-country by the late colonial period.[94] In this context, wealth in the Lower Cape Fear was undeniably unequal, but not excessively or surprisingly so.

Contemporaries did not perceive a significant or unusual degree of inequality in the Lower Cape Fear. On the contrary, several commentators found a leveling tendency in the region. When Scotus Americanus described the merchants and planters in the vicinity of Wilmington, he claimed that "poverty is almost an entire stranger among them."[95] John Brickell, in his *Natural History of North Carolina,* shared these sentiments and also wrote that the planters "live after the most easie and pleasant Manner of any People I have ever met with." Brickell also expressed astonishment that "there are no Beggars or Vagabonds to be met with Strowling from place to place as it is too common amongst us."[96] Less enthusiastically, the elite visitor Janet Schaw complained that Lower Cape Fear society had "a most disgusting equality."[97]

All of these comments depended on the various authors' frame of reference, but there were good reasons why the Lower Cape Fear would have seemed to be more equal than other regions in the early-modern world. For one thing, the Lower Cape Fear, as a more recently settled region, did not yet have as fully elaborated social and economic differences. As long as the land and resources of the region remained comparatively plentiful for the population, this was likely to continue on some level. Most important, all of these quantitative and qualitative assessments of social structure in the Lower Cape Fear apply only to the free population. The region's enslaved majority provided the bulk of its labor and utilized a relatively miniscule proportion of its resources. Even the poorest Anglo-American settlers could claim a more elevated status than most of the region's population, and this undoubtedly softened the implications of social hierarchy for some European Americans. Yet, however they viewed these circumstances, the region's wealthiest planters were still quite unlikely to bond with its poorest laborers, and, as some consideration of slave life will starkly demonstrate, economic relations could place enormous obstacles before individuals attempting to build social networks. For free people, at least, the distribution of wealth in the Lower Cape Fear can be summed up as a distinct midpoint between more-stratified conditions in South Carolina and less-stratified conditions in other parts of North Carolina, and this characterization, too, became part of the region's reputation.

Hierarchical differences related to wealth and other factors became even more important because they influenced attitudes toward individual patronage and reputations. Positive perceptions could make enormous differences in the prospects of Lower Cape Fear residents, and Murray's letters reveal a constant effort to assess and influence perceptions of friends, business partners, and acquaintances. Lower Cape Fear settlers sometimes acquired considerable wealth, but they also often felt compelled to appear well bred, educated, and genteel.

For African Americans in the Lower Cape Fear, social interaction proved to be even more circumscribed. While social hierarchies remained fluid among free people, European Americans readily achieved a consensus on the lowly status of enslaved African Americans. Of course, slaves continually contested the demeaning status colonists imposed on them, but their opportunities for interaction were clearly limited. It seems doubtful that many social relationships with European Americans would have remained untainted by racism. Schaw must have shared the virulently intolerant attitude of many early North Carolinians: she said she enjoyed a reprieve from "yelping Negroes with their discording voices to grate my ears and disturb my thoughts."[98] Ironically, the very proximity of European Americans probably imposed the greatest obstacles on slaves' attempts to foster meaningful social networks. Where slaves were subject to the most supervision, they also had the least autonomy. In the Lower Cape Fear, however, it proved much more difficult for European Americans to supervise and coerce slaves than in most other places in colonial America.

For example, slaves in colonial America had even less access to reliable transportation than free people, but many slaves in the Lower Cape Fear had unusual opportunities for spatial mobility. These opportunities derived from the importance of slave labor in transportation. Slaves supplied the manpower for transportation, whether by wagon, boat, animal power, or foot. The scarcity of labor, the heavy transportation requirements of the region's forest industries, and the centrality of the Cape Fear River made enslaved watermen especially important. These unusually mobile slaves could be found throughout the southern British colonies, but they seem to have been especially common in the Lower Cape Fear. Richard Marsden, for example, showed that he recognized the importance of these watermen in the region. Marsden complained of the difficulty of travel in the Lower Cape Fear, "being often obliged to take negroes for three or four days in a week to transport me by water." People of West African descent often associated water with spiritual powers, and these watermen consequently may have obtained a special cultural status.[99] Of even greater importance for the formation of social networks, watermen could undoubtedly travel great distances without European American interference. Not surprisingly, one study has found that slave watermen ran away more often and more successfully than other North Carolina slaves.[100]

Even when European Americans relied on land transportation, they turned to slaves. When Hugh Finlay attempted to establish a regular post between North Carolina towns, the response of the Lower Cape Fear elite was easy to anticipate. They proposed "to hire a negroe boy to go down to Brunswick twice a week."[101] Such traveling slaves may have provided other Africans and African Americans with comparatively sophisticated communication networks, even if most slaves had more confined face-to-face interactions.

Slave-hiring practices also gave some Lower Cape Fear slaves opportunities for mobility. Skilled slaves obtained a degree of bargaining power, and masters were compelled by economic circumstances to allow these slaves to hire themselves out. On the other hand, most slaves who were hired out had little bargaining power and may have dreaded the enforced mobility it entailed. For all kinds of networks, geographic movement could be disruptive as well as enabling. It is impossible to say precisely how widespread slave hiring was in the Lower Cape Fear, but innumerable contemporary references, together with the region's heavy reliance on slave labor and a relatively diverse economy, strongly suggest that it was relatively common.[102]

In most cases, however, social networks among slaves remained confined within small geographic spaces. In the Lower Cape Fear, as elsewhere in colonial America, enslaved people of African descent perpetuated cultural practices and formed social networks most effectively when they were near one another. The population of the entire region, enslaved or free, African or European, lived in a dispersed manner across the countryside, and this pattern of population distribution made social interaction more of a challenge for everyone.[103] But under the circumstances, slaves in the Lower Cape Fear lived in quite concentrated groups. When Tryon, the future governor, first visited North Carolina, he was so impressed by the concentrated slave population that he wrote, "The Negroes are very numerous I suppose five to one White Person in the Maritime Counties." Tryon's statement must have referred to the large plantation populations of the Lower Cape Fear and would have been an exaggeration even there. More accurately, he also wrote that "in the Counties on the Sea Coast Planters have from fifty to 250 Slaves. A Plantation with Seventy Slaves on it is esteemed a good property." But Tryon's observation reflected a certain reality about the Lower Cape Fear: on a plantation of seventy slaves, Africans and African Americans were unlikely to see many European Americans beyond their master, his overseer, and their families. Large plantations meant large slave communities and, therefore, greater opportunities for interaction.[104] Tryon could not have known it, but slaveholdings in the Lower Cape Fear were very concentrated by the standards of mainland Anglo-American plantation societies.[105] In British North America, only areas of the South Carolina lowcountry had plantations with comparable concentrations of slaves.[106]

Even when other slaves were nearby, the brutal plantation work regime could deprive laborers of the time and energy to nurture social connections. Labor routines on colonial American plantations were generally allocated according to one of two patterns: the gang system or the task system. Evidence on labor in the Lower Cape Fear is too limited to make any certain statements, but it seems likely that the task system prevailed in the region. In the task system, masters attempted to motivate laborers by allowing them free time after they had completed a specific amount of work, or task. The gang system was more common in the Chesapeake Bay region and elsewhere. The task system is generally associated with South Carolina rice plantations, but tasking could easily have spread to Lower Cape Fear plantations, with or without rice cultivation. Scotus Americanus wrote that North Carolina slaves' "work is performed by a daily task, allotted by their master or overseer, which they have generally done by one or two o'clock in the afternoon, and have the rest of the day for themselves."[107] More ambiguously, Schaw wrote about how "a number of Negroes follow each other's tail the day long, and have a task assigned them."[108] Schaw may have witnessed an example of the gang system, the task system, or some kind of hybrid of the two. Perhaps slaves assigned to a task utilized African patterns of communal labor to make their work more bearable and familiar.[109] In any case, it seems probable that many Lower Cape Fear slaves labored in the task system, which, while it may or may not have alleviated the difficulty of their toil, gave them a degree of autonomy and more time to foster social relationships.

Despite the requirements of labor and the difficulties of travel, slaves found ways to organize social gatherings and to give structure to their networks and interactions. Masters and overseers could do little to prevent members of such a large enslaved population from moving from plantation to plantation on various occasions and from preserving or adapting their own cultural practices. The location of slaves on plantations did, however, shift the focus of slave social networks away from the towns, where free people gathered. Slave social gatherings could take place on the plantations themselves, during slaves' leisure time, after tasks were completed, at night, or on special occasions or holidays. Perhaps even more important, slaves could meet clandestinely. The forests of the Lower Cape Fear provided the logical site for such gatherings. Slaves knew these wooded areas well from their work in the naval stores industry, lumbering, and other forms of labor. In a number of cases, masters even licensed slaves to carry guns in the forests in order to hunt.[110] Wilmington residents perhaps should not have been surprised, then, when, amid rumors of a slave insurrection, "there had been a great number of them discovered in the adjoining woods the night before, most of them with arms."[111]

Funerals clearly provided the most important public slave gatherings on Lower Cape Fear plantations. Schaw noted slave funeral rituals in the region, commenting that "the Negroes assembled to perform their part of the funeral rites, which they did by running, jumping, crying and various exercises."[112] However curious Schaw might have found these activities, for slaves they no doubt expressed powerful African cultural understandings of death, which made funerals a joyous celebration of the deceased's triumphant entry into the world of spirits. Murray recognized that his slaves found a festive aspect to their community's funeral rituals: in 1755 he wrote that his slaves were "at a great loss this Christmas for want of a death to play for."[113] In contrast, John Brickell found slave weddings to be relatively unceremonious events that slaves "generally performed amongst themselves."[114]

However effective slaves might have been at preserving social connections and arranging community gatherings, slave society was not undifferentiated: a variety of social and cultural markers could even influence social relations within slave quarters. Perhaps the biggest differences occurred between African-born and Creole slaves. Existing data make it impossible to determine the proportion of African-born slaves in any part of North Carolina during the colonial period, but their numbers were undoubtedly significant.[115] To slaves recently wrenched from their African homes, Creole slaves might have seemed like representatives of a completely different worldview. Some American-born slaves, for example, adopted the Christian religion, and, as John Brickell observed, that gave them "an abhorance of the Temper and Practice of those who are brought from Guinea."[116] In some dissenting congregations, people of African descent were even permitted to preach the gospel.[117] While neither Africans nor African Americans were as likely as Brickell to see this in the same bipolar terms of righteousness and paganism, such different attitudes clearly had the potential to cause rifts in the slave community.

Indeed, many more-assimilated slaves and those who were especially skilled received privileged treatment from masters, and such treatment must have caused tension with other slaves. Such tensions played a complex and important role in power relations and could often have violent consequences. For example, in 1760 information came before the New Hanover County Court "that a Negro man named Jack—belonging to Mr. John Dalrumple was shot by a Negro man named Paris belonging to Mr. Dalrumple aforesaid for stealing sundry things out of his said Masters House." The situation was complicated by the fact that "Paris had positive Orders from his Mistress to shott any Negroes whome he cou'd apprehend breaking open the House." Paris's decision to shoot Jack could have reflected a variety of motives. Most obviously, Paris could have feared repercussions from his mistress if the thieves escaped; or Paris could have had personal animosities toward Jack that made this a welcome opportunity; or, perhaps less likely, Paris might even have internalized Anglo-American attitudes toward property and felt obliged to shoot Jack for stealing. Whatever forces drove Paris's decision, the result undoubtedly would have caused controversy in the slave quarters. Nor was the situation likely to be unique. Countless other slaves must have faced similar dilemmas because of their compromised position in the plantation system.

Ultimately, though, the very pressures of enslavement probably convinced most slaves that they had more common interests than differences. Social and support networks were all the more necessary for people coping with the horrors of slavery. Moreover, no matter how different Africans and African Americans might have been from one another, they almost certainly had more points of commonality with each other than with Anglo-Americans. In the Lower Cape Fear, as throughout Anglo-American slave societies, slaves used support networks to assist each other in resisting their oppression. Networks could be especially helpful to slaves who ran away. The surviving runaway slave ads from colonial North Carolina newspapers offer a much smaller base of evidence than those from Virginia and South Carolina, but they tend to confirm what scholars have suspected about runaways.[118] They also make it clear that slaves sometimes helped runaways. William Wilkinson, of Wilmington, suspected that his runaway slave Ben was "harboured up the North East of the Cape Fear, or on the sound."[119] Similarly, when Cuffee escaped from Cornelius Harnett, Harnett offered "a further reward of Forty shillings . . . to any person who will give information of his being harboured by a Negro."

Of course, runaway slaves also would not hesitate to accept assistance from Anglo-Americans, and Harnett, recognizing as much, also offered five pounds additional reward if Cuffee was being assisted by a free person.[120] But fellow slaves undoubtedly provided more frequent, sympathetic, and reliable support for Africans and African Americans who resisted enslavement, whatever form the resistance took. In the end, no matter how Schaw understood the meeting of slaves in the adjoining woods that she heard about in 1775, such meetings were not only an opportunity for social interaction among slaves but also a moment when social conditions encouraged those present to be united and armed.[121] Slave life in the Lower Cape Fear also involved a constant negotiation between the conditions imposed by slave-owning settlers in accordance with the region's distinctive labor needs and the slaves' own autonomous social concerns and efforts at resistance. For slaves, as for many people who lived in the Lower Cape Fear settlement, the development of social networks and bonds became most necessary as a way to counter other forces that divided people from one another.

Historians studying slavery and other topics have long acknowledged important regional divisions within the political confines of eighteenth-century North Carolina.[122] For the vast majority of colonists and slaves in the Lower Cape Fear, social interactions and experiences were overwhelmingly likely to take place with other residents of the Lower Cape Fear region itself. Unlike settlers in the seventeenth-century Chesapeake, their social networks usually stretched somewhat beyond intensely localized networks. At the same time, there is little evidence that many inhabitants of the Lower Cape Fear participated in social networks that crossed into other regions of Anglo-America. Thus, in 1770, John Barnett could write from Northampton County in Albemarle that "in this part of the Province we have hardly any communication with Cape Fear."[123] Along similar lines, Murray's letters contain a litany of complaint

TABLE 4.9 **Nonresident Ties in Neighborhoods**

	Lockwoods Folly	*Town Creek*	*Rocky Point*	*Total*
Nonresident Ties	19	25	22	56
Total ties	528	704	1,168	2,400
% of ties nonresident	3.6	3.6	1.9	2.3
Residents with nonresident ties	13	14	13	34
Total residents	69	61	61	191
% with nonresident ties	18.8	22.9	21.3	17.8

about the difficulty of communication with the world beyond the Lower Cape Fear.[124]

In the three neighborhoods of Lockwoods Folly, Town Creek, and Rocky Point, settlers seldom recorded interactions with people from beyond the Lower Cape Fear (see table 4.9). County recording procedures may have been somewhat biased toward local transactions, but conveyances, wills, powers of attorney, and other documents usually identified individuals from distant locations. Consequently, county records provide a reasonable way of tracing ties to the world beyond the Lower Cape Fear. Even with this imperfect source of data, the results are compelling. More than 97 percent of all recorded interactions with residents of these neighborhoods took place with other identifiable Lower Cape Fear residents. More than eighty of the neighborhood residents had no recorded interactions with those from outside the Lower Cape Fear. Only slight variations occurred across the three neighborhoods, and these can easily be dismissed as products of the small data set.

Not only were recorded interactions with those outside the Lower Cape Fear very rare, when they did occur they still demonstrated the constraints of distance. Fully ten of the fifty-six nonresident ties were with individuals from Bladen County, North Carolina, which bordered Brunswick and New Hanover and had even absorbed a segment of Brunswick County. These Bladen County ties could scarcely be considered as being beyond the Lower Cape Fear: they may well have been a product of shifting county lines. Another ten ties came from other North Carolina counties, while seven more came from neighboring South Carolina. Only nineteen ties demonstrated any kind of transatlantic connection.

A comparison of county tax lists also provides evidence about interactions beyond the Lower Cape Fear region. Lower Cape Fear settlers were likely to have some contact outside of the region with residents of the adjacent counties of Bladen and Onslow. Analysis of the Bladen County tax list for 1763 and the Onslow County tax list for 1770 reveals some interaction across county and regional boundaries. A total of 120 names from the Bladen County tax list and 105 names from the Onslow County tax list appeared in the records of the Lower Cape Fear region. Various reasons help to explain the overlap between these tax lists. Some settlers appear to have migrated from one place to another, some merchants brought suit over business matters that crossed significant distances, some wealthy planter families owned multiple residences in different counties, and some individuals shared common names with others in nearby counties. Thus, the boundaries of the Lower Cape Fear region could be both fluid and permeable. On the other hand, evidence about residents of Bladen and Onslow counties confirm the basic pattern of regional interaction because they were clearly atypical. For example, the names on the 1763 New Hanover County tax list appeared in the Lower Cape Fear records more than ten times as frequently as the names on the Bladen County tax list for the same year.[125] Moreover, even when individuals did move in or out of the region, they tended to move within the most elite, mobile, and commercially oriented groups of the population.

Thus, different kinds of data confirm the regional nature of social interaction in the colonial Lower Cape Fear. To identify a predominantly regional pattern of interaction, however, does not suggest that the Lower Cape Fear was isolated from the outside world. On the contrary, many Lower Cape Fear inhabitants had important and meaningful social relationships with those in other regions or across the Atlantic. Such relationships could only be expected, because many, if not most, of the residents of the colonial Lower Cape Fear had emigrated from other locales. High levels of physical mobility in the early-modern Atlantic world acted against isolation and localism, even in the most peripheral locales. Even more important, all of the early- and mid-eighteenth-century Anglo-American colonies experienced rapid integration into Atlantic markets and economic networks. The growth of print culture also gave some individuals ways of identifying and communicating with those in distant places. Finally, the British Empire provided colonists with still another set of broader identifications and concerns.

Population movement had special importance for the colonial Lower Cape Fear. Enormous numbers of immigrants came to North Carolina in the mid-eighteenth century, many of them through Lower Cape Fear ports. While it seems clear that most of these newcomers only passed through the region on their way westward, it remains unclear whether this transitory population added a less stable element to the Lower Cape Fear's population. Indeed, very little data on population turnover exists at all for the colonies south of Virginia. Because information on the Lower Cape Fear's population has to be derived largely from tax lists, and no reliable measures of death rates remain extant, it is impossible to obtain precise information regarding population turnover in the region. Nonetheless, it is possible to make some crude estimates.

An examination of the two complete annual tax lists for the region, for the years 1755 and 1763 reveals that between these years about 60 percent of New Hanover County heads of households disappeared from the county tax lists, a rate of turnover of about 7.5 percent per year. No precise mortality rates exist for the Lower Cape Fear during this period, but it seems reasonable to assume, based on contemporary accounts, that the environment in the Lower Cape Fear killed less frequently than the South Carolina lowcountry and more frequently than much of the late-seventeenth-century Chesapeake. Peter Coclanis found crude mortality rates in Charles Town to be at least 5.2 percent per year, whereas James Horn and others have found annual mortality in the Chesapeake to be less than 3.5 percent. It seems plausible to say, then, that between 3.5 and 5.2 percent of Lower Cape Fear householders died during a typical year. Thus, using the figures from the 1755 and 1763 tax lists, between 4.0 and 2.3 percent of Lower Cape Fear heads of households left the region in a typical year, and given the unusually severe and contagious conditions in Charles Town, it seems probable that the real number was closer to 4.0 percent. Indeed, unless mortality rates in the Lower Cape Fear were close to the staggering levels that Coclanis suggests for Charles Town, population turnover played a far greater role in the Lower Cape Fear than in most parts of the supposedly highly mobile late seventeenth-century Chesapeake.[126]

So population turnover probably complicated the development of the Lower Cape Fear as a coherent and identifiable region. Some evidence suggests that even enslaved Lower Cape Fear inhabitants sometimes moved beyond the geographic confines of the region. When slaves ran away, some Lower Cape Fear masters advertised for runaways in South Carolina newspapers, expecting that their slaves would leave North Carolina.[127] They might well have done so in an attempt to utilize networks from previous homes.

Many of those engaged in trade also developed extensive and important networks that went beyond the Lower Cape Fear. Indeed, for merchants involved in transatlantic trade in naval stores and other commodities, their very financial security depended on the strength of their connections in London and elsewhere. The letters of a number of merchants trading with the Lower Cape Fear provide testimony to the impressive development of these economic networks. Moreover, maritime commerce structured the economy of the entire region, and all of the Lower Cape Fear's inhabitants participated in markets influenced by overseas trends.

Perhaps the most substantive evidence of extraregional business activities in the Lower Cape Fear comes from powers of attorney (see table 4.10). In the eighteenth century, it was common for merchants and entrepreneurs to give someone else a power of attorney in order to transact business for them in distant places. Not all powers of attorney were used for commercial purposes, however, because they also proved useful in settling estates and other more

TABLE 4.10 **Geographic Connections in Powers of Attorney**

Place	*Number of Powers of Attorney*
Bladen County, North Carolina	10
Other North Carolina counties	10
England	9
South Carolina	7
New England	6
Other transatlantic locations	5
Middle Colonies	3

personal economic transactions. Surviving Lower Cape Fear records include 289 powers of attorney, but only 104, slightly more than one-third of these, involved one party who could be identified as a nonresident. In any case, they do indicate that, throughout the colonial period, important economic exchanges occurred between Lower Cape Fear inhabitants and people in London, Charles Town, New York, Boston, and other trading centers.

Reading and writing gave Lower Cape Fear residents another means of interacting in worlds beyond the region. Books could provide them with vivid descriptions of very different worlds—worlds they could never visit in person. Perhaps even more important, correspondence and printing presses made it possible for Lower Cape Fear residents to communicate with, and participate in, those other worlds. Unfortunately, postal services that carried letters beyond the Lower Cape Fear often left a lot to be desired. Shortly after the migration of South Carolinians into the Cape Fear, the South Carolina assembly offered to fund one Lower Cape Fear settler's proposal to establish a regular postal delivery with the new settlement.[128] Even so, Gabriel Johnston, the North Carolina governor, later complained that "it is a great misfortune that Letters are so long in coming to hand in this Country." He also lamented "the want of an opportunity to transmit answers unless one sends them to the neighboring Colonies of Virginia and South Carolina where they often lye a long time and are sometimes entirely neglected."[129] In this context, it is not surprising that James Murray forlornly began one letter by writing, "Have had no Letters this 12 Months."[130]

Existing evidence suggests that neither writing nor printing fully engrossed the attention of many North Carolinians. The large library in Edward Moseley's estate, plantation names such as Lilliput, and James Murray's inquiries about issues of the *Gentleman's Magazine,* the *Spectator,* and the *Pennsylvania Gazette* all indicate that some colonists actively engaged in the world of print culture, but all of these examples appear very atypical in the colonial Lower Cape Fear.[131] While Murray left a respectable collection of letters, he wrote: "As for my Mrs her aversion to writing is grown by disuse to almost insuperable."[132] Along similar lines, Maurice Moore Jr. complained that, due to a lack of education in his youth, "writing . . . is the most painful Exercise to me in the world."[133] Other Lower Cape Fear elites appear to have taken more pains to have their children educated than did the Moores, but they evidently viewed print culture as something more to be respected and appreciated from afar than as something to indulge in. Lower Cape Fear estate inventories suggest that most readers in the region used books instrumentally. Most owned a Bible or prayerbook. If they owned any other book, it would usually be a law book or a treatise on some other area of practical endeavor. The sporadic and limited nature of efforts at newspaper publication in North Carolina also indicated relative apathy toward literary concerns.

It would also be difficult to overlook the Lower Cape Fear's commitments to broader, extraregional political configurations. Like other Anglo-American settlers, those in the Lower Cape Fear undoubtedly felt deep ties to British culture and government. The imperial crisis leading up to the Revolution constituted as much an assertion of these ties as a rejection of them. When the break with Britain finally came, colonists in the Lower Cape Fear and elsewhere had begun to form continental political ties through the Continental Congress and other forms of intercolonial association.

None of these external influences, however, changed the essentially regional character of society in the colonial Lower Cape Fear. Indeed, limited exposure to outsiders and others probably only strengthened ties to the Lower Cape Fear because it made regionally distinctive characteristics and experiences more evident. Further, all of these forces remained distant to most people in the Lower Cape Fear, who neither constantly migrated, engaged in transatlantic trade, read voluminously, nor attended the Continental Congress. Those who did may have been harbingers of important changes, but, during the colonial period, they remained atypical, and their influence did not immediately overwhelm older patterns of social interaction. Once changes began to integrate fully the people of the Lower Cape Fear into those broader areas of concern and interaction, the region had already become an entity unto itself.

Chapter 5

POLITICS AND AUTHORITY

In 1752, the Moravian leader August Gottlieb Spangenberg described a continuing problem in the political development of North Carolina. "North Carolina," he noted, "is a rather large Province, and the conditions of [the] inhabitants varies so greatly that often what is good for the southern part is bad for the northern, and vice versa." He went on to complain that this problem led to "a continual strife between the two sections."[1] While few modern historians have paid much attention to these brief comments, they present a perceptive and highly persuasive explanation for colonial North Carolina's notoriously fractious political culture.

Spangenberg's observations derive partly from his own perspective on North Carolina. He and the other Moravians who accompanied him on his journey through North Carolina in 1752 fit into a long tradition of religious dissenters seeking an American haven from intolerance. After traveling thousands of miles from their place of origin in eastern Europe, the radical German-speaking pietists who became known as the Moravians obtained permission to settle a community of believers on one hundred thousand acres in North Carolina. Spangenberg, the leader of this group, seeking the best location for this Moravian settlement, carefully considered the dynamics of North Carolina politics and society. The Lower Cape Fear region had filled with settlers by this time, and Spangenberg and his followers ultimately chose a promising area of land in the Carolina Piedmont region, hundreds of miles to the west.

As the Moravian settlement grew and developed in the years before the American Revolution, the size and divided character of North Carolina proved to be somewhat of a mixed blessing. At times, the pacifistic Moravians found themselves desperately trying to stay out of bitter conflicts. As a general rule, however, they benefited from the fact that a comparatively divided and weak North Carolina government lacked the authority to interfere with their distinctive and carefully guarded way of life.[2] The Moravians differed in many and profound ways from the residents of the Lower Cape Fear region, but as they expanded into new areas of settlement, both groups recognized and adapted to the reality that North Carolina's political boundaries contained several distinct and surprisingly autonomous regions.

For Anglo-American colonists such as those who dominated the Lower Cape Fear settlement, the expansion of settlement included the extension of British ideas about politics and authority in ways that proved far more important than the development of entities such as the province of North Carolina.

Only a small and elite minority had any regular interaction with the provincial government during the colonial period, but large numbers of colonists experienced authority through local institutions such as county courts, Anglican vestries, municipal governments, road commissions, and militia units. Even those who involved themselves in provincial politics were at times undoubtedly influenced by more local political concerns. Consequently, the establishment of governing institutions played a key role in the development of the colonial Lower Cape Fear as a region. Just as colonists strove to obtain land and fostered social networks, they also participated in elections, selected leaders, and negotiated their own place within broader political frameworks. They did this as they considered the function of authority on a more local level, as they brought grievances before the county court, sought to protect their own rights and property, and struggled to obtain control over their slaves. The rise of the Lower Cape Fear marked the simultaneous development of a new region and a set of local political interests and perspectives.

Lower Cape Fear settlers accepted the political structures and boundaries already established in colonial North Carolina. Conventional wisdom about political authority in colonial North Carolina emphasizes the colony's supposed instability, poverty, and fractiousness. Indeed, even by the standards of colonial America, North Carolina has acquired a reputation for tenuous political authority.[3] While this reputation reflects some important realities about colonial North Carolina, a look at politics and authority in the Lower Cape Fear provides a somewhat different and more complex interpretation. As Spangenberg recognized, no matter how important the artificial and political boundaries of North Carolina could be, for most North Carolinians they were not as important as regional divisions within the colony.

Thus, these characterizations of authority in colonial North Carolina do not necessarily apply to the experience of Lower Cape Fear residents. Most obviously, if the rest of North Carolina lacked a clearly differentiated political elite because of economic limitations, the Lower Cape Fear transcended these limitations and developed a far more secure and wealthy group of elite leaders. Equally important, the resolution of disputes in local forums such as the county court system could legitimize authority and limit internal divisions within North Carolina's regions. The presence of large numbers of enslaved Africans and African Americans in the Lower Cape Fear also created special imperatives for unified authority among Anglo-American settlers as slaves resisted these and other authority structures. Finally, many Lower Cape Fear settlers undoubtedly embraced the relatively decentralized authority structure of colonial North Carolina and viewed it as beneficial.

Yet decisions made outside of the Lower Cape Fear continued to have great importance for the region, and settlers tried to exercise whatever agency they could in these decisions. More regional and local concerns often took precedence for most settlers, but they also remained interrelated with provincial politics. The same regional differences that could provide local unity and coherence in the Lower Cape Fear could also cause intense political conflict with other regions. Indeed, differing regional interests probably served as the primary catalyst in the brutal fights that made colonial North Carolina politics so notorious. Participation in North Carolina politics also meant participation in colonial politics, and the relationship between Lower Cape Fear residents and the metropolitan authorities in Britain would prove increasingly important in the years leading up to 1776. Ultimately, all of these levels of authority underscored the relatively strong regional unity of the Lower Cape Fear in contrast to the region's weaker ties to other, more far-reaching political entities.

Before the earliest permanent settlements in the Lower Cape Fear around 1725, the region functioned as a liminal borderland between the settled areas of North and South Carolina. To contemporaries, its eventual absorption into North Carolina did not seem like a foregone conclusion. The border between the colonies remained vaguely defined: settlement from South Carolina stayed north of the Santee, and few North Carolinians had moved south of the Neuse. Indeed, the official boundary between the two colonies remained indeterminate in some areas for decades. Because the Moores and their allies settled the region as private individuals and lived far enough away to be beyond the coercive power of either colony, it was their decision to ally themselves with North Carolina instead of South Carolina that made all the difference.

The most powerful of the Lower Cape Fear region's earliest settlers clearly preferred to be within the political confines of North Carolina, and, in essence, they drew the boundary between the two colonies accordingly. Once Maurice Moore sought the assistance of North Carolina's governor, George Burrington, it became evident that the new settlement would become part of that colony. This may seem like a curious choice, not only because of Moore's South Carolina ties but also because, according to many modern historians, North Carolina's early government resembled a carnival of ineptitude and virulence. Yet the same weak government that has earned the scorn of so many scholars provided the Moores and their allies with important incentives. To begin with, it provided them with a refuge from Charles Town's tax collectors and creditors. But even beyond these obvious material advantages, North Carolina offered elites an opportunity to impose their will in ways that, by that time, had become impossible for men of their means within the reach of the burgeoning South Carolina government and society.

In contrast, it was widely believed that North Carolina's government could barely control its inhabitants, let alone infringe on their rights or status. Along these lines, in his famous *New Voyage to Carolina,* written in 1709, John Lawson praised North Carolina for having a government "so mild and easy, in respect to the Properties and Liberties of a Subject, that . . . it is the mildest and best establish'd Government in the World." For Lawson and perhaps for the Lower Cape settlers, North Carolina was a "Place where any Man may peaceably enjoy his own."[4] Most other observers proved far less kind, and the colony rapidly obtained a reputation as an impoverished and chaotic haven for criminals and debtors. Burrington wrote that, when he first became governor in the early 1720s, "North Carolina was little known or mentioned," and he "found the Inhabitants few and poor."[5] But, because North Carolina's established authorities remained weak, aspiring and wealthy newcomers could be relatively strong and form a society according to their own preferences and interests.

Contemporaries in South Carolina recognized that the Moores and their followers gravitated toward the Lower Cape Fear at least partly because of this power vacuum.[6] As South Carolinians characterized the situation several decades later, "in order to avoid payment of Taxes and to be in a situation on account of its distance beyond the reach of Process," some families migrated from South Carolina to the banks of the Cape Fear River and founded Brunswick. In a short time, however, "it became necessary that they should be under the actual authority of Government," and, "the People of Brunswick . . . [who were] moved by their own private Interest, chosed rather to be deemed Inhabitants of North Carolina." Consequently, the Crown established a new boundary between North and South Carolina.[7]

The integration and rise of Lower Cape Fear leaders within North Carolina politics proved to be a gradual and difficult process, however. The political elite in northern North Carolina may have been less wealthy, less secure, and less authoritative than their peers in South Carolina or Virginia, but they were firmly ensconced in positions of political power and were very jealous of their governing status. Moreover, after several generations, political systems acquire a momentum of their own that renders them resistant to rapid alterations. Beyond these obvious difficulties, the political leadership of the Lower Cape Fear faced three important obstacles after settlement.

First, during the years immediately following the region's settlement, North Carolina government became especially contentious and turbulent, partly because of the limited leadership skills of its governors. After several decades, the situation improved considerably, but only after infusing considerable controversy into the relationship between the Lower Cape Fear and the rest of North Carolina. Second, in order to claim political legitimacy, the leaders of the Lower Cape Fear first had to settle and develop the new region. North Carolinians would not allow their colony to be governed from an uncivilized wilderness, and a strong correlation tied the growth of the Lower Cape Fear and the importance of its leadership. By the late colonial period, the Lower Cape Fear had a relatively secure elite and an important role in North Carolina to underscore their influence. Third, North Carolina's regions differed in fundamental ways and therefore could not always be expected to share common interests. Economic, cultural, and social contrasts inevitably led to political conflict between regions, and this often prevented Lower Cape Fear leaders from accomplishing their goals. Ultimately, tensions between regions played as large a role in North Carolina as anywhere else in colonial British America and persisted into the American Revolution. Nonetheless, even with all these obstacles, by the American Revolution, the Lower Cape Fear region occupied the central position in North Carolina politics.

In the years immediately after the Moores began their new settlement in 1725, however, colonists in the region had to work hard to establish the most basic routines of law and government. If Burrington's office gave formal recognition and support to the Lower Cape Fear settlement, his personal characteristics and leadership proved to be an incalculable liability to his new allies in Brunswick. Moreover, in colonial North Carolina, the title of governor could carry as much opprobrium as authority. The governor, after all, represented executive authority, something contested in virtually every British American colony, but especially resented in North Carolina. Burrington himself recognized that North Carolinians "allways behaved insolently to their Governours." He could point to continuous hostility toward North Carolina executives in past decades: "some they have Imprisoned, [they] drove others out of the Country, [and] at other times [they] sett up two or three supported by Men under Arms." In short, Burrington concluded, "all the Governors that ever were in this Province lived in fear of the People (except myself) and D[r]eaded their Assemblys."[8] Yet Burrington, having quickly associated himself with the Brunswick settlement, and boasting that he had exerted great effort "Perfecting the Settlement on Cape Fear River," then proceeded to match any of his predecessors for evoking ire in North Carolina.[9]

Burrington pursued his own material interests in a manner that most contemporaries found surprisingly blatant and egregious. During the aggressive and unscrupulous rush to claim land in the Lower Cape Fear, no one, with the possible exception of the Moores, appeared more ruthlessly concerned with material gain than Governor Burrington. He obtained tens of thousands of prime acres of land that could be claimed only because he violated his instructions from the proprietors.[10] These land disputes resulted in countless aspersions on Burrington's character.[11] He also involved himself in disputes over other kinds of property, including a drawn-out dispute with John Baptista Ashe over some horses.[12] In another notable incident, Burrington allegedly extorted livestock from a poor, elderly man by threatening to have him imprisoned.[13]

Burrington's "mad extravagant behaviour" extended well beyond simple greed, however, and the governor's personal relationships seemed calculated to divide North Carolina politicians. Most obviously, his aggressive and self-interested support for the settlement of the Lower Cape Fear polarized many. He also caused enormous controversy by appointing to high office men who were less popular and reputable, encouraging tension between appointive and informal elites.[14] Further, Burrington changed allies in a seemingly arbitrary and unpredictable way that made it difficult to form stable political coalitions. Such important Lower Cape Fear figures as John Baptisa Ashe, Maurice Moore, and Edward Moseley changed political allegiances during these years because of Burrington's behavior. Most strikingly, Burrington showed an unusual willingness to resort to personal violence in an attempt to resolve political disputes.[15] Ultimately, Burrington's two, nonconsecutive, terms as governor resulted in little consensus among North Carolinians over the meaning of settlement in the Lower Cape Fear, or, for that matter, little coherent extralocal government.

Lower Cape Fear residents did not rely solely on Burrington's assistance during these early years, however. Throughout the late 1720s, persistent rumors circulated claiming that Burrington and the Moores planned to make the Lower Cape Fear a separate colony, distinct from both North and South Carolina. While such an outcome was undeniably unlikely, its mere suggestion gives some indication of the aspirations and influence of the Lower Cape Fear leadership. Richard Everard served as North Carolina's governor from 1725 until 1731, between Burrington's two terms, Burrington having been removed because of complaints from North Carolina officials about his misdeeds. But Everard changed little. Not only did he, too, pursue his own interests and offend many North Carolinians, he, like Burrington, yielded to pressure from Lower Cape Fear settlers and continued the granting of large tracts of land against the proprietors' wishes. Even more important, during Everard's administration Lower Cape Fear leaders voiced open criticisms of the deteriorating proprietary system. Indeed, contemporaries cited among the reasons for his removal rumors that Burrington and his allies planned to attempt an overthrow of the proprietors.[16] When machinations in both London and North Carolina led to the purchase of the colony by the Crown and Burrington's return to office in the place of Everard, Lower Cape Fear leaders expected a return to business as usual. When these changes led to increasing personal difficulties with Burrington and attempts by the Crown to centralize authority in the province and raise more revenue from quitrents, the Lower Cape Fear elite ultimately turned against Burrington and resisted any pretensions of prerogative power.[17] When Burrington was removed for the second time, this time by the Crown, Gabriel Johnston became governor of the colony and, as with Burrington and Everard, men from the Lower Cape Fear made overtures and expressed their concerns for the newly settled region.

By the time Johnston had arrived to assume the governorship, the Lower Cape Fear still occupied a precarious position. It had become known as a refuge for undesirable and lawless settlers, its leaders had participated in violent and fractious power struggles under Burrington and Everard, and the role of Crown government remained uncertain and contested. But the situation clearly showed the potential for improvement. The years of chaotic government had allowed Lower Cape Fear elites to organize and accumulate resources in the region without interference, so that, by Johnston's administration, they owned considerable wealth by North Carolina standards and now had to be taken seriously by the rest of the colony. At the same time, the process of settlement had continued steadily, and, even while the political disputes raged, New Hanover became a precinct and its inhabitants began to follow the same routines of law and authority that characterized other early modern British societies. In this vein, even Burrington could write, in 1733, that "Peace and good order subsist[ed] throughout the whole Province."[18] Finally, Crown rule may have involved encroachments by the metropolitan government and some jarring changes at first, but it also instilled a much more organized and energetic vision of leadership than had been present under North Carolina's proprietors. All in all, politics and government in the Lower Cape Fear had developed about as rapidly as could reasonably be expected in the first fifteen years of a new settlement, even with Burrington's difficult personality and the other problems associated with inclusion within the boundaries of North Carolina.

If Governor Johnston's arrival began a period of declining tension in North Carolina colonial politics, it also exacerbated some tensions within the Lower Cape Fear. The region's early inhabitants proved to be less homogenous than charter groups in some other colonial settlements, and they brought a variety of perspectives to the settlement process. In the early years, disagreements inevitably occurred and often remained unresolved. Governor Johnston tapped into two potential sources of conflict in the Lower Cape Fear almost immediately. He drew attention to ethnic differences by aligning himself very strongly with other Scottish people, and he reintroduced concerns about Crown rule by trying to enforce quitrent legislation to raise revenue. Johnston's Scottish interests never became as important in the Lower Cape Fear as they did farther up the river, and the Lower Cape Fear elite achieved a compromise with Johnston over quitrents and blank patents. Shortly thereafter, however, Johnston caused even more controversy by challenging the centrality of the Moores' town at Brunswick.

Consequently, during the first few years of Johnston's administration, the Lower Cape Fear divided into two factions, one revolving around Johnston, the other around the Moore family. James Murray, as a close ally of Johnston's, vented his rage against the Moores in a number of letters and commented that if Johnston did not succeed in improving the region he would "almost despair of it."[19] The principal focus of animosities was the rivalry between two towns, the Moores' Brunswick and Johnston's Newtown, later known as Wilmington. When Johnston's faction successfully got a bill to establish Wilmington past the Lower House of the North Carolina Assembly, a four-to-four tie in the colony's council was broken by William Smith, who claimed that his status as senior member entitled him to a second vote in such circumstances. When the Moore faction questioned the dubious legality of Smith's second vote, the pro-Wilmington councilors responded that the Moores and their followers demonstrated "such a violent, restless and arbitrary Spirit that We are sure it will not admit of a parallel in any Province of America from the first Settlement."[20] This heated competition between the interests of Brunswick and Wilmington expanded into economic activities, the recruitment of clergymen, and other areas.

Yet within several years of the official establishment of Wilmington, the issue was seldom mentioned. By the late 1740s, even the Moores must have recognized that Brunswick would quickly be eclipsed by Wilmington and that they would be better off to compromise. So, while Brunswick and Wilmington continued to represent different interests and served as a reminder of past political disputes, they no longer divided Lower Cape Fear politics in any significant way. Maurice Moore's death in 1743 also probably softened animosity toward the Moores.[21]

Thus, within twenty years of the first settlement in the region, the Lower Cape Fear leaders had begun to achieve a degree of consensus in some areas. A number of factors contributed to this increasingly cooperative attitude in the Lower Cape Fear. Increasing wealth in the region likely played a key role. A. Roger Ekirch, whose classic interpretation of eighteenth-century North Carolina politics emphasizes the link between economic underdevelopment and political instability, has claimed that the Lower Cape Fear leaders "in no customary sense . . . constitute[d] an indigenous elite, confident in its material circumstances." Yet a number of men in the Lower Cape Fear certainly constituted an economic elite and had reason to be confident in their material circumstances.[22] Customs data that will be much more fully discussed in chapter 6 reveals that about one-half of the wealth in overseas trade for the colony of North Carolina probably went through the Lower Cape Fear ports. Export profits in the region came much closer to those in the South Carolina lowcountry or in tidewater Virginia than to those usually associated with North Carolina. Lower Cape Fear officeholders and other elites possessed much greater wealth in slaves than did their peers in other regions of North Carolina.[23] Ekirch argued that these leaders' behavior could be attributed to an "intense concern with their precarious material status," but their focus on economic improvement in no way conflicted with or stood out from the economic ideology that characterized much of the early-modern Anglo-American world.[24]

Perhaps even more significant, after 1740 a relatively small and stable group of Lower Cape Fear elites maintained control over the region's major political offices. In the most important process for selecting local leaders, assembly elections, the voters of the Lower Cape Fear showed few signs of dissent. In eighty-one elections between the arrival of Governor Johnston and the signing of the Declaration of Independence, Lower Cape Fear voters returned incumbents more than 82 percent of the time. Thus, legislative turnover in the region for these years averaged a staggeringly low 17.3 percent, lower than in any mainland colony in British America during these years and much lower than in most. By contrast, some contemporaries believed that frequent legislative turnover could have unfortunate effects on North Carolina's government. In a letter to the Board of Trade in London, Governor Johnston complained that "there must be a new election every two years which is too short a time to settle a Country which has been so long in confusion." As a consequence, "men of sense who sincerely mean the Publick good are so much afraid of the next Elections that they are obliged to go in with the majority."[25] North Carolina as a whole averaged 47 percent legislative turnover during the colonial period.[26]

In the Lower Cape Fear, legislators could act with more security, knowing that their terms were likely to last much longer than a mere two years. Some assembly seats seemed particularly secure, like the one assembly seat given to the town of Wilmington in the late 1730s. Cornelius Harnett won every election to this seat between 1753 and 1776. John Ashe and several other Lower Cape Fear leaders enjoyed similar success with the voters. Even some instances of legislative turnover clearly do not suggest the presence of significant political dissent. When Maurice Moore died in office in 1743 and a new representative had to be sent to the assembly, New Hanover County voters elected his eldest son, George. Indeed, after the early 1740s, a Moore family member would sit in the assembly for the Lower Cape Fear, and he was generally accompanied by an Ashe and a Swann. As table 5.1 illustrates, no other region of North Carolina exhibited such a low rate of turnover in assembly elections.

The consistent reelection of assembly representatives could be interpreted in one of two ways. Either leaders suppressed dissent in some coercive manner or they managed local politics successfully enough to keep dissent to a minimum and established an effective consensus. Clearly, some elements of both explanations may apply. The accumulated economic and social capital of the Moore, Ashe, and Swann families could not have encouraged prospective opponents. Murray probably did not exaggerate in 1743 when he complained that "The Family carry everything before them . . . without Opposition & have much the Majority in [the] Council."[27] Yet, in the Lower Cape Fear, other evidence strongly suggests a less coercive and more consensual political climate. After all, early-modern English political ideology and rhetoric emphasized the relatively free and participatory nature of English politics, and eighteenth-century political bodies lacked the coercive mechanisms associated with modern nation-states.[28]

Equally important, even if incumbents did get reelected an unusually high percentage of the time, elections were contested. Indeed, some legislative turnover in the Lower Cape Fear occurred in most assembly elections; it merely stayed at a very minimal level. The only exception took place in 1746, when

TABLE 5.1 **Turnover Rates in North Carolina Assembly Elections, by Region, 1725–75**

Region	*Turnover Rate*
Lower Cape Fear	17.3%
Upper Cape Fear*	39.0%
Neuse-Pamlico†	39.7%
Backcountry‡	42.6%
Albemarle§	44.5%

Notes: Information in this table derives from the sources described for tables 4.1, 4.2, and 4.3. The placement of counties within regional categories for this table should be considered a necessarily imprecise and not definitive attempt to demarcate regional boundaries within North Carolina. My thanks to Chris Snow and Joe Smyth for their help in compiling the data for this table.

*This region includes the counties of Bladen, Cumberland, and Duplin.

†This region includes the counties of Beaufort, Carteret, Craven, Hyde, Onslow, and Pitt.

‡This region includes the counties of Anson, Bute, Chatham, Dobbs, Granville, Guilford, Johnston, Mecklenburg, Orange, Rowan, Surry, Tryon, and Wake.

§This region includes the counties of Bertie, Chowan, Currituck, Edgecombe, Halifax, Hertford, Northampton, Pasquotank, Perquimans, and Tyrrell.

only one of three incumbents gained reelection.[29] Even these low levels of turnover demonstrate the possibility for dissent. Moreover, on several occasions, elections appear to have been very openly and heatedly contested. In January 1735, when the provost marshal returned Job Howe as the winner of an assembly seat for New Hanover, Maurice Moore protested that the provost marshal was in error and that Moore had obtained more votes than Howe. After reviewing the election results, the assembly sided with Moore, but it seems clear that neither Moore nor Howe could claim uncontested control of the electorate.[30] Similarly, in a relatively close 1764 Brunswick County assembly election, John Paine protested his defeat by Thomas McGuire. McGuire had won the election by forty-seven votes to thirty-nine, but Paine objected specifically to three votes, claimed many voters were not freeholders and were ineligible to vote, and also asserted that McGuire himself was ineligible for election. In this case, the assembly could find no evidence to support Paine's claims and let the election stand.[31]

An even more startling view of contested elections comes from a petition regarding an election for the vestry of St. James Parish. Large numbers of New Hanover County voters complained that candidates in a 1764 election conveyed small and uncultivatable pieces of land before the election to increase the number of freeholders eligible to vote. The vestry was dissolved by the North Carolina assembly.[32] Such behavior might also account for John Paine's concerns about the Brunswick County assembly election in the same year. Not nearly enough is known about Lower Cape Fear vestry elections to determine whether or not this kind of competitive strategy was the norm or if vestry elections usually proved more harmonious. James Murray's personal distaste for the Moores and The Family certainly indicates the existence of significant political dissent. In 1739, he wrote that "our Elections of Assembly Men have been turned out in favour of Mr. Moore & friends for three Southern Counties but w[i]th much ado their Power [is] Declining Dayly." This appears to have been wishful thinking on Murray's part, however, because several years later he acknowledged that The Family was as powerful as ever.[33] A couple of years earlier, Murray had complained bitterly that Roger Moore interfered with all "designs for settling ye country" and that Moore wrote letters to discourage immigration from Ireland for fear that the new settlers would "be a weight against him in ye Assembly."[34] Some of this behavior may well have subverted the ideology of participatory politics, but that ideology remained important enough that Lower Cape Fear politicians took elections very seriously. In any case, evidence about assembly elections strongly suggests that political behavior could vary considerably from one constituency to another regardless of provincial political concerns. As John G. Kolp has noted, a similar pattern of local variation in assembly elections operated in colonial Virginia during the eighteenth century.[35]

Limited sources make it difficult to learn more about the context for these elections, but at least one source reveals much about the political culture of the colonial Lower Cape Fear. In the mid-1770s, as Lower Cape Fear leaders positioned themselves in relation to the emerging imperial crisis, an anonymous Lower Cape Fear writer, using the pen name Musquetoe, crafted two sets of brief caricatures of the most prominent men in the region.[36] Like most caricatures, many of these descriptions are far from flattering, and, in many cases, their biting tone suggests very real tensions and animosities within Lower Cape Fear politics. But, if Musquetoe does not describe a climate of perfect political harmony and consensus, his writings strongly indicate that in the Lower Cape even sincere and deeply felt political criticisms could best be expressed within the appropriate forms of polite society.[37] Most telling, Musquetoe apparently did not write for publication. In a disclaimer at the beginning of his caricatures, Musquetoe pointed out that the accompanying sketches were intended "to be viewed at the private apartments of the different proprietors, being too base for public inspection."[38] Along the same lines, when his first document caused excessively sharp criticism of some individuals and led to misguided claims about the author's identity, Musquetoe carefully apologized and corrected these misconceptions.

Musquetoe clearly wrote for a small, relatively articulate, and elite audience. The form of his caricatures suggests an effort to follow metropolitan literary trends, perhaps in imitation of Alexander Pope or others, in a way that would have been recognizable only to well-read Lower Cape Fear residents. Interestingly, Musquetoe articulated his ideas in very local terms. Not only did he use metaphors evocative of the warm, swampy environs of the Lower Cape Fear, and even of the region's naval stores industry, but he limited his characters to local individuals and he described them in ways that would have made them unrecognizable to readers outside the Lower Cape Fear.[39] Musquetoe, therefore, provides a limited but fascinating literary portrait of a relatively consensual regional political culture that was shaped by ideas of civility as well as by political interest.

The character of the Lower Cape Fear's political elite can also be elucidated by their role in the colonial government. Here again, the Lower Cape Fear's political leadership appears to have been increasingly secure and unified. Membership on the provincial council conferred the highest nonelective political office available to local leaders. Because these appointments were made by the Crown with the advice of the colonial governor, they provide a generally reliable indicator of the political influence of the recipients. Council and assembly memberships both indicate that leadership within the Lower Cape Fear was usually a prerequisite for leadership beyond the Lower Cape Fear. At both levels, those holding office owned many more slaves than did those householders who did not serve in some kind of office.[40] Of the twenty-four Lower Cape Fear residents who gained assembly seats, all but five had been justices of the peace in the New Hanover County Court. Of the thirty-seven council members, at least twenty-two had been justices of the peace.[41] Provincial council appointments, however, because their role in the executive branch of the colony made them more susceptible to influence from London, were not always as dependent on local stature. In at least two cases, individuals living in the Lower Cape Fear obtained seats on the council primarily through external influence. Governor Johnston secured council seats for his Scottish allies John Rutherford and James Murray. Similarly, Governor Arthur Dobbs's son received a seat on the council almost upon arrival in North Carolina. The provincial council, therefore, provided an arena of negotiation for imperial, colonial, and more local interests.

Even at the colonial level, the Lower Cape Fear political elite continued its ascent. In the two councils appointed during the 1720s by Burrington and Everard, Lower Cape Fear residents received only three of twenty-eight appointments. By 1734, when Burrington appointed the first royal council, eight of twenty-one councilors came from the Lower Cape Fear. Governor Johnston's administration constituted the real breakthrough for the Lower Cape Fear elite, however, as they gained fourteen out of seventeen council seats. With the exception of several months under James Hasell before the arrival of

Governor Josiah Martin in 1771, for the rest of the colonial period Lower Cape Fear residents occupied at least 60 percent of the council seats during every administration. The most impressive show of regional representation was in 1752 and early 1753, however, when Nathaniel Rice, the temporary governor and Old Town Creek resident, presided over a council of eight members, all of whom resided in the Lower Cape Fear.[42] Thus, after the first fifteen years of settlement, the Lower Cape Fear's political elite dominated the North Carolina colonial council and exerted a level of influence far out of proportion to the region's share of North Carolina's population.

The transformed stature of the Lower Cape Fear's political leaders can also be discerned from the letters of the colony's governors. In 1732, Governor Burrington complained that John Baptista Ashe was "unworthy of sitting in the Council of this Province" and that Cornelius Harnett Sr. "is now known to have traded with other men's goods, nor [is he] worth anything, and [he is] reduced to Keep a Publick House."[43] By the time of Governor Dobbs's administration in the 1750s, the Lower Cape Fear leadership commanded respect. Maurice Moore Jr. gained Dobbs's nomination for the council as "a young gentleman of distinguished character and very good fortune at Cape Fear."[44] He also found George Moore to be a good candidate because "he has a great fortune and good allowances."[45] In the 1770s, Governor Martin of North Carolina held the local leaders in low esteem because they held a differing view about the imperial relationship, but his writing still acknowledged the political influence and popularity of Lewis DeRosset and other Lower Cape Fear leaders.[46] After fifty years of settlement, politicians in the Lower Cape Fear could even weigh their own regional political authority against the favor of metropolitan authorities. Political development and participation in the Lower Cape Fear had begun to pay dividends.

Political participation in the provincial assembly and council may have been the most ostentatious display of authority in North Carolina government, but, for most residents of the Lower Cape Fear, it must have seemed far more distant and less important than the exercise of local power in the county court. The function of local authority has been neglected by scholars studying the Carolinas, and, in the case of North Carolina, this neglect has led to the widespread assumption that fractious provincial politics must coincide with disorder within county governments.[47] It would be difficult, however, to overestimate the importance of the ideology of legal authority in Anglo-American societies. Because early-modern elites often lacked the coercive power to compel obedience, they often relied on widespread acceptance of and participation in court systems to legitimate and reinforce their authority.[48] As the inhabitants of the region tried to resolve disputes and achieve some level of mutual understanding, law played a crucial role in Lower Cape Fear society. Indeed, North Carolina county courts helped to shape settlers' cultures and views of the world.

County courts performed a vast array of useful functions that maintained order and assisted in the development of local social relations. Of course, these functions included criminal and civil actions, which helped to resolve disputes, stabilize property relations, and maintain public order. But North Carolina county courts, like those in the Chesapeake and elsewhere, also took responsibility for probating estates and keeping records; formalizing sales and deeds; supervising the treatment of orphans, apprentices, servants, and slaves; and administering public buildings, roads, county, finance, and commerce. As Richard Bushman has noted in a perceptive recent essay, colonial North Carolina courts "made farms from texts" and constituted "the dominant influences in the formation of the farmer as a political subject."[49]

Few records exist from the New Hanover County Court for the years before 1750, and the early stage of settlement may have combined with political disputes to prevent much agreement about the law. Some scattered contemporary references certainly suggest discontent over legal matters in the Lower Cape Fear. George Burrington, in his many complaints about North Carolina leaders, wrote that, when he arrived in North Carolina, the justices of the peace "were mostly illiterate persons, & of no Authority."[50] Although Burrington claimed to have resolved these problems, several years later an Anglican missionary described the Lower Cape Fear as a "lawless place."[51] As late as 1747, another missionary discouraged litigation because "a lawsuit here is so tedious and expensive."[52] Perhaps because of these early years, Hugh Finlay reported in the 1770s that in South Carolina the Lower Cape Fear was reputed to have no laws.[53]

It seems likely, however, that as the region's population grew and local institutions were established, the situation improved rapidly. As early as 1731, Hugh Meredith wrote, "They have now at Brunswick Quarterly courts of Common Pleas and Officers of the peace and begin to fall into something like a regular Common-Weal."[54] Moreover, as Clarence Ver Steeg has pointed out, nothing indicates that North Carolina's political tribulations interfered with the function of its legal system.[55] To some degree, all Anglo-American colonies necessarily lacked the legal training and sophistication that could be found in London. It is not surprising, therefore, that metropolitan officials lamented the neglect of procedural details and niceties in local North Carolina courts. But, if county officers lacked impressive credentials and litigation proved to be inefficient during the first fifteen years of settlement, Lower Cape Fear residents at least could grow accustomed to having recourse to English legal customs, including the ability to bring suit, to have trials by jury, and the recognition of at least the most significant common law precedents. Most important, civil matters, which made up the vast majority court activity in most Anglo-American societies, could be addressed.[56]

Evidence from New Hanover County Court dockets between 1750 and 1775 clearly indicates widespread awareness and use of civil law in the Lower

TABLE 5.2 **Participation in New Hanover County Civil Suits, 1750–75**

	No. of Suits	*No. of Litigants*	*% of Litigants*
All heads of households	1,035	397	38.4
1755 tax list	260	140	53.8
1763 tax list	404	224	55.4
1767 tax list	338	182	53.7

Note: Lower Cape Fear computer biographical files. Extant Lower Cape Fear tax lists are available for the years 1755, 1762, 1763, 1765 (incomplete), and 1767 for New Hanover County, and for 1769 and 1772 for Brunswick County. All these lists are available in the North Carolina Department of Archives and History, Raleigh.

Cape Fear during the late colonial period.[57] Information exists on the outcome of 1,771 civil cases from the county court (see table 5.2).[58] First, this data reveals that a surprisingly high percentage of Lower Cape Fear residents participated in civil litigation. Of 1,035 heads of households that can be identified from tax lists, at least 397 took part in civil suits in the New Hanover County Court. In other words, more than one in three households experienced involvement in a legal dispute. These numbers are probably also quite deflated by the total lack of data on Brunswick County Court cases after the counties were divided in 1764. Sampling three exclusively New Hanover county tax lists—for the years 1755, 1763, and 1767—indicates that between 53 and 56 percent of New Hanover county households became involved in civil litigation at least once in the New Hanover County Court. Thus, most Lower Cape Fear residents must have had some close contact with civil suits. This participation extended beyond merely being sued: almost as many different litigants brought suit as were sued.[59]

There does not appear to have been much of a difference in the economic status of plaintiffs and defendants.[60] The widespread use of law in dealing with local disputes strongly indicates that it provided the Lower Cape Fear with a generally accepted and often-used means for maintaining social consensus. Of course, it also indicates that Lower Cape Fear residents must have had quite a few disputes to bring suit so frequently, but, in economically and culturally diverse societies like those of eighteenth-century America, disagreements could not have been uncommon, and it thus was especially important that individuals accepted legal procedures instead of resorting to violent conflict. While all legal systems sometimes use coercive measures, considerable incentives encouraged lawmakers in early modern governments to try to resolve disputes amicably whenever possible. William M. Offutt's innovative study of law and dispute resolution in the Delaware River Valley demonstrates that law could serve as a powerful mechanism for maintaining order and forging social consensus in colonial British America.[61] When colonists chose to use legal means to resolve

TABLE 5.3 **Outcomes of Civil Cases in New Hanover County Court, 1750–75**

Outcome	*No. of Cases*	*% of Cases*
Settled	642	36
Uncontested	332	19
Contested	797	45

Note: Lower Cape Fear computer biographical files.

their disputes, they reinforced the legitimacy of the law. Indeed, the degree to which litigants accepted the likely outcome of a lawsuit and chose to settle or plead no contest reflected the power of consensus or level of agreement within the society about the rule of law. By contrast, strongly contested cases indicated that, while litigants recognized the value of bringing disagreements into court, they disagreed about which principles resulted in the most appropriate and equitable legal outcomes. As Offutt has expressed it, "Where consensus exists, cases are low-intensity, predictable, and routinely dispatched; without consensus, cases more often involved high-intensity, in-court conflict, and unpredictable results."[62]

As table 5.3 illustrates, most New Hanover County litigants did not contest their civil disputes in court. Out of all the civil suits, 974 (55 percent) involved situations in which litigants chose not to pursue their cases into open conflict in a courtroom. Most of these cases (642, or 36 percent) could be settled without any formal legal damages whatsoever.[63] These cases probably represent only a small proportion of all the disputes in the Lower Cape Fear that could be handled through extralegal means, but the fact that individuals were willing to bring them before the court at all suggests their serious nature. In another 332 cases (19 percent) the suits went uncontested, indicating that the defendant did not choose to challenge the predictable and commonly accepted legal outcome.[64]

The remaining 797 cases (45 percent) resulted in legal contests.[65] Legal contests, therefore, occurred more frequently in the Lower Cape Fear than in the Delaware River Valley, where only about 24 percent of all civil cases resulted in this kind of resolution.[66] But the Quaker legal system of the Delaware Valley has been praised for its unusual degree of consensus, while the Lower Cape Fear, like the rest of colonial North Carolina, has been considered a hotbed of tension and discord. In the end, even from the perspective of the Lower Cape Fear, civil law muted a considerable amount of conflict: contested cases did not prove to be the norm. Moreover, even contested cases could end a dispute, if both parties respected the judgment of the court.[67]

Also, few litigants appear to have challenged decisions by appealing to a higher court. While the docket records may be incomplete, a mere 26 cases (fewer than 2 percent) appear to have involved any kind of appeal. Comparing case lists from the court of appeal one tier above the county court, the Wilmington District Superior Court, confirms that only rarely did cases receive an appellate hearing. Fewer than 4 percent, or 4 out of 123, of the superior court cases between 1760 and 1765 also appeared in the New Hanover County Court records.[68] The low percentage of appeals must reflect some level of satisfaction with county court decisions, though some motions for appeal could have been denied. The limited importance of appeals also means that, for most litigants in the Lower Cape Fear, the law functioned on a relatively local level. Decisions were made almost entirely by Lower Cape Fear judges, juries, and litigants.

Unfortunately, the county court docket records have significant limitations. Perhaps most important, in most cases the dockets reveal that some kind of verdict was reached without specifying whether the verdict had been for the plaintiff or defendant. Consequently, it is impossible to assess the degrees of success for various litigants. Also, due to a lack of technical legal expertise, the court officers rarely recorded the appropriate legal actions used in each case, listing almost all of them under "case," an unspecific form of action.[69] Because of the limited use of different legal actions, combined with the lack of depositions or other legal records, it is difficult to ascertain why most suits took place.

The gaps in information about county court cases can be filled with information from the Wilmington Superior Court, however. In a sample of years from the Lower Cape Fear's superior court, more than 95 percent (45 of 46 cases) completed cases went in favor of the plaintiff.[70] For Lower Cape Fear plaintiffs in the superior court, therefore, successful outcomes proved to be even more likely and predictable than in the Delaware River Valley.[71] While it is certainly possible that plaintiffs' success rates did not reach such high levels in the county court or, in other years, even in the superior court, these numbers provide strong evidence of the predictability of and, by extension, consensus about procedures and outcomes in Lower Cape Fear civil litigation.[72]

Superior Court case records are also complete enough to indicate the kinds of civil suits brought before the Lower Cape Fear bar. One particular type of action, "assumpsit," appeared in superior court cases most of the time. Assumpsit cases pertained to property rights in the fulfillment of contracts. They accounted for more than 61 percent (29 of 47 cases) of Wilmington Superior Court civil suits. As table 5.4 indicates, assumpsit cases also appear to have occurred more frequently than any other kind of case in the county court, though records there provide a less complete sample. In the county court, debt occurred next most often. No other type of action, aside from the generic action on the case, appeared with any significant degree of consistency in the Lower Cape Fear county court dockets.

The frequency of assumpsit and debt cases reveals the intensely property-oriented nature of civil litigation in these courts. Other suits, such as slander and

TABLE 5.4 **Types of Civil Suits in New Hanover County Court, 1750–75**

Action	*No. of cases*
Assumpsit	89
Debt	68
Trover	9
Trespass	3
Assault	3
Slander	2

Note: Lower Cape Fear computer biographical files.

assault cases, that had no real bearing on property, appear to have been quite rare. Moreover, the prevalence of contract and debt-related litigation conforms to patterns for civil suits in other parts of colonial British America. It also helps to explain the high rate of success for plaintiffs. In these cases, plaintiffs merely had to demonstrate that the defendant had not met an obligation; given sufficient plaintiff records, there was little defendants could do to contest the case.[73] Murray's letters reveal the importance of civil litigation for the collection of debt. Murray constantly found himself using legal means to manage business transactions, to coax reluctant debtors into payment, and to protect property ownership. He acknowledged that law suits provided "a tedious way in getting in one's debts," tried to make use of opportunities for arbitration, and expressed satisfaction with debtors who were "willing to make Satisfaction without Standing trial at law."[74]

In the Lower Cape Fear county courts, which could hear only cases with relatively little at stake, small-debt and property cases most likely became even more common and easily dispatched.[75] On the other hand, larger sums of money provided the most important incentive for Lower Cape Fear residents to bring their case before the superior court instead of the county court. Between 1760 and 1765, almost one-half the civil suits in the superior court took place between two residents of the New Hanover and Brunswick Counties.[76] An additional one-third or so of the cases involved suits between Lower Cape Fear residents and individuals who could not be identified as Lower Cape Fear residents.[77] Such cases probably made up a significant part of the superior court's business because it had jurisdiction over cases that crossed county jurisdictions. Indeed, in Wilmington, the superior court must have played a key role in resolving economic disputes between all those parties making use of the Lower Cape Fear's port facilities.

The activity of the Wilmington Superior Court remained limited to a small segment of Lower Cape Fear society, however. Considerably fewer litigants participated in superior court suits than in county court suits; the court had far fewer administrative responsibilities; and not all of the courts' officers resided in or identified with the Lower Cape Fear. The superior court had jurisdiction over crimes that were deemed too serious for the county courts, but between 1760 and 1765 the court prosecuted only twenty-six Lower Cape Fear residents for crimes. Of course, criminal prosecutions could receive a great deal of attention and have a more qualitative than quantitative influence on a society. Still, a significant proportion of criminal prosecutions took place in county courts, most notably for crimes involving trespass, assault, and crimes against moral standards. Because women were more likely to be prosecuted for offenses within county court jurisdiction, most female criminals would have been prosecuted by the more local court. Crimes handled by county courts were also more likely to result in convictions.[78]

What we know about criminal court cases in the Lower Cape Fear, and in colonial North Carolina in general, suggests an increasingly sophisticated and effective system of criminal justice.[79] But the low percentage of the region's residents involved in criminal prosecutions underscores the fact that most transgressions in early-modern colonial societies could usually be handled more efficiently through extralegal means. Moreover, while court cases tell us much about dispute resolution and social order, most inhabitants of the Lower Cape Fear had no access whatsoever to the much-vaunted legal rights of free English subjects. Slaves and other dependents would have to find their own ways to resolve disputes. For free residents of the Lower Cape Fear, however, the law played a powerful role in resolving disputes within the region and in making outside authority superfluous for most settlers.

In the Lower Cape Fear, unlike in virtually all other locales within North Carolina, the population and labor force consisted primarily of slaves, and the region's European American residents had to rely on slaves for material prosperity and on unity and coercion to save themselves from violent revolt. Indeed, the presence of such large numbers of slaves gave Lower Cape Fear European Americans compelling reasons to overlook differences among themselves.[80] Whatever disputes may have existed within provincial politics or other elite arenas of activity, slavery on the Lower Cape Fear's plantations made the exercise of authority a constant concern and an important part of life.

An oppressive institution like chattel slavery required considerable levels of coercion that exceeded anything conceived of within the normal confines of English legal culture. European American slave owners implemented this coercion themselves, often on their own plantations and usually without reference to formal law or government. North Carolina society, like other colonial British societies, recognized slave owners' power to exert force over slaves and other dependents according to a hierarchical view of society that emphasized their role as patriarchs. But even with this rhetoric of patriarchal ideology, constructions of race also enabled European Americans to rationalize enormous physical brutality. Slaves received brutal and dehumanizing treatment in all New

World slave societies, but the character and extent of that treatment varied considerably with regional circumstances.[81]

Slave owners in the colonial Lower Cape Fear left little record of the coercion they used to maintain slavery on their plantations, but they did extend the logic of slave societies into the courtroom, where they modified common law practices to exert authority over their slaves. As in other British American colonies, they did this partly through legislation, but they also regulated the conduct of slaves through special slave courts. Limited extant records reveal that slaves before North Carolina slave courts received guilty sentences 93 percent of the time and that verdicts, though requiring only a simple majority, were almost always unanimous.[82] Slave executions in the Lower Cape Fear appear to have been more disproportionately severe than in other parts of North Carolina, where it may have been less imperative to make an example of rebellious slaves. Perhaps the most tortuous slave execution in colonial North Carolina was meted out in New Hanover County to a slave named Will, who was hanged alive in a gibbet and left to die.[83] This case may have been unique in colonial North Carolina, but burning slaves alive, castrating, and hanging seem to have been fairly common punishments. Moreover, limited records indicate that the most grisly forms of punishment took place more often in the Lower Cape Fear than in other parts of North Carolina.[84]

Public efforts to control slaves did not end with occasional executions. Physical force could be used to punish lesser crimes, too, and New Hanover County had such difficulty keeping slave criminals in the jails that the justices of the peace ordered a special cage to hold slaves, which, significantly, they placed next to the pillory.[85] To protect their property and to assuage anxieties about revolt, Lower Cape Fear leaders also attempted to maintain a consensus about the treatment of slaves. To this end, they removed two prominent justices of the peace, John Swann and Jehu Davis, because they refused to act in a slave trial.[86] Perhaps not surprisingly, given the possible forms of punishment, the Lower Cape Fear seems to have had a recurring pattern of slaves who drowned themselves to avoid being brought to justice.[87]

Despite demographic circumstances that must have made fear a tangible part of the master/slave relationship for both parties, no large-scale slave revolt took place in the colonial Lower Cape Fear. Yet at least one incident demonstrates the real potential for violent resistance in the region. In 1767, the New Hanover County Court was "inform'd that upwards of Twenty run away Slaves in abody Arm'd, and are now in this County." The court responded with alacrity and ordered the sheriff to "raise the power of the County not to be less then Thirty Men well Arm'd, to go in pursuit of the said run away Slaves." They also empowered the sheriff to "Shoot Kill & destroy all such of the said run away Slaves as shall not Surrender themselves." Remarkably, no other reference sheds light on this event. The county court minutes make no further mention of these slaves, and no other contemporary source comments on any kind of revolt.[88] Presumably the slaves escaped Lower Cape Fear authority without a confrontation. But, given the limited information about this event, it is easy to imagine that similar moments of open and active resistance escaped the historical records altogether and occurred with relative frequency in the Lower Cape Fear. No matter how infrequently they might have occurred, such events gave free Lower Cape Fear residents a powerful incentive to overcome the internal divisions that supposedly characterized all of colonial North Carolina.

Surviving evidence about escaped slaves also underscores the tense, unruly, and often violent character of slavery in the Lower Cape Fear region.[89] Newspapers from North and South Carolina before 1790 provide information about nineteen slaves whose owners published advertisements about their flight.[90] In many ways, these slaves fit the profile of runaway slaves that other scholars have already described in their research in colonial newspapers in Virginia and the Carolinas. For example, they seem to have been a typical group of runaways in terms of age and in the representation of skilled slaves and females. But numbers conceal the human anxieties that persuaded these individuals to flee their bondage on Lower Cape Fear plantations.

Lower Cape Fear slaves had ample reason to run from their oppressors. Some fled to try to preserve familial connections, and at least three of the nineteen slaves ran to places where they could be together with their spouses. Six more slaves may have fled for similar reasons because they had recently been sold to new locations. Alternatively, some of these slaves may have found their new owners more brutal, or somehow more difficult to tolerate, prompting an attempted escape from their new living conditions. Samuel Ashe's slave Mingo may have had a variety of reasons for running or he may have established a pattern; whatever his motives, he escaped repeatedly.[91]

All of these forms of behavior heightened white anxieties about slaves. Perhaps as a consequence of fears about what might happen if colonists failed to present a unified front against unruly slaves, one slave owner placed an ad suggesting that three of his slaves had been "decoyed" away by an unscrupulous overseer.[92] Henry Young's ad for his escaped slave Quamino may be the most telling. Quamino, a recently imported African, ran away with "a Collar about his Neck with two Prongs marked g p, and an Iron on each Leg."[93] Along similar lines, Robert Rowan noted that his slave Prince was "marked with the small-pox and whip."[94] As an immigrant from the West Indies and one of many Lower Cape Fear residents who came from locales with larger plantation systems, Rowan probably recognized whipping and other forms of physical coercion as a common and socially acceptable aspect of slavery. Quamino and Prince surely viewed the situation differently.

Regardless of one's perspective, these examples underscore the relationship between the scale of a plantation regime and the level of violence needed to sustain it.[95] Significantly, Lower Cape Fear slaves seem to have been more likely to flee larger plantations. Ten of the Lower Cape Fear runaways fled slave owners who, according to tax lists, owned at least twenty slaves; only three runaway slaves can be traced to smaller slaveholdings. Such a group of runaways would be far less likely anywhere else in colonial North Carolina, where slaveholdings of this size were much rarer. Even more surprising, three of the slaves escaped from slave owners who owned more than a hundred slaves. Holdings of this size were almost unique to the Lower Cape Fear region of the colony and only few men in the region had holdings of this size.[96] Such large numbers of slaves changed the dynamics of resistance among Lower Cape Fear slaves and made the region's slave owners acutely aware of the need for unity and orderliness.

The character of slave work in the Lower Cape Fear probably also contributed to European American concerns about slave resistance. The export economy of the Lower Cape Fear depended heavily on forest products, including tar, lumber, turpentine, and pitch.[97] Gathering wood for tar kilns, felling trees for lumber, and boxing trees for turpentine all had important common features. All of these activities required slaves to spread out in the forests in isolation or in relatively small groups for long periods of time and to do task work, rather work than in gangs. Given the number of trees required to produce the region's exports, the combination of forest industries would have taken up more of the slaves' time than any other form of labor. The expanses of forest made supervision unusually difficult and provided slaves with a significant degree of autonomy that would not have been available in most agricultural work. Consequently, Lower Cape Fear plantation owners, who exported forest products on a larger scale than did any other group of slave owners in Colonial British America, must have been especially concerned about the possibilities for slave resistance.[98]

In the Lower Cape Fear region as in other places in colonial British North America, the American Revolution heightened fears about slave resistance and brought long-standing tensions to the surface. In July 1775, colonists in another part of eastern North Carolina found evidence of a widespread slave conspiracy involving slaves in three counties. Whether the belief in such a threat was the product of hysteria remains difficult to determine, but European American North Carolinians took it seriously, jailing more than forty slaves.[99] A month later, the Wilmington Safety Committee showed considerable concern over an African American man selling gunpowder in the town.[100] In 1781, the British occupation of Wilmington further complicated slave owners' attempts to maintain authority over their slaves. Slaves defected from their owners throughout the war, but, with the arrival of the British, escape became considerably easier. Rumors about British support for a slave insurrection spread. The British commander was rumored to have the support of five hundred newly liberated slaves, and many more no doubt fled to escape slavery for their own benefit.[101]

The disorder of the Revolutionary War finally enabled some slaves to escape bondage, and in doing so they demonstrated the ways that dissension among the European American population could make the nightmare of slave resistance a reality for Lower Cape Fear slave owners.[102]

Janet Schaw's account of her visit to the Lower Cape Fear region on the eve of the American Revolution is another revealing source: her writings show how the deep-seated fears of a slave insurrection underscored a need for unity among Lower Cape Fear elites. When Schaw visited Wilmington in 1775, she discovered that "an insurrection was expected hourly"; indeed, she "found the whole town in an uproar." Wilmington's slave owners had clearly imagined the consequences of this insurrection because Schaw remarks that they believed the British had issued a proclamation "ordering the tories to murder the whigs, and promising every Negro that would murder his Master and family that he should have his Master's plantation." In the face of such a threat, Lower Cape Fear leaders had taken a number of precautions, such as attempting to disarm their slaves, conducting searches, and imposing a curfew. After a "great number" of slaves were discovered in the nearby woods at night, one slave, apparently going to meet a female slave after sundown, was shot.

Despite her Tory sympathies and status as a visitor, Schaw placed credence in these threats of violence from slaves. Her anxieties about slaves prevented her from traveling alone in the region at times and contributed to her sleeplessness. She hypothesized that the slaves would revolt. Even more significantly, Schaw noted that the slaves themselves seemed to believe some of the rumors of British support for a slave insurrection. This, in itself, may have made violent resistance more likely, and Schaw wrote that "'Tis ten to one they may try the experiment, and in that case friends and foes will all be one."[103] As Schaw recognized, even the American Revolution itself could not ultimately disrupt racial solidarity in a slave society like that of the Lower Cape Fear. Less tumultuous differences between Lower Cape Fear settlers could be transcended even more easily in the interest of the region's plantation system.

Thus, by the late colonial period, Lower Cape Fear leaders had quieted many political disputes, elevated themselves to a secure position in local and colonial politics, achieved a relatively high degree of consensus about the region's legal system, and implemented a large-scale system of plantation slavery. This did not completely change their relationship to the rest of North Carolina, however. Regional animosities persisted and, in some ways, increased as the Lower Cape Fear developed politically and economically.

Indeed, North Carolina's regional tensions could not be resolved by changes within the Lower Cape Fear alone. Before 1700, North Carolina had a small population concentrated near Albemarle Sound that seems to have shared a common geographic identity and showed few signs of conflict between different areas. In the early eighteenth century, though, Cary's Rebellion had a disruptive effect on North Carolina government. While scholars have often portrayed the rebellion as a struggle over Quaker influence, there is considerable evidence to suggest that it occurred primarily because of differences between the older Albemarle settlements and the newly settled Bath area.[104] By the late 1760s, the even more recently settled North Carolina backcountry became the site of the North Carolina Regulator movement, which led to the most widespread violent protests anywhere in colonial British America before the American Revolution. While many scholars have studied the Regulator movement and offered different explanations for it, the regional character of the movement, which John Spencer Bassett described more than one hundred years ago, remains a prominent part of any analysis of the Regulation.[105] The Lower Cape Fear was one of several very different regions within the jurisdiction of North Carolina, and these regions often found their various interests to be in conflict.

Given these persistent regional tensions, Lower Cape Fear leaders continued to struggle for their own interests in North Carolina politics throughout the colonial period. In the first stage of this process, they not only sought leadership positions in colonial government, as discussed above, but they also extended the institutional components of North Carolina government into the Lower Cape Fear. Next, they sought to remedy an inequitable system of assembly representation that favored the Albemarle counties. Finally, the Lower Cape Fear elite showed its security and aspirations by vying to become the location of North Carolina's capital. All of these tactics worked to a degree, but the resolution of North Carolina's regional problems would await a much more powerful transformation.

The integration of the Lower Cape Fear into North Carolina government formally began with the establishment of New Hanover Precinct.[106] Precincts soon became counties, and this legislation enabled the crucial proceedings of the county court and other normal routines of local government. Prior to this time, fundamental institutional functions fell under the control of the colony's General Court.[107] After this initial measure, however, attempts to establish additional counties in the Lower Cape Fear caused considerable controversy. Most notably, politicians from northern North Carolina resisted the establishment of new counties in the south because such legislation would give the Lower Cape Fear interests additional seats in the assembly.[108] Moreover, North Carolina officials disagreed over the criteria for separate county status. Northern county residents cited the Lower Cape Fear region's sparse settlement and relatively small European American population in their argument against more counties. Lower Cape Fear residents, on the other hand, could point to their significant property interests, the additional population of slaves, and the difficulty of maintaining local government over large distances.[109] To make matters more complicated, some Lower Cape Fear residents opposed the formation of new counties because they felt that having the new political status did not justify the added expense and difficulty involved in creating new jurisdictions.[110] As a consequence, it took thirty years before a second Lower Cape Fear county, Brunswick, could be carved out of New Hanover. In the meantime, Lower Cape Fear leaders enhanced their position in colonial politics in ways that did not require the creation of new political units.

Indeed, during the 1740s the central issue in the distribution of power in North Carolina politics revolved around the number of representatives for each county, rather than the number of counties represented. Since the beginning of settlement in North Carolina, the Albemarle counties each had five representatives in the assembly, but new colonies, as they were created, generally received only two seats. Even with the dramatic expansion of settlement in the colony, in the late 1740s six northern counties maintained a majority in the assembly over the other ten counties to the south and west. Governor Johnston had allied himself with the Lower Cape Fear faction after the quitrent controversy had subsided and, to this end, he began calling the assembly into session in Wilmington, where distance made Albemarle's majority of representatives less likely to attend. In what appears to have been a planned boycott, not one member from the six Albemarle counties attended the assembly in 1746, and the southern representatives immediately passed legislation to equalize the inequitable representation system.[111] Astounded northern representatives questioned the legitimacy of this new legislation through authorities in London and resolved to continue boycotting the assembly. The consequences of this regional division grew over several years, as northern residents felt that their lack of participation in the assembly absolved them of obedience to provincial authority and everyone waited for a decision from the metropolis.

The rift began to heal after 1754, with the death of Johnston, new rulings from London, the arrival of Arthur Dobbs to replace him as governor, and a variety of other external forces that encouraged provincial cohesion. Ultimately, London ruled that the Albemarle counties could maintain their disproportionate representation, but that additional counties would be formed as settlement expanded to help level off regional differences in representation. At least one scholar has argued that this regional split in North Carolina between 1746 and 1754 resulted in deeper divisions than those experienced by any other Anglo-American colony in the early and mid-eighteenth century.[112] Dobbs lamented that "upon entering this Province; I found it had been divided into Parties, and in a very low state; and one half of the Province not obeying the laws made by the other, nor attending their Assemblies, refusing to pay the taxes which the Assembly raised."[113] But the crisis also demonstrated the Lower Cape Fear's emergence as a distinct political region and, despite the failure to achieve parity in assembly representation, indicated a clear shift in power to the southern part of North Carolina.

As the third key component of the Lower Cape Fear's integration and ascent in North Carolina politics, the region's leaders aspired to establish a new seat of provincial government in the region. Governor Johnston instigated a controversy over North Carolina's seat of government because he championed the cause of Wilmington. Johnston genuinely believed the establishment of a new capital on the Cape Fear would prove beneficial to the colony. Johnston complained of all the problems in North Carolina "entirely oweing to the want of a Town near the centre of the Country where all the Offices ought to be kept." While Wilmington certainly was not centrally located from the perspective of Albemarle, Johnston did believe it was "the most commodious in every respect, of any situation in the Province." Because of these considerations, Johnston clearly planned to move the capital of the province to Wilmington by 1740 and wrote, "In a year or two I hope to get all Publick Business done there. But this must be done by Degrees."[114] Apparently Johnston did not anticipate the intense regional animosity that followed his alliance with the Lower Cape Fear leaders over assembly representation and other matters. The location of the capital became a highly contested issue related to regional identity and politics. Moreover, the lack of an established location for the provincial government caused perennial procedural difficulties.[115] Before Johnston finally moved the government to Wilmington, the assembly had moved between Bath, Edenton, New Bern, and Wilmington.

As a compromise, the southern faction had committed themselves to New Bern as their preferred site for the capital by 1746, and when Dobbs arrived to replace Johnston and alleviate the regional controversy, the matter appeared to be resolved. Shortly thereafter, however, Lower Cape Fear residents began maneuvering to move the political center of the colony still farther south, to Wilmington. When Governor Dobbs expressed discontent with his expensive and poorly located home in New Bern, he was persuaded to move by "the Gentlemen upon Cape Fear having offered me a new convenient house . . . with convenient land to reside in there in a healthy dry open situation." Dobbs recognized the implications of his decision and promised to hold assemblies alternately at Edenton and Wilmington because "This however alarmed the Gentlemen in the north lest hereafter the seat of Government might be fixed at Cape Fear."[116]

Gradually, Dobbs began holding assemblies more frequently in Wilmington, which caused "great murmurings and Complaints among the people."[117] Dobbs's successor, William Tryon, quickly recognized the delicacy involved in where he made his place of residence and, when he first became governor, maintained three homes in different parts of the colony in order to placate the regional factions.[118] Ultimately, Tryon put an end to the debate by ordering the building of an opulent new gubernatorial mansion at New Bern and, after 1765, the provincial capital remained there. But on the very eve of the Revolution, animosities persisted between Wilmington and New Bern residents because of the location of the government.[119] Wilmington's increasing viability as a potential center for North Carolina politics provided yet another index of the burgeoning political influence and maturity of the Lower Cape Fear. The fact that the Lower Cape Fear leadership had to compromise on the seat of government only testified to the continually unpredictable and contested character of North Carolina's provincial politics.

North Carolina politicians also did not always negotiate their position solely between provincial and local authorities. North Carolina's political structure before 1775, like that of all the thirteen colonies that would become the United States, remained highly susceptible to British influence until the Revolution. As eager as politicians might have been to gain favor with their local constituencies, they also knew that metropolitan whims could gain them more desirable offices or overturn their most cherished legislative achievements. But the imperial relationship never became uncomplicated or predetermined. It continually changed as colonists gradually and subtly challenged the extent of metropolitan authority. Moreover, distance insured that some British assertions of authority remained just that.

North Carolinians had articulated opposition to metropolitan authority in a variety of forms for generations. Indeed, the residents of the Lower Cape Fear and other colonists did not see any contradiction between local rights and imperial authority. In 1732, Nathaniel Rice and John Baptista Ashe defended themselves from accusations by Governor Burrington by arguing that they acted in keeping with "our most gracious King as He is tender of his Prerogatives (which tend always to his peoples good) so is he of the rights and privileges of his subjects."[120] North Carolinians constantly echoed this refrain in their disputes with royal governors and other London authorities who tried to assert metropolitan authority and encroach upon local and representative authority. At the same time, this antiprerogative rhetoric proved useful in North Carolina politics as both parties tried to taint the other with the stigma of arbitrary authority. By the 1760s, then, Lower Cape Fear residents probably distrusted authoritarian interference from the metropolis as much as they worried about competing regional factions.

The Stamp Act Crisis laid bare all of these concerns about distant metropolitan authorities. News of the Stamp Act spread like wildfire through the colonies, leaving outraged colonists with various and growing expressions of political protest in its wake. The Stamp Act became the catalyst in an Anglo-American imperial crisis that lasted over a decade and resulted in the American Revolution. For a variety of reasons, North Carolina's resistance to the Stamp Act and to metropolitan authority in the years afterward centered around the Lower Cape Fear. The location of the colony's most important port in the Lower Cape Fear played a crucial role because the stamps arrived first in the main ports and gave the colonists their first opportunity for confrontation. Later, the maritime character of metropolitan punitive measures and taxation, as well as of colonial nonimportation and other resistance strategies, continued to keep the Lower Cape Fear more focused on the imperial crisis than any other region of North Carolina. Governor Tryon's residence on the Lower Cape Fear during the Stamp Act crisis also contributed to the centralization of resistance. Colonists faced off with stamp distributors and British officers in the streets of Wilmington and demonstrated a willingness to oppose British authority with violent force under some conditions. At one point, more than five hundred armed colonists gathered in Wilmington.[121]

The relatively secure position of the Lower Cape Fear elite was another factor that gave them confidence about resisting imperial authority. Evidence strongly suggests that the Stamp Act and other sources of conflict with the metropolis did not result in new leadership in the region. If anything, it probably solidified the popularity of local leaders by identifying them with a popular cause. Of course, some Lower Cape Fear leaders did pull away from colonial resistance and remain loyal to the Crown. These men abdicated their positions of leadership and, in many cases, left the region. Upper Cape Fear loyalists, allied with some predominantly Scottish interests in the Lower Cape Fear, even mounted armed opposition to the revolutionary forces before being crushed at the Battle of Moore's Creek Bridge. However, a sample of individuals chosen, up to 1776, to serve as members of the Lower Cape Fear Safety Committee or as representatives at the revolutionary provincial congress reveals a significant degree of continuity in Lower Cape Fear leadership. Of the seventeen officeholders, most had already been justices of the peace, more than one-third had been elected to North Carolina's assembly, and three had been members of the provincial council. Only four of the seventeen had not before held office in the Lower Cape Fear.[122]

Few detailed texts reveal how North Carolinians viewed their political relationship with Britain during these years, but one pamphlet provides a suggestive glimpse at one Lower Cape Fear leader's perspective. In 1765, Maurice Moore, son of the founder of Brunswick, published *Justice and Policy of Taxing the American Colonies in England*.[123] Essentially, Moore argued that the concept of virtual representation, whereby members of the House of Commons "virtually" represented constituents from geographic locales that did not get to elect their own representatives, did not justify Parliament's passage of the Stamp Act. Moore's pamphlet borrowed from a variety of political discourses and traditions, citing the natural rights thought of Samuel Puffendorff, English jurisprudential scholars, and *Cato's Letters,* and fit well with arguments lodged against the Stamp Act in other colonies.[124]

But Moore's argument might well have been more deeply rooted in his political experience in the Lower Cape Fear. At the heart of his argument against virtual representation, Moore emphasized that differing locales resulted in differing political interests.[125] English boroughs did not share the interests of the Lower Cape Fear, just as years of political strife had demonstrated that North Carolina's regions did not share the same interests. Moore articulated ideas about periphery rights that manifested themselves throughout Anglo-America between 1764 and 1776, but he did so with unusual attention to matters of geographic space and regional distinctiveness that had loomed large in the development of the Lower Cape Fear. Moore himself did not remain in the lead of North Carolina's revolutionary movement, however. As the ultimate decision to move away from Britain approached, he hesitated. Perhaps, in the end, personal or local concerns transcended broader questions of political philosophy for Moore. Or perhaps declining physical health played a role: Moore died in 1777.

In the Lower Cape Fear, the imperial crisis, beginning in 1764 and lasting into the American Revolution, did more than provide an opportunity for the expression of different political theories. The imperial crisis forced Lower Cape Fear residents to reconsider their own processes of identification. Revolt against Britain could not be accomplished by the relatively weak and disjointed regional and provincial political organizations that existed before 1764. After the Stamp Act, colonists throughout mainland British America worked vigorously to unify themselves with extralegal bodies like the Sons of Liberty, committees of correspondence, safety committees, nonimportation committees, and others. When they finally unified in the Continental Congress, they began the process of setting aside local and regional interests and establishing a national government.

The American Revolution, therefore, shaped the regional identity of the Lower Cape Fear in three ways. In the formative stages, the Lower Cape Fear's resistance to metropolitan authority made it the most influential region in North Carolina since residents in Albemarle and the backcountry followed the paths of opposition laid out in Wilmington. Next, during the military conflict, the need for unity temporarily muted the long-lasting tensions between the Lower Cape Fear and other regions of North Carolina. Finally, the formation of a national government began to make regional identifications irrelevant. This change took place gradually and clearly had not been completed a hundred years later. Yet the importance of extraregional identifications grew dramatically between 1764 and 1789, by which date the Lower Cape Fear at once functioned as a distinct region, as part of North Carolina, and as part of a broader, emerging nation.

Chapter 6

LOWER CAPE FEAR PLANTATIONS

Janet Schaw wrote the most detailed traveler's account of a visit to the eighteenth-century Lower Cape Fear. Schaw, an elite and refined Scottish visitor with strong loyalties to Great Britain, visited relatives in the Lower Cape Fear region late in 1775. Her journal makes no secret of her contempt for revolutionary political attitudes or for the seemingly less sophisticated and rougher mores of the region's settlers. Schaw also provides historians with the best description of one of the Lower Cape Fear's composite plantation enterprises. She visited John Rutherford's "fine plantation called Hunthill," where her host kept "a vast number of Negroes employed in various works." Hunthill produced tar and turpentine, operated a sawmill, utilized trees in adjoining woodlands, and tapped into an array of water-borne transportation routes and vessels. In addition, the plantation afforded "staves, hoops and ends for barrels and casks for the West India trade," Rutherford having "a great number of his slaves bred coopers and carpentars."[1]

Schaw was perhaps most impressed with Rutherford's sawmill, which she described as his "grand work" and "the finest I ever met with." Schaw estimated that the mill could cut three thousand boards a day "and can double the number when necessity demands it." Schaw also recognized the complex operation required to make the sawmill profitable, commenting that "the woods round him are immense, and he has a vast piece of water, which by a creek communicates with the river." Rutherford's operation used rafts "by which he sends down all the lumber, tar and pitch."[2] The visitor did not hide her admiration for the organization of this plantation system, remarking that its use of water transportation "appears to me the best contrived thing I have seen, nor do I think any better method could be fallen on." It is probable, of course, that, like Rutherford, all Lower Cape Fear sawmill owners also produced naval stores. It was also common for Lower Cape Fear entrepreneurs to combine saw milling with grist milling and other milling operations.[3] Schaw's description of Hunthill encapsulates the main characteristics of the Lower Cape Fear's plantation complex, an interrelated set of economic activities that required greater organization, utilized more slaves, and yielded more profit than anything else in the region.

Yet Schaw's patrician and metropolitan perspective still made her ambivalent about Hunthill. Despite its "show of plenty" and obvious prosperity, she described Hunthill as "a mere plantation" because it lacked a house to accommodate guests.

Schaw found herself uncomfortably residing in a building that was "little better than one of his Negro huts." The dispersed settlement patterns and rustic conditions of the Lower Cape Fear disturbed Schaw, but she recognized that in time Hunthill would be an even more appealing place. She also found the situation complicated by John Rutherford's attempts to make the Lower Cape Fear more civilized. Rutherford owned "an excellent library," globes, telescopes, "Mathematical instruments of all kinds," china, and good furniture.[4]

Schaw's discordant responses to her visit to Hunthill reflected both the dynamics of colonialism and the specifics of life in the Lower Cape Fear. As a metropolitan elite, she was bound to find life on the remote periphery wanting, but, in her admiration for Hunthill, Schaw recognized perhaps the most distinctive achievement of the Lower Cape Fear land owners. While Schaw had seen larger and more profitable plantations months before in Antigua, Hunthill and other diversified, forest-product-oriented plantations like it marked the development of a distinctive and relatively profitable regional economy. Schaw's comments about the large number of slaves at Hunthill also reveal the central role of enslaved labor in the region. For the region's free settlers, enslaved labor enabled the development of plantations and the achievement of economic independence and prosperity.

As the example of Rutherford's Hunthill plantation suggests, Lower Cape Fear settlers placed great weight on material considerations. Many of them clearly left previous places of residence in the hopes that they would become more prosperous, and even less individualistic and acquisitive settlers faced powerful Anglo-American cultural imperatives to achieve a certain level of economic independence, or "competency," for themselves and their families.[5] Attempts at economic success in the Lower Cape Fear, or anywhere else in British America, often required a considerable degree of adaptation to local economic conditions. At the same time, even the smallest economic operations depended on a degree of responsiveness to broader, often transatlantic, markets. The development of a distinct Lower Cape Fear economy occurred in the interstices of these two broader trends. Individuals responded to both local and transatlantic forces as they constructed economic enterprises, but they did so in ways that gave the Lower Cape Fear a distinct and active regional economic character.

The Lower Cape Fear shared some common characteristics with other colonial economic regions. To begin with, land remained relatively abundant throughout the colonial period. Compared with other resources like labor and capital, land could be obtained easily and people could move to newly settled areas. Of course, some lands proved vastly more suitable for cultivation and use than others, but alternative settlement locations prevented the kind of pressure on limited land resources that was becoming increasingly common in England. The availability of land also made labor more scarce and valuable. Colonial Americans found it difficult to find willing laborers when so many people could work for themselves on their own land in other accessible locales.[6] Equally important, colonists did not have access to the same amounts of capital to invest in economic enterprises as did their metropolitan counterparts.

Anglo-American colonists dealt with shortages of labor and capital in a variety of ways. Some solutions seemed to be much more practical, depending on different colonists' experiences and circumstances. In the New England colonies, families provided the most important pool of labor, for example, but in more southerly colonies demographic circumstances made this labor-finding strategy less plausible.[7] The relatively small and unhealthy European American population of the colonial Lower Cape Fear clearly made it unlikely that there would be an economy dominated by family farms, and as in neighboring regions, and especially in the South Carolina lowcountry, Lower Cape Fear planters and entrepreneurs preferred to rely heavily on enslaved African and African American labor. It should be noted that, though it would be misleading to reduce the use of slave labor to mere economic determinism in the Lower Cape Fear, powerful economic incentives made this a normative and frequent response to the same alternatives throughout European American colonies during the late seventeenth and early eighteenth centuries.

Similarly, colonists utilized two different ways of accumulating capital. On the one hand, the growth of population contributed to the development of domestic markets and argues for a Malthusian interpretation of colonial economic development. This view of the colonial American economy may have significant explanatory power for some other case studies, but the Lower Cape Fear's population grew comparatively slowly during the colonial period and, consequently, the region's domestic markets promised limited profits. Lower Cape Fear entrepreneurs and planters more often pursued the other capital accumulation strategy available to them by attempting to produce staples for overseas markets. The widely accepted "staples theory" of colonial economic growth argues that such exportable staples played a formative role in the economic structure and growth of several colonial regions. Tobacco in the Chesapeake, sugar in the West Indies, and rice in the South Carolina lowcountry all made crucial contributions to growth in colonial wealth and to the creation of rather distinctive modes of economic endeavor. Moreover, the comparative advantages bestowed on the colonies by their considerable natural resources made the exportation of some staples to the metropolis highly profitable.[8] Lower Cape Fear residents quickly recognized the advantages of exportable staples, partly because the rest of North Carolina, where the lack of ports made the direct exportation of commodities almost impossible, languished in relative poverty. Thus, the settlement of the Lower Cape Fear began, not accidentally, with the establishment of a port at Brunswick, and the almost immediate search for a profitable staple.

In a number of important ways, then, the economy of the Lower Cape Fear bears important affinities to other, more-studied staple-oriented economies relying on slave labor elsewhere in colonial British America. Studies of such similar economies necessarily inform any discussion of labor, production, and business in the colonial Lower Cape Fear. Perhaps most interesting, scholars have consistently emphasized the important social and cultural implications of the dominant form of organization in these economies, the plantation.[9] Plantations, as many scholars have shown us, could be far more than mere units of production: they could be, among many other things, sites for the assertion of paternalistic and patriarchal ideology, integrated and sophisticated economic enterprises, testing grounds for agricultural innovations and conceptions of modernity, protoindustrial labor systems, and key components of colonial elite identities.[10] Plantation societies have now been dissected, categorized, analyzed, compared, and mythologized.

Even within this broad and familiar context of plantation societies, however, the Lower Cape Fear remains anomalous in at least two important ways. First, the colonial Lower Cape Fear never experienced a transformation that changed it into a plantation society: it began as one. Limited records from the first couple of decades make it impossible to cite specific numbers, but it seems clear that slaves made up a very substantial proportion, and perhaps a majority, of the region's population within five years of the first settlement. Settlers in the Lower Cape Fear already had enough labor, but they needed to find a staple. Second, the Lower Cape Fear's staple orientation never led to the same kind of economic focus generally associated with a conventional agricultural staple such as sugar, tobacco, rice, or cotton. Naval stores, the main export of the Lower Cape Fear during the colonial period, fits the models associated with the production of plantation staples elsewhere in some ways, but not in others. It does not appear to have played the same role anywhere else in colonial America.

Ultimately, however, a close look at the economy of the Lower Cape Fear suggests that scholars need to be careful about generalizing about these matters based on other regional models, and that, in some ways, the models need to be refined or reconsidered. But it also suggests that even the most comprehensive models have their limits. The inhabitants of the Lower Cape Fear in the eighteenth century did not respond to these scholarly models; they responded to their own concerns and experiences. Partly because of the limited geographic scope of the regional economy they created, the residents of the Lower Cape Fear left a very incomplete record of their economic activities. But enough evidence exists to show that individuals worked with determination to use their agency in these processes, that economic life involved constant choice and negotiation, and that the economy of the Lower Cape Fear both shaped and was shaped by the regional character of life in the Lower Cape Fear.

TABLE 6.1 **Values of Recorded Lower Cape Fear and North Carolina Overseas Exports, 1768–72**

Year	*Lower Cape Fear Values (£s Sterling)*	*North Carolina Values (£s Sterling)*	*Lower Cape Fear Values as % of North Carolina Values*
1768	24,025	52,699	45.6
1769	38,692	66,703	58.0
1770	28,924	60,156	48.1
1771	41,503	77,598	53.5
1772	31,712	77,492	40.9
Total	164,855	334,652	49.3

TABLE 6.2 **Estimated Total Wealth from Exports from the Lower Cape Fear Ports and Other Selected Locales, 1768–72**

	Per Capita Wealth from Exports in Customs 16/1 (£s Sterling)	*Per Free Capita Wealth from Exports in Customs 16/1 (£s Sterling)*
South Carolina	3.7	9.5
Lower South	1.8	3.2
Upper South	1.8	3.0
Lower Cape Fear	1.6	2.4
Middle Colonies	1.0	1.1
New England	0.8	0.9
North Carolina	0.4	0.6

Scholars have overcome significant obstacles in recent decades in an attempt to assess the economic success of the American colonists. Probate records and account books, the most valuable sources for this purpose, cannot provide sufficient data to reach any conclusions about the wealth of the Lower Cape Fear. British customs records, which exist for all the ports of British America from 1768 to 1772, do allow some highly suggestive estimates of export wealth, however.[11] Moreover, the importance of exports for the economy of colonial America make export wealth one of the best indicators of total wealth. These customs records are not without problems, but, with careful use, they can reveal much.

To begin with, the Lower Cape Fear ports dominated the export economy of colonial North Carolina, as seen in table 6.1. About one-half of the colony's export wealth left the colony through either Wilmington or Brunswick. This may not appear surprising given the greater accessibility of the Lower Cape Fear ports; however, it also means that, because use of the Lower Cape Fear ports continued to be limited to a few counties throughout the colonial period, much of the colony's commercial profits went to residents of the Lower Cape Fear region. The difference in export profits between the Lower Cape Fear and the rest of North Carolina underscores the enormous economic disparity between the two geographic areas. Such large differences in wealth necessarily distinguished economic life in the Lower Cape Fear from elsewhere in North Carolina.

Equally important, in terms of exports, as documented in table 6.2, it appears that the Lower Cape Fear not only profited much more than the rest of North Carolina but also more than the Middle Colonies or New England, almost as much as the Chesapeake colonies, and far less than South Carolina or Georgia. In simple terms, this indicates that Lower Cape Fear residents, like most residents of colonial plantation societies, profited significantly from exports. At the same time, it means that Lower Cape Fear plantations did not appear to make as much as tobacco plantations to the north or rice and indigo plantations to the south. By the standards of colonial British America, the Lower Cape Fear became a prosperous place by the time of the American Revolution, but it clearly did not achieve the levels of wealth produced in some other staple-oriented regions.

Customs records also offer some preliminary conclusions about the character of the Lower Cape Fear's economy. As listed in table 6.3, commodities shipped from the region's ports provide a reliable indication of the value of various staples being produced for export. Most of the export wealth leaving the Lower Cape Fear ports consisted of tar, the most important kind of naval store in the eighteenth century. Lumber and another naval store, turpentine, made up the region's other most important exports. These three commodities accounted for the vast majority of the Lower Cape Fear's export sector—about 82 percent of the export wealth. Indeed, various forest-related products, including lumber, naval stores, staves, and headings, accounted for 86 percent of the export values. Tobacco, deerskins, and provisions provided the only non-forest-related exports of any notable significance.[12]

In terms of its share of regional export values, tar can be compared with other staple commodities of importance in different regions of colonial British America. Tables 6.4 and 6.5 make it clear that in this context tar brought significant profits into the Lower Cape Fear, although it did not dominate the region's economy the way that sugar dominated the West Indies, rice dominated South Carolina and Georgia, and tobacco dominated the Chesapeake.[13] Indeed, even grains and grain products in the Middle Colonies loomed larger in proportion of regional export tallies than tar from the Lower Cape Fear, and among broad regional economic categories in colonial British America, only New England lacked a more prominent export staple.

It would be misleading to assess the overall economic importance of an export staple purely in terms of the export value of one commodity, however.

Table 6.3 **Notable Commodity Export Values from the Lower Cape Fear Ports, 1768–72**

	Estimated Value (£s Sterling)	*% of Exports from Lower Cape Fear Ports*
Tar	91,091	55
Pine Boards	25,849	16
Turpentine	17,737	11
Tobacco	5,582	3
Staves and Headings	5,122	3
Deerskins	4,440	3
Beef and Pork	3,609	2
Bread and Flour	3,495	2
Flaxseed	2,141	1
Rice	1,294	>1
Indigo	549	>1
Wheat	294	>1
Maize	221	>1
Pitch	184	>1

Table 6.4 **Some Staple Commodities as Shares of Regional Export Wealth, 1768–72**

	Region	*% of Export Values*
Sugar	West Indies	82
Tobacco	Chesapeake	72
Grains	Middle Colonies	72
Rice	South Carolina, Georgia	64
Tar	Lower Cape Fear	55
Fish	New England	35

Table 6.5 **Some Combinations of Staples and Secondary Products as Shares of Regional Export Wealth, 1768–72**

	Location	*% of Export Values*
Sugar, Rum, Molasses	West Indies	100
Tobacco, Grains	Chesapeake	91
Rice, Indigo	South Carolina, Georgia	86
Forest Products	Lower Cape Fear	86

As proponents of the staples thesis have thoroughly demonstrated, a staple can influence the development of an economy in ways that transcend the mere accumulation of export profits. At least two other factors need to be considered. First, various export staples create different kinds of linkages through the allocation of resources and the organization of trade—a topic that is developed further in chapter 7. Second, some commodities can be produced more efficiently in tandem with one another. For example, the land and labor requirements of rice and indigo make them particularly complementary and, consequently, South Carolina planters often organized their resources in a system that enabled the production of both crops. Naval stores and other forest products provided a complementary combination for Lower Cape Fear planters, and a comparison of staple commodities combined with related secondary products should thus be taken into consideration. In these terms, the Lower Cape Fear's emphasis on forest products reveals a level of economic concentration comparable to that of other mainland plantation economic regions. Moreover, the size of port regions, differing factor distributions, and geographic variations would probably make much greater homogeneity in export production difficult for mainland economies.

Thus, forest products in the Lower Cape Fear played a central role similar to that played by other profitable export commodities elsewhere in British America. But if staples proved crucial to many plantation societies, different staples could have very different social and economic consequences. Not only did the Lower Cape Fear produce a different staple than any other region of colonial British America, it did so profitably. It also produced the only nonagricultural staple in colonial British America of comparable regional importance and used large amounts of slave labor. Clearly, the Lower Cape Fear's distinctive naval-stores economy raises important questions for scholars of early America, but any attempt to address these questions will first require a closer look at how various commodities could be produced.

In a sense, because the Moore family drew self-confidence and support from a South Carolina lowcountry economy that thrived on rice, rice made the settlement of the Lower Cape Fear possible. When the Moores went northward, South Carolina was still being transformed by the rice boom. Throughout the colonial period in the Lower South, rice planting remained the most desirable form of economic enterprise, the quickest route to greater wealth. Doubtless, many went to the Lower Cape Fear and, though aware of the inland swamps and warm climate that seemed so uncivilized to European eyes but that had proved so valuable to aspiring colonists elsewhere, began to plan rice plantations.

Modern historians have emphasized the Lower Cape Fear's place at the northern end of colonial America's rice-planting belt. Indeed, in the absence of more thorough study, many important scholars have implied that the presence of rice cultivation in the Lower Cape Fear made it much like the South Carolina lowcountry.[14] But, however important rice planting may have been as an ideal for early settlers and projectors, rice never played more than a minor role in the economic history of the colonial Lower Cape Fear. Few in the region grew any rice at all, and no one appears to have grown very large amounts; it always remained secondary to the production of naval stores and other forest products.[15]

Customs records provide only one indication of the limited role of rice in the Lower Cape Fear's economy. As several scholars have pointed out, customs records would not include any rice that had been transported overland and shipped out of Charles Town.[16] But no evidence exists to suggest that planters used such a route, and, because of the bulk of rice exports and the proximity of the Lower Cape Fear ports, it probably would have been much more efficient to have shipped any rice by water.[17] North Carolina legislation required inspection of rice along with other commodities even before the settlement of the Cape Fear and rice was made a rated staple commodity, but it does not appear to have been used in barter and three-way trade for Wilmington merchants.[18] The one substantial body of colonial merchant records extant for the Lower Cape Fear does not include, amid myriad other crops and products, any significant reference to rice.[19] Given the scarcity of specie in the Lower Cape Fear, this strongly argues against the likelihood of large quantities of rice in the region. Contemporaries also did not consider rice to be an important crop in the region. James Murray confirmed the figures in the customs records when he wrote, to another merchant regarding rice in the Lower Cape Fear, that "as we grow but a few 100 barrels yearly it is generally dearer than in South Carolina."[20] Similarly, William Faris complained that "Corn and Rice are very dear tho' this is a plentiful year," and, on other occasions, Murray remarked that rice was "hardly to be had" and that there would be "some difficulty in geting it."[21]

A variety of factors contributed to the minimal levels of rice cultivation in the Lower Cape Fear. Perhaps most important, only the wealthiest of Lower Cape Fear residents could marshal the considerable resources needed for a rice plantation. A profitable rice plantation required at least thirty slaves and also more initial capital than most agricultural enterprises.[22] At most, about twenty Lower Cape Fear planters had access to these minimal labor requirements, and labor needs clearly imposed the largest obstacle to rice cultivation in the region.[23] This can be seen in, for example, Governor Arthur Dobbs's comment on the need for more slave labor in North Carolina to enable rice growing and other enterprises.[24] Other factors must also have inhibited rice planting, however, or planters probably would have readily found a way to obtain capital for the purchase of slaves.[25]

Good rice land appears to have been more scarce in the Lower Cape Fear than in South Carolina. In the earliest years, it made sense that the best rice lands had to be found, settled, and cleared, and that cultivation, therefore, might develop slowly. However, in the Lower Cape Fear even a century later, when the region's rice industry had expanded dramatically, rice-planting areas remained comparatively small.[26] In 1755, Murray made reference to a mere twelve acres of his own land used for rice. He patented one hundred one acres more for a relative interested in planting that crop.[27] A number of other large eighteenth-century plantations in the Lower Cape Fear devoted only a small piece of land to rice cultivation.[28] Many planters probably found themselves in the position of one Lower Cape Fear resident who placed an advertisement in the *Cape Fear Mercury* expressing the hope that someone wanted to "dispose of from 500 to 1000 acres of land fit for rice."[29] Climate factors probably also played a role, because the Lower Cape Fear region does not have as long a growing season as some other rice-growing locales.[30]

Whether justifiably or not, the Lower Cape Fear's rice was believed to be of poorer quality. Murray had such strong doubts about cultivation in the region that in one letter he advised one correspondent "take no Rice at Cape Fear."[31] Lord Adam Gordon attributed the region's focus on other commodities to the fact that North Carolina rice "falls Short of that in South Carolina, being less heavy in equal quantities."[32] Finally, the smaller Lower Cape Fear ports did not offer such good opportunities for marketing rice as did Charleston, and the costs of additional transportation could be a huge disadvantage.[33] Along these lines, Henry McCulloh advised Murray that in bartering or trading for rice he should "always be ruled by the price in ye south."[34] None of these impediments would have proved determinative by itself, but labor scarcity, limited land, imperfect climate conditions, bad reputation, and poor location combined to give the Lower Cape Fear a significant comparative disadvantage in rice production.

Those in the Lower Cape Fear who did cultivate rice obviously represented an economic elite. Of the dozen or so individuals clearly identified as rice planters from Lower Cape Fear inventories and other contemporary references, all except one of those who appeared on tax lists or had slaves listed in their inventory owned more than thirty slaves, and a number owned more than fifty. The one exception, Henry Hyrne, listed twenty-six slaves in his inventory and only had twenty-five acres under rice cultivation.[35] Some planters probably hired slaves specifically for work on rice crops, but, as Murray discovered one season, poor growing conditions could make this a costly gamble.[36] A few other individuals probably grew rice on a small scale for purposes other than export. Several other inventories contained "rough" or small amounts of rice. Nothing indicates that anyone in the Lower Cape Fear focused exclusively on rice planting, and in every instance for which sufficient information is available, rice planting supplemented the production of other staples.

Though rice cultivation remained marginal to the economy of the Lower Cape Fear, its presence demonstrated the powerful drive to social and economic improvement that characterized the Lower Cape Fear and some other colonial American plantation societies.[37] North Carolina's location rested on the margins of lowcountry rice cultivation, but planters nevertheless worked to keep up with the latest agricultural techniques. Perhaps most notably, Hugh Meredith witnessed the use of tidal flows to irrigate rice swamps as early as 1731, when it would have still been a recent innovation in the South Carolina lowcountry.[38] Murray's letters reveal a constant concern with the improvement and success of his rice crop. When he began cultivating the crop, he remarked that little of it was grown in the Lower Cape Fear, but he optimistically commented that "next crop we expect 1500 or 2000 barrels."[39] In the following years he wrote about using his barn to mill rice, growing rice together with other crops, motivating his overseer with a share of the rice crop, and marketing rice in different locales.[40] Almost twenty years later and not long before leaving the province, however, he still complained that "My Crop of Rice comes much short."[41] Lower Cape Fear planters like Murray probably experimented with rice, using a variety of techniques, throughout the colonial period. Despite Murray's frustrations and the limited size of the region's rice crop, some planters achieved satisfactory results and added significantly to their profits. Thus, in 1742, Daniel Dunbibin could write to South Carolina merchant Robert Pringle about the Lower Cape Fear's promising rice crop.[42] Rather than diminishing, efforts to grow rice seemed be reaching a crescendo by the end of the colonial period. In 1772, Governor Josiah Martin wrote Lord Hillsborough of "a spirit of industry and improvement dawning in this Province exemplified by the beginnings that are making several planters on Cape Fear River to raise rice." Like other rice planters, they followed the example of South Carolina "in emulation of its prosperity."[43] Later the same year, Martin once again mentioned this "new spirit of industry and improvement." He wrote, "Mr Waters and Mr McGwire I am informed will ship this year between four and five hundred barrels of Rice."[44] But the following fall, Martin reported more setbacks, as the "experiments" with rice and indigo had "failed this year almost totally, owing to the extreme drought of the summer." Still holding out hope, Martin added, "I hope however that this discouragement will not occasion the Planters there to forsake the culture of those valuable commodities."[45] The Lower Cape Fear eventually produced large quantities of high-quality rice for export, but not during the colonial period.[46]

Indigo cultivation, which, as noted, was often closely associated with rice plantations, also became a potentially profitable agricultural experiment in the Lower Cape Fear and generated much interest. Murray's letters reveal an almost frantic excitement about the prospects for indigo production in 1755. In one letter, he writes that naval stores commanded less attention from Lower Cape Fear planters because "every boddy is going with all their might on Indigo."[47] In another, while commenting on new Governor Arthur Dobbs,

Murray remarks, "In a word I believe he and indigo are the greatest Blessings this Province has seen for a long time."[48] He refers to his hopes for indigo in many other letters from about the same time. On at least a couple of occasions, Murray claims to have produced about a thousand pounds of indigo in a season in the Lower Cape Fear.[49]

Clearly, Lower Cape Fear planters could find a number of reasons to be enthusiastic about indigo. At least one contemporary claimed that, in some areas of the Lower Cape Fear, "the soil is peculiar for Indigo."[50] A shortage of indigo in British markets led the metropolitan government to pay colonists a bounty for the exportation of indigo and added to planters' profits.[51] Indigo complemented rice production and could be grown in unison with corn and other crops as well.[52] Perhaps most important, indigo cultivation required considerably less capital and labor than rice.[53] But indigo cultivation still required significant amounts of labor and apparently remained dominated by a few plantations with large slaveholdings.[54] Murray's enthusiasm for indigo resulted partly from having grown a crop "reckoned of the best made here for the ensuing year" on "some of the finest Land in the Province" for indigo.[55]

Other evidence suggests that the economic benefits of indigo in the Lower Cape Fear remained limited. The Lower Cape Fear's climate proved to be a much more significant obstacle in indigo planting than in rice planting because cooler weather limited the number of cuttings in an indigo growing season.[56] Droughts, excessive rains, poor markets, and inexperience all hurt Lower Cape Fear indigo profits on different occasions.[57] Compared with some crops, indigo could be "very Intricate & difficult" to deal with, and Lower Cape Fear residents had to develop significant levels of expertise to make indigo a profitable export.[58] By 1758, a considerably less enthusiastic James Murray lamented that "Indigo proves a very precarious Crop."[59]

Sources do not permit a precise assessment of the importance of indigo cultivation in the economy of the colonial Lower Cape Fear, but they do make it evident that, much like rice, indigo played a comparatively minor role. Murray and perhaps a few others produced sizable crops, but no evidence reveals widespread indigo cultivation or any kind of barter with indigo.[60] Few inventories contain references to indigo equipment. Moreover, most contemporaries either dismissed the importance of indigo or named it as only one of many commodities produced in the region.[61] While customs data reveal the limited contributions of indigo to the region's export wealth, this source requires two important caveats. First, the low bulk of indigo makes it much more plausible that significant amounts went overland to more favorable markets in Charles Town and therefore did not show up in the customs records.[62] Second, customs records do indicate that indigo production was on the rise in the Lower Cape Fear during the later colonial period. The total for 1772, more than thirteen hundred pounds, marked an increase in excess of 500 percent from the year before, and port records indicate that the figure for 1775 reached almost seventeen hundred pounds. In this context, Governor Martin's excitement about indigo experiments may have been well founded.[63] The drought in 1773 may have been a temporary setback. In any case, the successful expansion of indigo cultivation in the Lower Cape Fear necessarily lasted only a short time. With the American Revolution, Lower Cape Fear planters lost access to the British bounties that made indigo profitable for them.

In a sense, the Lower Cape Fear efforts at rice and indigo production reflected the normative cultural imperatives of Anglo-American settlers. When the Moores moved north from South Carolina in the 1720s, they and their followers intended to replicate the same economic endeavors that had been successful near Charles Town. These included rice planting and, later, indigo planting. Lower Cape Fear settlers who came to the region from other locales also readily acknowledged the importance of these pursuits because they offered opportunities for enormous material gains. At the same time, economic behavior in early America could be profoundly influenced by more localized experiences and circumstances, and conditions in the South Carolina lowcountry could not be fully recreated along the Cape Fear River. From this perspective, the rapid accumulation of land and the relative availability of slave labor among Lower Cape Fear elites made it tremendously important to settlers that the region could utilize these resources efficiently. This required the production of profitable and exportable staple commodities. By the 1730s, the Lower Cape Fear resembled the South Carolina lowcountry around 1700. Both regions had a high percentage of slaves in their populations, and, consequently, they began the search for a profitable export staple.[64] In this region, however, rice and indigo would not do, and other commodities would have to be pursued. Economic enterprise in the Lower Cape Fear usually focused on the production of tar.[65]

Like other key economic activities in colonial British America, tar became more than merely a means to material gain, as Lower Cape Fear residents began to use tar as a metaphoric expression of their own regional culture. Janet Schaw's narrative of her visit to the Lower Cape Fear begins, appropriately enough, describing how she and her fellow travelers "proceeded thro' rows of tar and pitch to the house of a merch[an]t."[66] She and other commentators on the Lower Cape Fear repeatedly emphasized the significance of tar. Elkanah Watson must have been alluding to a well-known character type in the region when he remarked that, on one trip, he did not see "even a wild tar-burner's" house.[67] Lightwood, the wood that could be burned to produce tar, also figured prominently in the region's culture. Elites burned lightwood when hunting deer by night, and Schaw wrote that the "poorer sort" used lightwood in their homes in the absence of candles.[68] Most strikingly, Lower Cape Fear residents adapted their understanding of the natural environment to celebrate tar production as an example of human improvements to the region. As Johann D.

Schoepf wrote, areas along the Carolina coast could be prone to tropical diseases, but areas deeper in the forests were believed to be healthier. As Schoepf explained, "The people themselves are apt to ascribe their better condition of health to the beneficent effect of the pitch and tar odors they are almost constantly inhaling." As Schoepf shrewdly recognized later, the odor of tar did little to prevent the spread of malaria, but this willful misinterpretation speaks volumes about the cultural importance of the naval-stores industry.[69] Even the noxious smell of tar could be seen as a blessing. The enduring North Carolina nickname Tar Heel represents still further evidence of the broader local meaning attached to tar.

Lower Cape Fear entrepreneurs produced tar in response to market demands within the British Empire. Given the maritime character of the first British Empire, any commodity essential to the British navy acquired considerable significance. Tar, which could be used on ropes and rigging to prevent them from deteriorating, became the most important "naval store." British markets relied on Sweden and other Baltic nations to provide tar and other naval stores in the seventeenth century. When relations with these nations deteriorated and Swedish exporters tightened the terms of their economic monopoly at the beginning of the eighteenth century, the British government decided to offer a bounty to encourage the production of naval stores in its American colonies. In the Carolinas, the bounty combined with unusual concentrations of the necessary source, the long-leaf pine tree, the availability of large amounts of labor, and the desperate need for exportable staples to facilitate the rapid growth of a naval-stores industry. The production of tar expanded so rapidly, especially in South Carolina, that by the early 1720s a glutted London market convinced British authorities to repeal the naval-stores bounty. At this point, an important transition occurred. South Carolinians, recognizing a more profitable opportunity and discouraged by the loss of the bounty, shifted their resources from naval-stores production to rice cultivation. After this, the production of naval stores in South Carolina remained significant, but became relegated to locations and seasons that did not allow for the cultivation of rice or, later, indigo.[70]

Timing, then, played a key role in the development of the Lower Cape Fear's naval-stores industry. The Moores and other South Carolinians in the Lower Cape Fear had grown familiar with the processes and benefits of naval-stores production, but, in the midst of the lowcountry rice boom, rice cultivation would have been their first choice. When circumstances conspired to prevent the development of rice plantations on the Lower Cape Fear, naval stores seemed like a logical alternative. Any lingering doubts about the profitability of tar production could be dismissed in 1729, when merchants persuaded the British government to reinstate the naval-stores bounty, albeit with some restrictions.[71] By 1735, Roger Moore, James Murray, and other Lower Cape Fear elites began to involve themselves in the exportation of naval stores.[72]

Contemporary descriptions reveal that tar could be produced through a relatively simple process. Essentially, wood from the long-leaf pine had to be gathered in a large circular area, known as a tar kiln, and burned until tar ran out of the kiln bottom. One end of the kiln would be graded so that the resinous tar extract would run through a pipe into barrels. Kilns could vary greatly in size, but typically seem to have been about thirty feet in diameter and ten or twelve feet in height. A kiln of this size could produce between 150 and 200 barrels of tar in a burning, though some larger kilns could reputedly yield as much as 1,000 barrels. A small hole had to be left in the kiln to light the fire, and the wood could be left to smolder for long periods of time, but it was never allowed to burst into flames. Sometimes kilns would be burned continuously for eight or nine days. Dirt covering the kiln kept the heat within, and the temperature could be increased by punching holes in the kiln to allow the flow of more air. The basic technology used in this process had remained relatively unchanged since antiquity.[73]

If burning a tar kiln had few technological requirements, it did make demands on other resources. For one thing, tar kilns used large amounts of lightwood, and this required access to large amounts of forest land. One scholar has estimated that "a colonist with ten slaves who produced turpentine, tar, and pitch might have been able to exhaust one thousand acres of pines in as little as three years."[74] The early rush for land and the late settlement of the Lower Cape Fear, however, insured that land in the region remained concentrated and available to those with means to run a naval-stores operation of significant size. Nonetheless, naval-stores producers occasionally complained about the shortage of lightwood land.[75] It also became common in the Lower Cape Fear to take lightwood from forest lands that had not been claimed or had already been claimed by others.[76] When Murray was absent from his plantation, he expressed considerable anxiety about the possibility that others might "make waste of the Mill timber" by producing naval stores.[77] Murray's fears seem especially well founded given the condition of one abandoned Lower Cape Fear plantation that "had no trees for turpentine, or rails, nor a knot of lightwood left unpillaged."[78]

Partly in support of the argument that the Lower Cape Fear produced so much more tar than other regions because it had more slaves, scholars studying colonial North Carolina have also emphasized the labor requirements of tar production.[79] However, tar was nowhere near as labor intensive as other colonial American staple commodities, and naval-stores production does not correlate directly with slave ownership. The one known source recording regular allocations of slave labor for an early-eighteenth-century American tar kiln indicates that four slaves could run a relatively large kiln.[80] Estate inventories also reveal that some tar producers had few or no slaves.[81] Nathaniel Baron owned one-half of a tar kiln, but no slaves. James and Anne Pollard owned only five slaves, but their inventory also included a small kiln. Similarly, John Dallison's share of a tar kiln must have been worked by his six slaves. Richard Malpus's estate contained more than nine hundred barrels of naval stores, yet he does not appear ever to have owned more than five slaves. Unfortunately, the lack of distinctive implements and technology makes naval-stores production difficult to trace much further through inventories. But these examples demonstrate that tar kilns were burned in the Lower Cape Fear without significant concentrations of slaves. In this context, Elkanah Watson's reference to a "wild tar burner's" house suggests much. A poor and isolated family could burn tar to support itself because the capital requirements were low and lightwood could be obtained in a variety of ways, lawfully or unlawfully.

At the same time, tar production ultimately did involve significant amounts of labor, partly because the burning of the tar kiln was only one of several necessary activities before tar could be marketed. Gathering and cutting lightwood for the kiln could be laborious, especially as nearby forest areas became depleted and colonists had to go farther afield to get sufficient quantities of lightwood. Work crews in the forests of the Lower Cape Fear region often resided in temporary camps where long-leaf pine trees were readily available.[82] Tar burners often used oxen to haul carts of wood to the kiln.[83] The coopering of barrels for the storage of tar required skilled craftsmen, and the burning of the kiln itself involved a certain degree of expertise to prevent the tar from being overheated. The bulkiness of tar meant that the Lower Cape Fear invested much labor in transportation, and tar burners valued lightwood that was "convenient to a Landing."[84] As early as 1735, Murray noted that "timber fit for . . . [naval stores] grows generally at a distance from ye river," making it hard to utilize, especially when labor was scarce.[85] The use of waterways proved invaluable, and the proximity of the ports of Wilmington and Brunswick greatly reduced costs. Indeed, the relative ease of transporting naval stores in the Lower Cape Fear probably did as much to differentiate the scale of production from that in other regions of North Carolina as did the scale of slave ownership.[86] But as is demonstrated by the prominence of slave watermen in the region, slave labor also served to facilitate transportation.

If slave labor and the naval-stores industry did not depend on each other, in the Lower Cape Fear, at least, they clearly had a reciprocal relationship. In the first few years of settlement, Lower Cape Fear residents realized that they had a relatively abundant supply of slave labor and that their slaves could not be used for profitable, large-scale rice cultivation. They also knew that naval stores offered a profitable alternative activity that did not have to, but could, employ slave labor. Once they began using slaves to burn tar kilns, some slave owners increased the scale of production to a level that could be maintained only with significant numbers of slaves. Indeed, the importance of tar as an export sometimes led to the neglect of more conventional uses for slave labor. In a particularly prosperous moment in the naval-stores market, William Faris wrote "that those who have [the] most Negroes employ them in Burning Tar and buy Corn."[87] No doubt the sparse population, demographic disruption, and availability of other economic alternatives in the region made reliable free labor rather hard to obtain. By the late colonial period, these circumstances had made the naval-stores industry in the Lower Cape Fear practically synonymous with slavery, though some poorer families no doubt continued to produce small amounts of tar with free labor.[88]

Thus, tar production took some effort and resources, though less than other staples in colonial British America, and had several positive aspects that transcended its immediate profitability. First, because tar production was not especially labor intensive, it did not begin to exhaust the region's supply of slave labor. Lower Cape Fear slaves could therefore also be used in a variety of other ways that could bring profit or valuable goods to a plantation. Second, tar burning was not seasonal, so labor could be scheduled around growing seasons for crops or other, less-time-flexible, tasks without interfering significantly with productivity. Along these lines, Murray bought lightwood to keep his slaves busy during the winter and noted the "Dificulty of getting tar in the Crop time, especially now that several of our greatest Tar Burners employ their hands in Indigo."[89] Third, some of the same forest-oriented work regimes that yielded tar could overlap with the exigencies of other profitable forest activities, such as lumbering and boxing trees for turpentine. In this sense, the emphasis on tar burning in the Lower Cape Fear also enabled the development of an array of related forest-production activities.

Despite these advantages, Lower Cape Fear planters never seemed quite satisfied with the profits derived from exporting tar. Part of this attitude no doubt grew out of comparisons to the rice boom in South Carolina, but the tar business did have its limitations. No one described the importance of naval stores in the Lower Cape Fear more aptly than Murray, who, in a 1755 letter, wrote of "Naval Stores the Grand Export of the Province continuing still a very great Drug." But in the very next sentence Murray also revealed the region's impatience with these products, remarking that the economic situation would improve the following year because of indigo cultivation.[90] Another North Carolinian noted that wealthy South Carolinians left "the making of naval-stores" to their neighbors who "grapple with lightwood knots" and spend time "plodding over a tar kiln."[91]

In addition to the relatively minor difficulties associated with production and transportation, the Lower Cape Fear tar industry also struggled with precarious market conditions. While London authorities preferred to have a ready supply of naval stores within the empire, they also found tar produced in North Carolina to be notably inferior to tar imported from Sweden and elsewhere. Complaints about the poor quality of American tar continued unremittingly from the beginning of the eighteenth century until the American Revolution.

Attempts to improve naval stores through the careful packing and coopering of barrels or by the location of tar kilns on clay instead of sand showed that Cape Fear planters paid careful attention to production techniques, but they do not appear to have changed the reputation or quality of Carolina tar.[92] Complaints about the desirability of colonial naval stores did, in fact, have a legitimate basis: the colonists produced tar through a cheaper method that clearly diminished the quality of the product. Colonists refused to use carefully cut, fresh lightwood in kilns, preferring the far-easier method of gathering dead wood in the forests. Lower Cape Fear tar burners proved careless in other ways, too. Governor Gabriel Johnston complained that "they make so large and violent fires on their kilns as forces all the coarce juices of the lightwood along with the tarr." This "gives it so hot a Quantity that masters of Ships have observed it frequently burns their ropes which makes them very shy of meddling with it." Various other complaints about Carolina tar illustrated the same dilemma: the quality of Carolina tar was poor, but improving it with greater care would reduce the quantity significantly. Persistent quality problems combined with the increasing ease of production to drive London tar prices down and, as an enumerated commodity, tar could not be sold directly to potential non-British buyers.

Anecdotal evidence suggests that tar production and the fortunes of Lower Cape Fear planters in general were closely tied to the price of American tar in British markets. Prices rose sharply in the late 1730s, peaking a decade later at well over twice their previous price, only to plummet and bounce back again before 1760, when a more gradual decline started.[93] Consequently, Johnston wrote, tar earned "so low a price in London . . . that I find the Planters are generally resolved to make no more."[94] In the absence of a more profitable staple in the Lower Cape Fear, however, almost thirty years later Governor Dobbs reported that tar production in the region continued to increase.[95] Unfortunately for Lower Cape Fear tar producers, their profits also depended heavily on the bounty system made possible by their colonial status. When the American Revolution severed the imperial relationship with Britain, tar ceased to be a sufficient basis for the region's economy.

Turpentine provided the colonial Lower Cape Fear with its other valuable naval-store export and its third-most-valuable export commodity. From the perspective of economic development and linkages, turpentine bore a number of similarities to tar. Both fit into the broad classification of naval stores, both depended on British markets and bounties, and both involved similar storage and transportation requirements. Significantly, both also came from the longleaf pine trees common to the colonial Lower Cape Fear.[96] The much greater demand for tar in Atlantic markets, however, made it substantially more valuable to the Lower Cape Fear than turpentine.[97] Turpentine proved to be a valuable secondary commodity related to the production of tar, though in the nineteenth century this relationship would be reversed when new uses for turpentine pushed its demand higher.

The process of turpentine production differed markedly from that of tar.[98] Crude turpentine, or gum from the inside of pine trees, could be harvested by cutting incisions in trees and periodically gathering the substance as it gathered around the wound in the tree. The first stage, "boxing," in which an opening, or box, was cut near the bottom of a tree, began in the late fall and continued until spring. In the spring, the box would be "cornered," or cut, in order to start the turpentine flowing. Turpentine workers spent the rest of the year collecting the turpentine from the boxes and occasionally cutting around the wound in the tree when it again became clogged.[99] Crude turpentine had to be distilled for most purposes, but, during the colonial period, few Lower Cape Fear producers distilled their own turpentine; instead, they exported crude turpentine to avoid the rather complex and difficult distillation process, and European buyers distilled it.

Turpentine required a somewhat different allocation of resources than tar. Turpentine harvesting was far more labor-intensive than burning tar. Boxed trees required more continuous supervision, and laborers could not be shifted to other tasks as readily. The temperature requirements of gum extraction also made the turpentine industry seasonal. Consequently, in the Lower Cape Fear most turpentine production probably occurred only on larger units of production, where slave owners could afford to devote some of their labor to the task full-time.[100] On the other hand, where labor was plentiful enough, turpentine harvesting provided an excellent complement to tar production. Trade, labor, and transportation networks already in place for tar could also be employed to obtain additional profits from turpentine. Slaves in the forests could alternate tasks depending on the needs of the moment, and, when trees had been boxed too many times to yield more turpentine, they became lightwood for tar kilns. Moreover, both commodities exhausted land rapidly, but land could be used to produce both simultaneously without diminishing productivity significantly.

Pitch, the third category of naval store exported from the Lower Cape Fear, could be made from boiling tar. It served to insulate the exterior of wooden ships from potential leaking. Pitch does not appear ever to have made up a significant portion of the colonial American naval-stores industry, probably because, as with tar production and turpentine distillation, Lower Cape Fear businessmen found it more profitable to leave such refining techniques to English buyers and Baltic competitors. The Lower Cape Fear settlers' comparative advantage rested in the proximity of the long-leaf pine and in British bounties that could be obtained from tar as easily as pitch. In this sense, making pitch, like making tar from high-quality lightwood, simply was not profitable enough to justify the additional effort and resources. Although the presence of some pitch production for export from the Lower Cape Fear reveals another facet of the region's integrated complex of export-oriented forest activities, the combination of naval-stores products from the Lower Cape Fear region provided only a limited basis for a regional export economy. This situation prompted Murray, after his departure for Massachusetts, to write to a friend in the Lower Cape Fear region that "it is long since every thinking Man among you was sensible that the Province would never thrive till you make a better export than Pitch, Tar & Turpentine."[101]

The second-largest amount of export-based wealth in the Lower Cape Fear was brought in by pine boards, a product surpassed only by tar.[102] The regional lumber industry that produced these boards did not dominate the colonial American export market, however, as Lower Cape Fear naval stores did. New England exported the overwhelming majority of colonial British America's lumber, and the Lower Cape Fear was one of the few areas outside New England that exported significant amounts of boards. Indeed, lumber and related wood products played an important role in the material development of all settlements in colonial British America.[103] Settlers had to build houses, store goods in casks and barrels, and rely on local producers for a vast array of wood products, including fuel, firewood, casks, ships, shingles, furniture, and wagons. Only rarely did lumber become an export commodity—in New England, the Lower Cape Fear, and other places where production exceeded local needs. When colonists did turn to the exportation of lumber, they found ready markets in Britain, where population growth left few trees, and, even more conveniently, in the British West Indian colonies, where massive sugar cultivation led to deforestation and a labor force too profitable to have it spend time cutting down trees.

If the Lower Cape Fear did not have a monopoly on colonial lumber exports, however, its lumber industry did develop in a distinctive way. Elsewhere in British America, lumber industries developed gradually in response to local demand. Eventually, after considerable agricultural development and with settlement and population growth, economies of scale made it profitable to produce large amounts of lumber for export.[104] By contrast, the Lower Cape lumber industry began on a large scale and focused on exporting to overseas markets from the outset.[105] As early as 1732, Governor George Burrington wrote that in the Lower Cape Fear an "abundance of saw mills are erecting." Burrington also revealed that these mills were being built with the intention of exporting boards and timber.[106] A number of Lower Cape Fear residents expressed an interest in sawmilling during the 1730s, and, like elsewhere in colonial America, officials recognized the value of these enterprises to the local economy and attempted to encourage them by granting additional land to their proprietors.[107] By 1764, these incentives had clearly done their work because Governor Dobbs wrote that there were forty saw mills on the branches of the Cape Fear River, and a mere two years later Dobbs's successor, William Tryon, claimed the river had fifty saw mills, and more were being built. Other contemporary accounts agreed that the industry continued to expand.[108] Undoubtedly, some of these mills sold their products locally as settlement in the region expanded. Even by the end of the colonial period, however, the Lower Cape Fear's still relatively sparse population could not have exhausted a large share of the region's lumber production.

Unlike tar burning and other naval-stores operations, sawmilling could only be accomplished by those settlers with considerable resources. The eighteen identifiable sawmill owners in the Lower Cape Fear region appear to have owned on average between thirty and fifty slaves and more than sixty-five hundred acres of land.[109] For those with capital, however, the economy of the Lower Cape Fear provided everything necessary to obtain considerable profits from lumbering: land, labor, pine trees, water power, and water transportation could all be obtained comparatively easily. However, the construction of a mill required comparatively large amounts of start-up capital, and probably for this reason, some mills were jointly owned by two or three individuals.[110] The location of the mill was crucial because its profits depended heavily on the proximity of pine trees and water power. Trees appear to have been abundant in the Lower Cape Fear throughout the colonial period, but, over the years, transportation to the mills probably became increasingly burdensome. Where possible, logs were floated down inland waterways; otherwise draft animals, especially oxen, could be used. Water power appears to have been more of a problem at times. Governor Tryon remarked that, but for a shortage of power during the summer months, the region's sawmills would have been more productive.[111] James Murray became angry over the possibility that neighboring planters would alter the water flow and disrupt the function of his mill.[112] Janet Schaw, on the other hand, in praising the region's sawmills for the "vast command they have of water," recognized that hydraulic technology not only powered the mills but itself altered the geographic landscape.[113] If water-power needs slowed the mills in the summer, when water levels sometimes dipped, mill owners had the consolation that sawmills in the region could still run nearly year round, except when the water froze in the winter. The mills could also run both day and night.[114] Lumbering of course took a toll on forest land, using it up, but official incentives could provide mill owners with as much as five thousand acres of forest land near a mill.[115]

Sawmilling, like other Lower Cape Fear businesses, still had significant drawbacks. Some contemporaries claimed that pine could be used more profitably for tar burning than for producing lumber, but lumbering must have made economic sense when the two operations could be integrated and mechanized saws could run off hydraulic power.[116] Atlantic markets in lumber, as in naval stores, could be capricious, however. British authorities paid a bounty on lumber, as on naval stores, but the bounty scarcely covered the freight expenses for such a bulky product. Moreover, changes in demand could have sharp repercussions on such a large operation. Murray complained in 1757 about the low value of exports, "particularly Boards & Scantling for which there is no sort of Demand." He acknowledged that "this falls heavy on me who am a Saw Miller . . . my Mills being quite laid up."[117] Murray had embraced the lumber industry more than two decades earlier, when naval stores might not have seemed as promising. Back then he wrote that he could not carry on overseas trade with any commodity except lumber.[118] Customs records clearly indicate that the industry was on the rise again between 1768 and the American Revolution.[119] Indeed, the market for lumber may have been somewhat less volatile, if also less profitable, than the market for tar, and combining the two exports provided some protection against unpredictable price changes.

The Lower Cape Fear's abundant supply of slave labor must have also played an important role in the lumber industry. The mechanized mills themselves could be operated by as few as one or two workers, if they were properly trained.[120] But good sawyers were at a premium in the region, and Murray went so far as to inquire about hiring a sawyer from New York, offering him 10 percent of the mill's lumber as payment.[121] Ideally, Murray and other mill operators would have obtained a skilled slave who could function as a sawyer. However, even though the mills' labor requirements were small, large amounts of labor must have been expended in supplying the mills with trees. Slaves, using either axes or cross-cut saws, performed the exhausting task of felling the trees. Once again, the transportation networks used for tar would have proved valuable. Sawmill owners also bought trees cut down by other landowners or by other plantations' slaves. This would have been an accessible form of labor for anyone with extra slaves or land, and estate inventories reveal that most Lower Cape Fear households had implements suited for the task.[122] Lumbering offered a widespread opportunity for small profits, while sawmills offered more notable and centralized ways of accumulating profits. Many settlers would have been able to profit from selling forest products; however, the reason the Lower Cape Fear's lumber industry thrived was precisely because some planters were able to consolidate forest-based production in a variety of ways and on a relatively large scale. The Lower Cape Fear sawmills were, as H. R. Merrens has commented, "for their time, remarkably large units of commercial production."[123] Sawmills, then, even more than naval-stores operations, demonstrate the wide-ranging, composite, and export-oriented activities of the Lower Cape Fear's plantation owners.

Historians of southern plantation economies have emphasized the importance of export crops, but a successful plantation had to do much more than produce staples.[124] A large labor force and a wide variety of productive activities inevitably led to significant consumption needs. Planters could scarcely find food and other bare necessities in the Atlantic markets where they sold their staples, and they took it upon themselves to provide provisions from their own plantations. Thus, the myth of the monolithic, insular southern plantation grew from the recognition of an important reality: large plantations were among the few economic operations in colonial America that functioned on a large enough scale to be truly self-sufficient. When it was profitable to do so, planters shrewdly took advantage of this opportunity to meet their basic needs conveniently, and no colonial British society ever focused exclusively on the production of exports.[125] Moreover, practical plantation-management dilemmas illustrate the problematic nature of the distinction between internal and external economies.

In the Lower Cape Fear, planters allocated significant resources for the production of provisions that could be either consumed locally or exported. Obviously, they considered that feeding the plantation labor force enough to keep them working was a high priority. But a scarcity of provisions on the wealthy plantations of the British West Indies made export markets tempting and important to entrepreneurs throughout the Carolinas. Consequently, planters grew corn and herded livestock, simultaneously providing food for their slaves, diversifying their economic activities still further with activities that complemented other tasks, and enhancing their export profits.[126]

Livestock played a critical role in the Lower Cape Fear's provisioning. Beef and pork added another component to the region's export wealth, and livestock clearly occupied the attention of many of the region's planters. Indeed, the colony of North Carolina acquired a reputation among contemporaries for its large herds of high-quality livestock.[127] In a relatively poor colony, the limited labor and capital requirements of livestock offered a profitable opportunity to many. In the eighteenth-century Carolinas, livestock were allowed to roam free in the woods, planters fencing in their crops to protect them. North Carolina's large areas of unsettled or uncultivable land proved ideal for these purposes.

Other economic options probably made livestock less central to business in the Lower Cape Fear, but most Lower Cape Fear households still profited from livestock.[128] According to Burrington, the opening of the Cape Fear to settlement increased the scale and profitability of raising livestock in North Carolina.[129] Cattle ranching proved especially prominent in the Lower Cape Fear economy before the 1750s, when a disease carried north from South Carolina, causing a "great death of Cattle."[130] Estate inventories provide considerable evidence on livestock ownership because livestock were usually recorded in inventories. More than one-half of the inventories studied (94 of 181) included cattle. From the sample of inventories, it appears that cattle owners averaged about twenty-four cows each, but other evidence indicates that these figures are probably not representative. More complete evidence from the early 1780s reveals that New Hanover County cattle owners averaged about fifteen cows each—a figure that still makes cattle holdings in the Lower Cape Fear as large, though not as widespread, as elsewhere in North Carolina.[131] The inventories make it clear that both rich and poor Lower Cape Fear residents kept cattle.

Neither slave ownership, nor large areas of land, nor any other form of wealth was a prerequisite for cattle ownership. Cows required at least fifteen acres of land each for grazing, but both claimed land and empty woods were abundant in the Lower Cape Fear. The region's pine barrens, which proved so limited for agriculture and so valuable for naval stores and lumbering, could also be more than sufficient for grazing cattle.[132] An additional source underscores the frequency of livestock ownership among people of more limited means. Of the sixty-two individuals who had their livestock brand recorded before the New Hanover County Court, none owned large numbers of slaves.[133] At the same time, the inventories also demonstrate that some large-scale plantation operations included cattle ranching. Five individuals owned a hundred or more head of cattle; one owned two hundred. An estate with a hundred cows would require at least fifteen hundred acres for grazing. At least two of these estate owners also owned more than a hundred slaves, and most of those inventories with large slaveholdings also had significant numbers of cattle. The correlation between slave labor and cattle ranching should not be surprising: slaves had participated in every phase of cattle ranching in the Carolinas during the colonial period.[134] The ownership of other kinds of livestock in the Lower Cape Fear appears to have been much less common than cattle ownership. Only about 10 percent of inventoried estates contained hogs, and a few more contained sheep. Hogs and other livestock may have been more common than cattle but harder to count or keep track of. Yet, for some families, small livestock holdings could be quite important. According to at least one contemporary, hogs provided support for many families.[135]

Provision crops often complemented food supplies from livestock on Lower Cape Fear plantations, but it is difficult to know how much of these crops was being produced. Some bread, flour, and flaxseed exited through the Lower Cape Fear ports, but all of these products may have come downriver from the Upper Cape Fear. Contemporary accounts make it clear that corn and, to a lesser extent, wheat were grown in the region. Indeed, several early commentators described impressive corn crops in the Lower Cape Fear.[136] After about a decade of settlement, the region had begun exporting grain crops to the West Indies.[137] Corn and other crops would have been easy to produce if land was available. Slave labor was abundant, and the other significant economic activities in the region could readily be scheduled around a seasonal crop routine.

In provisioning, then, the distinctive regional economic characteristics of the Lower Cape Fear fade into the background as settlers adopted the small-scale livestock and grain-producing activities that played a central role on farms throughout colonial North Carolina and much of colonial America.[138] Indeed, these activities made a significant contribution to colonial America's reputation for abundance. One visitor to the Cape Fear River Valley claimed that "every proprietor of ever so small a piece of land, raises some Indian Corn and sweet potatoes, and breeds some hoggs and a calf or two."[139] Similarly, Scotus Americanus emphasized the ease of supporting a family with seventy or eighty cleared acres of land in North Carolina.[140]

Still, the results of the Lower Cape Fear's provisioning efforts remained mixed. The region seems to have alternated between grain surpluses and shortages. While contemporaries frequently noted exports, local leaders repeatedly felt compelled to implement grain embargoes from the region because of alarming shortages.[141] In sharp contrast to reports of grain surpluses in the Lower Cape Fear, Janet Schaw's brother and fellow traveler, Alexander Schaw, noted that the Lower Cape Fear settlements did not produce enough grain to meet their own demand, leading to large quantities of grain being sent down the river from Cross Creek in the Upper Cape Fear.[142] These conflicting images are hard to reconcile. In the earliest years of settlement, food shortages could be expected. In this vein, Murray wrote in 1736 that provisions remained scarce in the Lower Cape Fear because a large influx of new settlers made it difficult for the region to feed itself; even at this early date, however, Murray hoped soon to be able to export surplus provisions. When the exportation of corn was prohibited by the government, Murray still sought to export surpluses illicitly.[143] William Faris suggested a partial explanation in 1750. Faris wrote that tar burning had become profitable enough that many planters used their resources for naval-stores production and, because they neglected the cultivation of corn, were forced to buy corn at expensive prices. Indeed, corn often appears to have been quite expensive in the Lower Cape Fear.[144]

Unpredictable weather conditions also played a role. After a severe storm in 1769, William Tryon, estimating that one-half of the region's corn crop had been destroyed, expressed concern that the area would be short of provisions.[145] Thus a variety of factors combined to make provisioning, and particularly grain cultivation, an unpredictable component of economic life in the Lower Cape Fear. Environmental risks and fluctuating markets made farming an uncertain enterprise at any time and at any place in the early modern world. The Lower Cape Fear's limited farmland probably made many kinds of agriculture more difficult than in most regions.

Perhaps more important, provisioning does not appear to have been as high a priority in the Lower Cape Fear as elsewhere. If subsistence crops ran short down the river, they were abundant up the river and elsewhere in North Carolina, making importation convenient. Lower Cape Fear residents probably decided whether or not to invest resources in provisioning according to their opportunity costs at the time. If naval stores seemed especially profitable, they might forgo grain cultivation. If West Indian planters were paying higher prices for beef, they might buy more cows and combine subsistence with exporting. Most large-scale plantations probably devoted significant resources to provisions, but these could still fluctuate according to planter needs, preferences, and expectations.

Moreover, provisions did not necessarily function as a hedge against market instability in the Lower Cape Fear as they sometimes did in other parts of colonial America.[146] For one thing, the Lower Cape Fear region's focus on a variety of exports itself provided some security from sudden market shifts. Legislation insured that British bounties could also be relied on for some of these products, even if prices dropped. So market volatility, while still undeniably important, did not play as large a role as if the region's exports focused more on tobacco, rice, or sugar. At the same time, poor land probably made grain cultivation a less certain activity. Livestock, however, remained a stable source of provisions, and both wealthy planters and Lower Cape Fear families who were less economically secure probably relied on their animals for subsistence. In the Lower Cape Fear, then, provisioning functioned not only as a means of subsistence but also as one of many economic opportunities available to the region's residents.

Thus Lower Cape Fear plantations combined forest industries such as tar and pitch burning, boxing for turpentine, and lumbering with cattle ranching and traditional agriculture oriented toward both export staples and provisions. In a region with large numbers of enslaved laborers and no single and reliable route to large profits, plantations became more versatile and fluid, while labor had to become more flexible. As H. R. Merrens pointed out decades ago, these large, slave-labor operations that Lower Cape Fear residents referred to as "plantations" fit rather uncomfortably with the characteristics that American historians generally associate with plantations.[147] In part, this can be attributed to a transitional phase in the meaning of the term *plantation,* as common usage changed from considering such holdings as places planted in distant and conquered colonies to the static antebellum American model of the plantation. These Lower Cape Fear plantations could be seen as a combination of these two constructions, as settlers created and possessed "civilized" spaces in the Lower Cape Fear while also attempting to develop suitable units of production to meet the profit requirements of Atlantic markets. But even within these parameters, the Lower Cape Fear plantations seem anomalous. In contrast to the archetypal southern plantation focused on the production of one or, in some cases, two export crops, these Lower Cape Fear plantations used slaves to integrate a number of separate agricultural and, especially, nonagricultural activities for the production of a wide variety of different staples.

A paucity of sources and the relatively limited geographic scope of this Lower Cape Fear variation on the plantation model make it difficult to be precise about the details and operation of this kind of estate. No plantation account books exist, and there are few parallels beyond the colonial Lower Cape Fear.

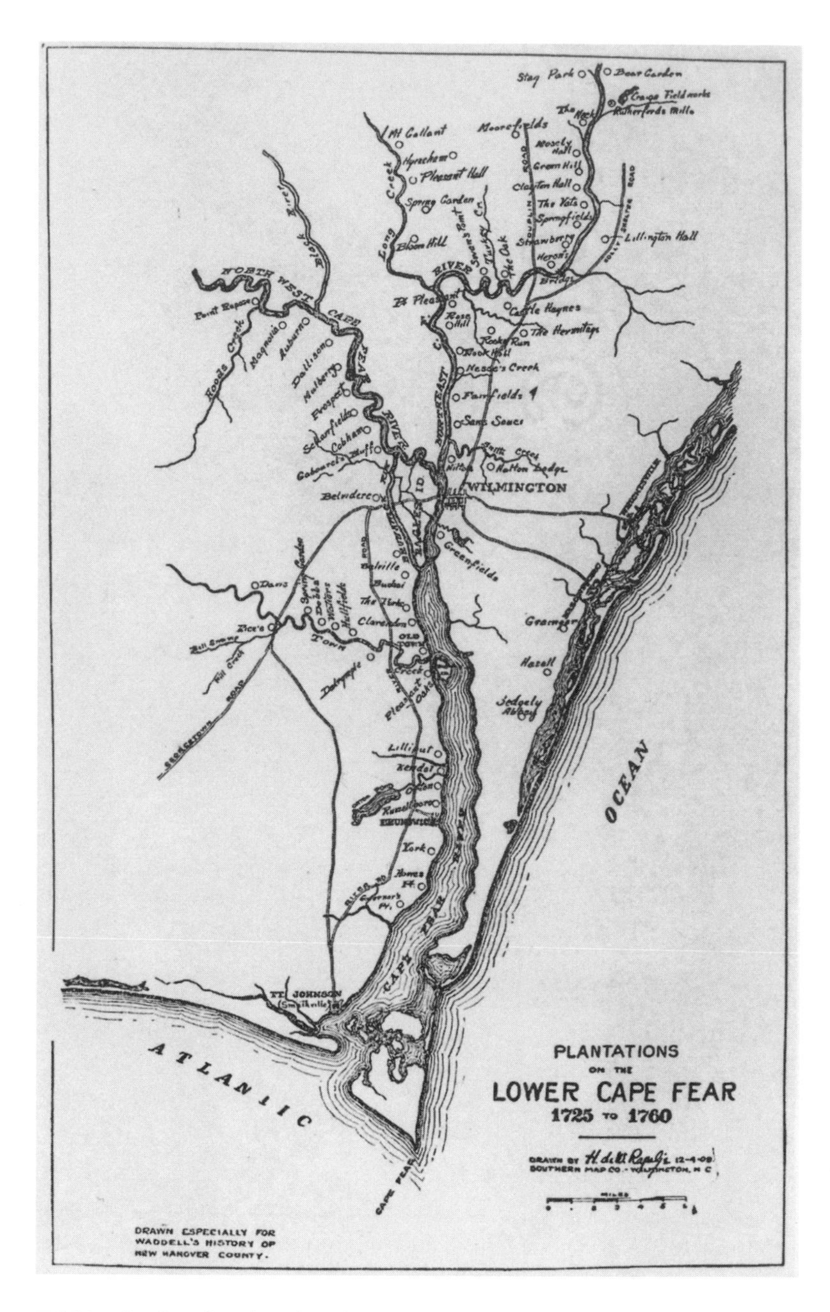

Within the first few decades of settlement, colonists filled the landscape along the Lower Cape Fear River with plantations suited to the region's distinctive forest-based system of enterprise.

Enough descriptions exist to confirm the general pattern, however. Janet Schaw witnessed at least one other plantation aside from her visit to Hunthill. She spent one day with Joseph Eagles and "saw his rice mills, his indigo works and timber mills."[148] Inventories also offer a few parallels. Mrs. Jean Corbin, a prominent Lower Cape Fear widow, for example, died with an estate containing ninety-seven slaves, thirty-one cows, skilled tools for coopers and carpentars, twenty-eight axes, including eight for chipping turpentine boxes, cross-cut and whip saws, rice sieves, and two hundred and sixty bushels of corn. Clearly, Corbin's slaves engaged in naval-stores production, lumbering, skilled crafts, and rice and corn cultivation. On a somewhat smaller but more typical scale, Thomas Merrick owned 36 slaves, 113 cows, 45 hogs, tools for coopers, carpenters, joiners, and shoemakers, and cross-cut saws, felling axes, a rice sieve, and more than three thousand feet of lumber. Of course, many colonial American plantations might have contained a variety of implements and been capable of a range of activities. Even wealthy Lower Cape Fear residents who did not consider themselves planters engaged in the region's distinctive economic system to make money, however. Thomas Cobham, a Scottish immigrant who was always identified in surviving records for his skills as a physician and never as a planter, owned twenty-nine slaves, a share of two sawmills on thirteen hundred acres of land, forty acres planted with rice, and several kinds of livestock.[149] In the Lower Cape Fear, export data and contemporary accounts demonstrate that varied economic activities were the norm, rather than an exception or peripheral variation.

Roger Moore was among the first settlers to build an example of this distinctive plantation system along the Cape Fear River. Some fragmentary business accounts reveal that by 1735 Moore already exported lumber, turpentine, and wood shingles from the Lower Cape Fear. At this time, Moore also traded with connections in both South Carolina and Barbados, perhaps participating in the West Indian provisions trade while importing a few slaves. These accounts probably provide only a small glimpse of the range of activities on Moore's two plantations, Orton and Kendall. Fifteen years later, Moore's will revealed that his resources included "Twenty Odd Thousand Acres of Land & Near Two Hundred & fifty Slaves," making him almost certainly the wealthiest plantation owner in North Carolina.[150] Moore's will also revealed other features of his economic enterprises, including one completed mill and another sawmill under construction, at least two lots and a wharf rented to others in the town of Brunswick, skilled slaves, at least four of whom were carpenters, as well as livestock, including horses, cattle, and sheep.[151] Few others could build plantations of such magnitude, but most Lower Cape Fear settlers could pursue at least some of these avenues to material gain by the 1730s.

James Murray's letters provide the best existing account of the business of a Lower Cape Fear plantation. Murray's Point Repose plantation embodied the

Roger Moore made the house pictured above his home and the center of Orton, his prosperous Lower Cape Fear plantation. The house was situated in close proximity to both Brunswick and the Cape Fear River. By the time this photo was taken, some additions had been made to the house, but the main part of the building is believed to have been built by Moore. Courtesy of the North Carolina Office of Archives and History, Raleigh, N.C.

same diversified economic approach as Hunthill and other plantations in the region. Between 1735 and his final departure from North Carolina, Murray engaged in the cultivation of rice and indigo, sawmilling, and tar and pitch production. When he first entered the Lower Cape Fear, Murray expressed great concern about the scarcity of provisions, found this to be an incentive for producing his own provisions at Point Repose, and ultimately managed to export some food products. He also recognized the need to procure significant numbers of slaves, skilled craftsmen, and a means of water transport for Point Repose. Nor did Murray conceive of Point Repose as an isolated enterprise. Indeed, Murray entered the Lower Cape Fear with the intention of profiting from trade, but found plantation ownership more congenial.

In one letter, Murray describes the use of plantation labor in the piney woods of the Lower Cape Fear region. When Sarah Allen left the Lower Cape Fear for England, Murray kept her appraised of the use of her slaves and the profits of her plantation, Lilliput. He reported that Allen's overseer had "made 8 & 900 lb of Indigo 1800 bushels of Corn & 300 bushels of pease." While this made her indigo crop one of the region's largest and no doubt reflected the influence of Murray's confidence in indigo, it would not suffice for the year's profits, partly because the price of corn was low. Consequently, after these crops were harvested, Allen's overseer, whom Murray considered the best available in the region, "went up the latter end of Nov[embe]r to Black River with all his hands to make tar." There would be plenty of lightwood because Murray had prepared for the winter by purchasing extra from another landowner. The location of their work was well positioned so that the tar they produced could be readily transported by water. Murray also sent his own slaves to work with Allen's and expected more production because he believed they were "spurr'd, one set by the other to excel."

Whether Murray possessed any real insight into the psychology of the slaves along the Black River remains questionable, but they had certainly labored productively by his standards because Allen's overseer was "on his second kiln" already and "from the first he expects about 200 barrels." Murray also assured Allen that tar was "likely to be in demand," increasing her profits further.[152] The plantation strategies and routines that Murray described probably would have been familiar to Allen after her decades of residence at Lilliput plantation, but to most of those unfamiliar with the Lower Cape Fear region, traveling into a wilderness during the middle of winter with several large groups of slaves in order to burn stores of prepurchased wood into tar might have seemed peculiar.

Murray's letters also reveal a constant concern with, participation in, and knowledge of markets and trade. He chose the location of his plantation in relation to Wilmington so that he could take advantage of urban connections and used correspondence to take advantage of far-flung business connections. Even after leaving North Carolina and retiring to New England, Murray dictated careful instructions through a number of distant acquaintances to make sure that his plantation was managed as skillfully and profitably as possible. In 1767, Murray estimated that his Lower Cape Fear estate was worth about £3,000, and the bulk of this, £2,000, he attributed to Point Repose. The remaining £1,000 came from mill lands worth £500, lots in Wilmington worth £250, and some separate landholdings on Rockfish Creek—a breakdown that suggests the range of Murray's economic activities. And Murray did not rest on his laurels. He constantly searched for new forms of profit. He showed the most enthusiasm for indigo, but he also grew some silk, tried growing corn and indigo together in the same fields, and turned his barn into a room for pounding rice. When his slaves had additional time without labor, Murray maximized his profits by hiring them out to other planters. The letters show satisfaction when his slaves became skilled at indigo cultivation and express frustration when his plans proved less successful; indeed, Murray's attitudes fit well with the portrait of modernizing and entrepreneurial planters in the Lower South drawn by historian Joyce Chaplin.

In developing his holdings, Murray was far from unique in the Lower Cape Fear. In 1762, when Murray reached a high of thirty taxables on the existing tax lists, a dozen other New Hanover County planters had more laborers, and seven years earlier he had been surpassed by at least eighteen others. More than forty other individuals in the Lower Cape Fear also accumulated more than Murray's 3,983 acres of land. Indeed, compared with Roger Moore's plantation system, Murray's economic activities might have seemed narrow and insignificant. But by the standards of Albemarle and many other places in colonial British America, Lower Cape Fear plantations like Point Repose were still an impressive achievement. Murray recognized the possibilities and limits of his position. He admitted that a man did not have "it in his power to make a great fortune at once" in the Lower Cape Fear. Yet he also pointed out that "a man with a moderate fortune & tolerable management may live very happily and plentifully here."[153]

One other source offers especially valuable insights into Lower Cape Fear plantation management. We know much less about Benjamin Heron, another Lower Cape Fear plantation owner, than we do about Murray, but some accounts from the administration of Heron's estate reveal important information about Heron's business. Born in Hampshire, England, in 1722, Heron was immigrated to the Lower Cape Fear region around 1755 after a career in the British navy that probably first introduced him to the Carolinas. It is impossible to determine where Heron acquired his wealth, but he was certainly aided by two marriages into elite Lower Cape Fear families—first the Howes and, after the death of his first wife, the Marsdens. Heron held numerous offices in the region during the 1760s, some of them at the provincial level, and also achieved notoriety as the builder of colonial America's first known drawbridge.

Better records exist for Heron's business partly because of the circumstances surrounding his death. In 1770, Heron had been ill and planned to take his family to England for a year's vacation. As a precaution, Heron drew up a will before his departure. This turns out to have been a wise decision because he died in Islington, London, that year. Heron's will left most of his estate to his children, to be divided when they reached adulthood or married. In the meantime, Heron's widow remained in England and the estate had to be administered by, Lewis DeRosset and Frederick Jones, Heron's friends in the Lower Cape Fear. In such cases, early-modern British courts were always extremely wary of the danger that others might take an unfair share of the estate; hence, unusually thorough records were kept.[154] In Heron's case, more than forty manuscript pages of estate accounts exist from between 1770 and 1774. Most of these pages are devoted to the expenses of educating and caring for Heron's children in London, but one section kept by Jones lists profits from the administration of Heron's Lower Cape Fear lands. At his death, Heron owned four plantations, and it remains unclear whether these accounts included profits from all or part

TABLE 6.6 **Credits to the Heron Estate Account, 1771–73**

	Number	*Value in £s*	*%*
Tar	14	1,877	37
Unidentified debts	20	1,300	25
Turpentine	13	876	17
Rent	25	441	9
Rice	6	330	6
Slave hiring	22	260	5
Crops	4	13	>1
Livestock	6	9	>1
Other	5	12	>1
Total	115	5,118	100

of Heron's property;[155] they do, however, provide some indication of the relative importance of various sources of income, as indicated in table 6.6.

Not surprisingly, most of the credits to Heron's estate came from naval stores. Tar proved especially important, with turpentine also making a significant contribution. The repayment to Heron's estate of unidentifiable debts also contributed a large portion of the income. It is difficult to determine where Heron was acquiring these sums of money. He could have been involved in a number of profitable economic activities in his life. It seems unlikely that these debts derived from the recent productivity of his plantations and merely were left unidentified. The other profitable staple sold from Heron's estate was rice. In this respect, Heron was certainly atypical because he was one of the few Lower Cape Fear planters with sufficient slaveholdings to engage in rice cultivation. Still, even given Heron's large estate, rice did not compete with naval stores.

Had Heron owned sawmills on his plantations, like many of his peers, the profits from forest products would no doubt have been an even larger share of his income. Heron also sold some livestock and provision products, but these commodities brought in little additional income, though they might well have helped to feed Heron's family and dozens of slaves.

Two other sources of income that made significant contributions to the Heron estate are in less-to-be-expected areas. First, two individuals, Lehansius Dekeyser and Henry Buford, paid Heron rent. They probably rented some of the lots Heron owned in Wilmington. In Dekeyser's case, this makes sense because Dekeyser kept an ordinary, and Wilmington would have been the best location for his business. Buford did not appear in the Lower Cape Fear records until the early 1770s so it is difficult to say anything conclusive about why he rented land from Heron. In any case, Heron's rental properties show another economic outlet available to the Lower Cape Fear elite. Most planters had various economic investments in the two Lower Cape Fear port towns. The goods and services necessitated by North Carolina's largest entrepot clearly offered many opportunities.[156]

Second, Heron accrued wealth by hiring out his slaves. In some cases, this included Heron's skilled carpenters, who would undoubtedly be a valuable commodity, though slaves were probably hired for a variety of reasons. Again, Heron's profits provide a valuable insight into the economy of the Lower Cape Fear because the hiring of slaves must have played an unusually significant role in a region with such an abundance of slave labor. Because none of the region's staple commodities had labor-intensive requirements or rigid seasonal schedules like rice, tobacco, or sugar, labor became more flexible. Planters could spare their slaves when another opportunity presented itself and, in many cases, this would have resulted in hiring. As long as Heron's rice crop remained small, he could pick up additional profits from hiring out his slaves quite frequently. Here again, the presence of a large slave population without a labor-intensive staple regime had profound economic consequences for the inhabitants of the Lower Cape Fear.

Another man who constructed an extensive and diverse plantation enterprise in the Lower Cape Fear region around the same time as Heron was Frederick Gregg. Gregg had arrived in the Lower Cape Fear from Ireland by 1748, owned land in Wilmington shortly afterward, and had made his mark in the region as a merchant, shipowner, and attorney. By 1766, Gregg had purchased three plantations from an aging settler, Charles Harrison, and by the early 1770s had accumulated thousands of acres. Gregg then decided to leave North Carolina and, in 1773, placed an advertisement to sell much of his estate. The most impressive part of his holdings may have been his residence in Wilmington, featuring a "dwelling House and Lott," along with a "Kitchen and Negro House, separate from each other, with other convenient out Houses." For business purposes, this home also included "a large Wharf" and seven storehouses, one of which was built with stone and could hold as much as eight hundred barrels of tar. In addition to this complex of buildings in town, Gregg also offered to sell "a pleasant Plantation on the Sound, containing upwards of 400 acres." This plantation included corn, indigo, vats and other equipment for producing indigo, sheep, horses, cattle, and hogs.

Gregg was reluctant to sell the most valuable parts of his Lower Cape Fear estate, however, so his ad also described a number of items that he was willing to hire out or rent. These items included "a good Grist-Mill ready to go," "a good Plantation on Hamilton's Creek for Rice & Indigo, on which there is a good Stream for a Saw-mill and plenty of Timber," plus "Lightwood, Oxen and Carts and a large stock of Cattle." While he did not mention them in his ad, other sources reveal that Gregg's plantations also produced tar, turpentine, pitch, and hemp. Gregg's slaves constituted the most significant part of his estate, however, since they provided the necessary labor for all of these business pursuits. In 1773 he offered to hire out forty slaves, the bulk of the sixty or so slaves that he owned in the region, including five of his six skilled coopers. Unfortunately for Gregg, most of his slaves and much of his profit in general would be lost during the American Revolution, prompting him to file a claim for reimbursement by the British government after the war.[157] The loss of his slaves weighed especially heavily on Gregg, and it was a dependence on enslaved labor that provides the most important common denominator between the plantation enterprises of Gregg, Moore, Murray, and Heron. In the Lower Cape Fear, abundant slave labor was treated as a given, while planters focused their creativity on the most effective ways to make slave labor profitable.

Slave labor made the economic development of the Lower Cape Fear possible, and the circumstances surrounding slavery did as much to differentiate the Lower Cape Fear from other regions as anything else. Contemporaries regularly acknowledged that there were many more slaves in the region than up the river, farther from the coast, or in Albemarle. They also drew sharp contrasts between the plantations in the Lower Cape Fear and those in the better rice country of South Carolina and Georgia. In many cases, these comparisons focused on the greater profitability of rice plantations.

Lower Cape Fear planters differed in the ways that they used their slaves as much as in the profits they obtained. Decades ago, H. R. Merrens characterized the difference between South Carolina lowcountry slavery and Lower Cape Fear slavery primarily in terms of scale.[158] More recent research and evidence from tax lists, however, demonstrate that slaves in the Lower Cape Fear made up almost as large a percentage of the population, and were as concentrated, as those in most parts of the South Carolina lowcountry.[159] Lower Cape Fear plantations did not bring their owners as much wealth, however, because the owners could not use slaves as profitability. Some of the region's planters had a labor force suited for rice planting, but they could not make as much from rice, and they fell back on a diversified economy that enabled them to take advantage of markets for several less profitable exports.

The large numbers of Lower Cape Fear slaves employed in seemingly non-labor-intensive activities raises questions about the choices made by the region's planter class. Present sources do not provide enough information to determine whether planters made the most rational economic choices. Because they did not have to import large numbers of slaves and pursued a wide range of economic activities, however, keeping and using slaves may have made the most business sense. Moreover, even if labor seemed much less badly needed in the Lower Cape Fear than in other staple-oriented regions, Lower Cape Fear residents demonstrated a strong desire to own slaves. John Brickell wrote that in North Carolina slaves "generally afford a good Price, viz. more or less according to their Goodness and Age, and are always sure Commodities for Gold or

Silver, most other things being purchased with . . . Paper Money."[160] The lack of direct shipments of slaves from Africa became a frequent source of complaint. In 1733, Burrington wrote that "Great is the loss this Country has sustained in not being supply'd by vessells from Guinea with Negroes." The governor expressed the earnest hope that "some Merchants in England will speedily furnish this Colony with Negroes, to increase the Produce and its Trade to England."[161]

Countless references reiterate the association between slave ownership and prosperity. Lower Cape Fear residents considered slaves the single most important marker of economic status and the primary prerequisite for further material advancement.[162] These attitudes may or may not have squared with estimates of profitability and preferred factor allocations, but they demonstrated powerful cultural imperatives. Slaves had been the fastest means to wealth for generations in various staple-oriented areas of British America by the time the Lower Cape Fear was first settled, and the region's inhabitants probably never doubted that the same pattern would apply in their locale. Certainly, the Moores and other immigrants from South Carolina had seen powerful evidence of the profitability of slave labor, and this prompted them to take slaves with them when they settled along the Cape Fear. Thus Lower Cape Fear settlers wanted slaves and were relatively successful at obtaining them. The many export-related activities in the region show the slave owners' creative efforts to find the most profitable uses for the region's slaves.

The production of different commodities required a different allocation of labor. This difference had far-reaching implications, not only for planters who had to manage their resources accordingly but also for the laborers themselves. In the past decade or so, historians have been increasingly attentive to the working lives of enslaved people, responding to Ira Berlin and Philip Morgan's plea that "The legacy of slavery cannot be understood without a full appreciation of the way in which slaves worked."[163] Indeed, scholars now have an impressive appreciation of the varied labor routines required for the production of rice, tobacco, and many other crops. The work of scholars focusing on slaves producing these staples obviously has significant, if limited, applicability for the diverse economy of the Lower Cape Fear. Without the same broad geographic base for source material, an equally detailed understanding for the Lower Cape Fear is impossible, but the broad contours of the experience of slavery in the region can be recovered, even if the perspectives of the slaves themselves often remain elusive.

To begin with, while no precise records of slave-work routines exist, export values, population figures, and estimates of labor requirements and productivity make it possible to estimate what tasks most frequently occupied Lower Cape Fear slaves. No other economic activity played as prominent a role in the region as tar burning, and contemporaries repeatedly stated that this work was performed by slave labor. By the late colonial period, the Lower Cape Fear's approximately five thousand slaves were producing about 50,000 barrels of tar, or 10 barrels per slave. Two contemporary sources, both from early-eighteenth-century South Carolina naval-stores operations, give some indication of the labor requirements of tar burning. Over a two-year period, Daniel Axtell recorded the production of 1,379 barrels of tar by four slaves at his kiln. This suggests that one slave working a kiln full-time produced in one year about 172 barrels of tar. Also, Thomas Smith, advising a correspondent about a piece of land, wrote that "had Mr. Hyrne on itt now twelfe good negroes he would gett off itt five hundred pounds worth off tarr yearly, for Carolina does nott afford a better tract off land for tarr and pitch."[164] Smith apparently believed that twelve slaves would produce more than 2,000 barrels of tar, under optimal conditions, and his estimates corroborate Axtell's account book, indicating that in one year slaves could produce between 150 and 200 barrels of tar. If these figures are correct, the Lower Cape Fear's seaborne exports of tar could theoretically have been burned by a few hundred slaves employed full-time.

Clearly, tar burning was not extremely labor-intensive, but these figures are misleading because Lower Cape Fear slaves were not used to burn tar full-time but in conjunction with many other activities. A more appropriate estimate comes from the author of *American Husbandry,* an eighteenth-century work about agriculture. He found that in one year, ten slaves could produce 114 barrels of tar, or slightly more than 11 barrels each, in a plantation routine that also included cultivating several relatively labor-intensive crops, producing shingles, tending to livestock, and performing various other tasks.[165] On this model, almost all of the Lower Cape Fear's slaves could have participated in the production of the region's large tar exports and also engaged in other productive plantation activities. Of course, the actual distribution of this work was probably nowhere near as uniform, but these estimates confirm that tar made up a significant but far from all-encompassing part of the laboring experience of Lower Cape Fear slaves.

Turpentine, in contrast, did require the full-time use of slaves. Contemporaries estimated that a slave could harvest about 100 barrels of crude turpentine per season.[166] Because the region produced somewhere between 8,000 and 16,000 barrels per year, the Lower Cape Fear's turpentine exports could realistically have come from a few hundred slaves. The more time-consuming nature of turpentine harvesting probably confined this work to slaves in large holdings who could be spared from more regular and rudimentary plantation tasks.

Work in the piney woods must have been a very different world for slaves, and, even if a relatively small proportion of the Lower Cape Fear's slaves spent time harvesting turpentine, many more slaves shared the experience of working in the forests.[167] Boxing trees for turpentine, gathering wood for tar kilns, and felling trees for lumber all had important common features. All of these

This antebellum illustration from *Harper's New Monthly Magazine* provides a glimpse of the routines at a tar kiln in the Lower Cape Fear's piney woods. Courtesy of the North Carolina Collection, University of North Carolina at Chapel Hill.

activities required slaves to spread out in the forests in isolation or in relatively small groups for long periods of time and to work at tasks, rather than in gangs. There is no way to determine quantitatively how much time slaves spent on any of these activities, but, given the number of trees required to produce the region's recorded exports, the combination would have taken up more of their time than any other form of labor.

The expanses of the forests made supervision unusually difficult and provided slaves with a significant degree of autonomy that would not have been available in most agricultural work. In turpentine harvesting, areas of the forests were most likely marked off in a grid since each slave was assigned a task of perhaps one-quarter of an acre.[168] Wood cutters and lightwood gatherers probably worked in small groups and must have devoted significant amounts of effort to transporting the wood to streams or some other means of getting it to the kiln or mill.[169] Both of these operations could take place on a very small scale, and even slaves on small holdings likely also participated in them on a regular basis. Large estates such as Benjamin Heron's sometimes purchased lightwood from small producers. Like elsewhere in early America, if slaves completed their tasks, masters might have let them earn money for themselves by accumulating additional wood.[170] Indeed, the challenges of supervision in the forests meant that slave owners combined traditional means of coercion with special incentives to try to control their slaves' labor despite significant difficulties. As one nineteenth-century white southerner explained, slaves in the forests were "employed in large, wooded tracts of country, out of the range of anything like close oversight and must be stimulated to their best work, as well by premiums for best crops as by so regulating their work that a portion of each week is their own." Slaves no doubt used their isolation, and sometimes even the opportunity to escape through the forests, in ways that demonstrated their agency and expressed discontent with their treatment.[171] The world of the piney woods was a world with positive and negative aspects that made it different from other kinds of work and other kinds of slavery.

Despite continual assertions to the contrary by both contemporaries and historians, laboring in the forests does not appear to have been any more pleasant for slaves than was agricultural work. If more isolation made supervision difficult, it also served as a serious impediment to participation in a slave community. Work songs and other common expressions of African and African American culture that were constantly infused into the plantation work regime must have provided less solace for lone slaves in the pine forests. Moreover, most phases of these activities were physically quite arduous and usually reserved for healthy male slaves.[172] Physical exhaustion combined with a skewed gender ratio to deny slaves rest and valuable companionship.[173]

Equally important, not even distance and isolation freed slaves from the harsh treatment of masters and overseers. In other British colonies, groups of slave woodcutters were often accompanied into the forests by a driver with a whip.[174] Colonial Lower Cape Fear planters probably used the same supervision tactics as their nineteenth-century descendants who sent men on horseback riding through the forests to make sure that slaves worked rigorously enough. Deep among the trees and far from neighboring planters, masters and overseers also would have faced little public pressure against using the most severe and alarming forms of discipline.[175] Distance and isolation also made it more difficult for masters to provide their slaves with clothes, provisions, and other necessities, and callous slave owners probably did not exert much effort to overcome these difficulties.

Here again, the rigors of the slave regime still depended on the master/slave relationship. Jones's account of Benjamin Heron's estate indicates that on Heron's plantations money was regularly spent to care for slaves in the forests. Jones frequently spent money on rum, molasses, and sugar for the slaves at Christmas or when they were ill, and at least on occasion had it sent to them while they worked at tar kilns. Jones's accounts also show a regular concern for the slaves' clothing and food. In contrast, when William Logan visited the Lower Cape Fear he discovered some "indolent & lazy" planters who "keep Negroes to do their work, which they half starve, allowing ym no more in general than a half peck of Indian Corn a week & a pint of Salt, & no Cloaths but a Breech Clout."[176] Some owners also subjected slaves to physical danger in their determination to produce more tar. As Brickell wrote, "It sometimes happens through ill management, and especially in too dry Weather, that these Kilns are blown up as if a train of Gun-powder had been laid under them by which Accident their Negroes have been very much burnt or scalded."[177] Most slaves probably experienced a middle ground between these extremes of paternalism and brutal neglect, and, on larger units of production, they were also more likely to encounter overseers than masters. Murray, who frequently expressed concern about his overseers, articulated a widely accepted planter ideal when he described "an exceeding good Overseer" who "keeps up Authority without Severity."[178] Of course, "without Severity" could be construed in a variety of ways, and all planters placed greater importance on the maintenance of their authority, even if it sometimes required coercion. In this respect and in others, the power relations at the base of plantation slavery did not vary much across regions of colonial British America.

While forest industries may have been central to the colonial Lower Cape Fear, diversity was the dominant characteristic of slaves' working experience in the region. A small number of slaves worked at rice cultivation, a routine unlike any other in the Lower Cape Fear. As Philip Morgan has expressed it, "The rice cycle was the most arduous, the most unhealthy, and the most prolonged of all mainland plantation staples."[179] But the total rice crop of the Lower Cape Fear could conceivably have been produced by fewer than a hundred slaves.[180] Maize and other crops probably occupied greater amounts of slave labor. The group of slaves described by Janet Schaw in chapter 4 as "follow[ing] each other's tail the day long" were working in corn fields.[181]

Important as collective labor patterns may have been for some slaves, a surprising number of Lower Cape Fear slaves worked at specialized and individualized tasks. Some of these activities bore a direct relationship to the forest industries. For example, a large network of slave watermen facilitated the movement of heavy export products through the region. Minding kilns and running sawmills also required specific forms of expertise, and both of these jobs could be filled by either slaves or colonists, depending on the owner's preferences and options. Perhaps most important of all, the many barrels of naval-stores sent out of the Lower Cape Fear required the work of numerous trained coopers. By one estimate, one in every five laborers used in the nineteenth-century North Carolina naval-stores industry was a cooper; consequently, these craftsman coopers drew a high value in the region.[182] Scattered advertisements from extant colonial North Carolina newspapers confirm that coopers, among other slaves in the region, brought a "good price."[183] A contemporary document estimating the value of the slaves in one estate appraised the two slaves identified as cooper at a higher value than all but one of the fifty-five other slaves.[184]

TABLE 6.7 **Occupational Structure of Frederick Gregg's Slaves, 1773**

Occupation	*Number*	*%*
Unspecified	41	66
Cooper	6	10
Domestic	5	8
Other Craftsmen	4	6
Watermen	4	6
Miscellaneous	2	4
Total	62	100

Note: *Domestic* includes cooks, washerwomen, housemaids, and bakers. *Other craftsmen* includes millers, tailors, shoemakers, and tanners. *Miscellaneous* includes fishermen and coachmen.

TABLE 6.8 **Differences in Occupation between Frederick Gregg's Male and Female Slaves, 1773**

	Number	*Specialized*	*% Specialized*
Male	41	17	41
Female	21	4	19

The role of coopers in the Lower Cape Fear underscores the ways that different regional economies and export products influenced the occupational structure of the slave population. Specialized skills became increasingly common as colonial economies became more elaborate and the scale of slaveholdings increased. Because most North Carolina estate inventories did not identify the occupations of skilled slaves, there is little evidence about this matter from the Lower Cape Fear. But because the requirements of slave fieldwork for the region's exports were comparatively limited, it can be hypothesized that slave owners were more willing to use their slaves in skilled crafts. The strong regional need for some of these skills—coopering, sawyering, boat piloting—made such specialization even more likely.

The records from Gregg's estate make an occupational analysis possible for a small sample of slaves.[185] A list of Gregg's sixty-two slaves and their occupations, listed in table 6.7, indicates a very high level of specialization among at least some Lower Cape Fear slaves. A staggeringly high twenty-one (34 percent) of Gregg's slaves had some kind of skill or specialized occupation. Such a proportion is impressive given the relatively early phase of settlement in the region and the comparatively limited scale of Gregg's holdings. But these figures are even more impressive because the sixty-two slaves listed almost certainly included a significant number of children who were too young to be trained in a specific skill.[186] In this context, Gregg's slaves showed as much occupational specialization as that for slaves anywhere on mainland colonial American plantations. Most significant parallels could be found on larger and more mature South Carolina plantations. As on most other colonial American plantations, the pattern of specialization among Gregg's slaves differed sharply along gender lines. More than 80 percent of his specialized slaves were male. All female slaves with specific occupations performed domestic task.[187]

Two estate inventories also shed light on Lower Cape Fear slave occupations. The thirty-six adult slaves listed in planter Joseph Blake's inventories included three coopers and a carpenter. Blake's skilled slaves constituted only about 11 percent of his labor force, a much lower proportion than Gregg's. This may or may not be a comprehensive listing for Blake's slaves, but, either way, Gregg's and Blake's slave occupational patterns suggest the varying circumstances on Lower Cape Fear plantations and the individual choices and options of planters. Perhaps Blake's smaller slaveholdings allowed him less room for specialization. Another inventory complicates the relationship between plantation size and specialization, however. William Gabie owned only eight slaves, but they included a cooper, a miller, and a housemaid. For Gabie, and probably for other small-scale owners of slaves, the ownership of skilled slaves offered a promising investment opportunity because coopers and other craftsmen played a much more central role in the Lower Cape Fear's labor force than fieldhands. Craftsmen could bring in steadier profits from hiring out. Thus, Gregg's and Gabie's labor forces provide strong indications that the Lower Cape Fear's relative abundance of slaves led to a more skilled and specialized slave population, whereas Blake's slaves serve as a reminder that this tendency would still have been subject to considerable variation from plantation to plantation.[188]

The diversity of Lower Cape Fear slaves' working conditions transcended narrow occupational categories, however. First of all, slaves worked in a greater variety of settings because the flexibility of labor supplies in the region permitted more hiring out. For most slaves, the benefits of a change in setting would have been outweighed by being distant from familiar social connections and by possibly being at the mercy of harsher masters and overseers. In some cases, coopers and other valuable skilled slaves may have been able to use hiring out as a bargaining chip to obtain more autonomy, but this was far from the norm.

Equally important, the region's large slave population enabled colonists to use slave labor for virtually every minor task, and contemporary accounts describe slaves performing a vast array of duties. Lower Cape Fear slaves cooked, served as guides, cared for children, killed alligators, hunted, gardened, made soap, and performed innumerable other tasks.[189] When no profitable work could be found for slaves, their owners hired them out, and the hiring of slaves seems to have been especially common feature of slave life in the region.[190] They performed these responsibilities not because of the requirements of a staple-driven, labor-intensive plantation system but because Anglo-American colonists had internalized the ideology of slave ownership and because, in the Lower Cape Fear, economic and population conditions made their labor readily available.

Finally, when all this labor had been performed, slaves went to work in still other ways, to further their own material condition and make their plight bearable. Independent economic production by slaves took place throughout the Americas.[191] Two tantalizing pieces of information show the importance of the slaves' own possessions. Janet Schaw, in sharply criticizing the agricultural practices of Lower Cape Fear settlers, at one point noted that "the Negroes are the only people that seem to pay any attention to the various uses that wild vegetables may be put to." Slaves received a small allowance of corn, she reported, but also "a little piece of land which they cultivate much better than their Master." In addition, they "rear hogs and poultry, sow calabashes, etc. and are better provided for in every thing than the poorer white people with us." This independent production, perhaps as much as planter efforts to keep livestock and grow corn, played a part in the Lower Cape Fear region's attempts at self-sufficiency and provision exporting. When European Americans ceased to be vigilant, Schaw noted, slaves "steal whatever they can come at, and even intercept the cows and milk them."[192]

Schaw's account provides the details of a potentially well-developed internal economy among slaves. Complaints from Lower Cape Fear authorities reveal the presence of marketing in this internal economy. Slave markets and trafficking played such a prominent role in the region, especially in Wilmington, that the authorities repeatedly found it necessary to try to curtail these activities. Their repeated protestations suggest that they had little success.[193] In the provision grounds and markets of the Lower Cape Fear, slaves found ways to own instead of be owned and to participate successfully in an economy built on their labor and designed to marginalize them. Thus, while Anglo-American colonists created a distinct regional economy, Lower Cape Fear slaves employed many of the same forms of self-assertion and perseverance that enslaved Africans and African Americans found useful throughout colonial America. In this, as in most things, Schaw recognized that "they are indeed the constant plague of their tyrants, whose severity or mildness is equally regarded by them in these Matters."[194] At the same time that slaves participated in broad patterns of resistance, however, their day-to-day lives within the Lower Cape Fear region gave meaning to geographic space both for them and their oppressors.

Lower Cape Fear slaves, plantation owners, merchants, and families, then, all acted within a regionally distinct set of economic parameters. Despite elaborate efforts by both modern scholars and contemporary observers to delineate clear agricultural patterns across large areas of geographic space, the inhabitants of the Lower Cape Fear developed a system of production and profit making unlike any others in the southern colonies because of the region's emphasis on forest resources, its relative abundance of enslaved labor, and its highly diversified export base. Perhaps even more impressive, they not only created this unusual regional economy, they also integrated it into a common intellectual and cultural framework that had been formed under very different and diverse experiences. In the Lower Cape Fear, Scottish entrepreneurs like James Murray, rice planters like Roger Moore, and yeoman farmers of limited means from Albemarle could view themselves as "planters" while exporting primarily nonagricultural products derived from the forests. Similarly, Creole and African slaves could utilize the same tactics of resistance, self-preservation, and cultural revitalization that played an important role throughout African American slave societies.

Cultural backgrounds and new experiences combined to reconfigure identities and root them in geographic space. Few individuals lived in complete isolation from broader trends and extraregional events and networks. At the same time, all those who considered the world beyond the Lower Cape Fear must have recognized significant differences. Labor, production, plantation management, and resource allocation played enormous roles in most peoples' lives. Rice, tobacco, sugar, and other export commodities had cultural meanings and, in each case, they ultimately became rooted in specific geographic spaces. For many, the regional identity of the Lower Cape Fear undoubtedly grew from the naval-stores industry and from the economy of the piney woods; others might have emphasized the absence of rice or tobacco production; but all must have been aware that circumstances differed in the Lower Cape Fear and that individuals in their region had to approach economic life on terms that varied significantly from those in South Carolina, Albemarle, or any other place around them.

Chapter 7

PORT TOWNS

Of the thousands of people who arrived in the Lower Cape Fear between the settlement of Brunswick and the American Revolution, few achieved greater notoriety than Thomas Godfrey. In 1759, at twenty-two years of age, Godfrey came to Wilmington partly because of an offer of employment in the Lower Cape Fear's growing commercial networks. Godfrey cared about much more than business, however, and his decision may have been even more influenced by positive accounts of North Carolina, including one from Benjamin Franklin in Godfrey's hometown of Philadelphia and one from his commanding officer in the Pennsylvania militia, Lower Cape Fear native Hugh Waddell. He resided in Wilmington for four years before an early death in 1763. During those four years, Godfrey left little record of his business transactions or role in Lower Cape Fear society, but he completed *The Prince of Parthia: A Tragedy,* the first work of drama by a native of the British colonies in America and the source of his fame. Most of *The Prince of Parthia* had been written in Pennsylvania, where Godfrey apparently hoped to have the play performed, but the migration of the first British American playwright to a relatively small North Carolina port town may reveal as much about the growth of the Lower Cape Fear region as it does about early American literature.[1]

Godfrey's writing continued while he lived in North Carolina, and surprisingly the coastal area known as Masonboro Sound appears more prominently in his work than Wilmington or any other specific place. There are indications that Godfrey hoped to find more peace and quiet in North Carolina than he had enjoyed in Philadelphia, and Masonboro provided a more likely place of retreat than a growing port town. In any case, Masonboro and its surroundings made enough of an impression on Godfrey that he placed them in a long and powerful tradition of pastoral imagery in literature:

> Come to Masonborough's grove
> Ye Nymphs and Swains away
> Where blooming Innocence and Love,
> And Pleasure crown the day.
> Here dwells the Muse, here her bright Seat
> Erects the lovely Maid
> From Noise and Show, a blest retreat,
> She seeks the sylvan shade.[2]

Godfrey was far from the only immigrant to the Lower Cape Fear who dreamed of a pleasant and restful retreat from the travails of the world. James Murray often reflected on his wish to abandon commerce and live in the more bucolic setting of his plantation, which he significantly named Point Repose.[3] Indeed, the pastoral ideal must have held widespread appeal for settlers in the Lower Cape Fear region: archaeological studies reveal that pastoral scenes provided the most common decorative motif on delftware tiles in Brunswick homes.[4]

Yet neither Godfrey's migration nor the growth of the Lower Cape Fear region more generally can be convincingly portrayed as a rejection of urban life. For Godfrey and other residents of the region, Masonboro Sound and Wilmington constituted different parts of the same world of experience. Godfrey's celebration of repose in Masonboro depended on and grew out of his familiarity with the bustling lifestyle of Philadelphia and his economic concerns in Wilmington. Similarly, Murray never fully abandoned his more urban activities, often moving back and forth from his plantation depending on the seasons and other concerns, and the pastoral tile motifs discovered by archaeologists in the Lower Cape Fear come from houses in a town. Lower Cape Fear residents apparently admired and sought to make use of both town and rural locale.

Godfrey's writing about Masonboro, then, reveals one more way that Lower Cape Fear residents attempted to impose their own meanings on geographic spaces. Ironically, Godfrey's life in the Lower Cape Fear illustrates the increasing importance of the region's town in several other ways. For one thing, Godfrey's literary endeavors provide an indication of the pursuit of civility and refinement in Lower Cape Fear society, and this pursuit tended to focus on more urban settings. It is uncertain whether an informal performance of *The Prince of Parthia* ever took place in the colonial Lower Cape Fear, but, at the very least, Godfrey found companions who shared similar aesthetic interests.[5] Also, it is difficult to lose sight of the fact that Godfrey, like many other settlers, made a living from trade in a Lower Cape Fear port town. In short, Godfrey's life in the Lower Cape Fear revolved around two of the defining characteristics of Atlantic world port towns: the exchange of ideas and the exchange of goods.

For many others, as for Thomas Godfrey, access to the Atlantic Ocean offered the most powerful impetus for settling in the Lower Cape Fear. Maurice Moore recognized as much when he carefully laid out the lots for Brunswick in 1725, providing the region with the blueprint for a port town. Generations of colonists to the north in North Carolina also recognized the significance of ocean ports, evident in their complaints about the lack of adequate port facilities. Such complaints were a dominant refrain in the early history of Albemarle.[6] Once the Lower Cape Fear region had been settled, contemporary commentators rarely neglected to point out the centrality of Brunswick and Wilmington to the region, acknowledging the towns' economic, social, cultural, and political centrality. Beyond these more explicit references, moreover, the behavior of Lower Cape Fear residents continually demonstrated the importance of these two port towns in their lives, as Wilmington and Brunswick not only provided urban functions but also eventually contributed to the centralization and definition of the region itself.

As vital as these port towns were in the colonial Lower Cape Fear, few colonial historians have paid much attention to them.[7] Indeed, the Lower Cape Fear, like other regions in the southern colonies, has become associated with the deeply rural mythology of the antebellum American South. Generalizations that overemphasize the rural character of the southern colonies and states have not gone unchallenged, and a relatively sophisticated body of scholarship has now shed valuable light on the once-neglected process of urban development in early America.[8] In this area, as in many others, however, scholars have generalized from models that are appropriate for some places but not for others.

The dominant interpretive schema regarding urbanization in the southern colonies emphasizes the economic linkages associated with certain staple exports and focuses primarily on the characteristics of the Chesapeake Bay region.[9] Scholars have focused so intensely on the Chesapeake because the pattern of urbanization there appears so anomalous. Despite the presence of large and increasingly well-populated hinterlands, few major towns appeared, and they never reached the size of such northern port towns as Philadelphia and Boston. Carville Earle, Ronald Hoffman, and Jacob Price, among others, have carefully demonstrated that tobacco cultivation required few linkages and combined with geography and other factors to stunt the growth of towns in much of the Chesapeake tidewater.[10] By contrast, wheat and rice seem to have encouraged centralization in the southern colonies, contributing significantly to the growth of Baltimore, Norfolk, and Charles Town. Of course, these tendencies cannot easily be generalized to areas, like the Lower Cape Fear, that were primarily oriented toward the production and exportation of completely different commodities, though the logic of tracing backward and forward linkages still bears much relevance.

Equally important, models that attempt to explain the peculiar disjunction between population growth and urbanization in the Chesapeake tend to obscure the powerful relationship between these variables elsewhere. In most parts of early America and even in the southern colonies, population growth did lead to urbanization, and central places did develop to accommodate new settlers. Except for Charles Town, no urban center south of Norfolk had a very large population at the time of the American Revolution, and the Carolinas and Georgia still remained quite sparsely populated during these years. A variety of factors also limited the potential hinterlands of some southern ports and prevented them from meeting the needs of settlers swarming into the backcountry in the late colonial period. But the Lower Cape Fear ports functioned on a relatively small scale primarily because of their late settlement and the small population of their hinterland, not solely because of the "colonial" character of southern economies or because of any cultural predisposition to decentralization.

The Lower Cape Fear ports and the plantations of the Cape Fear River Valley grew in unison, underscoring the fundamental continuity of urban and rural life in much of the early-modern world. Modern historians impose categories such as urban and rural, but the residents of the Lower Cape Fear moved easily between the worlds of Wilmington stores and of Rocky Point plantations. The development of Brunswick and Wilmington, then, encapsulate much of the development of the region. As settlers worked to mold the Lower Cape Fear into a prosperous and important region, they also attempted to give it a central focus, or, at times, two central foci.

When Maurice Moore tried to make Brunswick the first central focus of settlement in the Lower Cape Fear, his selection of a site for the town reflected some clear preferences and would have significant consequences. He positioned the town of Brunswick in a particularly exposed place in order to allow port access for the largest of eighteenth-century ships. The infamous "Flats" at the junction of Town Creek and the Cape Fear River above Brunswick prevented some ships from entering the river any further. From their experience in South Carolina, the Moores recognized the benefits of transatlantic commerce and knew that it required large vessels.[11] Rather than forgo the opportunity to develop a large export trade to European markets, the Moores decided to tolerate other deficiencies in the location of their town. By trying to make their own Charles Town on the Lower Cape Fear, the Moores neglected to consider the ways that the two regions differed. Over several decades, it became apparent that Brunswick would prove unsatisfactory.

Brunswick began promisingly enough. Not only the Moores but a number of other prosperous early settlers invested in the town. In 1735, John Brickell predicted that Brunswick "will be very considerable in a short time, by its' great Trade, the number of Merchants, and rich Planters that are settled . . . within these few Years."[12] But the town took time to develop. During these early years, Hugh Meredith also saw potential in Brunswick, but acknowledged that it was "at present but a poor, hungry, unprovided Place consisting of not above 10 or 12 scattering mean Houses, hardly worth the name of a Village."[13] Without an alternative port on the river, Brunswick might have become quite prominent, but in the mid-1730s, when Governor Gabriel Johnston and some other entrepreneurs acting independently of the Moores established another town upriver, the vast majority of newcomers went there instead of to Brunswick.

Lower Cape Fear residents hesitated to embrace the town of Brunswick for a variety of reasons. Perhaps most important, the town's location rendered it especially vulnerable to enemy attacks and severe weather. In the aftermath of one notable invasion by the Spanish in 1748, Brunswick appeared to be "ruined and Destroyed."[14] Also, while the whole Lower Cape Fear region faced persistent problems with tropical diseases, many people believed conditions to be particularly severe near Brunswick.[15]

Moreover, though Brunswick's location gave it clear advantages for large-scale transatlantic trade, its upriver competitor, Wilmington, proved better suited for the diverse and relatively small-scale trade that ultimately went through the Lower Cape Fear ports. Because the Cape Fear River easily surpassed all other means of transportation through the region and to the ports' hinterland, Wilmington merchants could readily entice most of the region's trade as it came down the river and before it got to Brunswick.[16] At the same time, only a relatively small minority of the vessels sailing to the Cape Fear had any difficulty traveling up the river as far as Wilmington, whereas it would have been dangerous for the upriver watercraft to have traveled to Brunswick.

The historian Lawrence Lee analyzed the tonnage of ships entering the two ports and provided reliable data that illustrates the comparative advantage of Wilmington. Lee found that only about one-quarter of the region's shipping would have been hindered beyond Brunswick. Wilmington dominated the Lower Cape Fear's coastal and West Indian commerce and still competed effectively with Brunswick for trade with Britain. Of course, Brunswick garnered most of the British commerce, including much of the lucrative naval-stores trade. But, because naval stores were enumerated in British legislation that required certain commodities to go to Britain before any foreign ports, and therefore to be inevitably monopolized by British markets, Lower Cape Fear merchants probably could not have made very large commercial profits marketing these commodities. The lack of backward linkages requiring personnel to market naval stores also limited the size of Brunswick's mercantile community. The West Indian and coastal trades leaving Wilmington offered significantly greater entrepreneurial opportunities because of competing markets. Not surprisingly, therefore, Wilmington attracted a considerably larger merchant community than Brunswick. Also, Lee found that despite the various geographic limitations of the two Lower Cape Fear ports, together they were able to clear ships that averaged about the same tonnage as those clearing Charles Town, and much more tonnage than those clearing other North Carolina ports.[17] In this sense, the two ports could be seen as complementary, rather than competitive; indeed, some prominent merchants owned lots in both towns.

Even if they fulfilled somewhat different economic functions, the existence of two port towns generated an impressive level of animosity within the Lower Cape Fear elite. As Murray observed, there was "a great emulation between the two towns."[18] The towns bid against each other for Anglican clergy, and they pushed the limits of North Carolina's political structure, fighting over legislation that enabled the incorporation of Wilmington and encouraged its development. Roger Moore even attempted to coerce his associates into avoiding business with Wilmington.[19]

Ultimately, though, the conventional characterization of persistent tension between Brunswick and Wilmington is misleading. After the earliest years of growth in Wilmington, such a large disparity existed between the two towns that realistic competition would have been impossible. Nor would it be accurate to say that the Lower Cape Fear had two separate and comparably important port towns, because Wilmington's emergence practically reduced Brunswick to insignificance except for its transatlantic port facilities.

Lower Cape Fear residents rapidly recognized the advantages of Wilmington, while the founders of Brunswick struggled to support their town. According to some of the region's residents, a preference for Wilmington became the "universal opinion of the People" as they praised the town for its "healthful Scituation," declared it "mighty convenient," and claimed it was "capable of receiving Vessels of great burthern and extremely safe in the most violent storms."[20] Many merchants probably followed the same course of action as James Murray. When Murray first arrived in 1735 he hoped to live in Wilmington, but he found that there were not yet enough houses in the town. In the meantime, he lived in Brunswick and acknowledged that, until Wilmington grew more, Brunswick was the preferable location. The following year, however, he purchased a house and lot in Wilmington and, in 1737, he stated that Wilmington would become "the Metropolis of the province."[21] When George Whitefield visited Wilmington in the early 1740s, he found it a "little but thriving place for trade."[22]

By contrast, the early enthusiasm and confidence about the prospects of Brunswick faded from the existing record. The town in fact evoked little comment from travelers. In official correspondence, the Moores and their allies protested the favoritism toward Wilmington and claimed that the incorporation of the new town had been unfair because many residents had already invested resources in Brunswick.[23] Evidence that their complaints and official protests had not been in vain came in 1745, when legislation sought to "encourage Persons to settle in the Town of Brunswick."[24] The small population of the town made it even more vulnerable to invasion, and the construction of nearby Fort Johnston ultimately proved a better response to the problem because legislation apparently did little to increase the size of the town.

Quantitative data confirms that Wilmington had easily surpassed Brunswick in size and resources by 1740. Between 1735 and 1740, in particular, land in Wilmington was conveyed 94 times, while land in Brunswick was conveyed only 14 times, reflecting a pronounced difference in the demand for land in the two towns. Through the rest of the colonial period, conveyances of land in Brunswick never made up more than 5 percent of the total conveyances in the

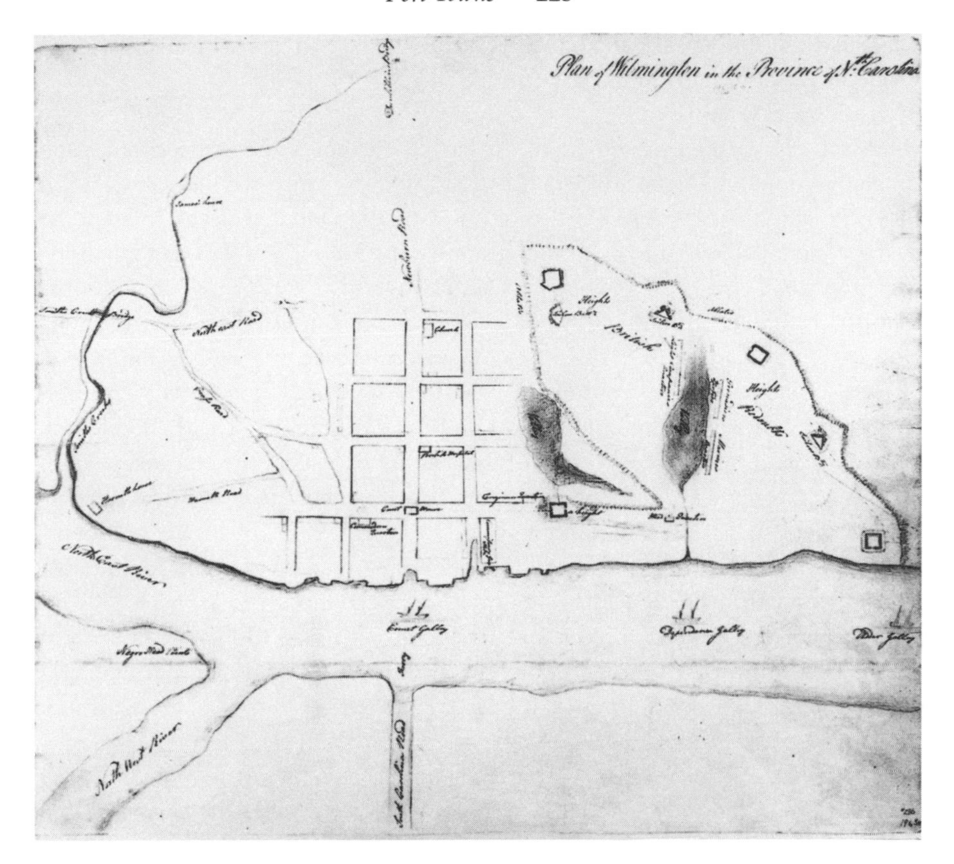

The British army occupied Wilmington during 1781 and made this map of North Carolina's most important port town. British fortifications can be seen at right center. Courtesy of the North Carolina Office of Archives and History, Raleigh, N.C.

region, but Wilmington conveyances always exceeded 10 percent of the region's total. Throughout the colonial period, land in Wilmington was conveyed 430 times, including 832 lots, but land in Brunswick was conveyed a mere 81 times, including 170 lots.[25] Various market factors dealing with land in the two towns probably contributed to patterns in the frequency of conveyances, but such a large difference in scale indicates that a much larger number of people were interested in Wilmington.

Records of the number of people owning lots or otherwise connected to the towns reveal a similar trend.[26] Between 1725 and 1775, 605 individuals had connections to Wilmington, and 358 owned land in the town, but only 109 had connections to Brunswick, and a mere 78 owned land.[27] All of this evidence suggests that Wilmington had a population approximately five or six times as large as that of Brunswick after 1740. Brunswick's population probably never exceeded two hundred, but Wilmington must have had about twelve hundred residents by the American Revolution.[28]

Aside from scale, the two towns differed in other notable ways. Brunswick's residents apparently invested in the town to further interests in other parts of the region. They most frequently received the occupational designation "planter," and they owned considerable amounts of land and slaves. Indeed, the average identifiable Brunswick lot owner possessed considerable wealth, including more than two thousand acres of land. Most of these lot owners probably identified closely with the Moores and envisioned themselves in the tradition of South Carolina's merchant rice planters. Compared with Wilmington, Brunswick's leaders played a disproportionately significant role in elite politics. Indeed, those included among the 109 individuals connected with Brunswick received appointment to provincial offices ten times during the colonial period. Brunswick's impressive level of representation probably made political opposition to much-larger Wilmington possible. At the same time, Brunswick residents seemed less oriented toward mercantile endeavors. Significantly, no identifiable maritime vessel owner or captain could be connected with Brunswick.

The character of Wilmington, on the other hand, owed much to the entrepreneurial spirit of the Atlantic world. Trade provided both a literal and metaphorical focus for Wilmington because the town's two busiest streets met at a market.[29] Its earliest residents were merchants, and the "merchant" designation remained the most common one among the town's residents and lot owners. Wilmington attracted a more heterogeneous elite that also included immigrants from various locations in the British Isles and from more distant colonies. They owned much smaller holdings of land in the region, suggesting the more commercial and less agricultural nature of their economic lives. Wilmington also had a more maritime character, as indicated by the nine vessel owners and four captains who possessed lots in the town. If Wilmington's residents did not demonstrate as much elite control of Lower Cape Fear wealth and offices as did Brunswick residents, they more than made up for the difference in numbers, accounting for almost three times as many of the region's justices of the peace.

Over several decades, these other differences became less crucial as Wilmington burgeoned and Brunswick atrophied. During the late colonial period, visitors to the region referred to Brunswick only as an afterthought or omitted mention of it altogether, focusing on Wilmington. In 1762, Moravian visitors from the backcountry, specifically comparing Wilmington with Brunswick, remarked that it was "a large city for this country."[30] Hugh Finlay called Wilmington "the most flourishing town in the Province," while Scotus Americanus echoed similar sentiments and neglected even to mention Brunswick.[31] William Mylne found Brunswick to be "a poor place and irregular built," but described Wilmington as "a place of considerable trade."[32]

Brunswick might have survived relatively unnoticed and underdeveloped, but a series of other difficulties diminished the town's already small population. Problems with defense and disease persisted. A particularly severe disease epidemic seems to have hit the Brunswick area sometime between 1769 and 1772.[33] Just before the American Revolution, Janet Schaw went to Brunswick and found that "tho' the best sea port in the province the town is very poor—a few scattered houses on the edge of the woods, without street or regularity."[34] Her brother Alexander also commented that Brunswick was "indeed but a straggling village."[35] The violence of the American Revolution dealt Brunswick its death blow, however. During the war, fear of British occupation caused many residents to flee the exposed site, and a fire destroyed some of the town's most prominent buildings. Some of the details remain sketchy, but visitors to the region in the years just after the British occupation confirmed that Brunswick had been abandoned and largely destroyed.[36] Maurice Moore's aspiring town lasted a mere fifty years, while up the river its rival had grown into the largest and most important urban center in North Carolina and, for many, the focal point of life in the Lower Cape Fear.

In both towns and the Lower Cape Fear region as a whole, trade took time to develop. While it is true that customs records for years beginning in 1768 indicate that the Lower Cape Fear ports brought in approximately one-half of North Carolina's export wealth, a lack of customs records makes the conditions of trade in earlier years less clear. In the early years, the Moores and other Lower Cape Fear elites probably depended on ties beyond the region to facilitate trade. Between 1727 and 1734, at least eighteen voyages between South Carolina and the Lower Cape Fear were recorded in surviving shipping lists from South Carolina. The first three voyages from the Lower Cape Fear to South Carolina, in 1730 and 1731, arrived in ballast, apparently because the new settlement lacked export commodities that would be valued in Charleston. By 1734, the region sent South Carolinians corn, lumber, and a variety of naval stores. The larger markets of Charleston provided the Lower Cape Fear settlers with various items that they held precious but could not obtain or make in their new homes, including molasses, rum, sugar, textiles, European goods, and slaves. South Carolinians also exported various provisions to the Lower Cape Fear, suggesting that even food may have been scarce during the earliest years of settlement in the region.

Gradually, as the region's population and institutions grew, Lower Cape Fear entrepreneurs became more established and less dependent on merchants in Charles Town and other colonial locales.[37] By the 1760s, enough contemporary comments exist to leave little doubt that the Lower Cape Fear dominated North Carolina's maritime trade, and as early as the 1730s the region's ports apparently surpassed any others in the colony. But even on a comparatively small scale, eighteenth-century transatlantic trading networks did not grow accidentally or overnight. Over five decades, aspiring Lower Cape Fear merchants and planters carved out a niche for themselves in highly competitive and potentially lucrative Atlantic markets.

North Carolinians recognized that the Lower Cape Fear offered them their most promising Atlantic port at an early stage, but they still had to work out the details of transporting, trading, producing, and marketing. In his first few years on the Lower Cape Fear, Murray saw little hope for the trade of the region. With the Lower Cape Fear's trade in naval stores, lumber, and provisions all in their infancy, Murray simply could not find goods valuable enough to support an extensive export trade. Local debts could not be collected; the price of naval stores in London remained low; he had to rely on ships from New England and other places; currency continued to be scarce; and the colony suffered from a gross trade imbalance. Unable to make remittances to carry on trade, Murray decided that mercantile ventures were not worth the freight costs. In later years, as regional markets fluctuated, Murray alternated between regret and thankfulness over his decision to move away from mercantile pursuits in Lower Cape Fear.[38]

Many of the problems about which Murray complained could be attributed to timing and went away as the region grew, but, throughout the colonial period, Lower Cape Fear merchants continued to face considerable impediments. Even though the Lower Cape Fear differed substantially from other regions of North Carolina in many ways, the region's merchants found themselves encumbered by the colony's unfavorable reputation. Beyond these perceptual problems, the Cape Fear offered a good oceangoing port by North Carolina standards, but still had some notable shortcomings that continued to plague the region's commercial endeavors.

North Carolina had and has one of the most treacherous coasts in the world for oceangoing vessels, making a trip to the Cape Fear ports unusually dangerous, even if the port facilities proved ample. Although a number of early commentators took great pains to point out that, as William Tryon put it, "the entrance of Cape Fear River is formidable only in its name," many merchants and sea captains no doubt remained wary.[39] Aside from the obviously considerable psychological implications of such sailing dangers, the frequency of mishaps along the North Carolina coast had real consequences for business in the Cape Fear. During the late colonial period at least, some merchants found that no one would insure vessels going to and from North Carolina, forcing them to bear an unusual burden of risk for oceangoing ventures in the region.[40]

The late beginning and small scale of trade from the Lower Cape Fear also hindered merchants in a number of significant ways. English and Scottish merchants had no great incentives to send ships with imports to the region because it offered but a small market for their goods. This situation, coupled with the natural impediments of the coast, contributed to the limited selection and notoriously high price of goods in Lower Cape Fear markets.[41] Small markets also meant limited means of exchange and less institutional development. Indeed, underdeveloped financial institutions became an acute problem as North Carolina currency inspired less and less confidence, specie remained scarce, and merchants lacked other reliable means of credit or payment. Efforts to encourage the issue of more currency to facilitate trade met with fierce opposition from Albemarle leaders, underscoring once again the significance of regional economic differences in North Carolina. Commodity money, three-way trade, barter, and currency emissions all made trade in the Lower Cape Fear possible, but each of these methods brought its own difficulties.[42]

Because commercial and transportation networks also took time to develop, Wilmington and Brunswick lagged in other key ways. Most important, credit drove almost all commercial transactions in the early modern Atlantic world, and Lower Cape Fear merchants had to find ways of obtaining credit. Some of the region's most prominent merchants brought sufficient credit reputations and capital with them, of course, making credit less of a problem. English and Scottish merchants like Murray, John Burgwin, Robert Hogg, Richard Eagles, and Benjamin Heron probably played a particularly helpful role in establishing transatlantic trade. But even well-prepared entrepreneurs such as these found themselves hindered by North Carolina's long-standing reputation as a poor credit risk.[43] Nor did naval stores and the region's other exports instill the same confidence in creditors as did rice, indigo, or some other colonial commodities. Robert Hogg and Francis Clayton complained that one trader with whom they did business did "not choose to order any of the Produce of this Province."[44] Just as Lower Cape Fear and other colonial merchants often relied on outside sources of credit, they also had to be willing to supply copious amounts of credit to other colonists.[45]

Because of the scarcity of specie and the difficulty of obtaining repayment, the burden of credit no doubt fell particularly heavily on merchants in the Lower Cape Fear. The few extant copies of the *Cape Fear Mercury,* the region's short-lived newspaper, include notices from merchants requesting payment of debts and expressing a desire to close their affairs, but in many cases these measures must have been in vain.[46] The extension of business interests and credit networks in the region also required improvements in transportation, which took time. The Cape Fear provided a valuable thoroughfare, but settlers first had to build roads and obtain access to the river, as well as acquire boats and make other adaptations.[47] These matters could be resolved more quickly than credit problems, but in the first decades of settlement, neither could they be taken for granted.

For the Lower Cape Fear to develop a substantial maritime trade, improvements in communication and transportation had to be extended into the Atlantic economy as well. Lower Cape Fear residents had to establish business relationships and connections in other ports. By the late colonial period, the Lower Cape Fear's transatlantic business connections appear to have been quite extensive. Of course, Murray and others began participating in trade with the West Indies and other distant locales in the 1730s, but it is impossible to say how widespread these activities were.[48] Murray continued to cultivate valuable economic ties, as illustrated by his dealings with prominent metropolitan merchant Richard Oswald. Murray gained access to Oswald through a long-time friend, merchant Robert Scott, and both Murray and Oswald gained from their interaction. Oswald sent Murray plantation supplies upon request, obtained insurance for Murray's cargoes, managed an account for Murray's sister, and even, each year, supplied Murray with fashionable wigs. Murray reciprocated by consigning indigo and other Carolina exports to Oswald, who received a commission for his services.

While Murray sometimes felt neglected in Oswald's vast trading network, metropolitan merchants like Oswald allowed colonial merchants like Murray to establish themselves in Atlantic world commerce.[49] By 1764, however, goods were selling well enough in the Lower Cape Fear that merchant Francis Clayton, of Charles Town, decided to relocate in Wilmington and join his business partner Robert Hogg. Clayton immediately put his ties to use and wrote the firm of Grubb and Watson in London, soliciting the interest of their friends in Bristol, Poole, and Liverpool, as well as London, about possibilities in the naval-stores trade.[50] Over the next few years, the firm maintained a brisk business between the Lower Cape Fear, London, South Carolina, and the British West Indies through ties with Richard Grubb and other important metropolitan merchants.

Trade with Charles Town played only a minor role in the Lower Cape Fear's oceangoing trade by the 1760s, but proximity often made it easy for merchants between the two ports to assist each other. Substantial extant business correspondence from Charles Town merchants Robert Pringle, John Guerrard, and Henry Laurens reveals the character of some Lower Cape Fear connections. The Lower Cape Fear exported much larger quantities of naval stores, so when South Carolina merchants could not fill naval-stores orders for British merchants, they referred them to reliable suppliers in the Lower Cape Fear.[51] In the struggle to obtain reputation and credit in Atlantic markets, South Carolina merchants spoke on behalf of Lower Cape Fear business associates. Pringle, for example, suggested that a London firm employ Lower Cape Fear merchant Daniel Dunbibin as its factor in North Carolina.[52] The two merchant communities also relied on each other for credit, helped one another recover debts, gave bills of exchange when circumstances warranted, and provided other business advice and services. The long list of Lower Cape Fear merchants mentioned in the business papers of Pringle and Laurens included Dunbibin, Hogg, and Eagles, and James Innes, Robert Walker, William Faris, Thomas Clark, William

Lithgow, Roger Moore, Lewis DeRosset, John Rutherford, Alexander Duncan, and Cornelius Harnett.[53] Significantly, most of these merchants did not participate in the migration from South Carolina to the Lower Cape Fear; they also represented more interests in Wilmington than in Brunswick. Clearly, then, Lower Cape Fear merchants had become active participants in a large maritime merchant community. If these communications with Charles Town do not indicate far-flung networks, their ancillary nature indicates that larger-scale trade must have necessitated even closer ties with merchants in the British Isles and the West Indies.

As useful as trade networks could be, Lower Cape Fear merchants could make more significant profits by controlling, as well as facilitating, the region's trade. Commercial profits varied considerably in colonial America because some merchants operated fully integrated enterprises that directed nearly every stage of the trading process, whereas whole regions left almost all of their commercial activities to merchants from the British Isles and other colonies. Late settlement, limited resources, and other circumstances made it necessary for Lower Cape Fear residents to share some of their trading activities with outsiders. Despite the reputation of the southern colonies for commercial underdevelopment, Lower Cape Fear merchants did participate in a significant degree of autonomous commercial activity by the late colonial period.

Mercantile opportunities in the eighteenth-century Atlantic depended heavily on shipping. Those who owned vessels not only had more say in choosing their destinations and markets, they minimalized considerable transportation costs. But oceangoing vessels required a large investment, and many small-scale merchants found themselves forced to pay high freight costs and rely on those who could afford to own vessels. Moreover, the expense of freight prompted most vessel owners to participate in the marketing of their vessel's cargoes, collapsing the distinction between maritime and mercantile businesses.[54] Before the settlement of the Lower Cape Fear, North Carolina's shipping had been dominated by ships owned by merchants from New England and other places outside the colony, and the problem persisted throughout the colonial period. Murray, for example, regularly negotiated to ship his cargoes on the most convenient and advantageous terms and sometimes had to send for vessels from New England and South Carolina in order to ship staples.[55] For a time, Murray gained more control over his trading endeavors through partial ownership of a vessel, *The Grenadier,* and his decision to sell his share in the vessel limited his trading opportunities.[56]

By the late colonial period, Lower Cape Fear merchants owned a significant share of the ships going in and out of their port towns. The fragmentary but substantial extant port records from the colonial Lower Cape Fear include the names of 390 vessel owners, 70, or approximately 18 percent, of whom can be positively identified as residents of the region.[57] Historian Christopher Crittenden has corroborated these findings, estimating that one-fifth of the tonnage of vessels in the port records had been registered in the region, and registration almost always indicated ownership.[58] While resident vessel owners constituted a minority, their numbers were clearly significant. Indeed, given the reputedly backward trade of North Carolina and the southern colonies in general, these numbers are surprisingly high.

The widespread ownership of vessels in the Lower Cape Fear ports by nonresidents reflected the inherently somewhat colonial character of the region's trade. The majority of the region's trade took place with British merchants, who controlled the structure of trade and shipped goods in their own vessels. The region's concentration on naval stores reinforced the superior position of British merchants because, as enumerated commodities dependent on a bounty and on demand from the British navy, naval stores could be exported only in large amounts to Britain. Without the opportunity to maximize profits by choosing between competing markets, colonial merchants had little incentive to justify such a large investment in shipping and marketing naval stores. The characteristics of naval stores, which made them both relatively cheap and bulky, also discouraged Lower Cape Fear traders from getting too involved in the overseas marketing of tar, pitch, and turpentine.[59] Along these lines, about three-quarters of the value of exports from the Lower Cape Fear went to ports in England or Scotland.[60]

Under such circumstances naval stores, like sugar, tobacco, and some other staple commodities, could more conveniently and efficiently be marketed in one of two ways. Merchants could consign their cargoes to British merchants or ship captains who would then sell them in England, or they could sell directly to factors or storeowners who would then ship and market them. In either case, much of the transporting and marketing processes fell to outside merchants.[61] Carolina merchants usually chose to consign their naval stores to British merchants.[62] It seems likely that a few of the region's more prosperous merchants undertook transatlantic trading ventures in naval stores, but they must have been a small minority of the merchants involved. Also, even though they operated at significant disadvantages compared with merchants in London and Bristol, most Lower Cape Fear merchants did operate their own businesses and were not mere agents of British firms like many of their peers in smaller North Carolina ports.[63]

Lower Cape Fear merchants did not limit themselves to a supporting role in commerce dominated by British merchants, however, and the region's export trade did not end with naval stores. Trading in other commodities and with other ports, especially in lumber and provisions with the British West Indian colonies, Lower Cape Fear merchants obtained a significant degree of commercial autonomy. Indeed, trade with the West Indies offered a promising if competitive commercial opportunity for merchants in a number of the mainland colonies because it could be carried on with more limited resources.[64]

If most of the value of the region's export trade went to the British Isles, about one-fifth also went to the West Indian colonies. The similarity between the scale of trade with the West Indies and the proportion of ships owned in the Lower Cape Fear strongly suggests that the region's merchants found significant opportunities through an alternative trade in provisions and lumber with the West Indian colonies. Indeed, trade with the West Indies interested James Murray before he even settled in the region, and his investment in *The Grenadier* enabled him to export lumbers and provisions to West Indian ports more readily.[65] Scotus Americanus mentioned trade with the West Indies as a prominent part of Wilmington's economy.[66] Whatever limitations trade with the British Isles may have imposed, then, Lower Cape Fear merchants achieved enough commercial autonomy to foster some economic growth and urban development in its ports. Of course, because Brunswick's trade remained confined to larger transatlantic vessels, much of the growth occurred in Wilmington.

If the conditions of trade in the Atlantic world constrained the commercial aspirations of Lower Cape Fear residents, they found themselves much more able to expand their trade inward, tapping the economic resources of the upriver hinterland. When the Moores first embarked on the settlement of the Lower Cape Fear, areas further up the river remained unsettled by Europeans, and the entire course of the Cape Fear remained sparsely populated for decades. After 1740, the population of the North Carolina backcountry grew at a staggering pace, and settlement on the Upper Cape Fear River also flourished. Opportunistic coastal merchants quickly recognized that large profits could be made by providing these new settlements with access to Atlantic markets. Initially, Wilmington merchants found that their fledgling port and marketing facilities faced a number of difficulties in competing with Charles Town businessmen for the trade of North Carolina's backcountry. Gradually, however, they managed to take advantage of their superior geographic position and developed a thriving trade with settlers near the upper reaches of the Cape Fear.

Moravian settlers at Salem, Bethabara, and Wachovia have left the best records of trade from the North Carolina backcountry. Initially, in the early 1750s, when they began their settlements, the Moravians identified Wilmington as the closest port and made inquiries about the town's markets. Upon investigation, however, they became less enamored of Wilmington because Charles Town merchants, such as Henry Laurens, offered better prices and a wider selection of goods made possible by Charles Town's larger scale of trade. Rather than giving up easily, distinguished emissaries from the Lower Cape Fear, including William Dry, Governor William Tryon, Maurice Moore Jr., John Rutherford, and James Hasell, the chief justice, sang the praises of Wilmington and attempted to lure Moravian trade down the Cape Fear. The Moravians wavered for a time and continued to direct some of their trade to Charles Town, but ultimately they found Charles Town less convenient for many of their needs.[67] No doubt many other settlers in the distant North Carolina backcountry also participated in Lower Cape Fear markets to at least some extent.

After 1750, the growth of the town of Cross Creek, in the Upper Cape Fear region, proved an invaluable aid in the extension of Lower Cape Fear trade. Business interests in the Lower Cape Fear encouraged the incorporation and development of Cross Creek with the express intention of redirecting trade from South Carolina into Wilmington and Brunswick. This new trading center linked commercial activities from as far away as Salem, Salisbury, Hillsboro, and Charlotte to Lower Cape Fear markets. By the 1760s, the Moravians, for example, probably traded indirectly with the Lower Cape Fear through Cross Creek more than they traded directly with either Wilmington or Charles Town. Cross Creek not only served as a midpoint between the Lower Cape Fear and the backcountry, it performed urban functions for the burgeoning population of the Upper Cape Fear itself. Flour, deerskins, provisions, and some lumber went down the Cape Fear River from Cross Creek in return for a wide variety of consumer goods shipped into Wilmington and Brunswick from London and other Atlantic ports. As Robert Hunter observed with only modest exaggeration shortly after the American Revolution, Wilmington owed its prosperity to Cross Creek.[68] Indeed, at least one contemporary commentator expressed doubt that the Lower Cape Fear region could feed itself without trade in provisions from Cross Creek.[69] Most prominent mercantile firms in Wilmington had agents and business ties in Cross Creek, and in many cases had their own stores. Thus, Lower Cape Fear merchants succeeded in expanding the geographic scope of their trade by leaps and bounds, through aggressive marketing, fostering growth in the Upper Cape Fear, and improving transportation and marketing facilities in the region. As a consequence, Scotus Americanus could credibly write of Wilmington that "all commodities from the southern and middle parts of the province centre there."[70]

The Lower Cape Fear ports, especially Wilmington, thus provided a vital link between distant Atlantic centers and settlers throughout much of North Carolina. While trade drove the urbanization process, towns often offered more than merely a commercial center: a variety of other services necessitated a central location and added to mercantile trade networks and facilities. To offer only one example, the thousands of barrels of naval stores leaving the Lower Cape Fear ports would have required extensive coopering facilities in town, if only for repair purposes.[71] Ultimately, these towns assisted the Lower Cape Fear region and its hinterland in organizing transportation, storage, processing, and inspection, as well as marketing. The Cape Fear River, of course, facilitated transportation, and pettiaugers, rafts, and large boats plied their way to Wilmington and Brunswick on it.

If transportation came easily in the Lower Cape Fear, storage proved to be a more difficult problem. The large quantities of naval stores and lumber exported from the region took up much space. Municipal records from the town of Wilmington reveal that these commodities were stored in the town and created an almost constant problem. Complaining that Wilmington's wharves, streets, markets, alleys, and docks were encumbered by lumber, tar, turpentine, and other items, frequent ordinances required that they be removed within forty-eight hours.[72] Storage facilities commanded a premium, as one local businessman recognized when he advertised the sale of "That convenient and valuable lot and tar house at the lower end of Wilmington formerly called Purviance's wharf and tar-house."[73] Others resorted to using space on Eagle's Island, a large island in the Cape Fear River adjacent to Wilmington. By the late 1760s, this practice had become so common that officials planned to appoint another customs inspector there because "there are large quantities of naval stores and other merchandises ship[p]ed from the Great Island opposite to Wilmington."[74] Of course, sites for the storage and marketing of commodities logically and quickly became sites for their inspection as well.[75]

Towns not only enabled access to distant markets for commodities, they also made an excellent location for the marketing of local services. Conventional wisdom dictates that free skilled craftsmen played an increasingly unimportant role in slave economies as plantation owners strove for greater self-sufficiency by allocating skilled work to their slaves. Free workers faced formidable competition from enslaved workers in many areas, but some achieved significant long-term success. Scotus Americanus claimed that Wilmington needed a wide variety of tradesmen.[76] Of the 42 individual heads of households identified on the Wilmington town tax list of 1755, for example, 11 can be identified as practicing some kind of skilled trade. Contemporaries described these 11 men as holding occupations that included tailor, cordwainer, shoemaker, cooper, carpenter, joyner, goldsmith, tanner, and silversmith. A broader sample of occupational descriptions in the extant Lower Cape Fear records reveals that of 222 artisans or craftsmen, at least 55 percent could be tied to residence in either Wilmington or Brunswick at some point in time.[77] In the vast majority of trades, most of those identified could be linked to one of the towns.[78] Not surprisingly, many more resided in Wilmington than in Brunswick, by a ratio of 109 to 20.[79]

At first, it may seem difficult to understand how these free skilled workers could make a living in a region with such an abundance of slave labor. Several factors help to explain this phenomenon. To begin with, income from these crafts appears inflated because many of these skilled workers held more than one occupation. This was true of 6 out of the 11 skilled workers on the 1755 Wilmington tax list, for example. Also, many of the skills provided in the more centralized urban market of Wilmington were too specialized to be worthwhile on a plantation. About one-half of the crafts or skilled occupational categories in the region applied to fewer than five people, and it is easy to see why few plantation owners would apprentice their slaves as goldsmiths, cabinetmakers, or printers.[80] Similarly, some skilled crafts, like blacksmithing, could be useful on plantations, but they required more equipment and capital than many plantations could readily muster.

The importance of slave craftsmen to the region can be seen more clearly in the limited number of free coopers available. Despite the fact that coopering played a central role in the naval-stores industry, records list fewer coopers than carpenters, blacksmiths, or tailors. Because slaves could be trained as coopers relatively easily and the region had an enormous demand for them on plantations, slaves must have done the overwhelming majority of the coopering in the Lower Cape Fear. Indeed, of the nineteen identifiable free coopers, at least two were described as mulattos, who might well have learned their trade as, or from, slaves. Here again, the emphasis on the forward linkages from staples that made use of slave labor and self-sufficient plantations applies in some situations but not in others. A practical distinction emerged between crafts that could be conveniently added into a plantation structure and those that functioned better under more urban conditions.[81] Thus, even with large numbers of slaves on their plantations, Lower Cape Fear residents found that they relied on their port towns as central marketing places for many vital and specialized skills. Whether such specialized, skilled labor came from these identifiable free workers or from unidentified skilled workers among Wilmington's considerable enslaved population, it often took place in towns. But, if the comparatively small population of the region kept the market for all skilled labor fairly contained, urban centers became important sites for obtaining a variety of goods and services, thereby unifying the region in much of its day-to-day business.

Trade and related economic functions no doubt created the greatest incentive toward centralization in colonial North Carolina.[82] Because some of the records of one of the region's most prominent merchants, Robert Hogg, have survived, some essential details about the patterns and structures of everyday economic activity in the Lower Cape Fear can be explored for one fairly representative set of transactions.[83] Hogg's business papers provide much valuable information about material life in early Wilmington, while also leaving references to other matters incomplete or tantalizingly obscure.[84]

The outline of Hogg's life in the Lower Cape Fear suggests that he was unexceptional in many ways, though probably much more successful than most Wilmington merchants, or even most colonial merchants. Hogg emigrated from Scotland in 1756, though he had bought land in the Lower Cape Fear in 1739, perhaps on the advice of Gabriel Johnston or other prominent Scots who came to the region about that time. Hogg prospered as a merchant and established one of the area's most prominent firms with Samuel Campbell. According to at least one estimate, the firm made £1,200 a year in profits by the late colonial period, and its total assets in North America came to £18,330 pounds in 1778. Hogg also participated in most of the civic activities that would be expected of a man of his prominence. Before the American Revolution, his responsibilities extended to service on the local safety committee, but, like many Scottish immigrants, Hogg drew back from actively supporting the Revolution. Contemporary accounts leave considerable doubt about Hogg's loyalties, and he may well have concealed his personal views in an attempt to protect his enormous property holdings.[85]

Perhaps the most valuable records left by Hogg are the account books from his store in Wilmington.[86] An analysis of the transactions recorded during 1768 shows that, that year, Hogg's store did business with 220 different people, conducting 1,168 recorded transactions, or an average of about 5 per customer. Several characteristics of these transactions are particularly striking. The store's business activities underscore the geographic limitations on trade for most residents of the Lower Cape Fear. Almost two-thirds of Hogg's customers can be identified as Lower Cape Fear residents, and they accounted for more than three-quarters of his transactions.[87] Almost all of the rest of his customers might be Lower Cape Fear residents, but they cannot be positively identified as such. Only four of Hogg's customers can be positively identified as nonresidents: a Scottish ship's captain who regularly visited the region, a Charles Town merchant, and two others from adjacent Bladen and Duplin Counties. Thus, it appears that much of Hogg's business revolved around linking local small-scale transactions at his store with much larger-scale transactions related to his other entrepreneurial activity. These activities proved useful for the region's residents, and almost one-third of the heads of households appearing on the tax lists for New Hanover County in 1767 and Brunswick County in 1769 did business with Hogg. Hogg undoubtedly had a significant number of competitors since few of the region's households were likely to do without the business offered by such stores. Given the Anglo-American cultural emphasis on the kinds of goods sold by Hogg and other merchants—tea, rum, sugar, and some manufactured goods—this finding perhaps should not be surprising. But it illustrates yet another way in which the internal development of the region, through central marketing in stores, coincides with external developments, as consumerism played a formative role in Atlantic economic patterns. Of course, such patterns had much more relevance for those who lived in or near towns, and more than one-half of the transactions that Hogg recorded took place with customers who could be linked to Wilmington.

Hogg's pool of customers seems to have been less circumscribed in other notable ways. Race clearly marked an important separation in the region's economic life: only one person identifiable as of mixed or non-European descent appeared in Hogg's journal. Another separation involved the sexes: the names of only thirteen women are recorded. But such distinctions probably apply more to Hogg's method of keeping records than to actual business activity: Hogg probably listed most credits and debits under the name of the head of a household even if business deals were actually made with their wives, children, slaves, or overseers. More detailed entries in his daybook for the firm of Hogg and Campbell indicate that all of these groups sometimes traded on the accounts of those considered more economically and legally independent. Other transactions with slaves may have been kept more secret, and Hogg was, in fact, fined once for breaking Wilmington regulations by trading with slaves. Business activity in Hogg's store also reinforced other important mercantile ties: other merchants or customers who were in some way involved in maritime activities consistently took part in more transactions than other customers. The vast majority of Hogg's customers required credit. Fewer than 10 percent of the transactions in Hogg's journal were marked as cash payments. Also, slightly more than two-thirds of the transactions were store purchases or credits to the store, with the remaining one-third accounting for all the payments to the store. Again, extending credit frequently figured into the role of almost all colonial merchants, and the problem appears to have been as acute in the Lower Cape Fear as anywhere.

The store journal sheds light on only a small portion of Hogg's business activities, but the rest can be roughly pieced together. The store sold not only imported commodities, it also purchased staples such as naval stores, lumber, and deerskins for export. Usually, these commodities would have to be stored before a sufficient quantity accumulated to justify shipping. Hogg and Campbell had a number of other stores, too, including ones in Cross Creek, Hillsboro, Bladen County, New River, and Swansboro. Altogether, Hogg and Campbell carried on an extensive trade with merchants in Britain, the British West Indies, and more-northern colonies.

Some shipping records document the flow of Hogg and Campbell's trade. Forty-one invoices exist for Hogg and Campbell between 1768 and 1773. These invoices reaffirm the importance of trade connections with Cross Creek. Fully twenty, or nearly one-half, of the invoices document trade between Cross Creek and Wilmington, as Cross Creek sent out flaxseed, butter, deerskins, tobacco, pork, bread, venison, corn, tallow, hides, beeswax, and, especially, flour. Evidently, Hogg's river trade also employed the regular services of a vessel named *The Rising Sun*. Of the remaining invoices, most record shipments bound for Hogg and Campbell in Wilmington, while most of the remaining shipping invoices describe shipments to Charles Town and to Kingston, Jamaica. Unfortunately, the terms of trade involved in these voyages remain somewhat unclear. At least eight of the voyages were made on Hogg and Campbell's own account and risk, but six others were on the account and risk of someone else. Hogg and Campbell did not indicate that they consigned any of the voyages to other merchants, but at least one invoice involved an agent, and on five other occasions they received goods on consignment from other merchants. Presumably, English merchants consigned consumer goods to Hogg and Campbell to be sold in their

North Carolina stores. These scanty details make generalization difficult, but they suggest that Lower Cape Fear merchants played a variety of roles in trade, as contingencies and circumstances dictated.

Hogg's store journal also makes reference to various shipping ventures. Twenty-eight voyages and destinations can be identified, though the details rarely reveal the trading agreements involved in these shipments. Hogg and Campbell clearly consigned at least two shipments—one bound for Charles Town and one headed for Philadelphia—to be sold by other merchants, who were not paid a commision, but there is little indication of why they were consigned. The other twenty-six journeys also indicate significant participation in coastal trade between the colonies. Only nine shipments went to the British Isles, while seven went to Philadelphia, five to Charles Town, three to Boston, one to Rhode Island, and one to Jamaica.

Hogg did not limit his business to the affairs of his partnership in Hogg and Campbell. He also participated in a partnership with Francis Clayton that included stores in Wilmington and Charles Town. Hogg and Clayton traded not only with North and South Carolina, but also with the British Isles and the West Indies, in the same vein as Hogg and Campbell. On the whole, none of the records from Hogg's two partnerships provides a portrait of the Lower Cape Fear's undeniably significant role in transatlantic trade, but together they reveal that some merchants in the Lower Cape Fear, like Hogg, participated in an impressive range of economic activities, showing their versatility and entrepreneurial acumen. Equally important, merchants like Hogg built trade networks that united the region's residents in a complex economic web.

Even slaves in the Lower Cape Fear made use of opportunities for greater centralization in towns, though in very different ways. For slaves, the towns offered opportunities for social gatherings, improvements in their material status, and, in some cases, more significant expressions of autonomy. Urban slavery followed these general patterns throughout the eighteenth-century southern colonies, though, again, the limited size of Wilmington and Brunswick led to significant differences from larger urban slave centers like Charles Town and Baltimore.

To begin with, slaves made up a smaller proportion of the total population in towns. Indeed, during much of the colonial period, Wilmington and Brunswick probably constituted the only locales in the Lower Cape Fear region where slaves could regularly expect to be outnumbered by free people. No precise figures record the enslaved population of colonial Wilmington, but 1755 tax lists from both the town and from New Hanover County can be compared, and they prove very suggestive. The 1755 tax list for Wilmington does not differentiate between free and unfree taxables, but, assuming that Anglo-American family organization and size did not differ dramatically between town and country, about 60 of the 106 recorded Wilmington taxables were not slaves.

Given that a higher percentage of slaves counted as taxables, this finding indicates that in 1755 Anglo-Americans outnumbered slaves in Wilmington by about three to one.[88] These figures contrast sharply with one historian's assertion that "Blacks were a majority in all Lower South towns," including not only Wilmington but, also rather improbably, New Bern and Edenton.[89] Of course, these population dynamics probably shifted toward a higher proportion of slaves as Wilmington's population continued to grow steadily after 1755, but the majority of the town's population most likely continued to be of European descent throughout the colonial period.[90] The small population of Brunswick also probably remained predominantly Anglo-American. Little evidence suggests that the town contained a large slave community.[91]

Southern towns also often provided refuge and opportunities for social interaction among African Americans because of relatively large concentrations of free people of African descent.[92] Surprisingly, this does not appear to have been the case in colonial Wilmington. Local records contain references to a mere eighteen individuals who may have been free people of African descent, most of whom were categorized as "mulatto," and only two can be linked to Wilmington or Brunswick in any way. Contemporaries also did not often comment on the presence of freed slaves in the region, perhaps partly because legislation discouraged those who were emancipated from staying in North Carolina.[93] Again, this situation would change with time, but the number of slave manumissions in the region remained small and had little time to accumulate before the end of the colonial period.

Even Africans and African Americans still held in bondage could sometimes obtain significantly greater autonomy in towns than in the countryside, however. The close confines of urban life required greater proximity to whites, but it also made anonymity and group activity more feasible, as slaves were able to concentrate in larger numbers. Anglo-American slave owners often complained about the difficulty of controlling slaves in urban settings, but, because slaves played a central role in urban economies and often exercised considerable agency in a variety of ways, they also recognized that there was little they could do about the matter.[94] Wilmington's enslaved population did not constitute a majority, but it certainly reached the critical mass necessary to trouble Wilmington's officials with its independence.

Several aspects of slave life in Wilmington demonstrate the less-constrained life of slaves there. Most striking, some slaves maintained their own residences within the town. Some masters probably found it more convenient to tolerate such independence from skilled slaves who could be hired out for considerable profits in the town or from other slaves who provided them with valuable services within the town. In any case, such circumstances would have posed severe challenges to slave discipline and supervision, and by extension this made slavery unusually close to freedom in some ways. Sensing the opportunities for autonomy among slaves who maintained their own residences, Wilmington officials sought to curtail these arrangements by passing regulations aimed at preventing slaves from renting "houses, Tenements, Kitchens and Outhouses" and from being able to "live at large." They feared that allowing slaves to live on their own would promote "Idleness, Revelling and disturbace, Thieving and Stealing and many other crimes."[95]

The centralization of markets in Wilmington also provided slaves with greater opportunities. Marketplaces allowed slaves to bargain with commodities that they had independently produced on economic terms that belied their slave status. Indeed, as Robert Olwell has noted regarding urban marketplaces in eighteenth-century Charles Town, Anglo-American adherence to the ideology of market relations enabled slaves to function in such places in a manner that "evaded the basic principles of the slave society."[96] Because of their numbers, their control over the proceedings, and their importance to local provisioning, slaves exercised as much power in the marketplaces of Wilmington as anywhere in the Lower Cape Fear. The domination of marketing by slave women and the frequent presence of runaway slaves in the markets made slave owners even more uneasy.[97] Wilmingtonians hoped to control slave marketing in ways that Charlestonians could not, and they repeatedly attempted to regulate such activities, but even the town's most prominent mercantile firms ignored these regulations with impunity and continued to deal with the slaves whenever it suited their interests.[98]

At the same time, slave owners probably became even more anxious when slaves in town behaved in ways that suggested their potential for violence. Authorities took immediate action, for example, when a black man named Nicholas tried to sell a "quantity of gunpowder" in Wilmington.[99] The threat of arson by slaves also loomed large, and fires could be particularly destructive. Along these lines, Janet Schaw complained of the "perverseness" of Wilmington slaves who failed to put out a house fire.[100]

As these white anxieties suggest, slaves did exercise more agency in Wilmington than in most parts of the Lower Cape Fear, but they seldom did so without opposition from slave owners and the authorities. The grim consequences of slave resistance and self-assertion can be seen in the 1768 trial in slave court of Quamino. Convicted of "several Robberies," Quamino received a death sentence. The court also ruled that, after Quamino had been hanged, his head should be placed on public display near Wilmington as a ghastly reminder of the potential physical coercion that limited slave autonomy. If few slaves received treatment as harsh as Quamino's, numerous town regulations reveal a persistent and determined effort to hinder slave aspirations in Wilmington. Authorities attempted to prevent slaves from defrauding citizens, from selling goods without permission, from hiring themselves out, from gathering in groups, from going out at night, from causing noises and "disturbances," from riding horses too fast, and from buying rum.[101] When free people and slaves committed the same offenses in Wilmington, free people received fines, but slaves were publicly whipped, a punishment that marked their transgressions on their bodies.[102] County authorities allocated funds for a cage and pillory in Wilmington for slaves who committed crimes.[103] Thus, for slaves, towns offered unusual opportunities for independent action, but no location within the Lower Cape Fear offered them freedom from bondage or removed them from the coercive power of slave owners.

Most Lower Cape Fear residents, whether free or enslaved, regularly participated in activities focused around either Wilmington or Brunswick, and a significant minority of the region's inhabitants lived within one of these two towns. A study of the 1755 tax lists shows that about 6 percent of all taxables lived in Wilmington—specifically, about 16 percent of white taxables and about 3 percent of black taxables. Brunswick no doubt constituted a smaller portion, but it still added to the number of urban residents in the region. A more comprehensive sample, including all those individuals who could be identified as Lower Cape Fear residents, indicates that 23 percent either owned land in a town or described themselves as "from" or "of" a town.[104] A much higher percentage must have regularly done business in town or visited the towns, but their numbers are impossible to estimate.

Indeed, the importance of the Lower Cape Fear towns defies quantification. Despite the towns' small size, Lower Cape Fear residents recognized their centrality, most obviously by referring to Wilmington as a "metropolis."[105] While such a designation did not mark the kinds of differences between urban and rural life familiar to more modern sensibilities, it did indicate that Wilmington offered different opportunities for spatial organization and experience. On one level, Lower Cape Fear towns offered an arena for new experiences because they served as a receiving point for goods and information from the far reaches of the Atlantic world. Obviously, transatlantic commercial ties played an important role in the lives of the vast majority of Lower Cape Fear residents who participated in the export economy. Even for those who did not sell naval stores or lumber for distant markets, the towns provided access to refined consumer goods from London and other locales, making them centers of civility for colonists. The latest fashions and most impressive forms of ornamentation could thus often be found in towns. But the crowded conditions of towns also allowed contagious diseases to spread more rapidly, and even small Atlantic ports could serve as focal points for epidemics. As sailors, merchants, and immigrants moved through Wilmington and Brunswick, then, they brought with them a variety of new experiences from the world beyond the Lower Cape Fear.

At the same time, Wilmington and Brunswick reaffirmed the regional identity of the Lower Cape Fear. Even with outsiders in the towns, the great majority of all interchanges within the towns occurred between local residents. The people of the Lower Cape Fear saw one another in Wilmington and Brunswick as they did business at stores and markets, went before county and superior courts, attended church, or participated in local social events. For many of them, networks fostered from plantations or homes in the countryside carried over without interruption into more urban but still very familiar and small-scale settings. Yet the presence of outsiders made a difference, turning the Lower Cape Fear towns into pivotal sites in the construction of otherness. In the towns, the region's residents found various exemplars of the highly diverse Atlantic world, and most of all they noted how these exemplars differed from those in their own region.

Wilmington and Brunswick, then, also added to the regional distinctiveness of the Lower Cape Fear. The towns gave the region its own center, marking it off from other places, focused around other centers. In Wilmington, Lower Cape Fear residents learned how they differed from individuals who lived in regions focused around New Bern, Charles Town, Boston, Bristol, and London. The towns also provided evidence that the Lower Cape Fear had developed enough that it could have its own center, rather than focusing on standards imposed from more distant and different centers in Britain's empire. In Wilmington and Brunswick, the many regionally distinct aspects of life in the Lower Cape Fear found possibilities for expression in urban settings.

EPILOGUE

Region, Revolution, and Nation

The American Revolution brought profound changes to all of the thirteen newly independent British colonies in North America, but these changes often came to specific people and places gradually, haltingly, or unevenly. New ideas about independence, political rights, and republicanism led to momentous changes as time passed, but they may not have made much immediate difference in the lives of those who were not part of the elite. In the Lower Cape Fear region, as elsewhere in the new states, educated and elite leaders grappled with the ideological implications of revolution and attempted to legitimate their authority amid political turmoil. For those unable or unwilling to participate in debates about politics, the American Revolution arrived first and most immediately in the form of war.[1] While more than a decade of protest prepared revolutionary leaders for the Declaration of Independence, nothing in the first fifty years of European settlement along the lower reaches of the Cape Fear River prepared the region's residents for the ultimately devastating consequences of the war for American independence.[2]

At first, the war between Britain and its rebellious colonies reinforced older patterns of regional difference within North Carolina. The anxieties of Lower Cape Fear revolutionaries focused on the widespread Loyalist sympathies in the Upper Cape Fear region surrounding the town of Cross Creek. The Upper Cape Fear had been dominated for decades by immigrants from the Scottish Highlands, and Scottish highlanders resisted the independence movement as fervently as any group in North America. The Loyalist presence in the Upper Cape Fear region contrasted sharply with political attitudes in the Lower Cape Fear region, where local leaders took an early lead in North Carolina's protests against British rule. Because the persistent and fierce loyalty of the Scottish Highland enclave along the Cape Fear River was unusual in British North America, it also quickly attracted the attention of British military officers and political officials as they probed for weaknesses in the American resistance. Consequently, the early months of war with Britain brought considerable tension to the Lower Cape Fear as both sides tried to determine what, if anything, would become of the Upper Cape Fear region's anomalous situation.

Early in 1776, Governor Josiah Martin finally persuaded the British military to mount an attack on the Lower Cape Fear region using armed Upper Cape Fear Loyalists. The Loyalist threat had been exaggerated by both sides, however, and by the time the makeshift pro-British forces moved southward into the Lower Cape Fear region, they were already poorly armed, confused, disappointed, and outnumbered by their opponents. In the early hours of the morning on February 27, 1776, the Loyalists were surprised by well-positioned Revolutionary forces as they tried to cross an already slippery and partly disassembled bridge over Moore's Creek in northern New Hanover County. What became known to North Carolinians as the Battle of Moore's Creek Bridge really amounted to little more than a one-sided skirmish, and it shattered British hopes for a Scottish Highlander assault on the Lower Cape Fear.[3] A British ship, venturing into the Cape Fear River in the hopes of aiding the Loyalists, caused panic in Wilmington, where the women and children and much of the residents' most valuable property were evacuated before it became apparent that the town was in no danger.[4] One letter writer, sympathetic to the revolutionary cause, asserted that it was "inconceivable" for one to "imagine what joy" news of the victory at Moore's Creek "dif[f]used" through North Carolina.[5] Once the only enemy military forces in southeastern North Carolina had been eradicated in the months after their failure at Moore's Creek, concern about the American Revolution seems to have waned throughout the Lower Cape Fear region. Thus, the first significant military conflict of the revolutionary war in North Carolina played out as a conflict between two regions.

The Moore's Creek campaign raised legitimate concerns about the American Revolution in the Lower Cape Fear region, and these concerns did not become any less relevant as the war raged on in other locales. For one thing, the relationship between Revolutionaries and Loyalists was problematic everywhere during the American Revolution, and the close proximity to such a staunchly antirevolutionary enclave insured that the Battle of Moore's Creek Bridge would not dispel this problem for Lower Cape Fear settlers.[6] Loyalism continued to cause anxiety in the region for years, even without support from the British military, partly because Loyalists within the Lower Cape Fear found themselves emboldened by nearby support.[7] Moreover, perhaps too confident from their rapid success in February 1776, the region's residents became more ambivalent about the war effort, suggesting that ammunition should be removed from Wilmington to avoid the danger of fire and even refusing to hold militia musters.[8] For a variety of reasons, considerable disorder seems to have continued in the region throughout the war.

In January 1781, the violence of war returned to the Lower Cape Fear, but this time it proved far more sustained, destructive, and disturbing. A British invasion force arrived in the region to provide support to the British forces led by General Charles, Earl Cornwallis. At this time, Cornwallis and his troops were engaged in a fierce military campaign against Nathanael Greene's Revolutionary forces in North Carolina. The British invasion force, which was led by Major James Henry Craig and consisted of about three hundred men, took

Wilmington with little difficulty.[9] Local militia gathered and made a stand upriver near the site of Benjamin Heron's drawbridge, but they were no match for Craig's troops.[10] Loyalists in the region looked on Craig's arrival as a chance at revenge for their defeat at Moore's Creek Bridge; Revolutionaries in the region dug in and tried to resist British and Loyalist control; and the Lower Cape Fear region began to imitate the pattern of brutal, chaotic, and partisan warfare that had already characterized much of the fighting elsewhere in the Carolinas.

Those who lived in southeastern North Carolina during Craig's occupation of Wilmington and its environs must have found the behavior of both Revolutionaries and their opponents disturbing. In the first fighting after Craig's invasion, Revolutionary General Alexander Lillington protested that two wounded men had been "inhumanely butchered" after the battle by African Americans who were with the British troops.[11] On various occasions, Revolutionary leaders accused Loyalists and British soldiers in the Lower Cape Fear region of nearly starving prisoners of war, plundering, kidnapping, impressing slaves, and murdering in cold blood.[12] Craig used Wilmington as a base and, operating in conjunction with local Loyalists, regularly wreaked havoc in different places between New Bern and the South Carolina border. But neither side had a monopoly on excess or brutality, and the British leaders made similar complaints about their opponents. Revolutionary soldiers and civilians allegedly burned down Loyalist houses, robbed, destroyed, and murdered. They even harassed and robbed those who sympathized with their cause.[13] Sir Henry Clinton, Cornwallis's superior officer, expressed his ire at "the atrocious barbarity of the Rebel Militia, which has been beyond what I ever heard of among the most savage nations."[14] The violence had spun out of the control of leaders on both sides, as suggested by repeated letters from Revolutionary Governor Thomas Burke expressing concern about the behavior of his own troops.[15] Each side blamed the other and threatened retaliation.[16] When the combatants sometimes also victimized the opposing soldiers' wives and children, empowered slaves, and destroyed homes, they added the ultimate insults to their opponents' injuries.[17] Indeed, large numbers of slaves in the Lower Cape Fear region must have experienced the year of 1781 as a fleeting opportunity at greater autonomy and at challenging their bondage in new ways.[18]

One particular incident from the partisan violence of 1781 acquired a special place in the folklore of the Lower Cape Fear region. The "massacre of the eight-mile house," as it came to be known, took place in the spring of that year when some of Craig's troops surprised a group of Revolutionaries late at night in a tavern outside Wilmington. The British soldiers set the door on fire and, upon entering, bayoneted all sixteen men. Local legend claims the men were at the tavern to meet some local women, and Robert Rowan reported that the men "begged quarter, some of them on their knees, in the most supplicating manner."[19] It is difficult to know how much of this story is accurate and how much of it represents an anti-British interpretation of stories and rumors, but its psychological effect on contemporaries must have been considerable. If the North Carolina–South Carolina Boundary House provides a convenient symbol for the shifting boundaries and constructions of place in the eighteenth century, then the Eight Mile House provides a convenient symbol for the dramatic and violent changes in the lives of Lower Cape Fear residents in 1781.

By the time Revolutionary troops entered Wilmington on November 14 and watched the distant sails from Craig's departing ships moving down the Cape Fear River, the outside world had brought powerful changes into the Lower Cape Fear region. By 1782, the Lower Cape Fear region seemed very distant from the world imagined by the members of The Family, the Moores, when they founded Brunswick. A look at some of the region's prominent individuals provides one index of change. Two of founder Maurice Moore's sons, General James Moore and Judge Maurice Moore, played important roles in the events of the 1770s. Both of these men died within a matter of days, in 1777.[20] Edward Moseley, Roger Moore, Eleazer Allen, Sarah Allen, Benjamin Heron, and Thomas Godfrey all died before the arrival of the American Revolution, signifying both the region's high mortality rate and the passing of the region's first waves of immigration. James Murray spent most of the war in New England, where his strong opinions and sympathies for the British government made him among the most-hated Loyalists in Massachusetts.[21] The naturalist William Bartram chose a different course of action, traveling extensively during the Revolutionary era, conducting his study of the plants and animals of the southeast in a way that seemed oddly unaffected by devastating war going on around him.[22] Cornelius Harnett, the region's most prominent opponent of British government in the years leading up to the Declaration of Independence, died after being captured and mistreated by British troops in 1781.[23]

Numerous individual stories can tell only part of the story, however, and broader, less-personal processes also changed the Lower Cape Fear region. The Lower Cape Fear's naval-stores economy had depended heavily on British markets and a bounty from the British navy. After the American Revolution and North Carolina's separation from the British mercantile system, the Lower Cape Fear naval-stores industry, in its eighteenth-century form, had little future. The region's economic distinctiveness was bound to fade, though in the nineteenth century some of the region's planters shifted the emphasis of the naval-stores industry from tar to turpentine and also finally produced significant and profitable rice crops along the Cape Fear River. Technological changes would also gradually alter the geographic organization of North Carolina, making it easier to extend networks farther and giving a very different role to Wilmington, the

Cape Fear River's surviving port town. Brunswick, the once-promising center of Maurice Moore's new settlement that had been destroyed by fire, would remain in ruins for two more centuries.

The most profound changes in the Lower Cape Fear region after 1775, however, related to the new American nation. The creation of the Continental Congress, participation in a united military effort, and the rhetoric of republicanism that accompanied the War for Independence all eventually made it imperative to subordinate more local concerns and to emphasize the unity of the thirteen new American states. The violent fighting in and around the Lower Cape Fear during 1781 no doubt underscored the growing significance of these extralocal concerns. In order for a new republic to be created during the war and strengthened by the Constitution in 1787, Americans also had to adopt new ways of thinking about cultural identities, political jurisdictions, and geographic spaces.[24]

In places like the Lower Cape Fear region, nationalism did not overwhelm other concerns immediately, of course, but both the Continental Congress and the Constitution of 1787 made it far more necessary to pay attention to politics at the state and national level. A long tradition of more regional and decentralized government may help to explain the hesitancy of some North Carolinians to accept the Constitution, but, once it had been ratified, the Constitution established very different political traditions of its own. By the early nineteenth century, the Lower Cape Fear functioned as a small part of the larger political systems revolving around the State of North Carolina and the United States government. In some ways, the Lower Cape Fear, like many other parts of the United States, maintains a distinct regional culture in the twenty-first century, but regions like the Lower Cape Fear no longer perform most of the important political, economic, cultural, and social functions that they did in the eighteenth century.[25] As the eighteenth century ended, the Lower Cape Fear began to seem less relevant, because the region was the historical construction of an eighteenth-century world. Like all historical constructions, the Lower Cape Fear made sense in its context. For at least half a century, thousands of people found their lives organized and defined by the contours of a regional world.

NOTES

Introduction: "This Remote Part of the World"

1. For another discussion of Finlay's travels, see John R. Stilgoe, *The Common Landscape of America, 1580 to 1845* (New Haven: Yale University Press, 1982), 130–31.

2. Hugh Finlay, *Journal Kept by Hugh Finlay, Surveyor of the Post Roads on the Continent of North America, during His Survey of the Post Offices between Falmouth and Casco Bay in the Province of Massachusetts, and Savannah in Georgia; Begun the 13th September, 1773 and Ended 26th June 1774* (Brooklyn: F. H. Norton, 1867), 65.

3. The Boundary House was probably not a private residence. In the eighteenth century the word *house* could also be used to refer to taverns, ordinaries, or other "public houses" that sometimes provided rooms and/or board to travelers. Travelers' interest in and familiarity with the Boundary House suggests that *house* was being used in this sense.

4. William Tryon to Peter Timothy, February 20, 1767, in William Saunders, ed., *The Colonial Records of North Carolina* (Raleigh: State of North Carolina, 1886–90) (hereafter cited as *Colonial Records*), 7:440.

5. William Tryon to Peter DeLancy, April 24, 1767, *Colonial Records,* 7:454.

6. H. G. Jones, *North Carolina Illustrated, 1524–1984* (Chapel Hill: University of North Carolina Press, 1983), 51, 66. On the North Carolina–South Carolina boundary, see Marvin Lucian Skaggs, "The First Boundary Survey between the Carolinas," *North Carolina Historical Review* 12, no. 3 (1935): 213–32; Skaggs, "Progress in the North Carolina–South Carolina Boundary Dispute," *North Carolina Historical Review* 15, no. 4 (1938): 341–53.

7. John Barnett to SPG, August 22, 1767, *Colonial Records*, 7:515.

8. Mr. Christian to SPG, July 27, 1775, *Colonial Records,* 9:1022.

9. Council Journals, *Colonial Records,* 9:1238. For some other references to the Boundary House during these years, see Extract from a Revolutionary Journal by Hugh McDonald [November 1776], in Walter Clark, ed., *The State Records of North Carolina* (Goldsboro: State of North Carolina, 1895–1905) (hereafter cited as *State Records*), 11:834; Gen. H. W. Harrington to Maj. General Gates, October 2, 1780, *State Records,* 14:660.

10. William Hooper to Joseph Hewes [November 16, 1776], in Paul H. Smith, ed., *Letters of the Delegates to Congress,* vol. 5 (Washington, D.C.: Library of Congress, 1976–2000), 498.

11. Memorandum of Distances, *State Records,* 15:380, 382.

12. On this point, see, for example, D. W. Meinig, *The Shaping of America: A Geographical Perspective on 500 Years of History,* vol. 1, *Atlantic America, 1492–1800* (New Haven: Yale University Press, 1986), 231–35.

13. Peter Sahlins, *Boundaries: The Making of France and Spain in the Pyrenees* (Berkeley: University of California Press, 1989), 2–3.

14. [Gabriel Johnston to Board of Trade], April 30, 1737, *Colonial Records,* 4:249.

15. Boundary Line between North and South Carolina, December 21, 1769, *Colonial Records,* 8:558.

16. Governor Dobbs to Board of Trade, May 17, 1762, *Colonial Records,* 5:1:718–19.

17. William K. Boyd, ed., *William Byrd's Histories of the Dividing Line betwixt Virginia and North Carolina* (New York: Dover, 1967); Douglas Anderson, "Plotting William Byrd,"

William and Mary Quarterly 56, no. 4 (October 1999): 701–22. For an interesting commentary on indigenous peoples' perspectives on the boundary between North Carolina and Virginia, see Shannon Lee Dawdy, "The Meherrin's Secret History of the Dividing Line," *North Carolina Historical Review* 72, no. 4 (October 1995): 386–415.

18. For a valuable study of the historical construction of boundaries in one early-modern locale, see Sahlins, *Boundaries.*

19. Letter of the vestrymen and churchwardens of St. Phillip's Parish to the bishop of London, Easter Monday, 1730, in Robert J. Cain, ed., *The Colonial Records of North Carolina,* 2nd series (Raleigh: State of North Carolina, 1963–) (hereafter cited as *Colonial Records,* 2nd series), 10:324.

20. Murray to John Murray, January 10, 1736/37, in James Murray, *Letters of James Murray, Loyalist,* edited by Nina M. Tiffany (Boston: Printed, not published, 1901), 36.

21. James Moir to the secretary, October 29, 1740, *Colonial Records,* 2nd series, 10:408.

22. Mr. Reed to the secretary [of SPG], December 26, 1763, *Colonial Records,* 5:1:999.

23. Richard Hofstadter, *America at 1750: A Social Portrait* (New York: Knopf, 1971), 3.

24. Jack P. Greene, *Pursuits of Happiness: The Social Development of Early Modern British Colonies and the Formation of American Culture* (Chapel Hill: University of North Carolina Press, 1988), 176–84; Hofstadter, *America at 1750,* 18.

25. Greene, *Pursuits of Happiness,* 180–81.

26. I would argue that this fragmented and regionally divided pattern of settlement has contributed substantially to the relative neglect of North Carolina's colonial history. Because it is difficult to deal with North Carolina as one coherent place, scholars are reluctant to deal with it at all.

27. This definition of regions is in large part based on the definition and framework suggested in the work of Eric Van Young, a historian of colonial Mexico. See Van Young, *Hacienda and Market in Eighteenth-Century Mexico: The Rural Economy of the Guadalajara Region, 1675–1820* (Berkeley: University of California Press, 1981), esp. 3–4; Van Young, ed., *Mexico's Regions: Comparative History and Development* (San Diego: Center for U.S.-Mexican Studies, 1992), esp. 2–5.

28. Edward Ayers, Patricia N. Limerick, Stephen Nissenbaum, and Peter S. Onuf, *All over the Map: Rethinking American Regions* (Baltimore: Johns Hopkins University Press, 1996), 3–5. For other examples of approaches to regional history besides the valuable ones in this book by Ayers et al. and in the works by Van Young cited in note 27 above, see "AHR Forum: Bringing Regionalism Back to History," *American Historical Review* 104, no. 4 (1999): 1156–220.

29. Peter S. Onuf, "Federalism, Republicanism, and the Origins of American Sectionalism," in Ayers et al., *All over the Map,* 22–23.

30. On the emergence of a coherent southern identity as a primarily nineteenth-century development, see Jack P. Greene, "The Constitution of 1787 and the Question of Southern Distinctiveness," in Greene, *Imperatives, Behaviors, and Identities: Essays in Early American Cultural History* (Charlottesville: University Press of Virginia, 1992), 327–47, esp. 332–34. Two monographs that powerfully reinforce and elucidate this interpretive point are Christopher Morris, *Becoming Southern: The Evolution of a Way of Life, Warren County and Vicksburg, Mississippi, 1770–1860* (New York: Oxford University Press, 1995); and Joyce E. Chaplin, *"An Anxious Pursuit": Agricultural Innovation and Modernity in the Lower South, 1730–1815* (Chapel Hill: University of North Carolina Press, 1993).

31. For Benedict Anderson's definition of imagined communities, see his *Imagined Communities: Reflections on the Origin and the Spread of Nationalism* (1983; rev. ed., London: Verso Press, 1991), 6.

32. The best articulation of the relevance of the cultural hearth for early American history can be found in Robert D. Mitchell, "The Formation of Early American Cultural Regions: An Interpretation," in *European Settlement and Development in North America: Essays on Geographical Change in Honour and Memory of Andrew Hill Clark,* ed. James R. Gibson (Toronto: University of Toronto Press, 1978), 66–90. For another example of the influence of one core area, see Jack P. Greene, "Colonial South Carolina and the Caribbean Connection," *South Carolina Historical Magazine* 88, no. 4 (1987): 192–210.

33. Jack P. Greene and J. R. Pole, "Reconstructing British-American Colonial History: An Introduction," in *Colonial British America: Essays in the New History of the Modern Era,* ed. Greene and Pole (Baltimore: Johns Hopkins University Press, 1984), 12–13.

34. On staple production areas in the eighteenth-century Lower South, see most notably Peter A. Coclanis, *The Shadow of a Dream: Economic Life and Death in the South Carolina Low Country, 1760–1920* (New York: Oxford University Press, 1989); Chaplin, *Anxious Pursuit*; John J. McCusker and Russell R. Menard, *The Economy of British America, 1607–1789* (Chapel Hill: University of North Carolina Press, 1985); Stanley L. Engerman and Robert E. Gallman, eds., *The Cambridge Economic History of the United States,* vol. 1, *The Colonial Era* (Cambridge: Cambridge University Press, 1996). On labor regime areas in early America, see Philip D. Morgan, *Slave Counterpoint: Black Culture in the Eighteenth-Century Chesapeake and Lowcountry* (Chapel Hill: University of North Carolina Press, 1998); Ira Berlin, *Many Thousands Gone: The First Two Centuries of Slavery in North America* (Cambridge: Harvard University Press, 1998).

35. Mitchell, "Early American Cultural Regions," 73.

36. On the distinction between regionalism and regionality, see Van Young, *Mexico's Regions,* 2.

37. When these counties were redefined, a small area of the original New Hanover County area became part of a third county, Bladen. Consequently, this small area often functioned as part of the Lower Cape Fear. Where possible, I have tried to pay attention to developments in this part of Bladen County.

38. Lawrence Lee, *The Lower Cape Fear in Colonial Days* (Chapel Hill: University of North Carolina Press, 1965).

39. H. Roy Merrens, *Colonial North Carolina in the Eighteenth Century: A Study in Historical Geography* (Chapel Hill: University of North Carolina Press, 1964). On the Lower Cape Fear, see esp. 127–33.

40. James T. Lemon. *The Best Poor Man's Country: A Geographical Study of Early Southeastern Pennsylvania* (Baltimore: Johns Hopkins University Press, 1972); Robert D. Mitchell, *Commercialism and Frontier: Perspectives on the Early Shenandoah Valley* (Charlottesville: University Press of Virginia, 1972).

Chapter 1: Entries and Expectations

1. Laws, in Walter Clark, ed., *The State Records of North Carolina* (Goldsboro: State of North Carolina, 1895–1905) (hereafter cited as *State Records*), 23:239–43; Lawrence Lee, "Old Brunswick, the Story of a Colonial Town," *North Carolina Historical Review* 29, no. 2 (April 1952): 230–45.

2. *Dictionary of North Carolina Biography*, 1977–96, s.v., "Moore, Maurice" and "Moore, Roger," 6:303–4, 308; Lawrence Lee, *The Lower Cape Fear in Colonial Days* (Chapel Hill: University of North Carolina Press, 1965), 92.

3. For a brief overview of the growing historiography on colonial South Carolina and the lower southern colonies in general, see Jack P. Greene, "Colonial South Carolina: An Introduction," in *Money, Trade, and Power: The Evolution of Colonial South Carolina's Plantation Society,* ed. Jack P. Greene, Rosemary Brana-Shute, and Randy Sparks (Columbia: University of South Carolina Press, 2001), vii–xiii. On wealth, see Alice H. Jones, *Wealth of a Nation to Be: The American Colonies on the Eve of the Revolution* (New York: Columbia University Press, 1980), 357; and Peter A. Coclanis, *The Shadow of a Dream: Economic Life and Death in the South Carolina Low Country, 1760–1920* (New York: Oxford University Press, 1989), 48–111. On slavery, see, among many others, Philip D. Morgan, *Slave Counterpoint: Black Culture in the Eighteenth-Century Chesapeake and Lowcountry* (Chapel Hill: University of North Carolina Press, 1998); and Peter H. Wood, *Black Majority: Negroes in Colonial South Carolina from 1670 through the Stono Rebellion* (New York: Knopf, 1974). On South Carolina politics, see Robert M. Weir, "'The Harmony We Were Famous For': An Interpretation of Pre-Revolutionary South Carolina Politics," *William and Mary Quarterly* 26, no. 4 (October 1969): 473–501; and Richard Waterhouse, *A New World Gentry: The Making of a Merchant and Planter Class in South Carolina, 1670–1770* (New York: Garland, 1989). On the geographic growth of South Carolina society and culture, see Robert L. Merriweather, *The Expansion of South Carolina, 1729–1765* (Kingsport, Tenn.: Southern Publishers, 1940); Verner W. Crane, *The Southern Frontier, 1670–1732* (Ann Arbor: University of Michigan Press, 1929), 22–46; David R. Chesnutt, *South Carolina's Expansion into Colonial Georgia, 1720–1765* (New York: Garland, 1989); and George Lloyd Johnson Jr., *The Frontier in the Colonial South: South Carolina Backcountry, 1736–1800* (Westport, Conn.: Greenwood Press, 1997). On the dynamism of low country culture, see Joyce E. Chaplin, *"An Anxious Pursuit": Agricultural Innovation and Modernity in the Lower South, 1730–1815* (Chapel Hill: University of North Carolina Press, 1993).

4. Most significantly, see Robert D. Mitchell, "The Formation of Early American Cultural Regions: An Interpretation," in *European Settlement and Development in North America: Essays on Geographical Change in Honour and Memory of Andrew Hill Clark,* ed. James R. Gibson (Toronto: University of Toronto Press, 1978), 66–90; and Jack P. Greene, "Colonial South Carolina and the Caribbean Connection," *South Carolina Historical Magazine* 88, no. 4 (1987): 192–210.

5. *Dictionary of North Carolina Biography,* s.v., "Moore, Maurice," 4:303–4; R. D. W. Connor, "The Settlement of the Cape Fear," *South Atlantic Quarterly* 5, no. 1 (July 1907): 272–87; Lee, *Lower Cape Fear,* 92–94.

6. James Sprunt, ed., *Chronicles of the Cape Fear River, 1660–1916* (Raleigh, N.C.: Edwards & Broughton Printing, 1916), 14. The details of this incident cannot be verified with the surviving documents from this period, but references to any Native American presence in the Lower Cape Fear after 1725 are strikingly rare. As early as 1736 Murray explained the limited deerskin trade in the Lower Cape Fear by writing that merchants "have no Indians to trade with." See Murray to Henry McCulloh, May 5, 1736, James Murray Letters, Massachusetts Historical Society, Boston (hereafter cited as MHS).

7. *Records in the British Public Records Office Relating to South Carolina,* 8:24–26.

8. Lee, *Lower Cape Fear,* 100.

9. *Records in the British Public Records Office Relating to South Carolina,* 22:215–16.

10. For various discussions of the similarities between the Lower Cape Fear region and the South Carolina low country, see, among many others, Lee, *Lower Cape Fear,* 92–104; Marvin Michael Kay and Lorin Lee Cary, *Slavery in North Carolina, 1748–1775* (Chapel Hill: University of North Carolina Press, 1995), 4–5, 15–16; H. Roy Merrens, *Colonial North Carolina in the Eighteenth Century: A Study in Historical Geography* (Chapel Hill: University of North Carolina Press, 1964), 127–33; A. Roger Ekirch, *"Poor Carolina": Politics and Society in Colonial North Carolina, 1929–1776* (Chapel Hill: University of North Carolina Press, 1981), 21–23, 33–34; and Christopher C. Crittenden, *The Commerce of North Carolina, 1763–1789* (New Haven: Yale University Press, 1936), vii, 70.

11. Lower Cape Fear computer biographical files. Data on land ownership has been derived largely from land patents and real estate conveyances, which are more reliable and consistent than the more fragmentary and problematic warrants and quitrent records. It should be noted that, while land patents and conveyances provide some of the most important information about early settlement in the Lower Cape Fear, they present empirical difficulties. The remaining records are almost certainly incomplete, and colonial surveying was often unreliable. The quality of land also varied considerably. Some of it was acquired solely for speculative purposes; also, warrants were issued for some tracts of land that were never patented. Many of these problems result from disagreements about land distribution —discussed in chapter 2.

12. Lower Cape Fear computer biographical files. There are two important exceptions to this generalization. Authorities in England granted two large parcels of land in the region to individuals Henry McCulloh and Arthur Dobbs, in association with promotional schemes. This would make McCulloh the largest landholder, but these lands were never settled as intended and the patents eventually lapsed. Dobbs evidently used his land to encourage immigration from Ireland. Consequently, they have been excluded from all data on acres patented in this chapter.

13. Ibid.

14. Ibid. Most of these connections can be traced with references in real estate conveyances and other documents that reveal where an individual lived. Some others were obtained from references such as *Dictionary of North Carolina Biography* or genealogical sources. The unrepresentative nature of these references is obvious, but they are frequent enough that one can draw some careful inferences about the larger population. Also, the references have been limited to individuals who appear to have resided in the Cape Fear when linked with other records such as tax lists, jury lists, and wills. They are not, however, limited to one reference per individual. Some Lower Cape Fear inhabitants had multiple former places of residence, and they have been included in the data for each of these locations. Also, not every connection involves a simple and permanent migration from a previous residence into the Lower Cape Fear. In several cases, references suggest that individuals either moved back and forth from the region or appeared to claim residence status simultaneously in the Lower Cape Fear and elsewhere. Because all of these individuals have been included, the possibility remains that some of the connections to other regions in the sample did not occur until after the individual in question established residence in the Lower Cape Fear. It does not seem likely that these exceptions account for a significant portion of the sample, however. Those who can be identified have been listed as outmigrants in tables 1.3 and 1.4. For a more complete listing of this data, see tables 1.1, 1.2, 1.3, 1.4.

15. Five can be identified as South Carolinians. One cannot be traced.

16. The Case of Sundry Inhabitants of North Carolina Dwelling at Cape Fear River to Board of Trade [1735], *Colonial Records,* 4:308–15; Lower Cape Fear computer biographical files.

17. Report of Both Houses of the South Carolina Assembly [1757], *State Records,* 11:127–28; Ekirch, *Poor Carolina,* 7; Lee, *Lower Cape Fear,* 96–101.

18. Charles Garth to Board of Trade [1771], *Colonial Records,* 8:565.

19. Edmond Porter to the duke of Newcastle, December 22, 1729, *Colonial Records,* 3:51; Lee, *Lower Cape Fear,* 99.

20. Lower Cape Fear computer biographical files. These figures were derived from tax lists between 1755 and 1772. No regional group other than New England averaged as many slaves. Distance and other factors made it highly unlikely that settlers from New England brought many slaves with them, so this discrepancy is probably the result of the small size of the sample and of an unusually wealthy sample for New England.

21. At the same time, it should be emphasized that there is a notable dearth of evidence to support repeated assertions such as that by D. W. Meinig that the Lower Cape Fear was "entirely a creation from South Carolina and in every way bound to Charles Town." See Meinig, *The Shaping of America: A Geographical Perspective on 500 Years of History,* vol. 1, *Atlantic America, 1492–1800* (New Haven: Yale University Press, 1986), 178.

22. Thomas Lowndes to Board of Trade, December 8, 1729, *Colonial Records,* 3:49.

23. The historiography of the Albemarle settlement is considerably less developed than that of colonial South Carolina, but see Hugh T. Lefler and William S. Powell, *Colonial North Carolina: A History* (New York: Charles Scribner's Sons, 1973), 56–113; Ekirch, *Poor Carolina,* 3–50; Charles M. Andrews, *The Colonial Period of American History: The Settlements,* vol. 3 (New Haven: Yale University Press, 1934–38), 246–67. On politics, see John Paden, "'Several & Many Grievances of Very Great Consequences': North Carolina's Political Factionalism in the 1720s," *North Carolina Historical Review* 71, no. 3 (July 1994): 285–305. On legal authority, see Donna J. Spindel, *Crime and Society in North Carolina, 1663–1776* (Baton Rouge: Louisiana State University Press, 1989); and Jack P. Greene, "Courts and Society in Proprietary North Carolina: A Review Essay," *North Carolina Historical Review* 60, no. 1 (January 1983): 100–104. On gender and sexual attitudes, see Kirsten Fischer, *Suspect Relations: Sex, Race, and Resistance in Colonial North Carolina* (Ithaca, N.Y.: Cornell University Press, 2002). For Byrd's comments, see William K. Boyd, ed., *William Byrd's Histories of the Dividing Line betwixt Virginia and North Carolina* (New York: Dover, 1967). For one example of pirates in the Cape Fear River, see *Records in the British Public Records Office Relating to South Carolina,* 7:164.

24. See, among others, Jack P. Greene, "Search for Identity: An Interpretation of the Meaning of Selected Patterns of Social Response in Eighteenth Century America," *Journal of Social History* 3 (spring 1970): 189–220; Michael J. Rozbicki, "The Curse of Provincialism: Negative Perceptions of Colonial American Plantation Gentry," *Journal of Southern History* 68, no. 4 (November 1997): 727–52; Bernard Bailyn, *The Peopling of British North America: An Introduction* (New York: Vintage, 1986), 89–131; Kenneth Lockridge, "Colonial Self-Fashioning: Paradoxes and Pathologies in the Construction of Genteel Identity in Eighteenth-Century America," in *Through a Glass Darkly: Reflections on Personal Identity in Early America,* ed. Ronald Hoffman et al. (Chapel Hill: University of North Carolina Press, 1997), 274–339.

25. William Byrd, *William Byrd's Histories of the Dividing Line betwixt Virginia and North Carolina* (New York: Dover, 1967), 43.

26. Lower Cape Fear computer biographical files; *Dictionary of North Carolina Biography,* s.v., "Moseley, Edward," 4:332–33.

27. Ibid.

28. Lower Cape Fear computer biographical files. It should be noted that, as described here, northern North Carolina or northeastern North Carolina includes not only the Albemarle region but also the counties directly north of the Lower Cape Fear, an area that has been characterized by some other historians as the Neuse-Pamilico region. For one alternative typology of North Carolina regions delineated by counties, see Kay and Cary, *Slavery in North Carolina,* 221–22.

29. Lower Cape Fear computer biographical files. Those with South Carolina ties patented 114,482 acres. Those associated with northern North Carolina patented 92,500 acres. See also tables 1.1, 1.2, 1.3, 1.4.

30. On slaveholding patterns, see Kay and Cary, *Slavery in North Carolina,* 221–35.

31. This may have been somewhat less true with those traveling from South Carolina because the distance was sometimes comparable. At the same time, contemporary accounts indicate that, if traveling conditions from north of the Cape Fear were difficult, those from the south were often practically impassable by land. See, for example, Hugh Finlay, *Journal Kept by Hugh Finlay, Surveyor of the Post Roads on the Continent of North America, during His Survey of the Post Offices between Falmouth and Casco Bay in the Province of Massachusetts, and Savannah in Georgia; Begun the 13th September, 1773 and Ended 26th June 1774* (Brooklyn: F. H. Norton, 1867), 66–79; Elkanah Watson, *Men and Times of the Revolution; or Memoirs of Elkanah Watson, Including Journals of Travels in Europe and America, from 1777 to 1842,* ed. Winslow C. Watson (New York: Dana, 1857), 41.

32. Hugh Meredith, *An Account of the Cape Fear Country, 1731,* ed. Earl Gregg Swem (Perth Amboy, N.J.: C. F. Heartman, 1922), 27; Governor Burrington to Board of Trade, September 4, 1731, *Colonial Records,* 3:210.

33. It is unclear precisely what Meredith and Burrington meant by "neighboring colonies." Clearly this probably included South Carolina. Given the early timing of these comments, the relative isolation of the new Lower Cape Fear settlement, and the especially indeterminate status of the boundary between North and South Carolina before 1737, it seems probable that they considered the rest of North Carolina to be a "neighboring colony" to the Lower Cape Fear. The only other colony contiguous with North Carolina, Virginia, does not appear to have contributed a significant number of settlers to the Lower Cape Fear, and both references clearly indicate that immigrants were arriving from multiple colonies.

34. Bernard Bailyn, *Voyagers to the West: A Passage in the Peopling of America on the Eve of the Revolution* (New York: Knopf, 1986), 15–16.

35. Lower Cape Fear computer biographical files. Specifically, these counties include Bladen, Duplin, and Cumberland. Also, the number of Lower Cape Fear connections with Bladen County may be slightly exaggerated because a portion of Bladen County became part of the Lower Cape Fear counties with the formation of Brunswick County in 1764. While there is no way to correct for this problem with the data, there does not appear to have been any large shift of residents taking place at the same time as the redrawing of these boundaries. For the rest of this data, see tables 1.1, 1.2, 1.3, 1.4.

36. It appears that forty-six of the connections were instances of migration from the Upper Cape Fear to the Lower Cape Fear and fifteen were instances of migration from the Lower Cape Fear to the Upper Cape Fear. Of course, the data are biased toward those who spent more time in the Lower Cape Fear and may understate the levels of outmigration. For more on population turnover and mobility, see chapter 4.

37. Lower Cape Fear computer biographical files. These counties include Dobbs, Rowan, Johnston, Orange, and Granville. See also tables 1.1, 1.2, 1.3, 1.4.

38. James Murray, *Letters of James Murray, Loyalist,* ed. Nina M. Tiffany (Boston: Printed, not published, 1901); *Dictionary of North Carolina Biography,* s.v., "Murray, James," 4:351. The rest of Murray's letters can be found in the James Murray Papers in the North Carolina Department of Archives and History, Raleigh, or in James Murray Letters, MHS, 28.

39. Murray to Andrew Bennet, May 13, 1735, in Murray, *Letters,* 17–19.

40. "Memorandum from Mr. McCulloh," "Rules rec[eiv]ed from H[enry] M[cCulloh]," September 1736: James Murray Letters, MHS.

41. Murray to Andrew Bennet, May 13, 1735, in Murray, *Letters,* 17–19.

42. Lower Cape Fear computer biographical files.

43. James Murray to Henry McCulloh, May 3, 1736, James Murray to Andrew Bennet, November, 1736: James Murray Letters, MHS.

44. James Murray to Andrew Bennet, November, 1736, James Murray to Henry McCulloh, November 4, 1736, James Murray to Hutchinson and Grimke, November 4, 1736: James Murray Letters, MHS.

45. James Murray to Henry McCulloh, December 1735: James Murray Letters, MHS.

46. Murray to David Tullideph, December 15, 1735: James Murray Letters, MHS.

47. Murray to Henry McCulloh, May 30, 1736: James Murray Letters, MHS.

48. Murray to Henry McCulloh, November 6, 1736: James Murray Letters, MHS.

49. On the migration of Scots to North Carolina during the colonial period, see, among others, Duane Meyer, *The Highland Scots of North Carolina, 1732–1776* (Chapel Hill: University of North Carolina Press, 1957); Bailyn, *Voyagers to the West,* 15–16, 204–39, 499–544; and Janet Schaw, *Journal of a Lady of Quality; Being the Narrative of a Journey from Scotland to the West Indies, North Carolina, and Portugal, in the Years 1774 to 1776,* ed. Evangeline W. Andrews and Charles M. Andrews (New Haven: Yale University Press, 1923), 257–59.

50. Scotus Americanus, "Informations Concerning the Province of North Carolina, Addressed to Emigrants from the Highlands and Western Isles of Scotland," in *Some Eighteenth Century Tracts Concerning North Carolina,* ed. William K. Boyd (Raleigh: State of North Carolina, 1927), 417–51.

51. Lower Cape Fear computer biographical files. See also tables 1.1, 1.2, 1.3, 1.4. Fourteen of the thirty-three Scots in the Lower Cape Fear described themselves as merchants, while several others for whom there is no occupational data owned ships appearing in the records for the Port of Brunswick customs district, suggesting that they were at least involved in the transportation end of overseas trade. In contrast, only six of the Scots described themselves as planters, and some of these, like Murray, alternated between using *planter* and *merchant.* It should also be noted that the ties to Scotland are, if anything, probably overrepresented in the sample because evidence relating to Scots is more complete. Not only are there several lists of Scottish passengers arriving in North Carolina from ships, but Dr. Robert Cain, of the North Carolina Office of Archives and History, allowed

me to use a list of Scots involved in North Carolina history. In each case, the percentage of Scots who show up in the records of the Lower Cape Fear counties is quite low.

52. On Scottish merchants in the Lower Cape Fear, see also the remarks by Merrens in *Colonial North Carolina,*152–53.

53. See Bailyn, *Voyagers to the West,* 189–203, 232–39.

54. Lower Cape Fear computer biographical files. See also tables 1.1, 1.2, 1.3, 1.4. While there was a significant contingent of ethnically Welsh settlers in the Lower Cape Fear, none of them could be traced to a specific location in Wales; hence, they cannot be included in the sample either separately or as English. Further, no attempt has been made to differentiate settlers who were, or were not, Anglo-Irish because the evidence reveals only places of residence.

55. They patented more land than any group except the North and South Carolinians, and twenty-six of them identified themselves as merchants, more than in any other group, compared with a mere nine of them who identified themselves as planters. See tables 1.1, 1.2, 1.3, 1.4.

56. Ian K. Steele, *The English Atlantic, 1675–1740: An Exploration of Communication and Community* (New York: Oxford University Press, 1986), 261.

57. Bailyn, *Voyagers to the West,* 94–104.

58. Lower Cape Fear computer biographical files. Most of these were probably Anglo-Irish, but it is impossible to be precise about the percentage. Only four of the nineteen identified themselves as planters. See tables 1.1, 1.2, 1.3, 1.4.

59. Lower Cape Fear computer biographical files. Seventeen out of the fifty-six individuals with ties to England and eight of the nineteen with ties to Ireland can also be traced to other colonies. It is also noteworthy that only four individuals can be traced to non-English-speaking parts of Europe, and at least two of these appear to have been Englishmen living abroad. Presumably, the Lower Cape Fear did not provide enough encouragement to those who would have to overcome such enormous linguistic and cultural barriers. See tables 1.1, 1.2, 1.3, 1.4.

60. Lower Cape Fear computer biographical files. On the settling of South Carolina, see Richard S. Dunn, "The English Sugar Islands and the Founding of South Carolina," *South Carolina Historical Magazine* 72, no. 2 (April 1971): 81–93; Richard Waterhouse, "England, the Caribbean, and the Settlement of Carolina," *Journal of American Studies* 9, no. 3 (December 1975): 259–81; and Greene, "Colonial South Carolina and the Caribbean Connection."

61. Meredith, *Account of the Cape Fear Country,* 13.

62. Letter of the vestrymen and churchwardens of St. Phillip's Parish to the bishop of London, Easter Monday, 1730, in Robert J. Cain, ed., *The Colonial Records of North Carolina,* 2nd series (Raleigh: State of North Carolina, 1963–) (hereafter cited as *Colonial Records,* 2nd series), 10:324.

63. Taxables included all white males at least sixteen years of age and all "black" or "mixed" persons over age twelve, whether enslaved or free, as well as the small number of white women who married black men. Individuals were considered mixed if they had black ancestors within the last four generations. See Laws, in Walter Clark, ed., *The State Records of North Carolina* (Goldsboro: State of North Carolina, 1895–1905) (hereafter cited as *State Records*), 23:106–7, 210–12, 345–46, 526–31.

64. In this matter, I have followed the procedures used by Kay and Cary in *Slavery in North Carolina,* 221–25. They determined that the population of North Carolina counties

consisted of approximately 4.1 people per white taxable and 1.89 people per black taxable. Because black women and some children were taxed, the number of black taxables is closer to the total population.

65. See tables 1.5 and 1.6. While these lists probably provide the most reliable information on taxables in colonial North Carolina counties, they are still incomplete because some indigent individuals and officeholders were exempt from taxes. See Alan D. Watson, "County Fiscal Policy in Colonial North Carolina," *North Carolina Historical Review* 55, no. 3 (July 1978): 294–96. All these lists are available at the North Carolina Office of Archives and History, Raleigh, North Carolina.

66. See tables 1.7, 1.8, 1.9. A third source provides a continuous list estimating the total number of taxables in North Carolina from 1748 to 1770. I have not used this source, however, because it gives numbers that conflict with those in the county tax lists and in the *Colonial Records* and because it seems to be the least reliable of the three choices. Also, this list does not differentiate between white and black taxables, making the statistical procedure of converting to total population estimates less accurate. Apparently the list was compiled by John Burgwin in 1770 to learn more about fiscal matters in the colony. On this source and on the data in the *Colonial Records,* see Evarts S. Greene and Virginia D. Harrington, *American Population before the Federal Census of 1790* (New York: Columbia University Press, 1932), 156–72. On North Carolina taxables and population, see also Merrens, *Colonial North Carolina,* 194–201.

67. See table 1.10.

68. See tables 1.5, 1.6, 1.7, 1.8, 1.9, 1.10.

69. See esp. Walter E. Minchinton, "The Seaborne Slave Trade of North Carolina," *North Carolina Historical Review* 71, no. 1 (January 1994): 1–61; Kay and Cary, *Slavery in North Carolina,* 19–22.

70. "Captain Burrington's Representation of the Present State and Condition of North Carolina, January 1st. 1732/33," *Colonial Records,* 3:430.

71. Murray to Richard Oswald, November 16, 1752: James Murray Letters, MHS.

72. David Eltis, Stephen D. Behrendt, David Richardson, and Herbert S. Klein, eds., *The Transatlantic Slave Trade: A Database on CD-ROM* (Cambridge: Cambridge University Press, 1999). These voyages bear the database's "unique identity numbers" 90370, 90787, 77714, 77759, 75900, and 91413. In all of these cases, the editor's database procedures have been used to estimate the number of slaves disembarked in North Carolina.

73. Port of Brunswick Records, 1765–75, North Carolina Department of Archives and History, Raleigh, 10.

74. Minchinton, "Seaborne Slave Trade," 8.

75. Proceedings of the Wilmington Safety Committee, *Colonial Records,* 9:1050–51, 1098.

76. Minchinton, "Seaborne Slave Trade," 21–25.

77. Naval Office Shipping Lists for South Carolina, Colonial Office 5/508–9, British Public Records Office, London. Copies of these lists and many other documents relating to the maritime trade of colonial South Carolina can be found in the Thomas Tobias Papers, South Carolina Historical Society, Charleston.

78. Council Journals, *Colonial Records,* 4:333–34. For two similar examples, see Journal of the Commons House of the Assembly, in J. H. Easterby, ed., *The Colonial Records of South Carolina* (Columbia: State of South Carolina, 1951–62), 5:273, 314.

79. *South Carolina Gazette,* October 12, 1739; Wood, *Black Majority,* 339.

80. Murray to Henry McCulloh, May 20, 1736; Murray to Hutchinson and Co., July 21, 1736; Murray to Hutchinson and Grimke, February 19, 1737; Murray to Hutchinson and Grimke, July 28, 1737; Murray to unnamed, December 23, 1738; Murray to Hutchinson and Grimke, May 14, 1739; Murray to Hutchinson and Grimke, July 4, 1739; Murray to Andrew Bennet, October 6, 1739; Murray to Henry McCulloh, November 10, 1739; Murray to Henry McCulloh, June 23, 1740; Murray to Watson and McKenzie, June 23, 1740; Murray to Mrs. Bennet, September 1740; Murray to John Watson, December 2, 1740; Murray to James Rutherford, March 1, 1751; Murray to Richard Oswald and Co., November 16, 1752; Murray to Richard Oswald and Co., July 19, 1756: James Murray Letters, MHS.

81. Indeed, the very existence of runaway slave ads placed in the early South Carolina newspapers by Lower Cape Fear planters suggests that slave owners assumed that their slaves often had ties to South Carolina. For examples of Lower Cape Fear runaways, see *Cape Fear Mercury,* November 2, 1769, January 13, 1773, August 7, 1775; *Wilmington Centinel and General Advertiser,* June 18, 1788; *South Carolina Gazette,* January 15, 1750, February 19, 1754, November 27, 1755, October 2, 1758, May 25, 1769; *Charleston South-Carolina Gazette and General Advertiser,* July 12, 1783.

82. See table 1.10. For data on the population of the rest of North Carolina, see Kay and Cary, *Slavery in North Carolina,* 221–28.

83. *Records of the Executive Council, 1664–1734, Colonial Records,* 2nd series, 7:269.

84. Petition of Several People at New Hanover at Cape Fair to the Society, undated, SPG Records, Library of Congress Manuscripts Division, Washington, D.C.

85. Murray to David Tullideph, February 2, 1735/36: James Murray Letters, MHS.

86. James Moir to SPG, April 22, 1742, *Colonial Records,* 4:605.

87. For data on rates of population increase in colonial North Carolina, see Kay and Cary, *Slavery in North Carolina,* 228.

Chapter 2: Land and Region

1. For John and William Bartram's relationship to southeastern North Carolina, see Edward J. Cashin, *William Bartram and the American Revolution on the Southern Frontier* (Columbia: University of South Carolina Press, 2000), 2–3, 242–44; Thomas P. Slaughter, *The Natures of John and William Bartram* (New York: Knopf, 1996), 124–31; Ernest Earnest, *John and William Bartram: Botanists and Explorers* (Philadelphia: University of Pennsylvania Press, 1940), 96–99; Eric G. Bolen, "The Bartrams in North Carolina," *Wildlife in North Carolina* 60 (May 1996): 16–21; William Bartram, *The Travels of William Bartram: Naturalist's Edition,* ed. Francis Harper (New Haven: Yale University Press, 1958), 298–302, 418–21, 449; John Bartram, *The Correspondence of John Bartram, 1734–1777,* ed. Edmund Berkeley and Dorothy Smith Berkeley (Gainesville: University of Florida Press, 1992), 490–91, 499, 509, 511–19, 524, 531–45; John Bartram, "Diary of a Journey through the Carolinas, Georgia, and Florida from July 1, 1765 to April 10, 1766," annotated by Francis Harper, *Transactions of the American Philosophical Society,* n.s., 33, part 1 (December 1942): 14–19, 59–61.

2. Bolen, "Bartrams in North Carolina," 16.

3. Technically, Colonel William Bartram's plantation and place of residence was in Bladen County and therefore beyond the definition of the Lower Cape Fear region given in the introduction above. Francis Harper located the present-day site of Ashwood six

miles northeast of Council, N.C., in Bladen County and not many more miles from the Lower Cape Fear counties of Brunswick and New Hanover. As noted earlier, these boundaries are necessarily imprecise indicators of the limits of the Lower Cape Fear region. It is possible that many of the features of the Lower Cape Fear region extended into parts of Bladen County, though several factors, including economic activity, patterns of wealth, and immigration, suggest otherwise. Farming activities on Colonel William Bartram's plantation, for example, seem to bear more resemblance to those in the Upper Cape Fear than to those in the Lower Cape Fear. Bladen County's surviving records are unusually sparse and make this matter difficult to explore fully, but some further discussion is included in chapter 4, below. See also H. Roy Merrens, *Colonial North Carolina in the Eighteenth Century: A Study in Historical Geography* (Chapel Hill: University of North Carolina Press, 1964), 128 n. 96. In any case, the nephew William's business on the Cape Fear River apparently revolved around trade in the Lower Cape Fear counties.

4. John Bartram, "Diary of a Journey," 59; William Bartram, *Travels,* 300, 449.

5. William Bartram to John Bartram, May 20, 1761, in John Bartram, *Correspondence,* 515–16.

6. D. W. Stahle, M. K. Cleaveland, and J. G. Hehr, "North Carolina Climate Changes Reconstructed from Tree Rings: A.D. 372 to 1985," *Science* 10, issue 240, no. 4858 (June 1988): 1517–19.

7. Colonel William Bartram to John Bartram, May 18, 1761, in John Bartram, *Correspondence,* 514–15. For additional contemporary remarks on the damage caused by a hurricane that struck the Lower Cape Fear, see letter from Governor Tryon to Lord Hillsborough, September 15, 1769, in William L. Saunders, ed., *The Colonial Records of North Carolina* (Raleigh: State of North Carolina, 1886–90) (hereafter cited as *Colonial Records*), 8:71; letter from Governor Tryon to Earl Hillsborough, September 24, 1769, ibid., 8:72–75; House Journals [?], ibid., 8:89; letter from Mr. Stewart to the secretary, December 6, 1769, ibid., 3:159–60.

8. William Bartram, *Travels,* 300.

9. Slaughter, *The Natures of John and William Bartram,* 128; John Bartram to William Bartram, June 7, 1765, in John Bartram, *Correspondence,* 651–52; Cashin, *William Bartram and the American Revolution,* 2–3, 243–44.

10. John Bartram to William Bartram, undated, in John Bartram, *Correspondence,* 524.

11. William Bartram, *Travels,* 300.

12. Quoted in Earnest, *John and William Bartram,* 98.

13. Difficulties related to the distribution of land were not unique to the Lower Cape Fear, but the intensity of problems reached an unusual level and responded to specific problems within the region. For two other early American locations with significant problems related to land acquisition and ownership, see Brendan J. McConville, *These Daring Disturbers of the Public Peace: The Struggle for Property and Power in Early New Jersey* (Ithaca, N.Y.: Cornell University Press, 1999); Alan Taylor, *Liberty Men and Great Proprietors: The Revolutionary Settlement on the Maine Frontier, 1760–1820* (Chapel Hill: University of North Carolina Press, 1990).

14. On the Outer and Inner Coastal Plains, see Merrens, *Colonial North Carolina,* 37–44.

15. Merrens, *Colonial North Carolina,* 44–45; Timothy Silver, *A New Face on the Countryside: Indians, Colonists, and Slaves in South Atlantic Forests, 1500–1800* (New York: Cambridge University Press, 1990), 16.

16. On Native Americans and pre-Columbian North American ecology, see, among others, Silver, *New Face on the Countryside;* William Cronin, *Changes in the Land: Indians, Colonists, and the Ecology of New England* (New York: Hill & Wang, 1983).

17. For further details, see Paul Quattlebaum, *The Land Called Chicora: The Carolinas under Spanish Rule with French Intrusions, 1520–1670* (Gainesville: University of Florida Press, 1956).

18. William S. Powell, *North Carolina through Four Centuries* (Chapel Hill: University of North Carolina Press, 1989), 14–15, 30–33.

19. "A Relation of a Discovery, by William Hilton, 1664," in *Narratives of Early Carolina, 1650–1708,* ed. Alexander S. Salley Jr. (New York: Charles Scribner's Sons, 1911), 47.

20. "A Brief Description of the Province of Carolina, by Robert Horne(?), 1666," in *Narratives,* ed. Salley, 67.

21. Samuel Mavericke to Lord Arlington, October 16, 1667, *Colonial Records,* 1:161.

22. For a much more detailed account of these events, see Lawrence Lee, *The Lower Cape Fear in Colonial Days* (Chapel Hill: University of North Carolina Press, 1965), 27–53. Also see Hugh T. Lefler and William S. Powell, *Colonial North Carolina: A History* (New York: Charles Scribner's Sons, 1973), 38–43.

23. Scotus Americanus, "Informations Concerning the Province of North Carolina, Addressed to Emigrants from the Highlands and Western Isles of Scotland," in *Some Eighteenth Century Tracts Concerning North Carolina,* ed. William K. Boyd (Chapel Hill: University of North Carolina Press, 1927), 448.

24. William Logan, "William Logan's Journal of a Journey to Georgia, 1745," *Pennsylvania Magazine of History and Biography* 36 (1912): 14.

25. Lower Cape Fear computer biographical files; Donald Lennon and Ida Brooks Kellam, eds., *The Wilmington Town Book, 1743–1778* (Raleigh: State of North Carolina, 1973), 3–4; Ida Brooks Kellam and Elizabeth Francenia McKoy, eds., *St. James Church, Wilmington, North Carolina, Historical Records, 1737–1852* (Wilmington, N.C.: I. B. Kellam, 1965), 10.

26. Hugh Meredith, *An Account of the Cape Fear Country, 1731,* ed. Earl Gregg Swem (Perth Amboy, N.J.: C. F. Heartman, 1922), 17, 19.

27. Lord Adam Gordon, "Journal of an Officer's Travels in America and the West Indies, 1764–1765," in *Travels in the American Colonies,* ed. Newton D. Mereness (New York: Antiquarian Press, 1916), 400–402.

28. Samuel B. Doggett, ed., "A Plantation on Prince George's Creek, Cape Fear, North Carolina," *New-England Historical and Genealogical Register* 52 (1898): 469–73.

29. Scotus Americanus, "Informations Concerning North Carolina," 446.

30. Murray to William Ellison, February 14, 1735/36, in James Murray, *Letters of James Murray, Loyalist,* ed. Nina M. Tiffany (Boston: Printed, not published, 1901), 24; Murray to Richard Oswald and Co., January 28, 1750/51: James Murray Letters, Massachusetts Historical Society, Boston (hereafter cited as MHS).

31. For an overview of this topic, see James M. Clifton, "Golden Grains of White: Rice Planting on the Lower Cape Fear," *North Carolina Historical Review* 50, no. 4 (1973): 365–93.

32. Meredith, *Account of the Cape Fear Country,* 27, 29; George Burrington to Board of Trade, October 13, 1735, *Colonial Records,* 4:303; Council Journals, April 11, 1753, ibid., 5:32–33; Council Journals, June 1766, ibid., 7:226–27; Scotus Americanus, "Informations Concerning North Carolina," 440–41. On the long-leaf pine and naval stores production, see Merrens, *Colonial North Carolina,* 85–89.

33. Jacquelyn H. Wolf, "Patents and Tithables in Proprietary North Carolina, 1663–1729," *North Carolina Historical Review* 56, no. 3 (1979): 263–67; Robert E. Gallman, "Influences on the Distribution of Landholdings in Early Colonial North Carolina," *Journal of Economic History* 62, no. 3 (1982): 549–75; Lefler and Powell, *Colonial North Carolina,* 151–53; Lee, *Lower Cape Fear,* 62–63; Merrens, *Colonial North Carolina,* 24–27; John Spencer Bassett, "Landholding in Colonial North Carolina," *Law Quarterly Review* 11, no. 2 (1895): 154–66; Council Journals, November 3, 1732, September 24, 1735, September 13, 1737, *Colonial Records,* 3:427, 4:60, 281; George Burrington to Board of Trade, February 20, 1731/32, ibid., 3:336–37; George Burrington to Board of Trade, March 11, 1735/36, ibid., 4:158. For valuable comparative information about the land-acquisition process in early South Carolina, see Meaghan N. Duff, "Creating a Plantation Province: Proprietary Land Policies and Early Settlement Patterns," in *Money, Trade, and Power: The Evolution of Colonial South Carolina's Plantation Society,* ed. Jack P. Greene, Rosemary Brana-Shute, and Randy J. Sparks (Columbia: University of South Carolina Press, 2001), 1–25.

34. Gallman, "Influences on the Distribution of Landholdings"; Wolf, "Patents and Tithables"; Lefler and Powell, *Colonial North Carolina,* 151–53. Gallman used multiple regression analysis to assess the influence of life events on the size of household landholdings in Perquimans County during the late proprietary period. He found widespread and relatively evenly divided landownership in Perquimans, as well as continuing economic opportunity. Gallman's focus on family relationships and events, however, underscored the importance of inheritance for the transmission and acquisition of land among colonial Americans. Using a very different approach, Wolf's work on patents revealed the average patent size under the proprietors to be 492 acres, well under the stipulated 640-acre maximum, though she also found a significant degree of inequality in landed wealth.

35. Edmond Porter to the duke of Newcastle, August 15, 1733, *Colonial Records,* 3:501.

36. See *Dictionary of North Carolina Biography,* 1979–96, s.v., "Burrington, George," 1:283–84; William S. Price Jr., "A Strange Incident in George Burrington's Royal Governorship," *North Carolina Historical Review* 51, no. 2 (1974): 149–58.

37. Council Journals, April 17, 1724, *Colonial Records,* 2:528–30; General Court Records, October 27, 1724, ibid., 2:557.

38. General Assembly of North Carolina to the king, May 22, 1731, *Colonial Records,* 3:137–38. And for Burrington's own account, see George Burrington to duke of Newcastle, March 1, 1732/33, ibid., 3:437–38.

39. North Carolina Council to the king, December 12, 1728, *Colonial Records,* 3:2–5; memorial of Henry McCulloh to Board of Trade [1750], *Dictionary of North Carolina Biography,* 2:171–72.

40. Murray to Henry McCulloh, May 3, 1736, in Murray, *Letters,* 31.

41. Lower Cape Fear computer biographical files; see table 2.1.

42. Ibid.; see tables 2.3, 2.4, 2.5, 2.6.

43. Ibid.; see table 2.1. The thirty-three patents in the years 1730–34 were presumably issued before Burrington arrived or after he departed.

44. Among the numerous contemporary documents mentioning the blank patent controversy, see esp. Edmond Porter to the duke of Newcastle, December 22, 1729, *Colonial Records,* 3:51–52; Board of Trade Journals, October 17, 1735, ibid., 4:30; Council Journals, March 6, 1734/45, September 13, 1737, ibid., 4:40, 280; Gabriel Johnston to Board of Trade, October 6, 1737, ibid., 4:265–68; Gabriel Johnston to Board of Trade, August 2,

1735, ibid., 4:296–99; George Burrington to Board of Trade, October 13, 1735, ibid., 4:299–307; The Case of Sundry Inhabitants of North Carolina Dwelling at Cape Fear River to Board of Trade [1735], ibid., 4:308–15; George Burrington to Board of Trade, October 28, 1735, ibid., 4:316–17; The Case of the Blank Patents [1738], ibid., 4:318–23; petition of T. Wragg to Board of Trade, June 12, 1738, ibid., 4:323–24. For two scholars' comments on the matter, see Lee, *Lower Cape Fear,* 104–6; and A. Roger Ekirch, *"Poor Carolina": Politics and Society in Colonial North Carolina, 1729–1776* (Chapel Hill: University of North Carolina Press, 1981), 57–59, 67–69.

45. Edmond Porter to duke of Newcastle, December 12, 1729, *Colonial Records,* 3:52.

46. Ibid., 3:51–52; representation of Board of Trade to the king, August 13, 1730, ibid., 3:87–88; The Case of Sundry Inhabitants of North Carolina Dwelling at Cape Fear River to Board of Trade, October 21, 1735, ibid., 4:308–9.

47. Meredith, *Account of the Cape Fear Country,* 25.

48. Gabriel Johnston to Board of Trade, November 29, 1736, *Colonial Records,* 4:203.

49. Ibid.

50. Representation of Board of Trade to the king, August 13, 1730, *Colonial Records,* 3:87–88; Robert Forster to George Burrington, August 8, 1731, ibid., 3:200; Burrington to Board of Trade, January 1, 1732/33, ibid., 3:431–32; Council Journals, March 6, 1734/35, ibid., 4:40; Gabriel Johnston to Board of Trade, November 29, 1736, ibid., 4:202–7; Eleazer Allen to Board of Trade, March 29, 1737, ibid., 245–47; Johnston to Board of Trade, October 6, 1737, ibid., 4:266–67; Lefler and Powell, *Colonial North Carolina,* 116–21; Ekirch, *Poor Carolina,* 58, 72–73, 85–86, 109.

51. Murray to Gabriel Johnston, February 8, 1750/51: James Murray Letters, MHS.

52. George Burrington to Board of Trade, September 4, 1731, *Colonial Records,* 3:209.

53. Murray to William Ellison, February 14, 1735/36, in Murray, *Letters,* 26.

54. George Burrington to Board of Trade, September 4, 1731, *Colonial Records,* 3:209; Burrington to Board of Trade, January 1, 1732/33, ibid., 3:431; Burrington to the council [1732], ibid., 3:460–61; Council Journal, November 29, 1735, ibid., 4:72–73; Temple Stanyan to the King's Council, April 29, 1736, ibid., 4:162–64; Charles G. Sellers Jr., "Private Profits and British Colonial Policy: The Speculations of Henry McCulloh," *William and Mary Quarterly* 8, no. 4 (1951): 535–57.

55. Memorandum from Mr. McCulloh, undated; Murray to Mr. David Tullideph, April 15, 1736; Murray to Henry McCulloh, May 3, 1736; Murray to Henry McCulloh, May 20, 1736; Murray to Walter Tullideph, June 23, 1736; Murray to Henry McCulloh, July 8, 1736: James Murray Letters, MHS.

56. George Burrington to Board of Trade, January 1, 1732/33, *Colonial Records,* 3:431–32.

57. Gabriel Johnston to Board of Trade, October 6, 1737, *Colonial Records,* 4:265.

58. Spangenberg diary, September 12, 1752, in Adelaide L. Fries, ed., *Records of the Moravians in North Carolina* (Raleigh, N.C.: Edwards & Broughton Printing, 1922–2000), 1:32.

59. Murray to David Tullideph, December 15, 1735: James Murray Letters, MHS.

60. Lower Cape Fear computer biographical files; see table 2.1.

61. Ibid.; Agreement with the Lords Proprietor for the Surrender of Their Title [1729], *Colonial Records,* 3:42; A Bill for Providing a Rent Roll and Securing Quitrents [1736], ibid., 4:180; Ekirch, *Poor Carolina,* 66–78, 109, 127.

62. Lower Cape Fear computer biographical files; see table 2.1.

63. Ibid.; see table 2.2

64. Ibid.; see table 2.3.

65. Murray to Henry McCulloh, May 20, 1736; Murray to Henry McCulloh, July 8, 1736; Murray to Henry McCulloh, January 30, 1739/40; Murray to Andrew Douglas, February 8, 1749: James Murray Letters, MHS.

66. Murray to John Ancrum, July 28, 1767: James Murray Letters, MHS.

67. Council Journals, *Colonial Records,* 4:802.

68. For some of the many examples of land-related disputes and problems in the Lower Cape Fear after 1740, see Deposition of James Moir [1750], *Colonial Records,* 4:1121–23; Council Journals, September 29, 1750, May 9, 1753, November 29, 1757, March 5, 1759, December 5, 1760, October 24, 1761, April 28, 1762, October 20, 1762, November 11, 1764, November 19, 1764, ibid., 4:1048, 5:1:33, 812, 821, 5:1:78, 343–44, 635, 761, 765, 1085, 1086.

69. Lower Cape Fear computer biographical files; see tables 2.3, 2.4, 2.5, 2.6.

70. Wolf, "Patents and Tithables"; Duff, "Creating a Plantation Province," 15. See also note 33 of chapter 2, above.

71. Francis Grave Morris and Phyllis Mary Morris, "Economic Conditions in North Carolina about 1780: Part 1, Landholdings," *North Carolina Historical Review* 16, no. 2 (1939): 107–33; see tables 2.4, 2.5.

72. Lower Cape Fear computer biographical files; see table 2.6.

73. Interestingly, slave ownership was also less widespread among households in Brunswick County than in New Hanover, though it was still more widespread throughout the Lower Cape Fear than virtually anywhere else in North Carolina. See Alan D. Watson, "Household Size and Composition in Pre-Revolutionary North Carolina," *Mississippi Quarterly* 31, no. 4 (1978): 551–69.

74. "A New Voyage to Georgia, By a Young Gentleman, Giving an Account of His Travels to South Carolina and Part of North Carolina . . . ," in *Collections of the Georgia Historical Society,* vol. 2 (Savannah, Ga., 1842), 58.

75. *Records of the Executive Council, 1735–1754,* in Robert J. Cain, ed., *Colonial Records of North Carolina,* 2nd series (Raleigh: State of North Carolina, 1963–) (hereafter cited as *Colonial Records,* 2nd series), 8:13–14. At the time of Gibbs's complaint, Moore owned more than twenty thousand acres of land and about two hundred slaves in the Lower Cape Fear; see Lower Cape Fear computer biographical files.

76. Council Journals, September 9, 1735, June 18, 1736, *Colonial Records,* 4:57, 220; Deposition of James Moir [1750], ibid., 4:1121–23.

77. George Burrington to Board of Trade, January 1, 1732/33, *Colonial Records,* 3:432.

78. *Colonial Records,* 3:431; Council Journals, November 11, 1732, June 18, 1736, ibid., 3:427, 4:220; *Records of the Executive Council, 1664–1734, Colonial Records,* 2nd series, 7:283–84; James Murray to Richard Oswald and Co., February 28, 1755, in Murray, *Letters,* 79.

79. Council Journals, March 6, 1734/35, April 4, 1745, May 26, 1772, *Colonial Records,* 1:41–42, 760, 9:294–95; Gabriel Johnston to Board of Trade, October 15, 1736, ibid., 4:176; Johnston to Board of Trade, November 29, 1736, ibid., 4:205; Deposition of James Moir [1750], 1122; *Records of the Executive Council, 1735–1754, Colonial Records,* 2nd series, 8:16.

80. John Bartram, "Diary of a Journey," 15 n. 1.

81. Murray to Thomas Clark, January 6, 1767: James Murray Letters, MHS.

82. Murray to John Ancrum, April 29, 1767: James Murray Letters, MHS.

83. Silver, *New Face on the Countryside,* 128.

84. Problems with malaria were common in the southern British American colonies, and particularly in the South Carolina low country, where residents adapted in a variety of ways. On this subject, see, among many others, Joyce E. Chaplin, *"An Anxious Pursuit": Agricultural Innovation and Modernity in the Lower South, 1730–1815* (Chapel Hill: University of North Carolina Press, 1993), 93–109; Peter A. Coclanis, *The Shadow of a Dream: Economic Life and Death in the South Carolina Low Country, 1760–1920* (New York: Oxford University Press, 1989), 38–47; Peter H. Wood, *Black Majority: Negroes in Colonial South Carolina from 1670 through the Stono Rebellion* (New York: Knopf, 1974), 63–91; John Duffy, *Epidemics in Colonial America* (Baton Rouge: Louisiana State University Press, 1953), 69, 103–4, 214, 315, 237–47; H. Roy Merrens and George D. Terry, "Dying in Paradise: Malaria, Mortality, and the Perceptual Environment on Colonial South Carolina," *Journal of Southern History* 50, no. 4 (1982): 533–50; Darret B. Rutman and Anita H. Rutman, "'Of Agues and Fevers': Malaria in the Early Chesapeake," *William and Mary Quarterly* 33, no. 1 (1976): 31–60.

85. Murray to Mrs. Bennet, March 25, 1758, in Murray, *Letters,* 96.

86. Janet Schaw, *Journal of a Lady of Quality; Being the Narrative of a Journey from Scotland to the West Indies, North Carolina, and Portugal, in the Years 1774 to 1776,* ed. Evangeline W. Andrews and Charles M. Andrews (New Haven: Yale University Press, 1923), 186.

87. LaPierre to SPG, October 25, 1728, SPG Records, Manuscripts Division, Library of Congress, Washington, D.C.

88. James Moir to SPG, April 22, 1742, November 4, 1746, *Colonial Records,* 4:605, 795.

89. John McDowell to SPG, April 17, 1760, *Colonial Records,* 5:1:36–37.

90. Nicholas Christian to SPG, July 27, 1774, *Colonial Records,* 9:1022.

91. Schaw, *Journal of a Lady,* 159; Johann D. Schoepf, *Travels in the Confederation, 1783–1784, from the German of Johann David Schoepf,* trans. and ed. Alfred J. Morrison (Philadelphia: Bergman, 1911), 103, 153; Robert Hunter Jr., *Quebec to Carolina in 1785–1786: Being the Travel Diary and Observations of Robert Hunter, Jr., a Young Merchant of London,* ed. Louis B. Wright and Marion Tinling (San Marino, Calif.: Huntington Library, 1943), 282; John Bartram, "Diary of a Journey," 18.

92. Murray to David Tullideph, March 31, 1736, Murray to Tullideph, April 15, 1736: James Murray Letters, MHS.

93. Murray to Richard Oswald and Co., February 28, 1755: James Murray Letters, MHS.

94. Lower Cape Fear computer biographical files; see tables 2.9, 2.10.

95. Gabriel Johnston to Board of Trade, October 15, 1736, *Colonial Records,* 4:176.

96. On the regional distinctiveness of the southern backcountry, see, among many others, Jack P. Greene, "Independence, Improvement, and Authority: Toward a Framework for Understanding the Histories of the Southern Backcountry during the Era of the American Revolution," in *An Uncivil War: The Southern Backcountry during the American Revolution,* ed. Ronald Hoffman, Thad W. Tate, and Peter J. Albert (Charlottesville: University Press of Virginia, 1985), 3–46; Carl Bridenbaugh, *Myths and Realities: Societies of the Colonial South* (Baton Rouge: Louisiana State University Press, 1952), 119–96; Robert W. Ramsey, *Carolina Cradle: Settlement of the Northwest Carolina Frontier, 1747–1762* (Chapel Hill: University

of North Carolina Press, 1964); Daniel B. Thorp, *The Moravian Community in Colonial North Carolina: Pluralism on the Southern Frontier* (Knoxville: University of Tennessee Press, 1989), 1–7.

97. See tables 2.7, 2.8.

98. Report of Commissioners Sent from Barbadoes to Explore the River Cape Fear [1663], *Colonial Records,* 1:69; William S. Powell, *North Carolina Gazetteer: A Dictionary of Tar Heel Places* (Chapel Hill: University of North Carolina Press, 1968, 424).

99. "A New Voyage to Georgia, By a Young Gentleman, Giving an Account of His Travels to South Carolina and Part of North Carolina . . . ," in *Collections of the Georgia Historical Society,* vol. 2 (Savannah, Ga., 1842), 68.

100. These individuals have been identified largely through land patents, real estate conveyances, contemporary maps, and references in county court minutes. It should be noted that this list may not be complete. Land records are not precise enough to identify the location of many tracts of land, though generally important markers such as Lockwoods Folly, Rocky Point, and Old Town Creek are mentioned in patents. Also, there is no reliable way to locate the residences of those who did not own their own land, though court minutes occasionally provide clues. Some pieces of land in these neighborhoods also may have been transferred in ways that cannot be traced in surviving records.

101. Lower Cape Fear computer biographical files; see tables 2.11, 2.12, 2.13.

102. Ibid.; see table 2.13.

103. Ibid.; see table 2.13.

104. *Cape Fear Mercury,* December 29, 1773.

105. "New Voyage to Georgia," 59; Powell, *North Carolina Gazetteer,* 294; Lee, *Lower Cape Fear,* 201–2.

106. John MacDowell to SPG, June 15, 1762, *Colonial Records,* 7:730.

107. On contemporary maps, see William P. Cummings, *The Southeast in Early Maps, with an Annotated Check List of Printed and Manuscript Regional and Local Maps of Southeastern North America during the Colonial Period* (Chapel Hill: University of North Carolina Press, 1962).

108. Lower Cape Fear computer biographical files; see tables 2.11, 2.12, 2.14.

109. Powell, *North Carolina Gazetteer,* 295.

110. Schaw, *Journal of a Lady,* 281.

111. Lower Cape Fear computer biographical files; see tables 2.11, 2.12, 2.14.

112. On Lockwoods Folly River, see Meredith, *Account of the Cape Fear Country,* 21–22; *Colonial Records,* 7:608.

113. Nicholas Christian to SPG, August 27, 1774, *Colonial Records,* 9:1022; Laws, ibid., 23, 447; Alexander M. Walker, ed., *New Hanover County Court Minutes* (Bethesda, Md.: A. M. Walker, 1958), 1:6, 34.

114. Lower Cape Fear computer biographical files; see tables 2.11, 2.12, 2.15.

115. It is important to acknowledge that this interpretation of the data could be somewhat predetermined by the decision to designate two neighborhoods in reference to waterways. One would, of course, expect settlers in the neighborhood of Lockwoods Folly and Old Town Creek to hold land on these two waterways. At the same time, the numbers are impressive and the data for Rocky Point have no such bias and demonstrate the same consistent trend.

116. Lower Cape Fear computer biographical files; see tables 2.11, 2.12, 2.13, 2.14, 2.15.

117. These three locales have been designated as neighborhoods for the purpose of this study. While no contemporary comments exist describing specific neighborhoods in the Lower Cape Fear, contemporaries used the term *neighborhood* to indicate a similar geographic area of interaction. Evidence does show that Lower Cape Fear residents placed significance on these three areas of settlement, and that some settlers identified themselves specifically as residents of each of these three places. On the use of the term *neighborhood,* see Lorena S. Walsh, "Community Networks in the Early Chesapeake," in *Colonial Chesapeake Society,* ed. Lois Green Carr, Philip D. Morgan, and Jean B. Russo (Chapel Hill: University of North Carolina Press, 1988), 228–31.

118. On transportation, see Christopher C. Crittenden, "Inland Navigation in North Carolina, 1763–1789," *North Carolina Historical Review* 8, no. 2 (1931): 145–54; Christopher C. Crittenden, "Overland Travel and Transportation in North Carolina, 1763–1789," *North Carolina Historical Review* 8, no. 3 (1931): 239–57; Alan D. Watson, "The Ferry in Colonial North Carolina: Vital Link in Transportation," *North Carolina Historical Review* 51, no. 3 (July 1974): 247–60.

119. Schaw, *Journal of a Lady,* 148, 158–59, 177–78, 184–85, 202.

120. Scotus Americanus, "Informations Concerning North Carolina," 443.

121. The development of these two towns is discussed more fully in chapter 7.

122. Lower Cape Fear computer biographical files; see tables 2.3, 2.4, 2.5, 2.6. It is impossible to demonstrate this precisely with quantitative evidence; however, neither patents nor real estate conveyances indicate a continuing opportunity to acquire concentrated holdings of land such as those obtained prior to 1740. Without comparable amounts of new land, culturally determined inheritance practices would have made a decline in the size of landed estates inevitable.

Chapter 3: Families

1. William Saunders, ed., *The Colonial Records of North Carolina* (Raleigh: State of North Carolina, 1886–90) (hereafter cited as *Colonial Records*), 5:xviii, 374–75.

2. At one point Allen appears to have held office in North Carolina at the same time that he was clerk of the South Carolina Assembly. See *Colonial Records,* 3:206, 209, 476.

3. Council Journals, *Colonial Records,* 4:762–63.

4. From MSS records in the Office of the Secretary of State, *Colonial Records,* 5:1:549–51.

5. Lower Cape Fear computer biographical files.

6. "The Slaves of Mrs. Allen & her Computation of their Value," James Murray Robbins Papers, Massachusetts Historical Society, Boston (hereafter cited as MHS).

7. Council Journals, *Council Records,* 5:33.

8. Mr. MacDowell to the secretary, April 16, 1761, *Colonial Records,* 5:1:55–56.

9. Henry Laurens to Thomas Frankland, April 17, 1756, in Henry Laurens, *The Papers of Henry Laurens,* ed. P. M. Hamer, G. C. Rogers, and D. R. Chesnutt (Columbia: University of South Carolina Press, 1968–2003), 2:173–74. For a similar interpretation of this passage, see Cara Anzilotti, "Autonomy and the Female Planter in Colonial South Carolina," *Journal of Southern History* 63, no. 2 (1997): 253. Anzilotti, however, believes Laurens's prediction and Hamer's incorrect footnote, both of which claim that Sarah Allen left the Lower Cape Fear and died in England. In fact, she was in the Lower Cape Fear five years later when her estate was probated. See Lower Cape Fear computer biographical files.

10. Murray to Mrs. Sarah Allen, February 11, 1757, Murray to Mrs. Sarah Allen, undated: James Murray Letters, Massachusetts Historical Society, Boston (hereafter cited as MHS).

11. Murray to Mrs. Sarah Allen, February 11, 1757: James Murray Letters, MHS.

12. Some of these details derive from the Lower Cape Fear computer biographical files, but Sarah Allen's will has been published in Bryan J. Grimes, ed., *North Carolina Wills and Inventories, Copied from the Original and Recorded Wills and Inventories in the Office of the Secretary of State* (Raleigh, N.C.: Edwards & Broughton Printing, 1912), 9–13.

13. While some scholars have depicted the history of British American colonies as a movement away from a family-centered environment toward a more individualistic society, in reality the formation and elaboration of family units constituted a key part of the development of these colonies. See Jack P. Greene, *Pursuits of Happiness: The Social Development of Early Modern British Colonies and the Formation of American Culture* (Chapel Hill: University of North Carolina Press, 1988), 196–97.

14. There is an enormous body of scholarship on families in colonial America. For some of those works most relevant to this study, see John Crowley, "Family Relations and Inheritance in Early South Carolina," *Histoire Sociale/Social History* 17, no. 33 (1984): 35–57; John Crowley, "The Importance of Kinship: Testamentary Evidence from South Carolina," *Journal of Interdisciplinary History* 16, no. 4 (1986): 559–77; James M. Gallman, "Determinants of Age of Marriage in Colonial Perquimans County, North Carolina," *William and Mary Quarterly* 39, no. 1 (1982): 176–91; Alan D. Watson, "Women in Colonial North Carolina: Overlooked and Underestimated," *North Carolina Historical Review* 58, no. 1 (1981): 1–22; Kirsten Fischer, *Suspect Relations: Sex, Race, and Resistance in Colonial North Carolina* (Ithaca, N.Y.: Cornell University Press, 2002); Lorri Glover, *All Our Relations: Blood Ties and Emotional Bonds among the Early South Carolina Gentry* (Baltimore: Johns Hopkins University Press, 2000); Lorena S. Walsh, "'Till Death Us Do Part': Marriage and Family in Seventeenth-Century Maryland," in *The Chesapeake in the Seventeenth-Century,* ed. Thad Tate and David Ammerman (Chapel Hill: University of North Carolina Press, 1979), 126–52; Daniel Blake Smith, *Inside the Great House: Planter Family Life in Eighteenth-Century Chesapeake Society* (Ithaca, N.Y.: Cornell University Press, 1980); Carole Shammas, "Anglo-American Household Government in Comparative Perspective," *William and Mary Quarterly* 52, no. 1 (1995): 104–66.

15. This number must have included slaves; see The Case of Sundry Inhabitants of North Carolina Dwelling at Cape Fear River to Board of Trade [1735], *Colonial Records,* 4:308–15.

16. Ibid., 315.

17. The following discussion of the Moore family's kinship networks and genealogy relies heavily on Mabel L. Webber, comp., "The First Governor Moore and His Children," *South Carolina Historical and Genealogical Magazine* 37, no. 1 (1936): 1–23. All other references to marriage and kinship in this section derive from Lower Cape Fear computer biographical files.

18. Murray to Capt. Innes, July 21, 1747: James Murray Letters, MHS.

19. Murray to Mr. Archibald Douglas, March 4, 1742/43: James Murray Letters, MHS.

20. Murray to Mary Lady Don, January 14, 1756; Murray to Hutchinson and Grimkie, July 28, 1757; Murray to Henry Howson, June 25, 1740; Murray to Gabriel Johnston, February 8, 1750/51: James Murray Letters, MHS.

21. Murray to William Ellison, July 15, 1737; Murray to John Murray, January 26, 1756: James Murray Letters, MHS.

22. Murray to Aeneus and Hugh McKay, September 12, 1749: James Murray Letters, MHS.

23. Murray to Dolly Murray, December 14, 1758: James Murray Letters, MHS.

24. Murray to Thomas Clark, July 22, 1767; Murray to John Rutherford, September 15, 1767; Murray to John Murray, December 15, 1767: James Murray Letters, MHS.

25. The ten landowners were Roger Moore, Maurice Moore, Samuel Swann, James Hasell Sr., George Burrington, John Porter Jr., John Baptista Ashe, Edward Moseley, Arthur Dobbs, and Robert Halton.

26. The top ten slave owners, based on averages from available tax lists, were William Dry, George Moore Sr., William Moore, William Ross Sr., Frederick Gregg, Richard Quince Jr., Maurice Moore Jr., Richard Eagles Jr., John Grange Jr., and Samuel Swann Sr.

27. Of course, the word *family* could include nonkin in eighteenth-century usage, but usually this broader use of the term was still restricted to members of an individual's household such as servants or other "dependents." It could also be argued that by referring to the Moore faction as The Family, Cape Fear residents were indicating their primacy with the article, *The,* more than their familial characteristics. This seems much less likely given the highly pluralistic characters of politics in this region, but in any case the choice of the word *family* is still suggestive.

28. Perhaps the most promising possibility would be to calculate life expectancies from information on tombstones, but even a survey of tombstone inscriptions from early North Carolina cemeteries provided an insufficient sample from which to draw any reliable conclusions. See, for example, the limited number of inscriptions from the eighteenth century in Ida Brooks Kellam and Elizabeth Francenia McKoy, eds., *St. James Church, Wilmington, North Carolina, Historical Records, 1737–1852* (Wilmington, N.C.: I. B. Kellam, 1965), 106–25.

29. James Moir to SPG, April 6, 1763, *Colonial Records,* 5:1:978.

30. Janet Schaw, *Journal of a Lady of Quality; Being the Narrative of a Journey from Scotland to the West Indies, North Carolina, and Portugal, in the Years 1774 to 1776,* ed. Evangeline W. Andrews and Charles M. Andrews (New Haven: Yale University Press, 1923), 153.

31. Hugh Meredith, *An Account of the Cape Fear Country, 1731,* ed. Earl Gregg Swem (Perth Amboy, N.J.: C. F. Heartman, 1922), 27.

32. "A New Voyage to Georgia, By a Young Gentleman, Giving an Account of His Travels to South Carolina and Part of North Carolina . . . ," in *Collections of the Georgia Historical Society,* vol. 2 (Savannah, Ga., 1842), 57–58; Harry J. Carmen, ed., *American Husbandry* (New York: Columbia University Press, 1939), 236, 242–43; "Journal of a French Traveller in the Colonies, 1765, I," *American Historical Review* 26 (July 1921): 735; Hugh Finlay, *Journal Kept by Hugh Finlay, Surveyor of the Post Roads on the Continent of North America, during His Survey of the Post Offices between Falmouth and Casco Bay in the Province of Massachusetts, and Savannah in Georgia; Begun the 13th September, 1773 and Ended 26th June 1774* (Brooklyn: F. H. Norton, 1867), 67; Johann D. Schoepf, *Travels in the Confederation, 1783–1784, from the German of Johann David Schoepf,* trans. and ed., Alfred J. Morrison (Philadelphia: Bergman, 1911), 103, 114, 116; Robert Hunter Jr., *Quebec to Carolina in 1785–1786: Being the Travel Diary and Observations of Robert Hunter, Jr., a Young Merchant of London,* ed. Louis B. Wright and Marion Tinling (San Marino, Calif.: Huntington Library, 1943), 280, 282.

33. On this point, see H. Roy Merrens, *Colonial North Carolina in the Eighteenth Century: A Study in Historical Geography* (Chapel Hill: University of North Carolina Press, 1964), 44–46, esp. fig. 15.

34. Schaw, *Journal of a Lady,* 179; "New Voyage to Georgia," 57–58.

35. Lawrence Lee, *The Lower Cape Fear in Colonial Days* (Chapel Hill: University of North Carolina Press, 1965), 161–67.

36. Murray to Archibald Douglas, March 4, 1742/43: James Murray Letters, MHS.

37. Bethabara Diary, September 25, 1766, in Adelaide L. Fries, ed., *Records of the Moravians in North Carolina* (Raleigh, N.C.: Edwards & Broughton Printing, 1922–2000), 1:335; Marshall's Report to UEC, April 9, 1770, ibid., 2:612.

38. Gabriel Johnston to SPG, October 15, 1748, *Colonial Records,* 4:876.

39. Murray to Henry McCulloh, April 12, 1741, in James Murray, *Letters of James Murray, Loyalist,* ed. Nina M. Tiffany (Boston: Printed, not published, 1901), 62.

40. Murray to Dorothy Murray, March 21, 1758, in Murray, *Letters,* 95–96.

41. Murray to John Murray, December 10, 1761: James Murray Letters, MHS.

42. John Crowley asserts that testators "almost always" named everyone in their immediate families in their wills in eighteenth-century South Carolina; see Crowley, "Importance of Kinship," 565. Undoubtedly, there were exceptions, but they were probably not numerous enough to skew the data dramatically, and there are few alternatives for an analysis of family structure in the colonial Lower Cape Fear.

43. Lower Cape Fear computer biographical files. A nuclear family is defined here as a spouse and at least one child.

44. John Crowley found that more than one-half of South Carolina testators lacked nuclear families, barely one-half were married, and one-third of husbands were childless. South Carolina couples averaged between as few as 2.8 children, in the period prior to 1720, and as high as 3.4 children, in the 1730s. The numbers for the Lower Cape Fear generally suggest a slightly less severe demographic disruption. See Crowley, "Family Relations and Inheritance," 42–43.

45. Murray to John Murray of Phillipspaugh, November 10, 1750; Murray to Andrew Bennet, September 5, 1741: James Murray Letters, MHS.

46. Murray to Mary Lady Don, January 14, 1756: James Murray Letters, MHS.

47. Murray to John Murray, February 9, 1757: James Murray Letters, MHS.

48. Murray to Mrs DeRosset, July 22, 1767; Murray to Dolly Murray, March 21, 1758: James Murray Letters, MHS.

49. In eighteenth-century Anglo-American society, *orphan* referred to a child without a father but not necessarily one without a mother.

50. Laws, in Walter Clark, ed., *The State Records of North Carolina* (Goldsboro: State of North Carolina, 1895–1905), 23:578; 25:313, 405. For a more detailed account of this legislation and a useful discussion of the treatment of orphans in early North Carolina, see Alan D. Watson, "Orphanage in Colonial North Carolina: Edgecombe County as a Case Study," *North Carolina Historical Review* 52, no. 2 (1975): 105–19. On the courts' role in the care of orphans, see Paul M. McCain, *The County Court in North Carolina before 1750* (Durham, N.C.: Duke University Press, 1954), 74–84.

51. Watson, "Orphanage in Colonial North Carolina"; McCain, *County Court;* Alan D. Watson, "Public Poor Relief in Colonial North Carolina," *North Carolina Historical Review* 54, no. 4 (1977): 347–66. On orphans' courts and the treatment of orphans elsewhere in the

colonial South, see Lois Green Carr, "The Development of the Maryland Orphans' Court, 1654–1715," in *Law, Society, and Politics in Early Maryland,* ed. Aubrey C. Land et al. (Baltimore: Johns Hopkins University Press, 1977), 41–62; Walter J. Fraser Jr., "The City Elite, 'Disorder,' and the Poor Children of Pre-Revolutionary Charleston," *South Carolina Historical Magazine* 84, no. 3 (1983): 167–79; Robert M. Weir, *Colonial South Carolina: A History* (Millwood, N.Y.: KTO Press, 1983), 235.

52. Watson, "Orphanage in Colonial North Carolina," 108.

53. Ibid., 111–12.

54. Alexander M. Walker, ed., *New Hanover County Court Minutes* (Bethesda, Md.: A. M. Walker, 1958), 1:25.

55. Ibid., 1:10, 11.

56. Ibid., 1:89; Lower Cape Fear computer biographical files.

57. Approximately one-fourth of testators who mentioned minor children made specific reference to a guardian. In most cases, however, they did specify some provisions for the children, and often these terms implied that the widow or executors would function as guardians.

58. McCain, *County Court,* 74–75; Carr, "Development of the Maryland Orphans' Court," 46–50; Watson, "Orphanage in Colonial North Carolina," 119.

59. For a thoughtful analysis of the nature and function of extended kinship relationships in the southern colonies, see Crowley, "Importance of Kinship." I have followed Crowley's approach in treating wills as indicators of the relative importance of kin and nonkin relationships. It is possible that in some cases the number of extended kin is underestimated because testators may not have made reference to their kinship ties with some individuals and not all extended kin share the same surnames.

60. For illuminating comparative information on responses to death and dying in colonial Virginia, see Patrick Henry Butler III, "Knowing the Uncertainties of This Life: Death and Society in Colonial Tidewater Virginia," doctoral dissertation, Johns Hopkins University, 1998.

61. Lower Cape Fear testators named nonkin as executors 289 times, compared with extended kin, who were named as executors only 89 times. See Lower Cape Fear computer biographical files, table 3.2.

62. Lower Cape Fear computer biographical files; see table 3.2. This apparently differs from testation practices in eighteenth-century South Carolina because John Crowley found that South Carolinians were more apt to mention nonkin than extended kin in their wills. See Crowley, "Importance of Kinship," 567–73. Also, it should be noted that this study treats being named as an executor as distinct from being mentioned in the will.

63. A total of 133 out of 278 wills make references to extended kin; see Lower Cape Fear computer biographical files, table 3.2.

64. On this point, see Carole Shammas, "Anglo-American Household Government in Comparative Perspective," *William and Mary Quarterly* 52, no. 1 (1995): 104–44.

65. In some cases they also had servants in their households, but these cases seem to have been much rarer in the Lower Cape Fear than in some other regions of the plantation colonies.

66. Philip D. Morgan, *Slave Counterpoint: Black Culture in the Eighteenth-Century Chesapeake and Lowcountry* (Chapel Hill: University of North Carolina Press, 1998), 258. For a much more detailed and elaborate discussion of patriarchalism, paternalism, and the ideologies

surrounding colonial slavery, see also 257–317. For two other insightful works among the many that discuss relations between slaves and slave owners in the eighteenth-century southern colonies, see Robert Olwell, *Masters, Slaves, and Subjects: The Culture of Power in the South Carolina Low Country, 1740–1790* (Ithaca, N.Y.: Cornell University Press, 1988); and Mechal Sobel, *The World They Made Together: Black and White Values in Eighteenth-Century Virginia* (Princeton, N.J.: Princeton University Press, 1987). For the construction of gender and race in colonial northeastern North Carolina, see Fischer, *Suspect Relations.*

67. For an important and highly sophisticated, if controversial, view of the ideology of master/slave relations in the antebellum South, see Eugene D. Genovese, *Roll, Jordan, Roll: The World the Slaves Made* (New York: Vintage, 1972); and Genovese, *The World the Slaveholders Made: Two Essays in Interpretation* (New York: Pantheon Books, 1969).

68. According to some tax lists, Chowan and Perquimans Counties, in the Albemarle region, may have been exceptions. See Alan D. Watson, "Household Size and Composition in Pre-Revolutionary North Carolina," *Mississippi Quarterly* 31, no. 4 (1978): 551–69; Merrens, *Colonial North Carolina,* 74–81.

69. Marvin Michael Kay and Lorin Lee Cary, *Slavery in North Carolina, 1748–1775* (Chapel Hill: University of North Carolina Press, 1995), 10–52, 221–30; Merrens, *Colonial North Carolina,* 74–81; Peter H. Wood, *Black Majority: Negroes in Colonial South Carolina from 1670 through the Stono Rebellion* (New York: Knopf, 1974), 131–66.

70. Morgan, *Slave Counterpoint,* 273–76.

71. Ibid., 40–41; Wood, *Black Majority,* 155–66; Philip D. Morgan, ed., "Profile of a Mid-Eighteenth Century South Carolina Parish: The Tax Return of St. James' Goose Creek," *South Carolina Historical Magazine* 81, no. 1 (1980): 51–65.

72. This phrase is borrowed from a monograph on antebellum yeoman households in the South Carolina low country; see Stephanie McCurry, *Masters of Small Worlds: Yeoman Households, Gender Relations, and the Political Culture of the Antebellum South Carolina Low-country* (New York: Oxford University Press, 1995). For an example of one North Carolinian who recognized the superior wealth and authority exerted by South Carolinians, see *South Carolina and American General Gazette,* July 29, 1768.

73. Marvin M. Kay and Lorin Lee Cary have provided copious quantitative documentation of the possibilities for slave family formation in the Lower Cape Fear and other regions of North Carolina, and their data inform this analysis; see Kay and Cary, *Slavery in North Carolina,* esp. 153–73, 229–34, 278–88.

74. Scotus Americanus, "Informations Concerning the Province of North Carolina, Addressed to Emigrants from the Highlands and Western Isles of Scotland," in *Some Eighteenth Century Tracts Concerning North Carolina,* ed. William K. Boyd (Chapel Hill: University of North Carolina Press, 1927), 445.

75. Kay and Cary, *Slavery in North Carolina,* 229, 230–34, 278, 288.

76. Schoepf, *Travels in the Confederation,* 147–49.

77. Elkanah Watson, *Men and Times of the Revolution; or Memoirs of Elkanah Watson, Including His Journals of Travels in Europe and America from 1777 to 1842,* ed. Winslow C. Watson (New York: Dana, 1857), 58.

78. John Brickell, *The Natural History of North-Carolina* (1737; repr., Raleigh, N.C.: Trustees of the Public Libraries, 1911), 275.

79. Kay and Cary, *Slavery in North Carolina,* 167–68.

80. Brickell, *Natural History of North-Carolina,* 274–75; Kay and Cary, *Slavery in North Carolina,* 156–59.

81. Kay and Cary have argued that previous scholars underestimated the number of slaves imported into North Carolina. They may be right, but they may also go to the opposite extreme and exaggerate with the size of their estimates. See Kay and Cary, *Slavery in North Carolina,* 19–21. For a valuable and persuasive corrective, see Walter E. Minchinton, "The Seaborne Slave Trade of North Carolina," *North Carolina Historical Review* 71, no. 1 (January 1994): 13–14. Also, not even Kay and Cary deny the significance of some natural population increase. For more on this topic, see chapter 1.

82. The following discussion of inheritance in the Lower Cape Fear draws on another large body of scholarship dealing with property and inheritance. Some of the most relevant works for this study include Crowley, "Family Relations and Inheritance"; Crowley, "Importance of Kinship"; Lee J. Alston and Morton Owen Shapiro, "Inheritance Laws across Colonies: Causes and Consequences," *Journal of Economic History* 44, no. 2 (1984): 277–87; Carole Shammas, Marylynn Salmon, and Michel Dahlin, *Inheritance in America from Colonial Times to the Present* (New Brunswick, N.J.: Rutgers University Press, 1987), 3–79; Holly Brewer, "Entailing Aristocracy in Colonial Virginia: 'Ancient Feudal Restraints' and Revolutionary Reform," *William and Mary Quarterly* 54, no. 2 (1997): 307–46; Smith, *Inside the Great House,* 231–48; Toby L. Ditz, *Property and Kinship: Inheritance in Early Connecticut, 1750–1820* (Princeton, N.J.: Princeton University Press, 1986). For a dissertation that explores matters related to the intergenerational transfer of property, see Glenn Donald Deane, "Parents and Progeny: The Demography of Inequality in Colonial North Carolina, 1680–1759," doctoral dissertation, University of North Carolina, 1993. Deane's findings pertain to Perquimans County, however, and should not be generalized to the Lower Cape Fear region.

83. Lower Cape Fear computer biographical files; see table 3.6.

84. Ibid.; see table 3.8.

85. New Hanover County Real Estate Conveyances, Book E, 206; see also Book AB, 96, 256; New Hanover Wills, Book C, 69, microfilm, North Carolina Department of Archives and History, Raleigh.

86. See Shammas et al., *Inheritance in America,* 32–33.

87. In 180 wills, only 8 cases could be found in which testators chose to give all their land to one son if they had more than one son. They also gave all their land to sons in only a mere 22 wills.

88. Out of 180 wills, entail was used in only 3; see Lower Cape Fear computer biographical files.

89. On the complicated but important subject of entail, see Brewer, "Entailing Aristocracy."

90. There is no comparable data available from scholars studying other regions of North Carolina. See James P. Horn, *Adapting to a New World: English Society in the Seventeenth-Century Chesapeake* (Chapel Hill: University of North Carolina Press, 1994), 228–29; Smith, *Inside the Great House,* 231–48; Crowley, "Family Relations and Inheritance," 44–47.

91. Of 154 Lower Cape Fear widows, 16 (about 10 percent) inherited all of their spouses' belongings. It is difficult to determine the precise number of widows who received less than dower because it is impossible to compare the value of different kinds of bequests. However, it appears that about 10 percent of widows received provisions less favorable than dower rights. See Lower Cape Fear computer biographical files; New Hanover County Will Books C, D; Real Estate Conveyances ABC, D, E, F, G; Brunswick County Real Estate Conveyances, Books A, B (microfilm) North Carolina Department of Archives and History, Raleigh.

92. Lower Cape Fear computer biographical files; see table 3.3. These numbers are roughly comparable to similar data for South Carolina, Virginia, and England; see Horn, *Adapting to a New World,* 226–27; Crowley, "Family Relations and Inheritance," 46–47.

93. Lower Cape Fear computer biographical files. Widows probably obtained much more land from inheritance, but wills, unfortunately, do not provide enough information on the size of land bequests to include inherited lands in these calculations.

94. Lower Cape Fear computer biographical files.

95. In table 3.8, for example, sons were more likely than daughters to receive all forms of property, but for landed property the difference proved to be particularly large. Also, laws regarding intestate inheritance generally gave sons a higher proportion of real property, or land, than of personal property, which included slaves.

96. William Tryon, "Tryon's 'Book' on North Carolina," ed. William S. Powell, *North Carolina Historical Review* 34, no. 3 (1957): 411.

97. Lower Cape Fear computer biographical files.

98. Watson, "Household Size and Composition," 561–62, 569; Lower Cape Fear computer biographical files.

99. Lower Cape Fear computer biographical files.

100. Murray to Archibald Douglas, March 4, 1742/43: James Murray Letters, MHS.

101. Watson, "Women in Colonial North Carolina," 9–11. The classic authority on marriage settlements is Marylynn Salmon, *Women and the Law of Property in Early America* (Chapel Hill: University of North Carolina Press, 1986).

102. New Hanover County Real Estate Conveyances, Book D, 471 (microfilm), North Carolina Department of Archives and History, Raleigh; Watson, "Women in Colonial North Carolina," 17.

103. As Elaine Forman Crane points out, the frequency of marriage problematizes interpretations that see a strong correlation between high sex ratios and improved opportunities for property acquisition among women in the southern colonies. See Elaine Forman Crane, "The Socioeconomics of a Female Majority in Eighteenth-Century Bermuda," *Signs* 15, no. 2 (1990): 231–58.

104. This paragraph draws heavily on Anzilotti, "Autonomy and the Female Planter," 239–68.

105. Lower Cape Fear computer biographical files.

106. Similarly, Elaine Forman Crane also found that conditions that improved the material status of women in eighteenth-century Bermuda also failed to undermine Anglo-American assumptions about power and gender; see Crane, "Socioeconomics of a Female Majority," 257–58.

107. An Abstract of a Letter from a Gentleman in No Carolina to his friend in Maryland dated June 7th. 1762, *Colonial Records,* 5:1:737–38; Lee, *Lower Cape Fear,* 198–99.

108. On the fluidity and complexity of gender hierarchies in colonial British America, see Kathleen Brown, "Brave New Worlds: Women's and Gender History," *William and Mary Quarterly* 50, no. 2 (April 1993): 311–28. For a case study with special relevance for the Lower Cape Fear, see Fischer, *Suspect Relations.*

109. Schaw, *Journal of a Lady,* 154–55.

110. Tryon, "Tryon's 'Book,'" 410.

111. Murray to John Murray, January 10, 1736/37, in Murray, *Letters,* 36.

112. Schaw, *Journal of a Lady,* 154; Murray to Henry McCullough, April 16, 1737: James Murray Letters, MHS.

113. Murray to Jean Bennet, July 24, 1749, in Murray, *Letters,* 70.

114. Scotus Americanus, "Informations Concerning North Carolina," 446.

115. John Lapierre to the bishop of London, April 23, 1734, *Colonial Records,* 3:624.

116. John MacDowell to SPG, April 16, 1761, *Colonial Records,* 5:1:556.

117. Walker, *New Hanover County Court Minutes,* 1:50. For other children of mixed descent, see ibid., 1:41, 51, 84, 96. For other illegitimate children, see ibid., 1:2, 26.

118. Francisco Miranda, *The New Democracy in America: Travels of Francisco de Miranda in the United States, 1783–1784,* trans. Judson P. Wood (Norman: University of Oklahoma Press, 1963), 14. On Howe, see also Schaw, *Journal of a Lady,* 167–68.

119. On this impulse among the Charleston elite, see esp. Richard Waterhouse, "The Development of Elite Culture in the Colonial American South: A Study of Charles Town, 1670–1770," *Australian Journal of Politics and History* 28, no. 3 (1982): 391–404.

120. But on the broader applicability of the concept of liminality for the study of early America, see Greg Dening, "Introduction: In Search of a Metaphor," in *Through a Glass Darkly: Reflections on Personal Identity in Early America,* ed. Ronald Hoffman et al. (Chapel Hill: University of North Carolina Press, 1997), 1–6.

121. It would be misleading to suggest that the Lower Cape Fear is unique in this respect. Colonial Georgia presents one significant parallel, for example. But I would argue that the rapidity of the region's movement from being completely unsettled to being a social and political center is at least unusual in the eighteenth century.

Chapter 4: Neighbors and Networks

1. Peter Dubois to Samuel Johnston, February [undated]; Peter Dubois to Samuel Johnston, 1757; Peter Dubois to Samuel Johnston, February 8, 1757, March 5, 1757: Hayes Collection, Johnston Series, filmed portion, box 1, Southern History Collection, Chapel Hill, N.C.

2. Over the past two decades, Rutman's has been the most persistent, articulate, and sophisticated voice advocating the use of networks analysis and attention to local concerns in early American history. The best introduction to Rutman's ideas on these matters can be found in Darret B. Rutman, with Anita H. Rutman, *Small Worlds, Large Questions: Explorations in Early American Social History, 1600–1850* (Charlottesville: University Press of Virginia, 1994), 34–54, 287–304. See also Darret B. Rutman and Anita H. Rutman, *A Place in Time,* vol. 1, *Middlesex County, Virginia, 1650–1750,* and vol. 2, *Explicatus* (New York: W. W. Norton, 1984). For some of the other important voices in this dialogue, see James R. Perry, *The Formation of a Society on Virginia's Eastern Shore, 1615–1655* (Chapel Hill: University of North Carolina Press, 1990); Lorena S. Walsh, "Community Networks in the Early Chesapeake," in *Colonial Chesapeake Society,* ed. Lois Green Carr, Philip D. Morgan, and Jean B. Russo (Chapel Hill: University of North Carolina Press, 1988), 200–241; and Richard R. Beeman, "The New Social History and the Search for 'Community' in Colonial America," *American Quarterly* 29, no. 4 (1977): 422–43. For the antebellum South, see Orville Vernon Burton, *In My Father's House Are Many Mansions: Family and Community in Edgefield, South Carolina* (Chapel Hill: University of North Carolina Press, 1985); and Christopher Morris, *Becoming Southern: The Evolution of a Way of Life, Warren County and Vicksburg, Mississippi, 1770–1860* (New York: Oxford University Press, 1995). For related issues in the historiography of colonial South Carolina, see George Terry, "'Champaign Country': A Social History of an Eighteenth Century Lowcountry Parish in South Carolina, St. Johns Berkeley, County," doctoral dissertation, University of South Carolina, 1981;

and George Lloyd Johnson Jr., *The Frontier in the Colonial South: South Carolina Backcountry, 1736–1800* (Westport, Conn.: Greenwood Press, 1997).

3. Those familiar with the Rutmans' work will note that I have avoided using the term *community,* though it is central to their discussion of these concepts. While I consider Darret Rutman's scholarship to be exemplary in many other respects, I take issue with his use of this intensely loaded and contested word to describe areas of social interaction in early America because, at this point in the discussion, it confuses far more than it clarifies.

4. Scotus Americanus, "Informations Concerning the Province of North Carolina, Addressed to Emigrants from the Highlands and Western Isles of Scotland," in *Some Eighteenth Century Tracts Concerning North Carolina,* ed. William K. Boyd (Raleigh: State of North Carolina, 1927), 443.

5. William Tryon, "Tryon's 'Book' on North Carolina," ed. William S. Powell, *North Carolina Historical Review* 34, no. 3 (1957): 408.

6. Josiah Quincy Jr., "The Southern Journal of Josiah Quincy, Junior, 1773," *Massachusetts Historical Society Proceedings* (October 1915–June 1916): 69, 459.

7. "A New Voyage to Georgia, By a Young Gentleman, Giving an Account of His Travels to South Carolina and Part of North Carolina . . . ," in *Collections of the Georgia Historical Society,* vol. 2 (Savannah, Ga., 1842), 54–60.

8. Governor Dobbs to Board of Trade, October 31, 1756, in William L. Saunders, ed., *The Colonial Records of North Carolina* (Raleigh: State of North Carolina, 1886–90) (hereafter cited as *Colonial Records*), 5:639.

9. Murray to John Murray, January 1759, in James Murray, *Letters of James Murray, Loyalist,* ed. Nina M. Tiffany (Boston: Printed, not published, 1901), 102.

10. Scotus Americanus, "Informations Concerning North Carolina," 443.

11. Samuel B. Dogget, ed., "A Plantation on Prince George's Creek, Cape Fear, North Carolina," *New-England Historical and Genealogical Register* 52 (1898): 471.

12. See, for example, Laws, in Walter Clark, ed., *The State Records of North Carolina* (Goldsboro: State of North Carolina, 1895–1905) (hereafter cited as *State Records*), 23:220.

13. Proceedings of the Safety Committee at Wilmington, January 20, 1776, *Colonial Records,* 10:419. "Waggamamar" probably refers to the area near Lake Waccamaw.

14. See table 4.1. Personal ties include interactions such as marriage or bequests in a will that indicate meaningful social or cultural ties, or such as guardianship, mastery, or powers of attorney that demonstrate high levels of either trust or proximity.

15. See table 4.1. Economic ties consist of significant property conveyances. In the vast majority of cases these involved land, but some conveyances of slaves, ships, and mills are also included. It should be noted that, because neighborhoods have been identified partly with land records, the use of these sources may overestimate interaction within neighborhoods.

16. The correlation coefficient for the distances in table 4.4 and all the personal ties in tables 4.1, 4.2, and 4.3 equaled –.84. The correlation coefficient for the economic ties equaled –.89. Both of these coefficients indicate a strong relationship, where 0 indicates no relationship, –1 indicates a perfect negative relationship, and 1 indicates a perfect positive relationship.

17. Walsh, "Community Networks," 219; Rutman and Rutman, *Place in Time,* vol. 1, *Middlesex County,* 120–21; Perry, *Formation of a Society,* 90–91.

18. Walsh, "Community Networks," 219.

19. James P. Horn, "Adapting to a New World: A Comparative Study of Local Society in England and Maryland, 1650–1700," in *Colonial Chesapeake Society,* ed. Carr et al., 165–74.

20. On Lower Cape Fear population densities, see chapter 2; Horn, "Adapting to a New World," 165.

21. Rutman, Darret B., "Community Study," *Historical Methods* 13, no. 1 (1980): 40–42.

22. On traveling in colonial North Carolina in general, see Christopher C. Crittenden, *The Commerce of North Carolina, 1763–1789* (New Haven: Yale University Press, 1936), 15–36; Alan D. Watson, *Society in North Carolina* (Raleigh: State of North Carolina, 1986), 100–11.

23. Hugh Finlay, *Journal Kept by Hugh Finlay, Surveyor of the Post Roads on the Continent of North America, during His Survey of the Post Offices between Falmouth and Casco Bay in the Province of Massachusetts, and Savannah in Georgia; Begun the 13th September, 1773 and Ended 26th June 1774* (Brooklyn: F. H. Norton, 1867), 67.

24. Robert Hunter Jr., *Quebec to Carolina in 1785–1786: Being the Travel Diary and Observations of Robert Hunter, Jr., a Young Merchant of London,* ed. Louis B. Wright and Marion Tinling (San Marino, Calif.: Huntington Library, 1943), 280.

25. Elizabeth Catherine DeRosset to John Burgwyn, September 10, 1775, in Kemp Battle, ed., *Letters and Documents, Relating to the Early History of the Lower Cape Fear,* vol. 4 of *James Sprunt Historical Monographs* (Chapel Hill: University of North Carolina Press, 1903), 26.

26. For other contemporary comments on the difficulty of traveling through the region by roads, see Janet Schaw, *Journal of a Lady of Quality; Being the Narrative of a Journey from Scotland to the West Indies, North Carolina, and Portugal, in the Years 1774 to 1776,* ed. Evangeline W. Andrews and Charles M. Andrews (New Haven: Yale University Press, 1921), 279; George Whitefield, *George Whitefield's Journals, 1737–1741,* ed. William V. Davis (Gainesville: University of Florida Press, 1969), 378; Richard Marsden to the bishop of London, July 7, 1735, *Colonial Records,* 4:12; Nicholas Christian to SPG, July 27, 1774, ibid., 9:1022.

27. For a more thorough discussion of this topic, see Alan D. Watson, "Regulation and Administration of Roads and Bridges in Colonial Eastern North Carolina," *North Carolina Historical Review* 45, no. 4 (October 1968): 399–417.

28. Records of the General Court [1727], *Colonial Records,* 2:698.

29. Watson, "Regulation and Administration of Roads and Bridges," 402–3.

30. Ibid., 411–17; Marvin Michael Kay and William S. Price Jr., "'To Ride the Wood Mare': Road Building and Militia Service in Colonial North Carolina, 1740–1775," *North Carolina Historical Review* 57, no. 4 (October 1980): 361–409.

31. Schaw, *Journal of a Lady,* 202.

32. Laws, *State Records,* 25:506–7; Schaw, *Journal of a Lady,* 202.

33. Alan D. Watson, "Ordinaries in Colonial Eastern North Carolina," *North Carolina Historical Review* 45, no. 1 (January 1968): 67–83.

34. Alan D. Watson, "The Ferry in Colonial North Carolina: A Vital Link in Transportation," *North Carolina Historical Review* 51, no. 3 (July 1974): 247–60.

35. On inland watercraft in early North Carolina, see Crittenden, *Commerce of North Carolina,* 15–18.

36. For two colonists experiencing problems with water transportation, see Murray to David Tullideph, March 31, 1736, in Murray, *Letters,* 27; and Hugh Meredith, *An Account*

of the Cape Fear Country, 1731, ed. Earl Gregg Swem (Perth Amboy, N.J.: C. F. Heartman, 1922), 21–22.

37. Murray to Henry McCulloh, May 11, 1741, in Murray, *Letters,* 64.

38. Schaw, *Journal of a Lady,* 171.

39. Ibid., 177.

40. For a much more detailed consideration of the importance of towns in the development of the Lower Cape Fear, see chapter 7.

41. Rutman, "Community Study," 41–46. See also Rutman and Rutman, *Place in Time.*

42. The best description of the function of the county court system in colonial North Carolina is still Paul McCain's classic *The County Court in North Carolina before 1750* (Durham, N.C.: Duke University Press, 1954).

43. Statistical analysis yields a correlation coefficient of –.24, which indicates a weak correlation that could easily be attributed to chance; see also table 4.5.

44. See, for example, Laws, *State Records,* 23:790–801.

45. Watson, "Ordinaries in Colonial Eastern North Carolina," 80; Governor Tryon to the earl of Hillsborough, February 8, 1771, *Colonial Records,* 8:496.

46. Francisco Miranda, *The New Democracy in America: Travels of Francisco Miranda in the United States, 1783–1784,* trans. Judson P. Wood (Norman: University of Oklahoma Press, 1963), 15.

47. Schaw, *Journal of a Lady,* 149; Proceedings of the Safety Committee at Wilmington, March 1, 1775, *Colonial Records,* 9:1136.

48. Alexander M. Walker, ed., *New Hanover County Court Minutes* (Bethesda, Md.: A. M. Walker, 1958), 1:79, 86, 95.

49. Laws, *State Records,* 23:79. On ordinaries in general, see Watson, "Ordinaries in Colonial Eastern North Carolina."

50. Watson, "Ordinaries in Colonial Eastern North Carolina," 78; William Logan, "William Logan's Journal of a Journey to Georgia, 1745," *Pennsylvania Magazine of History and Biography* 36 (1912): 10.

51. Miranda, *New Democracy in America,* 15; Elkanah Watson, *Men and Times of the Revolution; or Memoirs of Elkanah Watson, Including His Journals of Travels in Europe and America from 1777 to 1842,* ed. Winslow C. Watson (New York: Dana, 1857), 41; Schaw, *Journal of a Lady,* 149.

52. Proceedings of the Safety Committee at Wilmington, November 11, 1774, *Colonial Records,* 9:1090–91.

53. Governor Tryon to SPG, July 31, 1765, *Colonial Records,* 7:103.

54. James Moir to SPG, September 4, 1742, *Colonial Records,* 4:606; Memorial of the churchwardens . . . of Hanover County in favor of Mr. Smith, October 1, 1759, ibid., 5:1:58.

55. James Moir to SPG, September 4, 1742, *Colonial Records,* 4:607–8.

56. James Moir to SPG, February 15, 1741/42, *Colonial Records,* 4:603.

57. John LaPierre to the bishop of London, November 29, 1732, *Colonial Records,* 3:391–92; John LaPierre to the bishop of London, October 9, 1733, ibid., 3:529–30; John LaPierre to the bishop of London, April 23, 1734, ibid., 3:623.

58. John LaPierre to the bishop of London, April 23, 1734, *Colonial Records,* 3:623; James Moir to SPG, April 22, 1742, ibid., 4:605; Arthur Dobbs to Board of Trade, January 4, 1755, ibid., 5:314; Mr. Woodmason's Account of North Carolina made in 1766, ibid., 7:284–86.

59. Murray to George Whitefield, June 24, 1740: James Murray Letters, Massachusetts Historical Society, Boston (hereafter cited as MHS).

60. Murray to William Ellison, July 10, 1736: James Murray Letters, MHS.

61. John MacDowell to SPG, February 9, 1760, *Colonial Records,* 5:1:225; John MacDowell to SPG, June 15, 1762, ibid., 5:1:729.

62. John LaPierre to the bishop of London, November 29, 1732, *Colonial Records,* 13:391–92; Richard Marsden to the bishop of London, ibid., 4:11–13.

63. Laws, *State Records,* 23:535–37, 660–62, 25:243, 298–304, 424, 459; Watson, *Society in Colonial North Carolina,* 98–99; Ida Brooks Kellam and Elizabeth Francenia McKoy, eds., *St. James Church, Wilmington, North Carolina, Historical Records, 1737–1852* (Wilmington, N.C.: I. B. Kellam, 1965), 1.

64. James Moir to SPG, April 22, 1742, *Colonial Records,* 4:605; James Reed to SPG, July 20, 1766, ibid., 7:241.

65. Memorial of the churchwardens of Hanover County, October 1, 1759, *Colonial Records,* 5:1:58.

66. John Barnett to SPG, February 3, 1766, *Colonial Records,* 7:164.

67. John Brickell, *The Natural History of North-Carolina* (Dublin, Ireland: Printed for James Carson, 1737), 35–36.

68. Early Presbyterian Settlements in North Carolina, *Colonial Records,* 5:1:198–212.

69. John MacDowell to SPG, February 9, 1760, *Colonial Records,* 5:1:225.

70. On dissent in one North Carolina Scottish community, see Duane Meyer, *The Highland Scots of North Carolina, 1732–1776* (Chapel Hill: University of North Carolina Press, 1957), 113–16.

71. John LaPierre to the bishop of London, April 23, 1734, *Colonial Records,* 3:623; James Moir to SPG, April 22, 1742, ibid., 4:605.

72. Mr. Woodmason's Account of North Carolina made in 1766, *Colonial Records,* 5:1:284; Laws, *State Records,* 25:243; Kellam and McKoy, *St. James Church,* 1, 106.

73. Tryon to SPG, July 18, 1767, *Colonial Records,* 7:514; Laws, *State Records,* 23:535–37, 25:391.

74. Kellam and McKoy, *St. James Church,* 9, 110.

75. Ibid., 3–20.

76. The classic work on the hierarchical social role of the Anglican Church in the southern British colonies is Rhys Isaac, *The Transformation of Virginia, 1740–1790* (New York: W. W. Norton, 1982).

77. See John M. Garland, "The Nonecclesiastical Activities of an English and a North Carolina Parish: A Comparative Study," *North Carolina Historical Review* 50, no. 1 (January 1973): 32–51; Watson, *Society in Colonial North Carolina,* 83–99.

78. Barnett to the secretary, February 3, 1766, *Colonial Records,* 7:164.

79. For some of the works on ethnicity in colonial America that bear the most relevance to this study, see, among others, Daniel B. Thorp, *The Moravian Community in Colonial North Carolina: Pluralism on the Southern Frontier* (Knoxville: University of Tennessee Press, 1989); Meyer, *Highland Scots;* David Dobson, *Scottish Emigration to Colonial America, 1607–1785* (Athens: University of Georgia Press, 1994); Bernard Bailyn, *The Peopling of British North America: An Introduction* (New York: Vintage, 1986); Jon Butler, *The Huguenots in America: A Refugee People in New World Society* (Cambridge: Harvard University Press, 1983); Stephanie G. Wolf, *Urban Village: Population, Community, and Family Structure in Germantown, Pennsylvania, 1683–1800* (Princeton, N.J.: Princeton University Press, 1976);

Joyce D. Goodfriend, *Before the Melting Pot: Society and Culture in Colonial New York City, 1664–1730* (Princeton, N.J.: Princeton University Press, 1972).

80. See James Murray Letters, MHS; and Murray, *Letters,* esp. Murray to Andrew Bennet, May 13, 1735, in Murray, *Letters,* 17–19; Murray to John Murray, January 10, 1736/37, ibid., 38–39; Murray to James Hazel, February 28, 1743/44, ibid., 266.

81. Schaw, *Journal of a Lady,* 160.

82. The Scottish tendency toward loyalism was a complex phenomenon that has been discussed in great detail by other scholars. For Scottish loyalism, see, among others, Elizabeth Murray to Dorothy Forbes, June 16, 1776, in Murray, *Letters,* 266; Schaw, *Journal of a Lady,* 189–93, 319–33; Governor Martin to the earl of Dartmouth, August 28, 1775, *Colonial Records,* 10:236; Meyer, *Highland Scots,* 131–62.

83. See table 4.6.

84. Thirty-five identifiable Scottish residents are referred to 753 times in the database, or 2.6 percent of the total database references. The procedures followed for identifying interactions are the same as above.

85. For some of the more important works in the burgeoning literature on civility in early America, see Richard Lyman Bushman, *The Refinement of America: Persons, Houses, Cities* (New York: Vintage, 1993); David S. Shields, *Civil Tongues and Polite Letters in British America* (Chapel Hill: University of North Carolina Press, 1997); and Cary Carson, Ronald Hoffman, and Peter J. Albert, eds., *Of Consuming Interests: The Style of Life in the Eighteenth Century* (Charlottesville: University Press of Virginia, 1994). The classic studies of the civilizing process are Norbert Elias, *The History of Manners,* trans. Edmund Jephcott (New York: Urizen Books, 1982); and Norbert Elias, *The Court Society,* trans. Edmund Jephcott (New York: Urizen Books, 1983).

86. Murray to Richard Oswald and Co., December 12, 1749: James Murray Letters, MHS.

87. For a perceptive commentary on the concept of economic class in early American history, see Ronald Schulz, "A Class Society? The Nature of Inequality in Early America," in *Inequality in Early America,* ed. Carla Gardina Pestana and Sharon V. Salinger (Hanover, N.H.: University of New England Press, 1999), 203–21.

88. For some of the most important works on wealth in colonial America, see Alice H. Jones, *Wealth of a Nation to Be: The American Colonies on the Eve of the Revolution* (New York: Columbia University Press, 1980); John J. McCusker and Russell R. Menard, *The Economy of British America, 1607–1789* (Chapel Hill: University of North Carolina Press, 1985), 258–76; James A. Henretta, "Wealth and Social Structure," in *Colonial British America: Essays in the New History of the Modern Era,* ed. Jack P. Greene and J. R. Pole (Baltimore: Johns Hopkins University Press, 1984), 262–89.

89. Despite these handicaps, some scholars have devoted attention to wealth and social structure in colonial North Carolina. While many of these works use creative methodologies to compensate for the dearth of source material, they sometimes provide dubious interpretations of the evidence and are, for a variety of reasons, of limited relevance for this study. Marvin Michael Kay and Lorin Lee Cary offer the best-known of these interpretations, using reductionist class-conflict models to analyze the North Carolina regulation. They contribute some useful data on the stratification of slaveholdings in the Lower Cape Fear, but they also attempt to equate slaveholding with total wealth and changes in slave ownership with economic mobility. See, among others, Kay and Cary, "Class, Mobility, and Conflict in North Carolina on the Eve of the Revolution," in *The Southern Experience in*

the American Revolution, ed. Jeffrey J. Crow and Larry E. Tise (Chapel Hill: University of North Carolina Press, 1978); and Marvin M. Kay, "The Institutional Background to the Regulation in Colonial North Carolina," doctoral dissertation, University of Minnesota, 1962. Another body of scholarship, produced largely by Kay and William S. Price, emphasizes the importance of elite material interests in colonial North Carolina political decision making. See Kay and Price, "To Ride the Wood Mare"; William S. Price Jr., "'Men of Good Estates': Wealth among North Carolina's Royal Councillors," *North Carolina Historical Review* 49, no. 1 (January 1972): 72–82; and Kay, "Provincial Taxes in North Carolina during the Administrations of Dobbs and Tryon," *North Carolina Historical Review* 42, no. 4 (October 1965): 440–53. The third body of scholarship is less problematic but focuses solely on the proprietary period; see Jacquelyn H. Wolf, "Patents and Tithables in Propriety North Carolina, 1663–1729," *North Carolina Historical Review* 56, no. 3 (July 1979): 263–77; Jacqueline Wolf, "The Proud and the Poor: The Social Organization of Leadership in Proprietary North Carolina, 1663–1729," doctoral dissertation, University of Pittsburgh, 1977; Charles B. Lowry, "Class, Politics, Rebellion, and Regional Development in Proprietary North Carolina," doctoral dissertation, University of Florida, 1975.

90. Lower Cape Fear computer biographical files. See tables 4.7 and 4.8.

91. See chapters 2 and 6.

92. McCusker and Menard, *Economy of British America,* 272–73.

93. Total wealth distribution estimates for Bertie County are about as stratified as the land and slave distribution patterns for the Lower Cape Fear, while total wealth distribution for Orange County is somewhat, but not dramatically, less stratified than the Lower Cape Fear patterns. These data support the above comparisons because total wealth is likely to be less stratified than slave- and landholdings.

94. Richard Waterhouse, "Economic Growth and Changing Patterns of Wealth Distribution in Colonial Lowcountry South Carolina," *South Carolina Historical Magazine* 89, no. 4 (1988): 203–17.

95. Scotus Americanus, "Informations Concerning North Carolina," 443.

96. Brickell, *Natural History of North-Carolina,* 30.

97. Schaw, *Journal of a Lady,* 153.

98. Ibid., 169.

99. Richard Marsden to the bishop of London, July 7, 1735, *Colonial Records,* 4:12. For some other examples, see Schaw, *Journal of a Lady,* 175, 177; and Battle, *Letters and Documents,* 26. On African and African American watermen and understandings of water travel, see W. Jeffrey Bolster, "An Inner Diaspora: Black Sailors Making Selves," in *Through a Glass Darkly: Reflections on Personal Identity in Early America,* ed. Ronald Hoffman et al. (Chapel Hill: University of North Carolina Press, 1997), 422–28. More generally, see David Cecelski, *The Waterman's Song: Slavery and Freedom in Maritime North Carolina* (Chapel Hill: University of North Carolina Press, 2001); W. Jeffrey Bolster, *Black Jacks: African American Seamen in the Age of Sail* (Cambridge: Harvard University Press, 1997).

100. Marvin Michael Kay and Lorin Lee Cary, *Slavery in North Carolina, 1748–1775* (Chapel Hill: University of North Carolina Press, 1995), 126–27.

101. Finlay, *Journal,* 79.

102. Kay and Cary, *Slavery in North Carolina,* 48–50; Philip D. Morgan, *Slave Counterpoint: Black Culture in the Eighteenth-Century Chesapeake and Lowcountry* (Chapel Hill: University of North Carolina Press, 1998), 175, 351–52, 515–16.

103. Kay and Cary, *Slavery in North Carolina,* 22.

104. On the implications of the distribution of slave populations for family and kinship, see chapter 2; and William Tryon, "Tryon's 'Book' on North Carolina," ed. William S. Powell, *North Carolina Historical Review* 34, no. 3 (1957): 411.

105. But not, of course, by the standards of the British West Indian colonies, where slaves were concentrated in greater numbers than anywhere on the mainland because of the labor-intensive nature of sugar production.

106. Kay and Cary, *Slavery in North Carolina,* 24.

107. Scotus Americans, "Informations Concerning North Carolina," 445.

108. Schaw, *Journal of a Lady,* 163.

109. Kay and Cary, *Slavery in North Carolina,* 36–37.

110. Walker, *New Hanover Court Minutes,* 1:24, 38, 43, 45, 59, 64, 66, 69, 81, 85, 95–96, 98; 2:12, 14, 16, 33.

111. Schaw, *Journal of a Lady,* 199.

112. Ibid., 171.

113. Murray to Sister Clark, December 26, 1755: James Murray Letters, MHS; Morgan, *Slave Counterpoint,* 640–44; Kay and Cary, *Slavery in North Carolina,* 180–83; Sylvia R. Frey, *Water from the Rock: Black Resistance in a Revolutionary Age* (Princeton, N.J.: Princeton University Press, 1991), 41–42.

114. Brickell, *Natural History of North-Carolina,* 274.

115. Kay and Cary attempt to estimate the numbers of Africans in colonial North Carolina, but they rely on a dubious empirical foundation and acknowledge the problems with their data; see Kay and Cary, *Slavery in North Carolina,* 2, 25–26, 58, 127. See also Walter E. Minchinton, "The Seaborne Slave Trade of North Carolina," *North Carolina Historical Review* 71, no. 1 (January 1994): 1–61.

116. Brickell, *Natural History of North-Carolina,* 274.

117. John Barnett to SPG, February 3, 1766, *Colonial Records,* 7:164.

118. For one work that provides a thorough analysis of all the available runaway slave ads for North Carolina but makes some dangerous generalizations given the evidence, see Kay and Cary, *Slavery in North Carolina,* 121–36.

119. *North Carolina Gazette,* July 4, 1777.

120. *Cape Fear Mercury,* August 7, 1775.

121. Schaw, *Journal of a Lady,* 199.

122. See esp. A. Roger Ekirch, *"Poor Carolina": Politics and Society in Colonial North Carolina, 1929–1776* (Chapel Hill: University of North Carolina Press, 1981), 38–39.

123. John Barnett to SPG, September 15, 1770, *Colonial Records,* 8:229.

124. For two of many examples, see Murray to John Pringle, July 8, 1743; Murray to John Dubois, November 13, 1767: James Murray Letters, MHS.

125. New Hanover taxpayers for the year 1763 appeared in the database 10,618 times, whereas 1763 Bladen taxpayers appeared only 994 times. Bladen County residents also appeared more in the database than 1770 Onslow residents, who appeared 803 times. See Bladen County Tax List, 1763, and Onslow County Tax List, 1770, North Carolina Department of Archives and History, Lower Cape Fear computer biographical files.

126. James Horn, "Moving On in the New World: Migration and Out-Migration in the Seventeenth-Century Chesapeake," in *Migration and Society in Early Modern England,* ed. Peter Clark and David Souden (London: Hutchinson, 1988), 172–211; Peter A. Coclanis,

The Shadow of a Dream: Economic Life and Death in the South Carolina Low Country (New York: Oxford University Press, 1989), 161–74.

127. I thank Professor Robert Olwell for bringing these ads to my attention; see for examples, Lathan A. Windley, ed., *Runaway Slave Advertisements: A Documentary History from the 1730s to 1790,* vol. 3, *South Carolina* (Westport, Conn.: Greenwood Press, 1983), 95, 126, 138, 165, 278, 717.

128. Journal of the Commons House of the Assembly, in J. H. Easterby, ed., *The Colonial Records of South Carolina* (Columbia: State of South Carolina, 1951–62), 1:631.

129. Gabriel Johnston to Board of Trade, December 17, 1740, *Colonial Records,* 4:423.

130. Murray to Mrs. Bennet, June 1, 1752: James Murray Letters, MHS.

131. On Murray's reading, see, for example, "Memorandum of Books from among my other books at Chesters," July 22, 1745; Murray to Hutchinson and Grimkie, July 28, 1757, "Books": James Murray Letters, MHS.

132. Murray to Mrs. Bennet, February 28, 1755: James Murray Letters, MHS.

133. Maurice Moore to unidentified, January 27, 1770, *Colonial Records,* 8:173.

Chapter 5: Politics and Authority

1. Spangenberg diary, September 14, 1752, in Adelaide L. Fries, ed., *Records of the Moravians in North Carolina* (Raleigh, N.C.: Edwards & Broughton Printing, 1922–2000), 1:35.

2. The Moravian settlement in North Carolina has attracted the attention of many historians. The most useful analysis of the Moravians' place in North Carolina society is Daniel B. Thorp, *The Moravian Community in Colonial North Carolina: Pluralism on the Southern Frontier* (Knoxville: University of Tennessee Press, 1989). On the Moravians' attitude toward government, see esp. 148–77.

3. While there is a long tradition emphasizing the fractious character of colonial North Carolina politics, its most important expression in recent decades can be found in A. Roger Ekirch, *"Poor Carolina": Politics and Society in Colonial North Carolina, 1729–1776* (Chapel Hill: University of North Carolina Press, 1981). For other influential work on colonial North Carolina politics and authority, see Hugh T. Lefler and William S. Powell, *Colonial North Carolina: A History* (New York: Charles Scribner's Sons, 1973); Marvin Michael Kay and Lorin Lee Cary, "Class, Mobility, and Conflict in North Carolina on the Eve of the Revolution," in *The Southern Experience in the American Revolution,* ed. Jeffrey J. Crow and Larry E. Tise (Chapel Hill: University of North Carolina Press, 1978), 109–51; Donna J. Spindel, *Crime and Society in North Carolina, 1663–1776* (Baton Rouge: Louisiana State University Press, 1989); Marjoleine Kars, *Breaking Loose Together: The Regulator Rebellion in Pre-Revolutionary North Carolina* (Chapel Hill: University of North Carolina Press, 2002); Donald R. Lennon, "Development of Town Government in Colonial North Carolina," *East Carolina Publications in History* 5 (1981): 1–25; R. D. W. Connor, *History of North Carolina,* vol. 1, *The Colonial and Revolutionary Periods, 1584–1783* (Chicago: Lewis Publishing, 1919); James P. Whittenburg, "Planters, Merchants, and Lawyers: Social Change and the Origins of the North Carolina Regulation," *William and Mary Quarterly* 34, no. 2 (1977): 215–38; John Paden, "'Several & Many Grievances of Very Great Consequences': North Carolina's Political Factionalism in the 1720s," *North Carolina Historical Review* 71, no. 3 (July 1994): 285–305.

4. John Lawson, *A New Voyage to North Carolina,* ed. Hugh T. Lefler (Chapel Hill: University of North Carolina Press, 1967), 169.

5. George Burrington to Board of Trade, January 1, 1732/33, in William L. Saunders, ed., *The Colonial Records of North Carolina* (Raleigh: State of North Carolina, 1886–90) (hereafter cited as *Colonial Records*), 3:436.

6. Paragraph of a Letter from Carolina dated 24th. May 1727, in *Records of the British Public Records Office Relating to South Carolina,* 12:215–16.

7. Charles Garth to Board of Trade [1768], *Colonial Records,* 8:565–66; Report of both Houses of the South Carolina Assembly with respect to a Boundary Line [1757], ibid., 11:127–29.

8. George Burrington to Board of Trade, January 20, 1731/32, *Colonial Records,* 3:338.

9. George Burrington to Board of Trade, January 1, 1732/33, *Colonial Records,* 3:436.

10. For more on the process of land acquisition in the Lower Cape Fear and related difficulties, see chapter 2.

11. For one of many examples, see Edmund Porter to duke of Newcastle, August 15, 1733, *Colonial Records,* 3:501.

12. Nathanial Rice, John Baptista Ashe, and John Montgomery to Board of Trade, November 17, 1732, *Colonial Records,* 3:377.

13. Nathanial Rice, John Baptista Ashe, and John Montgomery to duke of Newcastle, September 16, 1732, *Colonial Records,* 3:366–67.

14. The Case of Ye Inhabitants of North Carolina in respect to Mr. George Burrington's being Reappointed their Governor [1730], *Colonial Records,* 3:123.

15. See, for example, ibid., 3:121–24; Edmund Porter to the duke of Newcastle, August 15, 1733, *Colonial Records,* 3:501.

16. Journal of the Lower House of Assembly, April 12, 1726, *Colonial Records,* 2:618–19.

17. Lefler and Powell, *Colonial North Carolina,* 113–19; Ekirch, *Poor Carolina,* 51–66.

18. George Burrington to Board of Trade, January 1, 1732/33, *Colonial Records,* 3:429, 433; Nathanial Rice and John Baptista Ashe to the governor and council [1733], *Colonial Records,* 3:450.

19. Murray to David Tullideph, January 10, 1736/37, in James Murray, *Letters of James Murray, Loyalist,* ed. Nina M. Tiffany (Boston: Printed, not published, 1901), 29; Murray to Henry McCulloh, July 8, 1736, ibid., 33; Murray to Henry McCulloh, January 30, 1739/40, ibid., 54; Murray to unidentified, March 25, 1740, ibid., 58–60; Murray to William Ellison, July 10, 1736, Murray to Archibald Douglas, March 4, 1742/3: James Murray Letters, Massachusetts Historical Society, Boston (hereafter cited as MHS).

20. Council Journals, June 5, 1740, *Colonial Records,* 4:457.

21. Ibid., May 22, 1740, to June 5, 1740, *Colonial Records,* 4:449–58; Donald Lennon and Ida Brooks Kellam, eds., *The Wilmington Town Book, 1743–1778* (Raleigh: State of North Carolina, 1973), xv–xxiii; Ekirch, *Poor Carolina,* 70, 77–78, 89.

22. Ekirch, *Poor Carolina,* 84.

23. For one of many scholarly works using tax lists and other sources to demonstrate this point, see Kay and Cary, "Class, Mobility, and Conflict," 124–25.

24. C. B. MacPherson's classic work *The Political Theory of Possessive Individualism* (Oxford: Clarendon Press, 1962) provides a particularly powerful statement of the materialist character of this ideology.

25. Gabriel Johnston to Board of Trade, October 15, 1736, *Colonial Records,* 4:177–78.

26. The formula used to calculate legislative turnover and the comparative data have been taken from Jack P. Greene, "Legislative Turnover in Colonial British America,

1695–1775: A Quantitative Analysis," in *Negotiated Authorities: Essays in Colonial Political and Constitutional History* (Charlottesville: University Press of Virginia, 1994), 215–37. Lists of assembly members came from John L. Cheney Jr., *North Carolina Government, 1585–1974: A Narrative and Statistical History* (Raleigh: State of North Carolina, 1975), 25–59.

27. Murray to Archibald Douglas, March 4, 1742/43: James Murray Letters, MHS.

28. See Jack P. Greene, "Negotiated Authorities: The Problem of Governance in the Extended Polities of the Early Modern Atlantic World," in *Negotiated Authorities,* 1–24, esp. 15–17.

29. I have found no particular reason why there might have been any kind of change in the Lower Cape Fear's acknowledged leadership at this time, but given the small sample, it seems likely to be the result of coincidence. In particular, Samuel Swann, who owned large amounts of land in New Hanover and Onslow Counties, won seats from both counties in this election and had to choose to represent one or the other. He chose to represent Onslow. He also represented Onslow every other time he was elected to the assembly. Nonetheless, confusion about Swann's eligibility and loyalty might have complicated the vote considerably. See Legislative Journals, June 12, 1746, *Colonial Records,* 4:817.

30. Ibid., January 18, 1734/35, *Colonial Records,* 4:117.

31. October–November 1764, Lower House Committees, General Assembly Session Records, North Carolina Department of Archives and History, Raleigh.

32. October–November 1764, Bills, General Assembly Session Records; from MSS records in the Office of the Secretary of State, *Colonial Records,* 5:1:1308.

33. Murray to Henry McCulloh, January 30, 1739/40, Murray to Archibald Douglas, March 4, 1742/43: James Murray Letters, MHS.

34. Murray to Henry McCulloh, May 3, 1736: James Murray Letters, MHS.

35. See John G. Kolp, *Gentlemen and Freeholders: Electoral Politics in Colonial Virginia* (Baltimore: Johns Hopkins University Press, 1998), 67, 118. Kolp notes, "Parochial concerns often overshadowed provincial and imperial issues, producing at times localized patterns entirely at odds with colonywide trends." He also adds that "local politics in the prerevolutionary era reflected the attachment of most freeholders to the long-standing neighborhood communities."

36. These documents have been published, annotated, and commented on in Richard Rankin, ed., "'Musquetoe' Bites: Caricatures of Lower Cape Fear Whigs and Tories on the Eve of the American Revolution," *North Carolina Historical Review* 65 (April 1988): 173–207.

37. For much more on polite discourse and literary culture in colonial America, see David S. Shields, *Civil Tongues and Polite Letters in British America* (Chapel Hill: University of North Carolina Press, 1997).

38. Rankin, "'Musquetoe' Bites," 186.

39. Ibid., 185.

40. Kay and Cary, "Class, Mobility, and Conflict," 125.

41. Cheney, *North Carolina Government,* 17–54; Lower Cape Fear computer biographical files.

42. Cheney, *North Carolina Government,* 17–20; Lower Cape Fear computer biographical files.

43. George Burrington to Board of Trade, February 20, 1731/32, *Colonial Records,* 3:332.

44. Arthur Dobbs to Board of Trade, December 27, 1757, *Colonial Records,* 5:1:947–48.

45. Arthur Dobbs to Board of Trade, October 28, 1755, *Colonial Records,* 5:1:440.

46. Governor Martin to the earl of Dartmouth, April 6, 1774, *Colonial Records,* 9:972–73.

47. For a brief but important exception, see Clarence L. Ver Steeg, *Origins of a Southern Mosaic: Studies of Early Carolina and Georgia* (Athens: University of Georgia Press, 1975), 63–68. Spindel, *Crime and Society in North Carolina,* also devotes significant attention to crime in the county courts, but much of her study relies more on data for the North Carolina General and Superior Courts, which are more complete and handled proportionally more criminal cases. In many ways, the best complete study of North Carolina local government is still Paul McCain, *The County Court in North Carolina before 1750* (Durham, N.C.: Duke University Press, 1954). See also Jack P. Greene, "Courts and Society in Proprietary North Carolina: A Review Essay," *North Carolina Historical Review* 60, no. 1 (January 1983): 100–104.

48. William M. Offutt Jr., "The Limits of Authority: Courts, Ethnicity, and Gender in the Middle Colonies, 1670–1710," in *The Many Legalities of Early America,* ed. Christopher L. Tomlins and Bruce H. Mann (Chapel Hill: University of North Carolina Press, 2001), 357.

49. Richard Lyman Bushman, "Farmers in Court: Orange County, North Carolina, 1750–1776," in *Many Legalities of Early America,* ed. Tomlins and Mann, 388–89. Bushman also notes that the authority of the court system remained intact and relatively unchallenged even during the tumultuous Regulator revolt in the North Carolina Piedmont; see 411–13. For a similar finding, see also Carl Bridenbaugh, *Myths and Realities: Societies of the Colonial South* (Baton Rouge: Louisiana State University Press, 1952), 158–59.

50. George Burrington to the Lords Proprietors [August 1729], *Colonial Records,* 3:28.

51. John LaPierre to the bishop of London, October 9, 1733, *Colonial Records,* 3:530.

52. James Moir to SPG, SPG Records, Manuscripts Division, Library of Congress.

53. Hugh Finlay, *Journal Kept by Hugh Finlay, Surveyor of the Post Roads on the Continent of North America, during His Survey of the Post Offices between Falmouth and Casco Bay in the Province of Massachusetts, and Savannah in Georgia; Begun the 13th September, 1773 and Ended 26th June 1774* (Brooklyn: F. H. Norton, 1867), 66.

54. Hugh Meredith, *An Account of the Cape Fear Country, 1731,* ed. Earl Gregg Swem (Perth Amboy, N.J.: C. F. Heartman, 1912), 27.

55. Ver Steeg, *Origins of a Southern Mosaic,* 63–68.

56. Greene, "Courts and Society in Proprietary North Carolina," 101.

57. These dockets include New Hanover County Reference Dockets, 1750–58; New Hanover County Execution Dockets, 1758–70; New Hanover County Trial Dockets, 1771–75: North Carolina Department of Archives and History, Raleigh.

58. Gathering information on these cases involved comparing references from all three sets of dockets and from the county court minutes. When the same combinations of litigants appeared in different sources or were referred to in different stages of the litigation process, they were assumed to be the same. When the same combinations were referred to simultaneously within dockets either repeatedly in the same place or with different results, they were assumed to be different legal actions. All cases with multiple or corporate litigants were excluded from this analysis because of the difficulty of tracing estates under administration or execution from docket to docket and because of other problems. There

is no reason to believe that this omission would have created any systematic bias in the data, however. Finally, the analysis was limited to cases with surviving recorded outcomes, therefore excluding many cases that were continued for a time until disappearing from the records.

59. There were 261 different plaintiffs and 276 different defendants.

60. Plaintiffs were a little wealthier. Among the 261 plaintiffs, 115 (44 percent) patented land and 188 (72 percent) owned slaves. The average plaintiff who patented land ranked about 321st among patentees in acres; the average plaintiff who owned slaves ranked about 250th among slave owners. Of 276 defendants, 111 (40 percent) patented land; and 166 (60 percent) owned slaves. The average defendant who patented land ranked about 330th among patentees in acres, and the average defendant who owned slaves ranked about 253rd among slave owners.

61. William M. Offutt Jr., *Of "Good Laws" and "Good Men": Law and Society in the Delaware Valley, 1680–1710* (Urbana: University of Illinois Press, 1995). This work informs much of the following discussion of legal procedure and litigation. Offutt often discusses the use of law in dispute resolution in relation to Quaker ideology about governance and social harmony. I would argue that the most important principles behind his work could also be applied to legal systems in most other areas of colonial British America, with or without the presence or leadership of Quakers. For another classic work on colonial law that deals with the relationship between legal procedure and consensus, see David T. Konig, *Law and Society in Puritan Massachusetts: Essex County, 1629–1692* (Chapel Hill: University of North Carolina Press, 1979). Other works on the role of law in early-modern England and America that are of relevance for this study include, among many others, Bruce Mann, *Neighbors and Strangers: Law and Community in Early Connecticut* (Chapel Hill: University of North Carolina Press, 1987); John Brewer and John Styles, eds., *An Ungovernable People: The English and Their Law in the Seventeenth and Eighteenth Centuries* (New Brunswick, N.J.: Rutgers University Press, 1980); Cynthia B. Herrup, *The Common Peace: Participation and the Criminal Law in Seventeenth-Century England* (Cambridge: Cambridge University Press, 1987).

62. Offutt, *Of "Good Laws" and "Good Men,"* 106.

63. It should be noted, of course, that these cases may not have represented an ideal resolution of the dispute from the perspective of the plaintiff. Indeed, the dismissal of a case could have been infuriating for some plaintiffs. But the important point for this interpretation is that the parties arrived at some form of legal compromise that prevented an open and potentially even more acrimonious courtroom contest. Cases considered as settled include those that were dismissed, nonsuited, quashed, arbitrated, forgiven, or resolved without a verdict in some other manner.

64. Defendants in these cases either confessed judgment or defaulted.

65. These cases include all those in which the dockets clearly indicate that the suit resulted in some kind of verdict, judgment, or contested decision.

66. Offutt, *Of "Good Laws" and "Good Men,"* 104.

67. It should be noted that by looking at the behavior of litigants over five-year intervals, it is possible to discern two chronological trends. First, contested cases were the least frequent in the years between 1750 and 1755 and became more common between 1755 and 1770. While this trend may seem to contradict an expected trend toward an increasingly developed and reliable court system, it might be due to several potential sources of

social friction, including population growth and differing perspectives on declining relations with the metropolis. Or, of course, some other changes may have played an important role in litigation but remain hidden by the dearth of data on the cases. Second, after 1770 contested cases became less common again proportionally, and the total number of cases before the courts also declined sharply. This is probably a reflection of the fact that the North Carolina court cases were more interrupted and less accessible during these years because of a political dispute with Governor Martin that enabled the legislation governing the courts to lapse temporarily and prevent normal sessions and because of the intensification of the crisis with Britain. For whatever reason, many cases were resolved without being contested throughout the period from 1750 to 1775 and, except between 1765 and 1770, these cases made up a majority of the outcomes.

68. Wilmington Superior Court Minutes, 1760–65, North Carolina Department of Archives and History, Raleigh.

69. *Case* did constitute a specific and differentiated kind of action, but its almost universal appearance in the docket suggests that it was used indiscriminately regardless of the nature of the suit.

70. The years 1760 to 1765 were included in this analysis. Wilmington District Superior Court minutes exist from 1760 until the end of the colonial period.

71. Offutt, *Of "Good Laws" and "Good Men,"* 105.

72. It should be noted that proportionally fewer settled and uncontested cases showed up in the superior court minutes than in the county court dockets. This discrepancy is the result of different source materials, because court minutes generally are more likely only to include mention of completed and contested cases, whereas dockets are much more comprehensive. Such high success rates for plaintiffs also make it unlikely that defendants would have been willing to contest cases often.

73. Offutt, *Of "Good Laws" and "Good Men,"* 93–94, 106–8, 291; Michael Woods, "The Culture of Credit in Colonial Charleston," *South Carolina Historical Magazine* 99, no. 4 (1998): 358–80, esp. 358–65. On the importance of property in North Carolina courts, see Bushman, "Farmers in Court," 412; Greene, "Courts and Society in Proprietary North Carolina," 102.

74. Murray to Henry McCulloh, November 11, 1739, Murray to unidentified, December 23, 1738, Murray to William Guyther, December 4, 1743: James Murray Letters, MHS. For other examples of Murray's use of legal means to pursue debts, see Murray to Ingham Foster, July 25, 1749; Murray to Ingham Foster, July 30, 1751; Murray to Mackay and Co., January 31, 1751; Murray to Archibald Douglas, September 4, 1754; Murray to Elizabeth Smith, March 18, 1765: James Murray Letters, MHS.

75. On the jurisdiction of the North Carolina county courts, see McCain, *County Court,* 43, 50–53.

76. To be precise, 46.3 percent (57 of 123) of the cases involved two identifiable Lower Cape Fear residents. The superior court also had jurisdiction over cases from residents of Duplin, Bladen, Cumberland, and Onslow Counties, but most of these counties' residents had much greater distances to travel to bring suits in the Wilmington Superior Court and, in some cases, somewhat smaller populations than that of the Lower Cape Fear; see Marvin Michael Kay and Lorin Lee Cary, *Slavery in North Carolina, 1748–1775* (Chapel Hill: University of North Carolina Press, 1995), 221.

77. I found that 41 out of the 123 cases fit this category.

78. Spindel, *Crime and Society in North Carolina,* 46, 87, 98.

79. Ibid., esp. 138–46.

80. Ironically, Roger Ekirch argues that the relatively small numbers of slaves in North Carolina contributed to the lack of cohesion among the colony's elite. Once again, however, what is true for the rest of North Carolina fits poorly in the Lower Cape Fear, where slaveholdings were about as concentrated as in South Carolina or anywhere else on the North American mainland at this time. See Ekirch, *Poor Carolina,* 37.

81. Philip D. Morgan, *Slave Counterpoint: Black Culture in the Eighteenth-Century Chesapeake and Lowcountry* (Chapel Hill: University of North Carolina Press, 1998), esp. 1–101, 659–72; Ira Berlin, *Many Thousands Gone: The First Two Centuries of Slavery in North America* (Cambridge: Harvard University Press, 1998), esp., 1–14. Both Morgan and Berlin offer recent, thorough, and sophisticated interpretations of slavery in different regions of colonial America. While significant differences in approach separate the two works, they both offer powerful demonstrations of regional variation in the formation of slave systems.

82. Alan D. Watson, "North Carolina Slave Courts, 1715–1785," *North Carolina Historical Review* 60, no. 1 (1983): 24–36. On these slave codes, see Jeffrey J. Crow, *The Black Experience in Revolutionary North Carolina* (Raleigh: State of North Carolina, 1977), 19–25; Kay and Cary, *Slavery in North Carolina,* 61–67.

83. Kay and Cary, *Slavery in North Carolina,* 81. For a similar incident in the South Carolina lowcountry, see J. Hector St. John de Crevecoeur, *Letters of an American Farmer and Sketches of Eighteenth-Century America,* ed. Albert E. Stone (New York: Penguin Books, 1981), 177–79.

84. Lower Cape Fear slaves made up only 12 to 15 percent of North Carolina's slave population, but by comparing Lower Cape Fear records with a larger sample used by Kay and Cary, it appears that 33 percent of the slaves executed by burning, 50 percent of the slaves who were castrated and hanged, 20 percent of the slaves who were burned and hanged, 50 percent of the slaves who died in jail, 42 percent of the slaves who were killed in attempts to capture them, 80 percent of the slaves who drowned themselves in an attempt to escape, and 21 percent of the slaves who were castrated resided in or belonged to slave owners in the Lower Cape Fear. By contrast, there are fewer references to the most conventional form of execution, hanging. Also, because Kay and Cary have explored this issue over a longer period of time in their research and appear to have found some cases that I have not, these numbers are minimal percentages. Kay and Cary, however, make no note of this important regional difference and imply that such punishments were equally common in parts of North Carolina with a less intensive system of plantation slavery. In contrast, Alan D. Watson, who also pays little attention to these variations, implies that all of North Carolina punished slaves less harshly than did South Carolina and Virginia. See Kay and Cary, *Slavery in North Carolina;* Watson, "North Carolina Slave Courts"; and Alan D. Watson, "Impulse toward Independence: Resistance and Rebellion among North Carolina Slaves, 1750–1775," *Journal of Negro History* 63, no. 4 (October 1978): 317–28.

85. Alexander M. Walker, ed., *New Hanover County Court Minutes, 1738–1785* (Bethesda, Md.: A. M. Walker, 1958–59), 1:77.

86. Council Journals, June 5, 1740, *Colonial Records,* 4:460.

87. Walker, *New Hanover County Court Minutes,* 1:69, 92, 100; Report of the Committee of Public Claims, November 11, 1766, in Walter Clark, ed., *The State Records of North Carolina* (Goldsboro: State of North Carolina, 1895–1905) (hereafter cited as *State Records*), 22:8421; Report of the Committee of Public Claims, December 11, 1770, ibid., 22:859.

88. Walker, *New Hanover County Court Minutes,* 1:80.

89. On evidence about runaway slaves in North Carolina, see the detailed analysis in Kay and Cary, *Slavery in North Carolina,* 121–36. I have not applied the same detailed quantitative analysis because the limited sample of runaways from the Lower Cape Fear would cast doubt on the reliability of statistics.

90. These advertisements have been reprinted in Lathan A. Windley, ed., *Runaway Slave Advertisements: A Documentary History from the 1730s to 1790* (Westport, Conn.: Greenwood Press, 1983). See vol. 1, *Virginia and North Carolina,* 437, 441, 444, 451, 454, 460, 461–62, 464–65; and vol. 3, *South Carolina,* 95, 126, 138, 165, 278, 717.

91. Windley, *Runaway Slave Advertisements,* 2:95.

92. Ibid., 2:138.

93. Ibid., 2:441.

94. Ibid., 1:451.

95. While this is an old theme in the historiography of slavery, some especially helpful observations can be found in Berlin, *Many Thousands Gone,* 98, 106, 115–16, 150, 346.

96. Slave owners have been traced using New Hanover County tax lists, 1755, 1762, 1763, 1767; Brunswick County Tax Lists, 1769, 1772, North Carolina Department of Archives and History, Raleigh. On slaveholding patterns in colonial North Carolina, see Kay and Cary, *Slavery in North Carolina,* 230–31; H. Roy Merrens, *Colonial North Carolina in the Eighteenth Century: A Study in Historical Geography* (Chapel Hill: University of North Carolina Press, 1964), 74–81.

97. Merrens, *Colonial North Carolina,* 85–107.

98. On slave labor in the forests in early North Carolina, see Robert D. Outland III, "Slavery, Work, and the Geography of the North Carolina Naval Stores Industry, 1835–1860," *Journal of Southern History* 62, no. 1 (1996): 27–56; Percival Perry, "The Naval Stores Industry in the Old South, 1790–1860," *Journal of Southern History* 34, no. 4 (1968): 509–26; Merrens, *Colonial North Carolina,* 85–107; Kay and Cary, *Slavery in North Carolina,* 11, 14–17, 43–44; David S. Cecelski, *The Waterman's Song: Slavery and Freedom in Maritime North Carolina* (Chapel Hill: University of North Carolina Press, 2001), 131–33. I also thank Dr. Outland for allowing me to read some of his unpublished work on the antebellum North Carolina naval-stores industry.

99. Jeffrey J. Crow, "Slave Rebelliousness and Social Conflict in North Carolina, 1775 to 1802," *William and Mary Quarterly* 37, no. 1 (1980): 84–86; Sylvia Frey, *Water from the Rock: Black Resistance in a Revolutionary Age* (Princeton, N.J.: Princeton University Press, 1991), 59. Frey incorrectly locates this insurrection scare in Wilmington.

100. Proceedings of the Safety Committee at Wilmington, August 17, 1775, *Colonial Records,* 10:159.

101. Frey, *Water from the Rock,* 163–64; Crow, "Slave Rebelliousness," 86–87.

102. Also on North Carolina slaves in the American Revolution, see Crow, *Black Experience;* and Frey, *Water from the Rock,* 8–9, 58, 61, 129, 162–64.

103. Janet Schaw, *Journal of a Lady of Quality: Being the Narrative of a Journey from Scotland to the West Indies, North Carolina, and Portugal, in the Years 1774 to 1776,* ed. Evangeline A. Andrews and Charles M. Andrews (New Haven: Yale University Press, 1921), 199–202; Crow, "Slave Rebelliousness," 84; Frey, *Water from the Rock,* 59.

104. See Charles B. Lowry, "Class, Politics, Rebellion, and Regional Development in Proprietary North Carolina," doctoral dissertation, University of Florida, 1975.

105. The North Carolina Regulation has received more scholarly attention than any other topic in the colony's history and lies well beyond the scope of this study. Moreover,

the Regulation seems to have had little impact on life in the Lower Cape Fear. Some Lower Cape Fear leaders showed sympathy for Governor Tryon in his efforts to end the movement, but few of the individuals involved in the Battle of Alamance or other major events associated with the Regulation lived in the Lower Cape Fear. See Governor Tryon to Earl Hillsborough, April 12, 1771, *Colonial Records,* 8:547–48; and Return of the Army Whilst Encamped at Hermon Husbands on Sandy Creek, May 22, 1771, *Colonial Records,* 8:677. For an introduction to the historiography of the North Carolina Regulation, see Marjoleine Kars, *Breaking Loose Together: The Regulator Rebellion in Pre-Revolutionary North Carolina* (Chapel Hill: University of North Carolina Press, 2002); Wayne E. Lee, *Crowds and Soldiers in Revolutionary North Carolina: The Culture of Violence in Riot and War* (Gainesville: University of Florida Press, 2001); Ekirch, *Poor Carolina,* 161–209; James P. Whittenburg, "Planters, Merchants, and Lawyers: Social Change and the Origins of the North Carolina Regulation," *William and Mary Quarterly* 34, no. 2 (1977): 215–38; and Marvin Michael Kay, "The North Carolina Regulation, 1766–1776: A Class Conflict," in *The American Revolution: Explorations in the History of American Radicalism,* ed. Alfred F. Young (De Kalb: University of Northern Illinois, 1976), 84–103.

106. Laws, *State Records,* 23:119.

107. Records of the General Court, March 1727, *Colonial Records,* 2:698.

108. Council Journals, May 22, 1740, *Colonial Records,* 4:450; Legislative Journals, December 2, 1760, ibid., 5:1:507; Arthur Dobbs to Board of Trade, ibid., 5:1:598; Arthur Dobbs to Board of Trade, March 7, 1763, ibid., 5:1:972; Couchet Jouvencal to Board of Trade, May 16, 1763, ibid., 5:1:985–86; Dobbs to Board of Trade, March 29, 1764, ibid., 5:1:1036.

109. Couchet Jouvencal to Board of Trade, May 16, 1763, *Colonial Records,* 5:1:985–86.

110. Legislative Journals, December 12, 1760, *Colonial Records,* 5:1:507; Couchet Jouvencal to Board of Trade, May 16, 1763, ibid., 5:1:986.

111. Gabriel Johnston to the duke of Bedford [1749], *Colonial Records,* 4:919; Gabriel Johnston to Board of Trade, March 9, 1746/47, ibid., 5:1152–55; Johnston to Board of Trade, December 28, 1748, ibid., 5:1164–66; Deposition of John Wynns, April 13, 1749, ibid., 5:1171–72; Inhabitants of Chowan, Perquimans, Pasquotank, and Currotuck to Board of Trade [1749], ibid., 5:1215–17; Ekirch, *Poor Carolina,* 92–93.

112. Ekirch, *Poor Carolina,* 91–111; Lefler and Powell, *Colonial North Carolina,* 121–28.

113. Governor Dobbs to the earl of Loudoun, July 10, 1756, *Colonial Records,* 5:1:595.

114. Gabriel Johnston to Board of Trade, December 17, 1740, *Colonial Records,* 4:424.

115. Numerous references indicate contemporary discontent over the location of the government and its implications for institutional efficiency. See George Burrington to Board of Trade, September 4, 1731, *Colonial Records,* 3:204; Legislative Journals, April 28, 1731, ibid., 3:303; Nathanial Rice, John Baptista Ashe, and John Montgomery to the duke of Newcastle, September 16, 1732, ibid., 3:357–58; Gabriel Johnston to Board of Trade, December 17, 1740, ibid., 4:204, 206–7; Johnston to Board of Trade, ibid., 4:423; Council Journals, July 4, 1744, October 2, 1749, ibid., 4:701, 961; Arthur Dobbs to Board of Trade, November 9, 1759, ibid., 5:146; Mr. Lucas to Board of Trade [1761], ibid., 5:1:604.

116. Arthur Dobbs to Board of Trade, January 22, 1759, *Colonial Records,* 5:1:1.

117. Mr. Lucas to Board of Trade [1761], *Colonial Records,* 5:1:604.

118. William Tryon, "Tryon's 'Book' on North Carolina," ed. William S. Powell, *North Carolina Historical Review* 34, no. 3 (1957): 413.

119. Samuel Johnston to Alexander Elmsley, September 23, 1774, *Colonial Records,* 9:1071.

120. Nathanial Rice and John Baptista Ashe to governor and council [1733], *Colonial Records,* 3:451.

121. Lefler and Powell, *Colonial North Carolina,* 240–88; Lawrence Lee, *The Lower Cape Fear in Colonial Days* (Chapel Hill: University of North Carolina Press, 1965), 242–80; Donna J. Spindel, "Law and Disorder: The North Carolina Stamp Act Crisis," *North Carolina Historical Review* 57, no. 1 (January 1980): 1–16.

122. Lower Cape Fear computer biographical files.

123. This pamphlet has been republished in William K. Boyd, ed., *Some Eighteenth Century Tracts Concerning North Carolina* (Raleigh: State of North Carolina, 1927), 157–74.

124. Moore, *Justice and Policy,* 159–61, 165, 166, 173.

125. Ibid., 169–70.

Chapter 6: Lower Cape Fear Plantations

1. Janet Schaw, *Journal of a Lady of Quality: Being the Narrative of a Journey from Scotland to the West Indies, North Carolina, and Portugal, in the Years 1774 to 1776,* ed. Evangeline A. Andrews and Charles M. Andrews (New Haven: Yale University Press, 1921), 184–85.

2. Ibid., 184–85; H. Roy Merrens, *Colonial North Carolina in the Eighteenth Century: A Study in Historical Geography* (Chapel Hill: University of North Carolina Press, 1964), 98.

3. For two examples, see "Journal of a French Traveller in the Colonies, 1765, I," *American Historical Review* 26 (July 1921): 735; and William Faris to Arthur Dobbs, February 18, 1749/50, Arthur Dobbs Papers, North Carolina Department of Archives and History, Raleigh.

4. Schaw, *Journal of a Lady,* 185.

5. On the concept of competency, see Daniel Vickers, *Farmers and Fishermen: Two Centuries of Work in Essex County, Massachusetts, 1630–1850* (Chapel Hill: University of North Carolina Press, 1994), 14–23; and Vickers, "Competency and Competition: Economic Culture in Early America," *William and Mary Quarterly* 47, no. 1 (1990): 3–29.

6. On this situation and on labor in early America in general, see Stephen Innes, "Fulfilling John Smith's Vision: Work and Labor in Early America," in *Work and Labor in Early America,* ed. Stephen Innes (Chapel Hill: University of North Carolina Press, 1988), 3–47.

7. On family labor in New England, see Vickers, *Farmers and Fishermen.*

8. On the staples and Malthusian interpretations of colonial American economic history, see John J. McCusker and Russell R. Menard, *The Economy of British America, 1607–1789* (Chapel Hill: University of North Carolina Press, 1985), 17–34. For several other overviews of colonial economic history, see Stanley L. Engerman and Robert E. Gallman, eds., *The Cambridge Economic History of the United States,* vol. 1, *The Colonial Era* (Cambridge: Cambridge University Press, 1996); Jacob M. Price, "The Transatlantic Economy," in *Colonial British America: Essays in the New History of the Early Modern Era,* ed. Jack P. Greene and J. R. Pole (Baltimore: Johns Hopkins University Press, 1984), 18–42; Richard B. Sheridan, "The Domestic Economy," in *Colonial British America,* ed. Greene and Pole, 43–85; Gary M. Walton and James F. Shepherd, *The Economic Rise of Early America* (Cambridge: Cambridge University Press, 1979).

9. For an important attempt at defining the characteristics and consequences of plantations in the early-modern Atlantic world, see Philip D. Curtin, *The Rise and Fall of the Plantation Complex: Essays in Atlantic History* (Cambridge: Cambridge University Press, 1990).

10. For some important works on New World plantations, see Eugene D. Genovese, *Roll, Jordan, Roll: The World the Slaves Made* (New York: Vintage, 1974); Joyce E. Chaplin, *"An Anxious Pursuit": Agricultural Innovation and Modernity in the Lower South, 1730–1815* (Chapel Hill: University of North Carolina Press, 1993); Peter A. Coclanis, *The Shadow of a Dream: Economic Life and Death in the South Carolina Low Country, 1760–1920* (New York: Oxford University Press, 1989); Philip D. Morgan, *Slave Counterpoint: Black Culture in the Eighteenth-Century Chesapeake and Lowcountry* (Chapel Hill: University of North Carolina Press, 1998); Robert W. Fogel, *Without Consent or Contract: The Rise and Fall of American Slavery* (New York: W. W. Norton, 1989); Richard B. Sheridan, *Sugar and Slavery: An Economic History of the British West Indies* (Baltimore: Johns Hopkins University Press, 1974); Lois Green Carr, Russell R. Menard, and Lorena S. Walsh, *Robert Cole's World: Agriculture and Society in Early Maryland* (Chapel Hill: University of North Carolina Press, 1991); Lewis C. Gray, *History of Agriculture in the Southern United States to 1860* (Clifton, N.J.: A. M. Kelley, 1933); and Stuart B. Schwartz, *Sugar Plantations in the Formation of Brazilian Society: Bahia, 1550–1835* (Cambridge: Cambridge University Press, 1985).

11. The following discussion has been based on Class 16, Volume 1, Customs, British Public Records Office; Port of Brunswick Customs Records, North Carolina Department of Archives and History, Raleigh; and James F. Shepherd, "Commodity Exports from the British North American Colonies to Overseas Areas, 1768–1772," *Explorations in Economic History* 8, no. 3 (fall 1970): 5–76.

12. Tobacco and deerskins exiting through the Lower Cape Fear ports were, however, almost certainly from other regions of North Carolina.

13. McCusker and Menard, *Economy of British America,* 130, 160; Engerman and Gallman, *Cambridge Economic History,* 285.

14. For three influential examples, see Jack P. Greene, *Pursuits of Happiness: The Social Development of Early Modern British Colonies and the Formation of American Culture* (Chapel Hill: University of North Carolina Press, 1988), 142; McCusker and Menard, *Economy of British America,* 170; and D. W. Meinig, *The Shaping of America: A Geographical Perspective on 500 Years of History,* vol. 1, *Atlantic America, 1492–1800* (New Haven: Yale University Press, 1986), 182–83, 190. For two notable exceptions, see Merrens, *Colonial North Carolina,* 131; and Christopher C. Crittenden, *The Commerce of North Carolina, 1763–1789* (New Haven: Yale University Press, 1936), 70.

15. On rice in the Lower Cape Fear, see James M. Clifton, "Golden Grains of White: Rice Planting on the Lower Cape Fear," *North Carolina Historical Review* 50, no. 4 (1973): 365–93; and Merrens, *Colonial North Carolina,* 125–33.

16. Clifton, "Golden Grains of White," 368 n. 16; Marvin Michael Kay and Lorin Lee Cary, *Slavery in North Carolina, 1748–1775* (Chapel Hill: University of North Carolina Press, 1995), 29.

17. In a suggestive parallel, Henry Laurens used a fleet of ships to transport rice and other commodities between his various South Carolina low-country plantations and Charleston; see S. Max Edelson, "Planting the Lowcountry: Agricultural Enterprise and Economic Experience in the Lower South, 1695–1785," doctoral dissertation, Johns Hopkins University, 1998, 341.

18. Laws, in William L. Saunders, ed., *The Colonial Records of North Carolina* (Raleigh: State of North Carolina, 1886–90) (hereafter cited as *Colonial Records*), 23:352, 380; 25:205–6, 313–19.

19. These various papers, all associated with the business of Wilmington merchant Robert Hogg, include account books, ledgers, and a letterbook; they are analyzed more fully in chapter 7. The volumes used in this study include the Robert Hogg Journal, Wilmington, 1767–72, Southern History Collection, Chapel Hill, N.C.; Robert Hogg Ledger, Wilmington, 1767–72, ibid.; Invoice Outward, Hogg and Campbell, Wilmington, 1767–82, North Carolina Department of Archives and History, Raleigh; Hogg and Clayton Letterbook, Charleston, 1762–71, William R. Perkins Library, Duke University, Durham, N.C.

20. Murray to John Pringle, July 8, 1743: James Murray Letters, Massachusetts Historical Society, Boston (hereafter cited as MHS).

21. William Faris to Arthur Dobbs, February 18, 1749/50, Arthur Dobbs Papers; Murray to Henry McCulloh, January 10, 1736/37, in James Murray, *Letters of James Murray, Loyalist,* ed. Nina M. Tiffany (Boston: Printed, not published, 1901), 36; Murray to Henry McCulloh, May 11, 1741: James Murray Letters, MHS.

22. Morgan, *Slave Counterpoint,* 35–37.

23. Tax lists indicate the size of slaveholdings. The number of households with thirty or more slaves for each tax list is as follows: 1755: 12; 1763: 15; 1767 (New Hanover County only): 11; 1769 (Brunswick County only): 9. On the importance of labor, see Clifton, "Golden Grains of White," 368–69; and Merrens, *Colonial North Carolina,* 130.

24. Report on the Boundary Line between North and South Carolina, December 21, 1769, *Colonial Records,* 8:558.

25. On how this occurred in South Carolina, see Russell R. Menard, "Financing the Lowcountry Export Boom: Capital and Growth in Early South Carolina," *William and Mary Quarterly* 52, no. 4 (1995): 280–303.

26. Clifton, "Golden Grains of White," 363, 381.

27. Murray to Barbara Clark, December 26, 1755, Murray to Mrs. Bennet, February 28, 1755: James Murray Letters, MHS.

28. The limited land available for rice may have been reduced by a lack of bottomland due to the tidal flows from the Lower Cape Fear River, which were relatively small compared with those from South Carolina rivers. Tidal rice cultivation appears to have been used on the Lower Cape Fear as early as 1731. See Clifton, "Golden Grains of White," 368, 371; Merrens, *Colonial North Carolina,* 131; and Hugh Meredith, *An Account of the Cape Fear Country, 1731,* ed. Earl Gregg Swem (Perth Amboy, N.J.: C. F. Heartman, 1922), 20–21.

29. *Cape Fear Mercury,* January 11, 1773.

30. Merrens, *Colonial North Carolina,* 126; Josiah Martin to the earl of Dartmouth, October 6, 1773, *Colonial Records,* 9:687.

31. Murray to David Thomson, June 22, 1745: James Murray Letters, MHS.

32. Lord Adam Gordon, "Journal of an Officer's Travels in America and the West Indies, 1764–1765," in *Travels in the American Colonies,* ed. Newton D. Mereness (New York: Antiquarian Press, 1916), 402.

33. For example, South Carolinian Henry Laurens incurred greater transportation and marketing costs at his Savannah River plantations because he shipped his rice to Charleston, where he could take advantage of more favorable markets. For Laurens, this remained profitable because of the unusual fertility of these lands and because of the efficient integration of his plantation enterprises. See Edelson, "Planting the Lowcountry," 325. On the advantages of a centralized market for the exportation of colonial rice, see

R. C. Nash, "Urbanization in the Colonial South: Charleston, South Carolina, as a Case Study," *Journal of Urban History* 19, no. 1 (1992): 16–18.

34. Rules Recd from HM, September 1735: James Murray Letters, MHS.

35. Lower Cape Fear computer biographical files. These individuals had either rice mills or rice sieves in their inventories or are referred to specifically as the owners of land planted with rice.

36. Murray to Barbara Clark, February 8, 1757: James Murray Letters, MHS.

37. On conceptions of improvement, innovation, progress, and rice cultivation in eighteenth-century South Carolina and Georgia, see Chaplin, *Anxious Pursuit.*

38. Meredith, *Account of the Cape Fear Country,* 20–21.

39. Murray, *Letters,* 30.

40. Murray to Henry McCulloh, May 3, 1736, in Murray, *Letters,* 41; Murray to Thomas Clark, December 23, 1738, ibid., 60; Murray to Barbara Clark, February 26, 1755, ibid., 77, 78; Murray to George Dunbar, January 27, 1757; Murray to Barbara Clark, December 26, 1755; Murray to Thomas Campbell, March 11, 1757: James Murray Letters, MHS.

41. Murray to Barbara Clark, February 26, 1755, in Murray, *Letters,* 77.

42. Robert Pringle to Daniel Dunbibin, September 7, 1742, in Robert Pringle, *The Letterbook of Robert Pringle, 1737–1745,* ed. Walter Edgar (Columbia: University of South Carolina Press, 1972), 410.

43. Governor Martin to Secretary Hillsborough, March 8, 1772, *Colonial Records,* 9:270.

44. Martin to the earl of Dartmouth, December 16, 1772, *Colonial Records,* 9:364.

45. Martin to the earl of Dartmouth, October 6, 1773, *Colonial Records,* 9:687.

46. Clifton, "Golden Grains of White," 369–93.

47. Murray to Mrs. Bennet, February 28, 1755: James Murray Letters, MHS.

48. Murray to James Abercromby, February 26, 1755: James Murray Letters, MHS.

49. Murray to Mrs. Sarah Allen, undated; Murray to George Dunbar, January 12, 1757: James Murray Letters, MHS.

50. Samuel B. Doggett, ed., "A Plantation on Prince George's Creek, Cape Fear, North Carolina," *New-England Historical and Genealogical Register* 52 (1898): 471.

51. See Murray's comment on the bounty in Murray to Richard Oswald and Co., February 28, 1755, in Murray, *Letters,* 79.

52. Murray to Barbara Clark, December 26, 1755: James Murray Letters, MHS.

53. Morgan, *Slave Counterpoint,* 37, 159–64.

54. Items used in the production of indigo appear in only a few estate inventories, but one contemporary letter identifies some of the most important indigo producers; see Merrens, *Colonial North Carolina,* 128–29; and Report on the Boundary Line between North and South Carolina, December 21, 1769, *Colonial Records,* 8:558–59.

55. James Murray to John Murray, January 26, 1756: James Murray Letters, MHS.

56. Merrens, *Colonial North Carolina,* 126.

57. Josiah Martin to the earl of Dartmouth, October 6, 1773, *Colonial Records,* 9:687; Arthur Dobbs to Board of Trade, March 29, 1764, ibid., 5:1:1029–30; Murray to Mrs. Sarah Allen, undated, Murray to Mrs. Bennet, December 26, 1755, and Murray to George Dunbar, January 27, 1757: James Murray Letters, MHS; James Abercromby to John Rutherfurd, December 29, 1757, in James Abercromby, *Letterbook of James Abercromby, Colonial Agent, 1751–1773,* ed. John C. Van Horne and George Reese (Richmond: Virginia State Library and Archives, 1991), 218, 220.

58. James Murray to John Murray, February 9, 1757; Murray to Mrs. Bennet, December 26, 1755; Murray to David Nicoll, February 28, 1755: James Murray Letters, MHS.

59. Murray to Lady Don, November 25, 1758: James Murray Letters, MHS.

60. For another significant producer, see Josiah Martin to the earl of Dartmouth, December 16, 1772, *Colonial Records,* 9:364.

61. For examples, see The Colony, its Climate, Soil, Population, Government, &c [1761], *Colonial Records,* 5:1:612; Arthur Dobbs to Board of Trade, March 29, 1764, ibid., 5:1:1029; Josiah Martin to the earl of Dartmouth, October 6, 1773, ibid., 9:687; Gordon, "Journal," 401; and Schaw, *Journal of a Lady,* 194.

62. Merrens, *Colonial North Carolina,* 127; R. C. Nash, "Urbanization in the Colonial South," 14. At least some planters in the North Carolina backcountry clearly transported indigo overland to Charleston and sold it there, though the difference in distance between Charleston and Wilmington would have been much smaller from the backcountry than from the Lower Cape Fear.

63. Josiah Martin to Secretary Hillsborough, March 8, 1772, *Colonial Records,* 9:270; Josiah Martin to the earl of Dartmouth, December 16, 1772, ibid., 9:364; Josiah Martin to the earl of Dartmouth, May 20, 1773, ibid., 9:644; Josiah Martin to the earl of Dartmouth, October 6, 1773, ibid., 9:687.

64. On South Carolina, see Clarence Ver Steeg, *Origins of a Southern Mosaic: Studies of Early Carolina and Georgia* (Athens: University of Georgia Press, 1975), 108.

65. The following discussion of the Lower Cape Fear's naval-stores industry has been informed by the work of other scholars on naval stores in early America. Among others, these include Merrens, *Colonial North Carolina,* 85–92; Robert D. Outland III, "Slavery, Work, and the Geography of the North Carolina Naval Stores Industry, 1835–1860," *Journal of Southern History* 62, no. 1 (1996): 27–56; Kenneth W. Robinson, "Port Brunswick and the Colonial Naval Stores Industry: Historical and Archaeological Observations," *North Carolina Archaeology* 46 (1997): 51–67; Percival Perry, "The Naval Stores Industry in the Old South, 1790–1860," *Journal of Southern History* 34, no. 4 (1968): 509–26; Michael Williams, *Americans and Their Forests: A Historical Geography* (Cambridge: Cambridge University Press, 1989), 94–104; Thomas Gamble, comp., *Naval Stores: History, Production, Distribution and Consumption* (Savannah, Ga.: Review Publishing, 1921), 18–23; Gray, *History of Agriculture,* 151–60; Percival Perry, "The Naval Stores Industry in the Antebellum South, 1789–1861," doctoral dissertation, Duke University, 1947; Melvin Herndon, "Naval Stores in Colonial Georgia," *Georgia Historical Quarterly* 52, no. 4 (1968): 426–33; Converse D. Clowse, *Economic Beginnings in Colonial South Carolina* (Columbia: University of South Carolina Press, 1971), 132–34, 170–78, 232–35; David S. Cecelski, *The Waterman's Song: Slavery and Freedom in Maritime North Carolina* (Chapel Hill: University of North Carolina Press, 2001), 131–32; W. W. Ashe, *The Forests, Forest Lands, and Forest Products of Eastern North Carolina* (Raleigh, N.C.: J. Daniels, 1894), 72–75; Alexander Moore, ed., "Daniel Axtell's Account Book and the Economy of Early South Carolina," *South Carolina Historical Magazine* 95, no. 4 (1994): 289–92; Charles L. Paul, "Factors in the Economy of Colonial Beaufort," *North Carolina Historical Review* 47, no. 4 (1967): 121–25; and Timothy Silver, *A New Face on the Countryside: Indians, Colonists, and Slaves in South Atlantic Forests, 1500–1800* (Cambridge: Cambridge University Press, 1990), 121–28.

66. Schaw, *Journal of a Lady,* 143.

67. Elkanah Watson, *Men and Times of the Revolution; or Memoirs of Elkanah Watson, Including Journals of His Travels in Europe and America from 1777 to 1842,* ed. Winslow C. Watson (New York: Dana, 1856), 41.

68. Ibid., 41; Schaw, *Journal of a Lady,* 202.

69. Johann D. Schoepf, *Travels in the Confederation, 1783–1784, from the German of Johann David Schoepf,* trans. and ed. Alfred J. Morrison (Philadelphia: Bergman, 1911), 114–15.

70. Justin Williams, "English Mercantilism and the Carolina Naval Stores Industry, 1705–1776," *Journal of Southern History* 1, no. 2 (1935): 169–85; Clowse, *Economic Beginnings,* 132–34, 170–78, 232–35; Gray, *History of Agriculture,* 151–57.

71. Justin Williams, "English Mercantilism," 184.

72. "Moore, Roger," Colonial Court Records, box 190, Personal Accounts, 1730–39, North Carolina Department of Archives and History, Raleigh; James Murray to Henry McCulloh, December, 1735, Murray to Andrew Bennet, November 17, 1736: James Murray Letters, MHS.

73. For some contemporary descriptions of this process, see, among others, Harry J. Carmen, ed., *American Husbandry* (New York: Columbia University Press, 1939), 244–45; Schoepf, *Travels in the Confederation,* 140–44; William Tryon, "Tryon's 'Book' on North Carolina," ed. William S. Powell, *North Carolina Historical Review* 34, no. 3 (1957): 411–12; John Brickell, *The Natural History of North-Carolina* (Dublin, Ireland: Printed for James Carson, 1737), 265–66; Mark Catesby, *The Natural History of Carolina, Florida and the Bahama Islands* (London: B. White, 1771), xxiii–xxiv; "Journal of a French Traveller," 733–34; Thomas Nairne, "A Letter from South Carolina," in *Selling a New World: Two Colonial South Carolina Promotional Pamphlets,* ed. Jack P. Greene (Columbia: University of South Carolina Press, 1989), 40–41.

74. Silver, *New Face on the Countryside,* 128.

75. See, for example, George Burrington to Board of Trade, January 1, 1732/33, *Colonial Records,* 3:431; Petition of Edward Moseley to the governor and council, April 5, 1733, ibid., 3:469.

76. For more on land use in the Lower Cape Fear and on illegal boxing and burning, see chapter 2.

77. Murray to Thomas Clark, January 6, 1767: James Murray Letters, MHS.

78. Robert Williams to the North Carolina Council of Safety, September 14, 1776, *Colonial Records,* 10:800–801.

79. See esp. Merrens, *Colonial North Carolina,* 85–92, 127–33.

80. Moore, "Daniell Axtell's Account Book," 290.

81. With only 181 extant estate inventories and a limited range of implements that were distinctive to tar production, only nineteen individuals can be identified as tar producers. Initially, I had hoped to identify more naval-stores producers from transactions in the Hogg accounts, but the importance of commodity trade in the Lower Cape Fear invalidates the assumption that individuals selling tar also produced it, and patterns in the Hogg accounts strongly suggest that tar often served as a medium of exchange as well as an export staple. The following references in the text attempt to demonstrate the minimal requirements for tar production. On the opposite extreme, Richard Eagles produced tar and owned 110 slaves at one time, while the average identifiable tar producer owned between 16 and 28 slaves, as well as close to one thousand acres of land. See Lower Cape Fear computer biographical files.

82. Robinson, "Port Brunswick," 55.

83. Schoepf, *Travels in the Confederation,* 142.

84. James Murray to Sarah Allen, undated: James Murray Letters, MHS.

85. James Murray to Henry McCulloh, December 1735: James Murray Letters, MHS.

86. The experience of Thomas Pollock in the Albemarle region provides an instructive contrast. Pollock, as one of the wealthiest men in North Carolina, had little problem

obtaining slaves, but he complained incessantly in his letters about difficulties and expenses he had with the naval-stores industry, many of them related to transportation and the lack of a navigable port nearby; see esp. Pollock to Nathaniel Duckinfield, December 20, 1741, and Pollock to Joseph Anderson, May 11, 1747, Thomas Pollock Letterbook, Pollock Family Papers, North Carolina Department of Archives and History, Raleigh. Similarly, when the Moravians planned their settlement in North Carolina, they dismissed naval-stores production because they lacked water transportation; see diary of Bishop Spangenberg, *Colonial Records,* 5:2.

87. Faris to Arthur Dobbs, February 18, 1749/50, Arthur Dobbs Papers.

88. For some contemporary references to the importance of slaves for the large-scale production of tar and other naval stores in the Lower Cape Fear, see Report on the Boundary Line between North and South Carolina, December 21, 1769, *Colonial Records,* 8:558–59; Tryon, "Tryon's 'Book,'" 411–12; Murray to Henry McCulloh, May 11, 1741, in Murray, *Letters,* 64; Samuel Johnston Sr. to Samuel Johnston Jr., February 1, 1752, filmed portion, box 1, Hayes Collection, Johnston Family Series, Southern History Collection, Chapel Hill, N.C.

89. James Murray to Barbara Clark, February 8, 1757, James Murray to Richard Oswald and Co., September 7, 1749: James Murray Letters, MHS.

90. Murray to Mrs. Bennet, February 28, 1755: James Murray Letters, MHS.

91. *South Carolina and American Gazette,* July 29, 1768.

92. Murray to William Dunbar, April 19, 1743; James Murray to Charles Rutherfurd, December 12, 1745; Murray to Richard Oswald and Co., January 18, 1752: James Murray Letters, MHS; John Bartram, "Diary of a Journey through the Carolinas, Georgia, and Florida from July 1, 1765 to April 10, 1766," annotated by Francis Harper, *Transactions of the American Philosophical Society* n.s., 33, part 1 (December 1942): 15.

93. Joseph J. Malone, *Pine Trees and Politics: The Naval Stores and Forest Policy in Colonial New England, 1691–1775* (Seattle: University of Washington Press, 1964), 148.

94. Gabriel Johnston to Board of Trade, December 12, 1734, *Colonial Records,* 4:5–6. Also on problems with quality and marketing in the Carolina naval-stores industry, see Considerations why Naval Stores cannot be Brought in Great Quantities from Her Majesty's Plantations, May 19, 1704, *Colonial Records,* 1:598–99; Board of Trade to Governor Johnston, September 12, 1735, ibid., 4:16; Arthur Dobbs to Lord Halifax, ibid., 5:1:1022; memorial of Bridgen and Waller, and Hindley and Needham, merchants trading to North Carolina, March 31, 1770, ibid., 8:186–90; Laws, ibid., 23:790–801; Murray to Henry McCulloh, May 3, 1736, in Murray, *Letters,* 30; Justin Williams, "English Mercantilism," 177, 181–84; Gray, *History of Agriculture,* 155–57; Outland, "Slavery, Work, and Geography," 30–31, 41–42; and Malone, *Pine Tress and Politics,* 148–50.

95. Arthur Dobbs to Board of Trade, March 29, 1764, *Colonial Records,* 5:1:1030.

96. On the distribution of the long-leaf pine, see Merrens, *Colonial North Carolina,* 86–87, 89–91, 226–27.

97. Tar played an important role in early-modern maritime ventures, but until the nineteenth century, turpentine only had minor uses; see Outland, "Slavery, Work, and Geography," 31.

98. For some contemporary descriptions of this process, see, among others, Carmen, *American Husbandry,* 244–45; Schoepf, *Travels in the Confederation,* 140–44; Tryon, "Tryon's 'Book,'" 411–12; Brickell, *Natural History of North-Carolina,* 265–66; and "Journal of a

French Traveller," 733–34. While sources on the production of turpentine in the colonial period remain sparse, the prominence of turpentine production in the nineteenth-century naval-stores industry has encouraged research on basic procedures that had probably changed little since the colonial period. This discussion owes a debt to that research. See esp. Outland, "Slavery, Work, and Geography"; Kenneth W. Robinson, "Archaeology and the North Carolina Naval Stores Industry: A Prospectus," unpublished paper prepared for the Office of State Archaeology, North Carolina Department of Archives and History, Raleigh; and G. Terry Sharrer, "Naval Stores, 1781–1881," in *Material Culture of the Wooden Age,* ed. Brooke Hindle (Tarrytown, N.Y.: Sleepy Hollow Press, 1981), 241–70.

99. For a much more detailed description of these procedures, see Outland, "Slavery, Work, and Geography," 34–38.

100. Only five identifiable turpentine producers can be traced to slaveholdings, providing an insufficient sample for any generalization; however, the demand for labor can be inferred from nineteenth-century practices. Turpentine production was still not as labor-intensive as the cultivation of sugar, rice, or some other agricultural staples, however.

101. Murray to Robert Palmer, March 31, 1768: James Murray Letters, MHS.

102. In the case of lumber exports, unlike naval stores, there is evidence to suggest that a significant share of the exports leaving the port of Brunswick came from areas outside the Lower Cape Fear. Several sawmills in the Upper Cape Fear near Cross Creek probably contributed to the export figures. Nonetheless, these differences must have been too small to call into question the significance or relative place of lumber production in the Lower Cape Fear. See Merrens, *Colonial North Carolina,* 98, 100.

103. On the colonial American lumber industry, see Michael Williams, *Americans and Their Forests: A Historical Geography* (Cambridge: Cambridge University Press, 1989), 94–104; McCusker and Menard, *Economy of British America,* 314–21; Silver, *New Face on the Countryside,* 116–21; and Victor S. Clark, *History of Manufactures in the United States* (New York: McGraw-Hill, 1929), 1:73. On the lumber industry in the Carolinas, see Merrens, *Colonial North Carolina,* 93–107; Paul, "Factors in the Economy," 121–22; and Moore, "Daniel Axtell's Account Book," 292–96.

104. Michael Williams, *Americans and Their Forests,* 94–95.

105. While I argue that this pattern of development is distinctive, I do not wish to suggest that it is unique. Victor Clark indicates that a similar process occurred in colonial Georgia, where some of the same influences may have been at work; see Clark, *History of Manufactures,* 1:73.

106. George Burrington to the secretary, November 2, 1732, *Colonial Records,* 3:369.

107. Council Journals, November 3, 1732, June 18, 1736, *Colonial Records,* 3:427, 4:220; George Burrington to Board of Trade, January 1, 1732/33, ibid., 3:432.

108. Arthur Dobbs to Board of Trade, March 29, 1764, *Colonial Records,* 5:1:1030; William Tryon to Board of Trade, April 30, 1766, ibid., 7:201–2; William Tryon to Board of Trade, January 30, 1767, ibid., 7:430; William Tryon to Board of Trade, February 22, 1767, 7:440–41; "Journal of a French Traveller," 735.

109. Lower Cape Fear computer biographical files.

110. See, for examples, the articles of agreement between Ezekiel Morgan and John James in 1771. Morgan and James both agreed to pay one-half of the expenses necessary to build sawmills and grist mills in New Hanover County. Similarly, Henry Johnston, Thomas Holloway, and William Anderson agreed to share responsibilities for another

Lower Cape Fear sawmill. See New Hanover County Real Estate Conveyances, 1734–75, Book F, 191–92; Hayes Collection, Johnston Series, filmed portion, box 1, folder 60, Southern History Collection, Chapel Hill, N.C.

111. Tryon, "Tryon's 'Book,'" 411–12.

112. Murray to James, April 30, 1767, Murray to Thomas Clark, July 28, 1767: James Murray Letters, MHS.

113. Schaw, *Journal of a Lady,* 148.

114. Michael Williams, *Americans and Their Forests,* 96; "Journal of a French Traveller," 735.

115. Council Journals, November 3, 1732, *Colonial Records,* 3:427; George Burrington to Board of Trade, January 1, 1732/33, ibid., 3:432.

116. For this claim, see Carmen, *American Husbandry,* 245.

117. Murray to George Dunbar, January 27, 1757: James Murray Letters, MHS.

118. Murray to David Tullideph, February 21, 1735/36: James Murray Letters, MHS.

119. Merrens, *Colonial North Carolina,* 99.

120. Michael Williams, *Americans and Their Forests,* 95.

121. Murray to John Wallace, September 4, 1756, in Murray, *Letters,* 81.

122. Out of 181 estate inventories, 94 had some kind of ax, 59 had some kind of saw, and 29 had the rarer and more specialized cross-cut saws that would dominate the lumbering industry in later decades.

123. Merrens, *Colonial North Carolina,* 99.

124. As scholars have pointed out, the intense study of staples and exportation has led to the neglect of research and comment related to the colonial American domestic economy. For a good overview of these matters, see Sheridan, "Domestic Economy."

125. Research has demonstrated that even in sugar-rich British Jamaica, planters devoted significant attention to provisioning and other economic activities. See Yu Wu, "Jamaican Trade, 1688–1769: A Quantitative Study," doctoral dissertation, Johns Hopkins University, 1996.

126. I use *corn* in this study to refer to maize, or Indian corn, rather than other kinds of grain.

127. Carmen, *American Husbandry,* 240–42; George Burrington to Board of Trade, January 1, 1732/33, *Colonial Records,* 3:430; Arthur Dobbs to Board of Trade, January 4, 1755, ibid., 5:315.

128. Evidence on cattle ownership from just after the American Revolution bears this out. New Hanover County had a lower percentage of households with cattle than any other county in North Carolina for which records exist, but a clear majority of households owned some cattle. See Francis Grave Morris and Phyllis Mary Morris, "Economic Conditions in North Carolina about 1780: Part 2, Ownership of Town Lots, Slaves, and Cattle," *North Carolina Historical Review* 16, no. 3 (1939): 316–26.

129. Captain Burrington's Representation of the Present State and Condition of North Carolina, January 1, 1732/33, *Colonial Records,* 3:436–37.

130. Arthur Dobbs to Board of Trade, March 29, 1764, *Colonial Records,* 5:1:1029; The Humble Petition of the Subscribers, Tanners, & Merchants in Behalf of Themselves and Others [1757], *Colonial Records,* 5:1:745–46; Murray to Barbara Clark, December 26, 1755: James Murray Letters, MHS.

131. Morris and Morris, "Economic Conditions, Part 2," 317.

132. John Solomon Otto, "Livestock-Raising in Early South Carolina, 1670–1700: Prelude to the Rice Plantation Economy," *Agricultural History* 61, no. 4 (fall 1987): 15–21.

133. It is difficult to ascertain what factors compelled certain individuals to record their brands. Law required that all livestock owners record brands, but clearly the vast majority did not. The economic and psychological importance of property in poorer households, the identifiability of different breeds of cattle, and relationships toward authority all probably played roles. On the courts' records of brands, see McCain, *County Court,* 68–69.

134. Otto, "Livestock-Raising," 22; Peter H. Wood, *Black Majority: Negroes in Colonial South Carolina from 1670 through the Stono Rebellion* (New York: Knopf, 1974), 106.

135. William Tryon to Lord Hillsborough, September 15, 1769, *Colonial Records,* 8:71.

136. Meredith, *Account of the Cape Fear Country,* 19–20; "New Voyage to Georgia," 56; Robert Pringle to Daniel Dunbibin, September 7, 1742, in Pringle, *Letterbook,* 410.

137. Arthur Dobbs to Board of Trade, March 29, 1764, *Colonial Records,* 5:1:1030; Murray to Pringle, July 3, 1743: James Murray Letters, MHS; "New Voyage to Georgia," 56.

138. On these activities in North Carolina generally, see Merrens, *Colonial North Carolina,* 108–19, 134–41. On precursors to cattle ranching in the Carolinas, see John Solomon Otto, "The Origins of Cattle-Ranching in Colonial South Carolina, 1670–1715," *South Carolina Historical Magazine* 87, no. 2 (1986): 117–24.

139. Schaw, *Journal of a Lady,* 281.

140. Scotus Americanus, "Informations Concerning the Province of North Carolina, Addressed to Emigrants from the Highlands and Western Isles of Scotland," in *Some Eighteenth Century Tracts Concerning North Carolina,* ed. William K. Boyd (Raleigh: State of North Carolina, 1927), 445.

141. Council Journals, April 12, 1753, June 1766, January 23, 1767, *Colonial Records,* 5:1:32–33, 7:226, 428; Laws, ibid., 25:25, 255.

142. Schaw, *Journal of a Lady,* 280–81.

143. Murray to Hutchinson and Grimke, May 3, 1736: James Murray Letters, MHS.

144. Faris to Dobbs, February 18, 1749/50, Arthur Dobbs Papers; Murray to Henry McCulloh, undated; Murray to John Pringle, July 8, 1743; Murray to David Tullideph, February 21, 1735/36: James Murray Letters, MHS.

145. William Tryon to Lord Hillsborough, September 15, 1769, *Colonial Records,* 8:71.

146. See, for example, Carr et al., *Robert Cole's World,* 80–81. In the early Chesapeake Bay area, a strong emphasis on unpredictable tobacco markets and the presence of fertile grain-growing areas made provisioning a comparatively stable source of income when tobacco profits dropped.

147. See Merrens, *Colonial North Carolina,* 132.

148. Schaw, *Journal of a Lady,* 148.

149. "Cobham, Thomas," American Loyalist Claims, microfilm copies, North Carolina Department of Archives and History, Raleigh.

150. In fact, Moore claimed closer to forty thousand acres of land by this time, but he may not have mentioned some of this land specifically in his will because of its limited development and value. See Lower Cape Fear computer biographical files; and "Moore, Roger," Colonial Court Records, box 190, Personal Accounts, 1730–39, North Carolina Department of Archives and History, Raleigh.

151. "Roger Moore's Will," in Bryan J. Grimes, ed, *North Carolina Wills and Inventories, Copied from the Original and Recorded Wills and Inventories in the Office of the Secretary of State* (Raleigh, N.C.: Edwards & Broughton Printing, 1912), 309–12.

152. Murray to Sarah Allen, undated; Murray to Sarah Allen, February 11, 1757; Murray to Sarah Allen, March 4, 1757: James Murray Letters, MHS.

153. The description of Murray's activities above derives from many of his letters, but especially from the following: Murray to William Ellison, February 14, 1735/36, in Murray, *Letters,* 24; Murray to John Murray, January 10, 1736/37, ibid., 38; Murray to Thomas Clark, December 23, 1738, ibid., 41; Murray to Henry McCulloh, May 11, 1741, ibid., 64; Murray to James Hazel, February 28, 1743/44, ibid., 67–69; Murray to Barbara Clark, February 26, 1775, ibid., 77, 78; Murray to Sampson Simpson, September 4, 1756, ibid., 80–81; Murray to John Murray, June 21, 1766, ibid., 156; and Murray to Sarah Allen, undated; Murray to Henry McCulloh, undated; Murray to David Tullideph, February 21, 1735/36; Murray to William Ellison, July 10, 1736; Murray to Hutcheson and Grimke, November 4, 1736; Murray to Henry McCulloh, March 30, 1737; Murray to Mrs. Bennet, February 28, 1755; Murray to Barbara Clark, December 26, 1755; Murray to Mrs. Bennet, December 26, 1755; Murray to Barbara Clark, undated: James Murray Letters, MHS. On plantations and modernity, see Chaplin, *Anxious Pursuit.*

154. For an innovative, much more detailed, and valuable use of similar source materials from the seventeenth-century Chesapeake Bay region, see Carr et al., *Robert Cole's World.*

155. Because Lewis DeRosset also qualified as an executor and is not mentioned anywhere in the estate records, it seems probable that both Jones and DeRosset kept track of part of the Lower Cape Fear estate but that only Jones's records have survived.

156. This topic receives more attention in chapter 7.

157. "Gregg, Frederick," American Loyalist Claims, microfilm copies; Lower Cape Fear computer biographical files.

158. Merrens, *Colonial North Carolina,* 131.

159. Kay and Cary, *Slavery in North Carolina,* 22–25; Morgan, *Slave Counterpoint,* 95–101.

160. Brickell, *Natural History of North-Carolina,* 272.

161. George Burrington to Board of Trade, January 1, 1732/33, *Colonial Records,* 3:430.

162. For some examples, see Arthur Dobbs to Board of Trade, January 4, 1755, *Colonial Records,* 5:1:315; John Macdowell to SPG, June 15, 1762, ibid., 5:1:730; Report on the Boundary Line between North and South Carolina, December 21, 1769, 8:558–59; Scotus Americanus, "Informations Concerning North Carolina," 445–46; Schoepf, *Travels in the Confederation,* 143; Murray to William Ellison, February 14, 1735/36, in Murray, *Letters,* 24; Murray to John Murray, January 10, 1736/37, ibid., 38; Murray to Thomas Clark, December 23, 1738, ibid., 41; Murray to Henry McCulloh, May 11, 1741, ibid., 64.

163. Ira Berlin and Philip D. Morgan, "Labor and the Shaping of Slave Life in the Americas," in *Cultivation and Culture: Labor and the Shaping of Slave Life in the Americas,* ed. Berlin and Morgan (Charlottesville: University Press of Virginia, 1993), 3.

164. H. R. Merrens, ed., *The Colonial South Carolina Scene: Contemporary Views, 1697–1774* (Columbia: University of South Carolina Press, 1977), 23.

165. Carmen, *American Husbandry,* 245–46.

166. "Journal of a French Traveller," 733.

167. Because there are no detailed descriptions of slaves working in the colonial Lower Cape Fear's forest industries, details must be inferred from information about regional circumstances and from useful parallels in other places and times. These parallels fall into three categories. First, the nineteenth-century North Carolina naval-stores industry focused much more heavily on turpentine harvesting, but a fairly detailed description of the labor routine can be found in Outland, "Slavery, Work, and Geography." On slavery in antebellum North Carolina, see also Cecelski, *The Waterman's Song.* Second, in the early years of

settlement, the settlers in British colonial Honduras developed an economy based primarily on the exportation of cut wood, especially mahogany. On this topic, I have relied primarily on O. Nigel Bolland, *The Formation of a Colonial Society: Belize from Conquest to Crown Colony* (Baltimore: Johns Hopkins University Press, 1977), 53–62; and B. W. Higman, *Slave Populations of the British Caribbean, 1807–1834* (Baltimore: Johns Hopkins University Press, 1984), 177–78. Much can also be deduced from information about lumbering and sawmilling at different times and places in early America. On this topic, see esp. Michael Williams, *Americans and Their Forests,* 94–104; Hindle, *Material Culture of the Wooden Age;* and John Hebron Moore, *Andrew Brown and Cypress Lumbering in the Old Southwest* (Baton Rouge: Louisiana State University Press, 1967). On tasking, see Philip D. Morgan, "Task and Gang Systems: The Organization of Labor on New World Plantations," in *Work and Labor in Early America,* ed. Innes, 191–92.

168. This was the norm in the nineteenth century; see Outland, "Slavery, Work, and Geography," 55.

169. In more isolated Belize, about two-thirds of the cost of woodcutting operations went into clearing a path for the fallen trees; see Higman, *Slave Populations,* 177.

170. Roderick A. McDonald, "Independent Economic Production by Slaves on Antebellum Louisiana Sugar Plantations," in *Cultivation and Culture,* ed. Berlin and Morgan, 283–84.

171. James B. Avirett, *The Old Plantation: How We Lived in Great House and Cabin before the War* (New York: F. Tennyson Nelly Co., 1901), 70; Cecelski, *Waterman's Song,* 130.

172. Higman, *Slave Populations,* 177; Bolland, *Formation of a Colonial Society,* 59–61; Outland, "Slavery, Work, and Geography," 43, 46; McDonald, "Independent Economic Production," 283–84.

173. This is not intended to imply that the Lower Cape Fear had an unusually imbalanced sex ratio among its slave population, but merely that the opportunities for interaction between sexes during work would have been significantly reduced from plantation norms. On sex ratios, see chapter 3.

174. Higman, *Slave Populations,* 177.

175. Outland, "Slavery, Work, and Geography," 47–48.

176. William Logan, "William Logan's Journal of a Journey to Georgia, 1745," *Pennsylvania Magazine of History and Biography* 36 (1912): 15.

177. Brickell, *Natural History of North-Carolina,* 266.

178. Murray to Barbara Clark, December 26, 1755; Murray to Mrs. Bennet, February 28, 1755; Murray to Sarah Allen, undated: James Murray Letters, MHS; Murray to David Tullideph, March 31, 1736, in Murray, *Letters,* 27.

179. Morgan, *Slave Counterpoint,* 149.

180. Using data on the productivity of slaves in the early years of South Carolina rice cultivation, estimates of the size of barrels, and export figures from Customs 16:1, it would take slightly more than forty-two slaves, but I assume that the export data understate the total size of the crop somewhat. See Morgan, *Slave Counterpoint,* 39; and Coclanis, *Shadow of a Dream,* 99.

181. Schaw, *Journal of a Lady,* 163.

182. Outland, "Slavery, Work, and Geography," 41; Murray to Henry McCulloh, May 11, 1741, in Murray, *Letters,* 64.

183. *Cape Fear Mercury,* December 8, 1769, March 9, 1770.

184. This document does not clearly indicate whether or not the *cooper* was intended as description of an occupation or as a name; see "The Slaves of Mrs. Allen & her Computation of their Value," James Murray Robbins Papers, MHS. For one interpretation, see Kay and Cary, *Slavery in North Carolina,* 147.

185. "Gregg, Frederick," No. 3, Letter C, American Loyalist Claims.

186. The slaves' ages are not included on the list, but significantly, none of the six slaves who are unnamed or referred to as "young" or "little" had a specialized occupation.

187. Kay and Cary, *Slavery in North Carolina,* 32–34, 245; Morgan, *Slave Counterpoint,* 204–12.

188. New Hanover County Estate Inventories, North Carolina Department of Archives and History; Lower Cape Fear computer biographical files.

189. For references to these activities, see James Moir to SPG, March 26, 1745, *Colonial Records,* 4:755; Schaw, *Journal of a Lady,* 146–47, 250, 157, 176–77, 196, 204.

190. It is impossible to be precise about the frequency of this practice. Even for the antebellum United States, the hiring of slaves is an understudied topic, but the configuration of the region's economy and countless contemporary references and anecdotes indicate that the practice was especially frequent in the colonial Lower Cape Fear. For some examples from James Murray's letters, see Murray to Charles Rutherfurd, December 12, 1745; Murray to Walter Tullideph, June 23, 1736; Murray to William Guyther, December 4, 1743; Murray to Elizabeth Murray, September 4, 1749; Murray to John Murray, September 7, 1749; Murray to Richard Oswald and Co., July 19, 1756; Murray to Sarah Allen, undated; Murray to Barbara Clark, February 8, 1757: James Murray Letters, MHS.

191. Ira Berlin and Philip D. Morgan, eds., *Cultivation and Culture: Labor and the Shaping of Slave Life in the Americas* (Charlottesville: University Press of Virginia, 1993), 203–99.

192. Schaw, *Journal of a Lady,* 176–77.

193. Lennon and Kellum, *Wilmington Town Book,* 160, 165–69, 210, 226; Walker, *New Hanover County Court Minutes,* 1:102.

194. Schaw, *Journal of a Lady,* 177.

Chapter 7: Port Towns

1. William E. McCarron, ed., *A Bicentennial Edition of Thomas Godfrey's* The Prince of Parthia, A Tragedy (Colorado Springs: United States Air Force Academy, 1976), 1–5; Thomas Godfrey, *Juvenile Poems on Various Subjects with the Prince of Parthia, a Tragedy* (Philadelphia: Henry Miller, 1765), iii–xxii.

2. Godfrey, *Juvenile Poems,* 79.

3. See, for example, Murray to William Ellison, February 14, 1735/36; Murray to Henry McCulloh, November 6, 1736; Murray to Mrs. Bennet, September 19, 1749; Murray to John Murray of Philipspaugh, November 10, 1750: James Murray Letters, Massachusetts Historical Society, Boston (hereafter cited as MHS).

4. Thomas Beaman Jr., "'Some Fragments of Blue Dutch Tiling' at Brunswick Town: Decorative Delftware Tiles from Russellborough, Prospect Hall, and the Public House," *North Carolina Archaeology* 46 (1997): 23, 31.

5. Godfrey clearly intended the play for performance. While it was performed in Philadelphia after his death, there is no strong evidence to support nineteenth-century claims that the play was performed in the Lower Cape Fear region. See McCarron, *Bicentennial Edition of* The Prince of Parthia, 5.

6. For some examples of the numerous complaints about the difficulty of coastal trade in North Carolina outside of the Cape Fear, see George Burrington to duke of Newcastle, July 2, 1731, in William Saunders, ed., *The Colonial Records of North Carolina* (Raleigh: State of North Carolina, 1884–90) (hereafter cited as *Colonial Records*), 3:155; The Case of the Inhabitants of the County of Albemarle in North Carolina bordering upon his Majestys Colony of Virginia, ibid., 3:196; George Burrington to the commissioners of customs, July 20, 1736, ibid., 3:169–73; Governor Dobbs to Board of Trade, February 23, 1763, ibid., 5:1:968–69.

7. For exceptions, see Donald R. Lennon, "Development of Town Government in Colonial North Carolina," *East Carolina Publications in History* 5 (1981): 1–25; Lawrence Lee, "Old Brunswick, the Story of a Colonial Town," *North Carolina Historical Review* 29, no. 2 (April 1952): 230–45; Alan D. Watson, *Wilmington: Port of North Carolina* (Columbia: University of South Carolina Press, 1992), 3–45; Donald Lennon and Ida Brooks Kellam, eds., *The Wilmington Town Book, 1743–1778* (Raleigh: State of North Carolina, 1973), xv–xxxvii; Lawrence Lee, *The Lower Cape Fear in Colonial Days* (Chapel Hill: University of North Carolina Press, 1965), 117–44, 161–67; H. Roy Merrens, *Colonial North Carolina in the Eighteenth Century: A Study in Historical Geography* (Chapel Hill: University of North Carolina Press, 1964), 143–55; and Edwin L. Combs III, "Trading in Lubberland: Maritime Commerce in Colonial North Carolina," *North Carolina Historical Review* 80, no. 1 (2003): 1–27.

8. Works in this vein that have been particularly important for this interpretation include Jacob M. Price, "Economic Function and the Growth of American Port Towns in the Eighteenth Century," *Perspectives in American History* 8 (1974): 121–86; Carville Earle and Ronald Hoffman, "Staple Crops and Urban Development in the Eighteenth-Century South," *Perspectives in American History* 10 (1976): 5–78; Joseph Albert Ernst and H. Roy Merrens, "'Camden's Turrets Pierce the Skies': The Urban Process in the Southern Colonies during the Eighteenth Century," *William and Mary Quarterly* 30, no. 4 (1973): 549–74; James T. Lemon, "Urbanization and the Development of Eighteenth-Century Southeastern Pennsylvania and Adjacent Delaware," *William and Mary Quarterly* 24, no. 4 (1967): 501–42; Darret B. Rutman, with Anita H. Rutman, "The Village South," in Rutman, with Rutman, *Small Worlds, Large Questions: Explorations in Early American Social History, 1600–1850* (Charlottesville: University Press of Virginia, 1994), 231–72; Daniel B. Thorp, "Doing Business in the Backcountry: Retail Trade in Colonial Rowan County, North Carolina," *William and Mary Quarterly* 48, no. 3 (1991): 387–408; Daniel B. Thorp, "Taverns and Tavern Culture on the Southern Colonial Frontier: Rowan County, North Carolina, 1753–1776," *Journal of Southern History* 62, no. 4 (1996): 661–88; R. C. Nash, "Urbanization in the Colonial South: Charleston, South Carolina, as a Case Study," *Journal of Urban History* 19, no. 1 (1992): 2–29; R. C. Nash, "The Organization of Trade and Finance in the Atlantic Economy: Britain and South Carolina, 1670–1775," in *Money, Trade, and Power: The Evolution of South Carolina's Plantation Society,* ed. Jack P. Greene, Rosemary Brana-Shute, and Randy J. Sparks (Columbia: University of South Carolina Press, 2001), 74–107; Gary B. Nash, *The Urban Crucible: The Northern Seaports and the Origins of the American Revolution* (Cambridge: Harvard University Press, 1979).

9. R. C. Nash has offered some valuable correctives based on his research on colonial Charleston. See R. C. Nash, "Urbanization in the Colonial South"; idem, "Organization of Trade and Finance"; and idem, "South Carolina and the Atlantic Economy in the Late

Seventeenth and Eighteenth Centuries," *Economic History Review* 45, no. 4 (1992): 677–702.

10. Earle and Hoffman, "Staple Crops"; Price, "Economic Function."

11. The main exports from Charleston—rice, indigo, deerskins, and naval stores—went primarily to transatlantic markets, though provisions trade to the West Indies also proved valuable.

12. John Brickell, *The Natural History of North-Carolina* (Dublin, Ireland: Printed for James Carson, 1737), 8–9.

13. Hugh Meredith, *An Account of the Cape Fear Country, 1731,* ed. Earl Gregg Swem (Perth Amboy, N.J.: C. F. Heartman, 1912), 15.

14. Account of the Spanish Wreck on the Coast of North Carolina Continued [1750], *Colonial Records,* 4:1306.

15. For one example, see William Smith, Robert Halton, Matthew Rowan, and James Murray to Gabriel Johnston [1740], *Colonial Records,* 4:458.

16. Merrens, *Colonial North Carolina,* 151.

17. Lee, *Lower Cape Fear,* 162–66.

18. Murray to William Ellison, February 14, 1735/36, in James Murray, *Letters of James Murray, Loyalist,* ed. Nina M. Tiffany (Boston: Printed, not published, 1901), 24.

19. Lennon and Kellam, *Wilmington Town Book,* xxiii n. 23.

20. Gabriel Johnston to Board of Trade, March 3, 1739/40, *Colonial Records,* 4:418; William Smith, Robert Halton, Matthew Rowan, and James Murray to Governor Johnston [1740], ibid., 4:458.

21. Murray to William Ellison, February 19, 1735/36, in Murray, *Letters,* 24, 26; Murray to Henry McCulloh, July 8, 1736, ibid., 34; Murray to Henry McCulloh, January 10, 1736/37, ibid., 38.

22. George Whitefield, *George Whitefield's Journals, 1737–1741,* ed. William V. Davis (Gainesville: University of Florida Press, 1969), 377.

23. Nathaniel Rice, Eleazer Allen, Edward Moseley, and Roger Moore to the House, February 25, 1740, *Colonial Records,* 4:486.

24. Laws, in Walter Clark, ed., *The State Records of North Carolina* (Raleigh: State of North Carolina, 1890–1912) (hereafter cited as *State Records*), 23:239–43.

25. See tables 2.9 and 2.10.

26. Those persons not owning land but connected to towns include primarily individuals who were described in records as "from" or "of" the town.

27. Lower Cape Fear computer biographical files.

28. Lee, *Lower Cape Fear,* 140; Watson, *Wilmington,* 8.

29. William Mylne, *Travels in the Colonies in 1773–1775: Described in the Letters of William Mylne,* ed. Ted Ruddock (Athens: University of Georgia Press, 1993), 65.

30. Diary of Bethabara and Bethania, May 14, 1762, in Adelaide L. Fries, ed., *Records of the Moravians in North Carolina* (Raleigh, N.C.: Edwards & Broughton Printing, 1922–2000), 1:260.

31. Hugh Finlay, *Journal Kept by Hugh Finlay, Surveyor of the Post Roads on the Continent of North America, during His Survey of the Post Offices between Falmouth and Casco Bay in the Province of Massachusetts, and Savannah in Georgia; Begun the 13th September, 1773 and Ended 26th June 1774* (Brooklyn: F. H. Norton, 1867), 66; Scotus Americanus, "Informations Concerning the Province of North Carolina, Addressed to Emigrants from the Highlands

and Western Isles of Scotland," in *Some Eighteenth Century Tracts Concerning North Carolina,* ed. William K. Boyd (Raleigh: State of North Carolina, 1927), 439.

32. Mylne, *Travels in the Colonies,* 64–65.

33. Alan D. Watson, "Household Size and Composition in Pre-Revolutionary North Carolina," *Mississippi Quarterly* 31, no. 4 (1978): 554–55.

34. Janet Schaw, *The Journal of a Lady of Quality; Being the Narrative of a Journey from Scotland to the West Indies, North Carolina, and Portugal, in the Years 1774 to 1776,* ed. Evangeline W. Andrews and Charles M. Andrews (New Haven: Yale University Press, 1921), 145.

35. Ibid., 281–82.

36. Elkanah Watson, *Men and Times of the Revolution; or Memoirs of Elkanah Watson, Including Journals of His Travels in Europe and America from 1777 to 1845,* ed. Winslow C. Watson (New York: Dana, 1857), 41; Johann D. Schoepf, *Travels in the Confederation, 1783–1784, from the German of Johann David Schoepf,* trans. and ed. Alfred J. Morrison (Philadelphia: Bergman, 1911), 145; Francisco Miranda, *The New Democracy in America: Travels of Francisco de Miranda in the United States, 1783–1784,* trans. Judson P. Wood (Norman: University of Oklahoma Press, 1963), 14.

37. Naval Office Shipping Lists for South Carolina, Colonial Office 5/508–9, British Public Records Office, London. Copies of these shipping lists, along with many other documents relating to maritime commerce in colonial South Carolina, can be found in the Thomas Tobias Papers, South Carolina Historical Society, Charleston.

38. Murray to David Tullideph, January 10, 1736/37, in Murray, *Letters,* 29–30; Murray to Henry McCulloh, July 8, 1736, ibid., 34; Murray to John Murray, January 10, 1736/37, ibid., 37; Murray to Thomas Clark, December 23, 1738, ibid., 40; Murray to David Tullideph, February 21, 1735/36; Murray to John Gordon, April 5, 1765: James Murray Letters, MHS.

39. George Burrington to Board of Trade, March 1730, *Colonial Records,* 3:77; Burrington to Board of Trade, September 4, 1731, ibid., 3:210; Burrington to Board of Trade, January 1, 1732/33, ibid., 3:430; William Tryon to Lord Hyde, December 8, 1764, ibid., 5:1:1059; Josiah Martin to the earl of Dartmouth, January 12, 1776, 10:408; "A New Voyage to Georgia, By a Young Gentleman, Giving an Account of His Travels to South Carolina and Part of North Carolina . . . ," in *Collections of the Georgia Historical Society,* vol. 2 (Savannah, Ga., 1842), 56; Scotus Americanus, "Informations Concerning North Carolina," 434; Schaw, *Journal of a Lady,* 279, 282; Miranda, *New Democracy in America,* 14.

40. Hogg and Clayton to George Parker, May 5, 1765, May 9, 1764, Hogg and Clayton Letterbook, Special Collections, William R. Perkins Library, Duke University, Durham, N.C.; Christopher C. Crittenden, *The Commerce of North Carolina, 1763–1789* (New Haven: Yale University Press, 19936), 109.

41. Ettwein's Visit to Governor Tryon at Brunschwig [1766], in Fries, *Records of the Moravians,* 1:339; Murray to Henry McCulloh, May 11, 1741, in Murray, *Letters,* 64; Murray to Richard Oswald and Co., February 28, 1755, ibid., 79; Murray to Henry McCulloh, March 30, 1737: James Murray Letters, MHS; Murray to Archibald Douglas, March 4, 1742/43, ibid.; Murray to George Dunbar, January 27, 1757, ibid.

42. For the best summary of currency problems in colonial North Carolina, see Alan D. Watson, *Money and Monetary Problems in Early North Carolina* (Raleigh: State of North Carolina, 1980). For selected contemporary comments from the Lower Cape Fear, see George Burrington to the assembly, November 8, 1733, *Colonial Records,* 3:622; Schaw,

Journal of a Lady, 281; Murray to William Ellison, February 14, 1735/36, in Murray, *Letters,* 25–26; Murray to John Murray, January 10, 1736/37, ibid., 37; Murray to Richard Oswald and Co., February 28, 1755, ibid., 79; and Murray to David Tullideph, February 21, 1735/36; Murray to Henry McCulloh, March 30, 1737: James Murray Letters, MHS.

43. Murray to Richard Oswald, January 1, 1752: James Murray Letters, MHS. For two examples of South Carolina merchants complaining about the difficulty of getting payments from debtors in the Lower Cape Fear, see Henry Laurens to Roger Moore, December 14, 1747, in Henry Laurens, *The Papers of Henry Laurens,* ed. P. M. Hamer, G. C. Rogers, and D. R. Chesnutt (Columbia: University of South Carolina Press, 1968–2003), 1:88–90; Henry Laurens to James Crockatt, March 12, 1747/48, ibid., 1:120; Laurens to Roger Moore, May 28, 1748, ibid., 1:140; Laurens to Lewis DeRosset, August 4, 1755, ibid., 2:311; Robert Pringle to Thomas Clark, December 18, 1740, in Robert Pringle, *The Letterbook of Robert Pringle, 1737–1745,* ed. Walter Edgar (Columbia: University of South Carolina Press, 1972), 1:277–78; Pringle to William MacKay, January 10, 1744/45, ibid., 2:791–92.

44. Hogg and Clayton to Burrough, Sealy, and Hudson, August 5, 1767, Hogg and Clayton Letterbook.

45. Murray to Henry McCulloh, undated: James Murray Letters, MHS. For some interesting parallels in the North Carolina backcountry, see Thorp, "Doing Business in the Backcountry," 392, 405–7.

46. *Cape Fear Mercury,* December 8, 1769, March 9, 1770, September 23, 1773.

47. Matters relating to transportation are discussed more fully in chapter 4. See George Burrington to Board of Trade, March 1730, *Colonial Records,* 3:77; diary of Bishop Spangenberg, September 13, 1752, ibid., 5:3.

48. Murray to William Rutherford, July 10, 1732: James Murray Letters, MHS; Murray to Thomas Clark, December 23, 1738, in Murray, *Letters,* 40.

49. David Hancock, *Citizens of the World: London Merchants and the Integration of the British Atlantic Community, 1735–1785* (Cambridge: Cambridge University Press, 1995), 125, 127, 128–30, 139; James Murray to John Murray of Philipspaugh, July 27, 1749; Murray to Elizabeth Dunbar, January 26, 1750; Murray, November 6, 1752; Murray to Richard Oswald, July 19, 1756; Murray to Sarah Allen, undated; James Murray to John Murray, February 9, 1757: James Murray Letters, MHS.

50. Hogg and Clayton to Grubb and Watson, September 10, 1764, Hogg and Clayton Letterbook.

51. Henry Laurens to James Crokatt, June 10, 1748, in Laurens, *Papers,* 1:145; Laurens to William Moore, July 30, 1748, ibid., 1:164–65; Laurens to Lewis DeRosset, May 8, 1764, ibid., 4:273; Laurens to Hugh Porter, February 5, 1766, ibid., 5:68; Laurens to Hogg and Clayton, October 25, 1767, ibid., 5:376.

52. Robert Pringle to Daniel Dunbibin, September 25, 1742, in Pringle, *Letterbook,* 1:419.

53. Robert Pringle to James Innes, May 17, 1739, in Pringle, *Letterbook,* 1:95; Pringle to Robert Walker, August 22, 1739, ibid., 1:128; Pringle to Walker, August 25, 1739, ibid., 1:129; Pringle to William Faris, August 1, 1740, ibid., 1:234–35; Pringle to Thomas Clark, August 1, 1740, ibid., 1:277–78; Pringle to Daniel Dunbibin, February 26, 1740/41, ibid., 1:297; Pringle to Daniel Dunbibin, February 19, 1741/42, ibid., 1:326; Pringle to William Lithgow, June 28, 1742, ibid., 1:384; Pringle to Daniel Dunbibin, September 7, 1742, ibid.,

1:410–11; Pringle to Dunbibin, September 25, 1742, ibid., 1:419; Pringle to Thomas Clark, March 9, 1742/43, ibid., 2:522; Pringle to Dunbibin, May 21, 1743, ibid., 2:557; Pringle to William MacKay, January 10, 1744/45, ibid., 2:791–92; Henry Laurens to Richard Grubb, November 21, 1747, in Laurens, *Papers,* 1:84; Henry Laurens to Roger Moore, December 14, 1747, ibid., 1:88–90; Laurens to James Crokatt, March 5, 1747/48, ibid., 1:120; Laurens to Roger Moore, May 28, 1748, ibid., 1:140; Laurens to James Crokatt, June 10, 1748, ibid., 1:145; Laurens to William Moore, July 30, 1748, ibid., 1:164–65; Laurens to Lewis DeRosset, August 4, 1755, ibid., 1:311; Laurens to Richard Smith, April 9, 1756, ibid., 2:153; Laurens to Henry Bright, May 17, 1756, ibid., 2:185; Laurens to James Innes, May 19, 1757, ibid., 2:495; Laurens to John Rutherford, May 8, 1764, ibid., 4:271–72; Laurens to Lewis DeRosset, ibid., 4:273; Laurens to Abraham Parsons, September 14, 1764, ibid., 4:425; Laurens to Hugh Porter, February 5, 1766, ibid., 5:68; Laurens to Hogg and Clayton, October 25, 1767, ibid., 5:376; Laurens to Reynolds, Getly and Co., December 18, 1773, ibid., 9:203; Laurens to Robert Hogg, January 4, 1774, ibid., 9:218; and John Guerrard to Cornelius Harnett, May 24, 1752; Guerrard to Harnett, June 10, 1752; Guerrard to Harnett, January 20, 1753; Guerrard to Harnett, October 23, 1753; Guerrard to Harnett, June 15, 1753; Guerrard to Harnett, January 9, 1753; Guerrard to Harnett, March 9, 1753: John Guerrard Letterbook, South Carolina Historical Society.

54. Gary M. Walton and James F. Shepherd, *Shipping, Maritime Trade, and the Economic Development of Colonial North America* (Cambridge: Cambridge University Press, 1972), 51.

55. Murray to Henry McCulloh, July 8, 1736, in Murray, *Letters,* 34; Murray to Hutchinson and Grimke, July 14, 1736; Murray to Hutchinson and Grimke, December 18, 1738; Murray to Henry McCulloh, July 4, 1739; Murray to Hutchinson and Grimke, September 1, 1739; Murray to Henry Howson, December 27, 1740; Murray to James Rutherford, undated; Murray to William Dunbar, July 24, 1749: James Murray Letters, MHS.

56. Murray to William Dunbar, July 24, 1749; Murray to Richard Oswald, December 12, 1749; Murray to Rev. Mr. Hooper, March 18, 1750/51: James Murray Letters, MHS.

57. Lower Cape Fear computer biographical files.

58. Crittenden, *Commerce of North Carolina,* 105; Walton and Shepherd, *Shipping,* 122–23.

59. R. C. Nash, "Organization of Trade and Finance," 81.

60. Enumerated goods could also not be exported to Ireland, which obtained another 2 percent of the region's export value, despite entreaties from Arthur Dobbs to open trade from North Carolina to Ireland. See Arthur Dobbs to Lord Halifax, January 14, 1764, *Colonial Records,* 5:1:1022; Arthur Dobbs to Board of Trade, March 29, 1764, ibid., 5:1:1030.

61. On the pros and cons of these marketing methods, see R. C. Nash, "Urbanization in the Colonial South," 11–21; Price, "Economic Function," 165–68, 173–74; Walton and Shepherd, *Shipping,* 51; John J. McCusker and Russell R. Menard, *The Economy of British America, 1607–1789* (Chapel Hill: University of North Carolina Press, 1985), 79–80.

62. R. C. Nash, "Organization of Trade and Finance," 81. For some Lower Cape Fear examples, see the invoices for cargoes of naval stores that Robert Hogg and Samuel Campbell consigned to London merchants, February 3, 1773, March 16, 1773, March 24, 1773, Hogg and Campbell Daybook, 1772–73, William R. Perkins Library, Duke University, Durham, N.C. For additional examples from throughout the Carolinas, see Robert Pringle to Thomas Clark, December 18, 1740, in Pringle, *Letterbook,* 1:277–78; Robert Pringle to Thomas Clark, March 9, 1742/43, ibid., 2:502; Henry Laurens to Lewis DeRosset, August

4, 1755, in Laurens, *Papers,* 1:311; Thomas Pollock Letterbook, August 3, 1714, July 6, 1717, Pollock Family Papers, North Carolina Department of Archives and History, Raleigh; Hogg and Clayton to Grubb and Watson, September 10, 1764, Hogg and Clayton Letterbook.

63. Crittenden, *Commerce of North Carolina,* 97.

64. Price, "Economic Function," 173.

65. Murray to William Rutherford, June 10, 1732, Murray to William Dunbar, July 24, 1749, Murray to Richard Oswald, December 12, 1749, Murray to Rev. Mr. Hooper, March 18, 1750/51: James Murray Letters, MHS.

66. Scotus Americanus, "Informations Concerning North Carolina," 440; George Burrington to the assembly, November 8, 1733, *Colonial Records,* 3:622.

67. Bethabara Diary, August 14, 1754, May 29, 1755, August 18, 1755, December 1, 1756, December 19, 1756, August 18, 1759, November 28, 1759, January 17, 1768, January 17, 1776, January 27, 1776, in Fries, *Records of the Moravians,* 1:105, 127, 136, 173, 174, 212, 214, 377; 2:1103–4; Bethabara Memorabilia, July 7, 1755, ibid., 1:121; Memorabilia of Outward Affairs, November 1756, ibid., 1:160; Wachovia Diary, January 3, 1757, April 19, 1767, November 22, 1767, ibid., 1:179, 352, 356; Diary of Bethabara and Bethania, January 23, 1762, May 14, 1762, ibid., 1:247, 260; Memorabilia of Bethabara and Bethania, 1763, ibid., 1:266; Visitors to Bethabara, January 19, 1765, March 25, 1765, ibid., 1:307; Ettwein's Visit to Governor William Tryon at Brunshwig, ibid., 1:338–39; Bishop Spangenberg to Count von Zinzindorff, June 11, 1760, ibid., 1:540; Merrens, *Colonial North Carolina,* 164–66; Lee, *Lower Cape Fear,* 172–78; Watson, *Wilmington,* 20–21; Daniel B. Thorp, *The Moravian Community in Colonial North Carolina: Pluralism on the Southern Frontier* (Knoxville: University of Tennessee Press, 1989), 134–38.

68. Robert Hunter Jr., *Quebec to Carolina in 1785–1786: Being the Travel Diary and Observations of Robert Hunter, Jr., a Young Merchant of London,* ed. Louis B. Wright and Marion Tinling (San Marino, Calif.: Huntington Library, 1943), 288.

69. Schaw, *Journal of a Lady,* 156.

70. Scotus Americanus, "Informations Concerning North Carolina," 440.

71. Kenneth W. Robinson, "Port Brunswick and the Colonial Naval Stores Industry: Historical and Archaeological Observations," *North Carolina Archaeology* 46 (1997): 65.

72. Lennon and Kellam, *Wilmington Town Book,* 72, 79, 94, 97, 118, 123, 146, 180.

73. *Cape Fear Mercury,* September 23, 1773.

74. Session Papers, December 1767 to January 1768, Bills, General Assembly Records, North Carolina Department of Archives and History, Raleigh; Laws, *State Records,* 23:748.

75. On the inspection of commodities in colonial North Carolina, see Laws, *State Records,* 23:443, 639–54, 748; 25:313–19.

76. Scotus Americanus, "Informations Concerning North Carolina," 449.

77. The terms *artisans* and *craftsmen* here include such occupational descriptions as baker, blacksmith, bricklayer, brick maker, cabinetmaker, carpenter, chair maker, cooper, cordwainer, goldsmith, house carpenter, housewright, ironmonger, jeweler, joiner, millwright, periwig maker, printer, saddler, sailmaker, ship carpenter, shipwright, shoemaker, silversmith, tailor, tanner, and watchmaker.

78. This was true for eighteen of twenty-four occupations. The exceptions were blacksmith, bricklayer or brick maker, cooper, millwright, saddler, and shoemaker.

79. Lower Cape Fear computer biographical files.

80. Ibid. This was true of twelve out of twenty-four categories, including baker, cabinetmaker, chair maker, goldsmith, ironmonger, jeweler, joiner, periwig maker, printer, sailmaker, silversmith, and watchmaker.

81. Jean B. Russo, "Self-Sufficiency and Local Exchange: Free Craftsmen in the Rural Chesapeake Economy," in *Colonial Chesapeake Society,* ed. Lois Green Carr, Philip D. Morgan, and Jean B. Russo (Chapel Hill: University of North Carolina Press, 1988), 429–32.

82. Merrens also makes this point in *Colonial North Carolina,* 145.

83. The manuscript sources in this analysis of Hogg's business include the following: Robert Hogg Journal, Wilmington, 1767–72, Southern History Collection, Chapel Hill, N.C.; Robert Hogg Ledger, Wilmington, 1767–72, ibid.; Invoice Outward, Hogg and Campbell, Wilmington, 1767–82, North Carolina Department of Archives and History, Raleigh; Hogg and Clayton Letterbook, Charleston, 1762–71, Hogg and Campbell Daybook, 1772–73, William R. Perkins Library, Duke University, Durham, N.C.

84. Another brief analysis of Hogg's business activities in the Lower Cape Fear region has been published recently in Combs, "Trading in Lubberland," 16–19, 21. My interpretation differs from Combs's in several important respects. First, Combs focuses almost exclusively on Hogg's correspondence in the Hogg and Clayton Letterbook and on the Hogg Wilmington store accounts. An examination of other sources, such as the Hogg and Campbell Invoice Outward and the Hogg and Campbell Daybook, reveals that Hogg's business activities were more complex than these other sources suggest. Second, Combs treats the economic activities described in Hogg's accounts as typical of Lower Cape Fear maritime trade. While Hogg seems to have run his store in a typical fashion for the region, he clearly did not participate in naval stores and other export trades in the same ways as other Lower Cape Fear merchants did. For example, an unusually high proportion of the voyages described in these sources was coastwise and reveals little about the large-scale trade between the Lower Cape Fear and the British Isles. According to these accounts, Hogg also only exported small quantities of naval stores, making his participation in the largest naval-stores export economy in North America marginal and atypical. Of course, Hogg may have participated in more large-scale exportations of naval stores and other Lower Cape Fear commodities to the British Isles, perhaps in conjunction with Samuel Campbell, Francis Clayton, or others, but it is impossible to know this from the surviving Wilmington store account books.

85. On Robert Hogg and his business, see Merrens, *Colonial North Carolina,* 153; Crittenden, *Commerce of North Carolina,* 96; and Schaw, *Journal of a Lady,* 180, 323–35.

86. A full analysis of all the volumes of material related to Robert Hogg's business accounts and partnerships lies beyond the scope of this study.

87. By contrast, surviving accounts from the years that James Murray ran a shop in the region suggest a heavy dependence on business associates beyond North Carolina. Only twelve of the forty-five names, or roughly one-quarter, could be traced to the Lower Cape Fear. This may indicate that in the earliest years of settlement, local trade remained simplistic and limited. On the other hand, it may merely be indicative of which Murray records happened to survive. Murray probably had other, more detailed records related to local transactions; see also Account Book, 1732–49, James Murray Accounts, MHS.

88. The 106 taxables came from 42 households. New Hanover County households listed on the 1755 tax list averaged 1.5 white taxables. If the Wilmington households followed the same trend, the 42 households would account for 63 white taxables, leaving only

43 black taxables. While this relies on a certain amount of continuity between different cultural settings, the average number of white taxables, who by definition had to be adult males, probably remained fairly constant from place to place. Following the ratios of taxables to nontaxables of 1.89 for whites and 4.1 for blacks suggested by Kay and Cary, this calculation would yield estimated populations of 258 whites and 81 blacks. See Marvin Michael Kay and Lorin Lee Cary, *Slavery in North Carolina, 1748–1775* (Chapel Hill: University of North Carolina Press, 1995), 221–25.

89. Philip D. Morgan, *Slave Counterpoint: Black Culture in the Eighteenth-Century Chesapeake and Lowcountry* (Chapel Hill: University of North Carolina Press, 1998), 663–64.

90. Based on his footnote, Morgan may be referring to the population figures in the federal census of 1802, when this claim may have been accurate, but the passage is unclear about timing; see Morgan, *Slave Counterpoint,* 663–64.

91. Archaeological evidence provides one exception. African American colonoware pottery, which was probably made and utilized by slaves, has been found at the Brunswick site. These ceramics may have been manufactured on nearby plantations. See Thomas C. Loftfield and Michael Stoner, "Brunswick Town Colonowares Re-examined," *North Carolina Archaeology* 47 (1997): 12.

92. For valuable insight into this process in one city, see T. Stephen Whitman, *The Price of Freedom: Slavery and Manumission in Baltimore and Early National Maryland* (Lexington: University Press of Kentucky, 1997). Michael P. Johnson and James L. Roark, *Black Masters: A Free Family of Color in the Old South* (New York: W. W. Norton, 1984) also bears much relevance to this topic.

93. Alan D. Watson, *Society in Colonial North Carolina* (Raleigh: State of North Carolina, 1986), 9–10, 21, 39–40.

94. Ira Berlin, *Many Thousands Gone: The First Two Centuries of Slavery in North America* (Cambridge: Harvard University Press, 1998), 154–57; Whitman, *Price of Freedom,* 61–92; Philip D. Morgan, "Black Life in Eighteenth-Century Charleston," *Perspectives in American History* 1 (1984): 187–232.

95. Lennon and Kellam, *Wilmington Town Book,* 148, 166, 204–5.

96. Robert Olwell, *Masters, Slaves, and Subjects: The Culture of Power in the South Carolina Low Country, 1740–1790* (Ithaca, N.Y.: Cornell University Press, 1998), 174.

97. Ibid., 167–78.

98. Lennon and Kellam, *Wilmington Town Book,* 160, 163, 164, 165, 204, 209, 210, 226.

99. Proceedings of the Wilmington Safety Committee, August 17, 1775, *Colonial Records,* 10:159.

100. Schaw, *Journal of a Lady,* 169–70; Lennon and Kellam, *Wilmington Town Book,* 197.

101. Lennon and Kellam, *Wilmington Town Book,* 148, 160, 165–69, 187, 204–5, 209, 226.

102. Ibid., 197, 204.

103. Alexander M. Walker, ed., *New Hanover County Court Minutes, 1738–1785* (Bethesda, Md.: A. M. Walker, 1958–59), 1:77.

104. Lower Cape Fear computer biographical files.

105. J. F. D. Smyth, *A Tour in the United States of America* (London: G. Robinson, 1784), 169–70.

Epilogue: Region, Revolution, and Nation

1. For a study that illustrates the localized character of the revolutionary conflict, see Albert H. Tillson, "The Localist Roots of Backcountry Loyalism: An Examination of

Popular Political Culture in Virginia's New River Valley," *Journal of Southern History* 54, no. 3 (1988): 387–404.

2. This is not intended to imply that the Lower Cape Fear settlers had not experienced violent conflict. Some had fought in the Seven Years' War and other conflicts, and a small Spanish invasion devastated Brunswick in 1748.

3. On the Battle of Moore's Creek Bridge, see, among others, Hugh F. Rankin, "The Moore's Creek Bridge Campaign, 1776," *North Carolina Historical Review* 30, no. 1 (1953): 23–60; Wayne E. Lee, *Crowds and Soldiers in Revolutionary North Carolina: The Culture of Violence in Riot and War* (Gainesville: University of Florida Press, 2001), 152–56; and Lawrence Lee, *The Lower Cape Fear in Colonial Days* (Chapel Hill: University of North Carolina Press, 1965), 264–69.

4. William Purviance to provincial council, February 23, 1776, in Walter Clark, ed., *The State Records of North Carolina* (Goldsboro: State of North Carolina, 1895–1905) (hereafter cited as *State Records*), 10:466–67.

5. Extract from a letter, dated North Carolina, March 10, 1776, *State Records,* 11:286.

6. On the Loyalists, see Robert M. Calhoon, *The Loyalists in Revolutionary America, 1760–1781* (New York: Harcourt Brace Jovanovich, 1973); Robert O. Demond, *The Loyalists in North Carolina during the Revolution* (Durham, N.C.: Duke University Press, 1940); and Carole Watterson Troxler, *The Loyalist Experience in North Carolina* (Raleigh: State of North Carolina, 1976).

7. See, for example, John Ashe to Governor Caswell, July 28, 1777, *State Records,* 11:546.

8. General Alexander Lillington to Governor Caswell, July 5, 1779, *State Records,* 14:140–41.

9. The most thorough description of British military activity in the region during 1781 can be found in Gregory De Van Massey, "The British Expedition to Wilmington, January–November, 1781," *North Carolina Historical Review* 66, no. 4 (1989): 387–411.

10. From General Alexander Lillington, March 21, 1781, in Nathanael Greene, *The Papers of General Nathanael Greene,* ed. Richard K. Showman et al. (Chapel Hill: University of North Carolina Press, 1976–2002), 7:457.

11. Ibid.

12. Ibid.; From George Fletcher, May 6, 1781, ibid., 8:214; Statement of John Montgomery, *State Records,* 22:152; Archibald MacLaine to Governor Thomas Burke, June 30, 1781, ibid., 22:537; Governor Thomas Burke to unidentified, October 17, 1781, ibid., 15:654; Robert Rowan to Nathanael Greene, April 18, 1781, Nathanael Greene Papers, 20:27, William L. Clements Library, Ann Arbor, Mich.

13. Governor Josiah Martin to Mrs. Anne Hooper and others, June 1782, *State Records,* 16:337; Senate Journal, 1790, ibid., 21:829; letter to Governor Alexander Martin, December 19, 1781, ibid., 22:602; Major Craig to Governor Abner Nash, June 20, 1781, ibid., 22:1023–25.

14. Sir Henry Clinton to Lord Rawdon, June 6, 1781, Sir Henry Clinton Papers, 162:6, William L. Clements Library.

15. From Governor Thomas Burke, North Carolina, August 31, 1781, in Greene, *Papers of Nathanael Greene,* 9:272; Governor Thomas Burke to General Alexander Lillington, February 2, 1782, *State Records,* 16:182; Governor Thomas Burke to General Alexander Lillington, February 27, 1782, ibid., 16:528.

16. Major Craig to William Hooper, July 20, 1781, *State Records,* 15:553–54; Major Craig to Governor Abner Nash, June 20, 1781, ibid., 22:1024–25; Governor Thomas Burke to Major Craig, June 27, 1781, ibid., 22:1026–28.

17. To Colonel Stephen Dayton, March 28, 1781, in Greene, *Papers of Nathanael Greene,* 7:475; Robert Rowan to Nathanael Greene, May 5, 1781, Nathanael Greene Papers, 20:27; Colonel Nathan Bryan to Governor Thomas Burke, September 6, 1781, *State Records,* 15:634–35; Extract from minutes of New Hanover Superior Court, October Term, 1832, ibid., 15:786; William Hooper to James Iredell, February 13, 1781, in James Iredell, *The Papers of James Iredell,* ed. Don Higginbotham (Raleigh: State of North Carolina, 1976), 2:207–9.

18. See Jeffrey J. Crow, *The Black Experience in Revolutionary North Carolina* (Raleigh: State of North Carolina, 1977); Sylvia Frey, *Water from the Rock: Black Resistance in a Revolutionary Age* (Princeton, N.J.: Princeton University Press, 1991).

19. Robert Rowan to Nathanael Greene, May 5, 1781, Nathanael Greene Papers, 20:27; Alfred Moore Waddell, *A History of New Hanover County and the Lower Cape Fear Region, 1723–1800* (Wilmington, N.C.: Printed, not published, 1909), 186; Massey, "British Expedition to Wilmington," 394.

20. Lee, *Lower Cape Fear,* 273.

21. For accounts of Murray's activities in New England, see Patricia Cleary, *Elizabeth Murray: A Woman's Pursuit of Independence in Eighteenth-Century America* (Amherst: University of Massachusetts Press, 2000), 98–99, 102–4, 111, 206, 208–9; and James Murray, *Letters of James Murray, Loyalist,* ed. Nina M. Tiffany (Boston: Printed, not published, 1901), 150–289.

22. See Edward J. Cashin, *William Bartram and the American Revolution on the Southern Frontier* (Columbia: University of South Carolina Press, 2000).

23. On Harnett, see Alan D. Watson et al., *Harnett, Hooper, and Howe: Revolutionary Leaders of the Lower Cape Fear* (Wilmington, N.C.: Lower Cape Fear Historical Society, 1979), 3–31.

24. See, for example, Peter S. Onuf, *The Origins of the Federal Republic: Jurisdictional Controversies in the United States, 1775–1787* (Philadelphia: University of Pennsylvania Press, 1983).

25. On the enduring cultural distinctiveness of the Lower Cape Fear region, see Janet K. Seapker, ed., *Time, Talent, Tradition: Five Essays on the Cultural History of the Lower Cape Fear Region, North Carolina* (Wilmington, N.C.: Cape Fear Museum, 1995).

BIBLIOGRAPHY

Primary Sources—Manuscripts and Microfilms

North Carolina Department of Archives and History, Raleigh

New Hanover County

Appointment of County Officials, 1774–75
Coroner's Records, 1768–75
County Court Execution Dockets, 1758–70
County Court Minutes, 1738–81
County Court Reference Dockets, 1750–56
County Court Trial Dockets, 1771–75
Estate Records, 1741–76
Miscellaneous Land Records, 1748–76
Miscellaneous Records, 1756–75
Officials' Bonds and Records, 1766–76
Real Estate Conveyances, 1734–75
Superior Court Civil Action Papers, 1758–76
Wills, 1734–80

Brunswick County

Real Estate Conveyances, 1764–75
Wills, 1764–80

Private Collections

Arthur Dobbs Papers
MacAllister Papers
Louis T. Moore Collection
James Murray Papers
Phillips Manuscripts
Pollock Family Papers
Colin Shaw Papers
Slavery Collection
John Walker Papers

General

Audit Office Papers, Class 12, vols. 13, 36, 117–20
Colonial Court Records
General Assembly Session Records
Invoice Outward, Hogg and Campbell, Wilmington, 1767–82
North Carolina Higher Court Records, 1730–76
Port of Brunswick Records, Shipping Register, 1765–75 (box 7); Return of Exports, 1775, 1785 (box 8)
Secretary of State Papers, Quitrent Records

Secretary of State Papers, Tax Lists, 1720–1839. Microfilm
Treasurers' and Comptrollers' Papers, Tax Lists in County Settlements with the State. Microfilm
Wilmington Superior Court Minutes, 1760–75

Southern History Collection, Chapel Hill, North Carolina

Manuscripts

DeRosset Family Papers
Cornelius Harnett Letters
Hayes Collection, Johnston Series
Robert Hogg Account Books
Robert Howe Papers
Fanning McCulloh Papers
Henry Bacon McKoy Collection
Strudwick Family Papers

William R. Perkins Library of Duke University, Durham, North Carolina

Manuscripts

Hogg and Campbell Daybook, 1772–73. 1 vol.
Hogg and Clayton Letterbook and Accounts, 1762–71. 1 vol.

Library of Congress, Manuscripts Division, Washington, D.C.

General

An Account of the Number of Ships Entering in and Clearing from the Several Ports in North Carolina for the Years 1739 and 1740. British Museum Additional Manuscripts, no. 33028, folio 400. Transcript
British Public Records Office. Photostatic copies
Customs 16: Accounts, Ledgers of Imports and Exports, 1768–73, 282 folios
Fulham Palace Papers
Records of the Society for the Propagation of the Gospel in Foreign Parts

Massachusetts Historical Society, Boston

Manuscripts

James Murray Account Books
James Murray Letterbooks
James Murray Robbins Papers

South Carolina Historical Society, Charleston

Manuscripts

John Guerrard Letterbook
Thomas Tobias Papers

William L. Clements Library, Ann Arbor, Michigan

Manuscripts

Sir Henry Clinton Papers
Lord Germain Papers
Nathanael Greene Papers
William Henry Lyttleton Papers

Primary Sources: Published Record Collections

Bradley, Stephen E., Jr. *Early Records of North Carolina from the Secretary of State Papers.* Keysville, Va.: S. E. Bradley, 1992.

Cain, Robert J., ed. *The Colonial Records of North Carolina.* 2nd series. Raleigh: State of North Carolina, 1963– .

Clark, Walter. *The State Records of North Carolina.* Goldsboro: State of North Carolina, 1895–1905.

Easterby, J. H., ed. *The Colonial Records of South Carolina.* Columbia: State of South Carolina, 1951– .

Fries, Adelaide L., ed. *Records of the Moravians in North Carolina.* Raleigh, N.C.: Edwards & Broughton Printing, 1922–64.

Grimes, Bryan J., ed. *Abstracts of North Carolina Wills.* Raleigh, N.C.: Edwards & Broughton Printing, 1910.

———, ed. *North Carolina Wills and Inventories, Copied from the Original and Recorded Wills and Inventories in the Office of the Secretary of State.* Raleigh, N.C.: Edwards & Broughton Printing, 1912.

Hofmann, Margaret, ed. *Colony of North Carolina: Abstracts of Land Patents, 1735–1775.* 2 vols. Weldon, N.C.: Roanoke News Co., 1982, 1984.

———, ed. *Province of North Carolina: Abstracts of Land Patents, 1663–1729.* Weldon, N.C.: Roanoke News Co., 1979.

Kellam, Ida Brooks, and Elizabeth Francenia McKoy, eds. *St. James Church, Wilmington, North Carolina, Historical Records, 1737–1852.* Wilmington, N.C.: I. B. Kellam, 1965.

Lennon, Donald, and Ida Brooks Kellam, eds. *The Wilmington Town Book, 1743–1778.* Raleigh: State of North Carolina, 1973.

Newsome, A. R. "Records of Emigrants from England and Scotland to North Carolina, 1774–5." *North Carolina Historical Review* 11, no. 2 (1934): 39–53, 129–43.

Records in the British Public Records Office Relating to South Carolina. Microfilm transcripts.

Saunders, William L., Stephen B. Weeks, and Walter Clark, eds. *The Colonial and State Records of North Carolina.* Raleigh: State of North Carolina, 1886–1912.

Paul H. Smith, ed. *Letters of the Delegates to Congress.* Washington, D.C.: Library of Congress, 1976–2000.

Walker, Alexander M., ed. *New Hanover County Court Minutes, 1738–1785.* Bethesda, Md.: A. M. Walker, 1958–59.

Windley, Lathan A., ed. *Runaway Slave Advertisements: A Documentary History from the 1730s to 1790.* Westport, Conn.: Greenwood Press, 1983.

Pre-1776 Newspapers

Cape Fear Mercury
North Carolina Gazette
North Carolina Magazine or Universal Intelligencer
South Carolina and American Gazette
South Carolina Gazette
South Carolina Gazette and Country Journal

Primary Sources: Published Writings

Abercromby, James. *The Letterbook of James Abercromby Colonial Agent, 1751–1773.* Edited by John C. Van Horne and George Reese. Richmond: Virginia Library and Archives, 1991.

Avery, Waightstill. "The Diary of Waightstill Avery." *North Carolina University Magazine,* 2nd ser., 4 (1885): 242–64.

Avirett, James B. *The Old Plantation: How We Lived in Great House and Cabin before the War.* New York: F. Tennyson Nelly Co., 1901.

Bartram, John. *The Correspondence of John Bartram, 1734–1777.* Edited by Edmund and Dorothy Smith Berkeley. Gainesville: University of Florida Press, 1992.

———. "Diary of a Journey through the Carolinas, Georgia, and Florida, from July 1, 1765, to April 10, 1766." Annotated by Francis Harper. *Transactions of the American Philosophic Society,* n.s., 33, part 1 (December 1942).

Bartram, William. *The Travels of William Bartram: Naturalist's Edition.* Edited by Francis Harper. New Haven: Yale University Press, 1958.

Battle, Kemp, ed. *Letter and Documents, Relating to the Early History of the Lower Cape Fear.* Volume 4 of *James Sprunt Historical Monographs.* Chapel Hill: University of North Carolina Press, 1903.

Blount, John Gray. *The John Gray Blount Papers.* Vol. 1. Edited by Alice Barnwell Keith. Raleigh: State of North Carolina, 1952.

Boyd, William K., ed. *William Byrd's Histories of the Dividing Line betwixt Virginia and North Carolina.* New York: Dover, 1967.

Brickell, John. *The Natural History of North-Carolina.* Dublin, Ireland: Printed for James Carson, 1737. Reprint, Raleigh, N.C.: Trustees of the Public Libraries, 1911.

Carmen, Harry J., ed. *American Husbandry.* New York: Columbia University Press, 1939.

Catesby, Mark. *The Natural History of Carolina, Florida, and the Bahama Islands.* London: B. White, 1771.

Cheney, John L., Jr. *North Carolina Government, 1585–1974: A Narrative and Statistical History.* Raleigh: State of North Carolina, 1975.

Commerce of Rhode Island, 1726–1774. In *Collections of the Massachusetts Historical Society,* 7th series, 9. Boston: [Massachusetts Historical Society], 1914.

Crevecoeur, J. Hector St. John de. *Letters of an American Farmer and Sketches of Eighteenth-Century America.* Edited by Albert E. Stone. New York: Penguin Books, 1981.

Doggett, Samuel B., ed. "A Plantation on Prince George's Creek, Cape Fear, North Carolina." *New-England Historical and Genealogical Register* 52 (1898): 469–73.

Finlay, Hugh. *Journal Kept by Hugh Finlay, Surveyor of the Post Roads on the Continent of North America, during His Survey of the Post Offices between Falmouth and Casco Bay in the Province of Massachusetts, and Savannah in Georgia; Begun the 13th September, 1773 and Ended 26th June 1774.* Brooklyn: F. H. Norton, 1867.

Godfrey, Thomas. *Juvenile Poems on Various Subjects with The Prince of Parthia, A Tragedy.* Philadelphia: Henry Miller, 1765.

Gordon, Lord Adam. "Journal of an Officer's Travels in America and the West Indies, 1764–1765." In *Travels in the American Colonies,* edited by Newton D. Merreness, 367–453. New York: Antiquarian Press, 1916.

Greene, Nathanael. *The Papers of General Nathanael Greene.* Edited by Richard K. Showman et al. Chapel Hill: University of North Carolina Press, 1976–2002.

Hunter, Robert, Jr. *Quebec to Carolina in 1785–1786: Being the Travel Diary and Observations of Robert Hunter, Jr., a Young Merchant of London.* Edited by Louis B. Wright and Marion Tinling. San Marino, Calif.: Huntington Library, 1943.

Iredell, James. *The Papers of James Iredell.* Vol. 1. Edited by Don Higginbotham. Raleigh: State of North Carolina, 1976.

"Journal of a French Traveller in the Colonies, 1765, I." *American Historical Review* 26 (July 1921): 726–47.

Laurens, Henry. *The Papers of Henry Laurens.* Edited by P. M. Hamer, G. C. Rogers, and D. R. Chesnutt. Columbia: University of South Carolina Press, 1968–2003.

Lawson, John. *A New Voyage to North Carolina.* Edited by Hugh T. Lefler. Chapel Hill: University of North Carolina Press, 1967.

Lemmon, Sarah McCulloh, ed. *The Pettigrew Papers.* Vol. 1. Raleigh: State of North Carolina, 1971.

Logan, William. "William Logan's Journal of a Journey to Georgia, 1745." *Pennsylvania Magazine of History and Biography* 36 (1912): 1–16.

McCulloh, Henry. "Miscellaneous Representatives Relative to Our Concerns in America." In *Some Eighteenth Century Tracts Concerning North Carolina,* edited by William K. Boyd, 141–56. Raleigh: State of North Carolina, 1927.

Meredith, Hugh. *An Account of the Cape Fear Country, 1731.* Edited by Earl Gregg Swem. Perth Amboy, N.J.: C. F. Heartman, 1912.

Miranda, Francisco. *The New Democracy in America: Travels of Francisco de Miranda in the United States, 1783–1784.* Translated by Judson P. Wood. Norman: University of Oklahoma Press, 1963.

Moore, Maurice. "Justice and Policy of Taxing the American Colonies in England." In *Some Eighteenth Century Tracts Concerning North Carolina,* edited by William K. Boyd, 157–74. Raleigh: State of North Carolina, 1927.

Murray, James. *Letters of James Murray, Loyalist.* Edited by Nina M. Tiffany. Boston: Printed, not published, 1901.

Mylne, William. *Travels in the Colonies in 1773–1775: Described in the Letters of William Mylne.* Edited by Ted Ruddock. Athens: University of Georgia Press, 1993.

Nairne, Thomas. "A Letter from South Carolina." In *Selling a New World: Two Colonial South Carolina Promotional Pamphlets,* edited by Jack P. Greene, 33–73. Columbia: University of South Carolina Press, 1989.

"A New Voyage to Georgia, By a Young Gentleman, Giving an Account of His Travels to South Carolina, and Part of North Carolina. . . ." In *Collections of the Georgia Historical Society,* vol. 2, 37–66. Savannah, Ga., 1840–1916.

The Present State of the British Empire. London: B. Law, 1768.

Pringle, Robert. *The Letterbook of Robert Pringle, 1737–1745.* Edited by Walter Edgar. Columbia: University of South Carolina Press, 1972.

Quincy, Josiah, Jr. "The Southern Journal of Josiah Quincy, Junior, 1773." *Massachusetts Historical Society Proceedings* (October 1915–June 1916): 69, 424–81.

Rankin, Richard, ed. "'Musquetoe' Bites: Caricatures of Lower Cape Fear Whigs and Tories on the Eve of the American Revolution." *North Carolina Historical Review* 65 (April 1988): 173–207.

Rutherford, John. "The Importance of the Colonies to Great Britain." In *Some Eighteenth Century Tracts Concerning North Carolina,* edited by William K. Boyd, 107–38. Raleigh: State of North Carolina, 1927.

Salley, Alexander S., Jr., ed. *Narratives of Early Carolina, 1650–1708.* New York: Charles Scribner's Sons, 1911.

Schaw, Janet. *The Journal of a Lady of Quality; Being the Narrative of a Journey from Scotland to the West Indies, North Carolina, and Portugal, in the Years 1774 to 1776.* Edited by Evangeline W. Andrews and Charles M. Andrews. New Haven: Yale University Press, 1921.

Schoepf, Johann D. *Travels in the Confederation, 1783–1784, from the German of Johann David Schoepf.* Translated and edited by Alfred J. Morrison. Philadelphia: Bergman, 1911.

Scotus Americanus. "Informations Concerning the Province of North Carolina, Addressed to Emigrants from the Highlands and Western Isles of Scotland." In *Some Eighteenth Century Tracts Concerning North Carolina,* edited by William K. Boyd, 419–51. Raleigh: State of North Carolina, 1927.

Smyth, J. F. D. *A Tour in the United States of America.* London: G. Robinson, 1784.

Sprunt, James, ed. *Chronicles of the Cape Fear River, 1660–1916.* Raleigh, N.C.: Edwards & Broughton Printing, 1916.

Tryon, William. *Correspondence of William Tryon and Other Selected Papers.* Edited by William S. Powell. Raleigh: State of North Carolina, 1980–81.

———. "Tryon's 'Book' on North Carolina." Edited by William S. Powell. *North Carolina Historical Review* 34, no. 3 (1957): 406–15.

Watson, Elkanah. *Men and Times of the Revolution; or Memoirs of Elkanah Watson, Including His Journals of Travels in Europe and America, from 1777 to 1842.* Edited by Winslow C. Watson. New York: Dana, 1857.

Whitefield, George. *George Whitefield's Journals, 1737–1741.* Edited by William V. Davis. Gainesville: University of Florida Press, 1969.

Published Secondary Sources

Alston, Lee J., and Morton Owen Shapiro. "Inheritance Laws across Colonies: Causes and Consequences." *Journal of Economic History* 44, no. 2 (1984): 277–87.

Anderson, Benedict. *Imagined Communities: Reflections on the Origin and the Spread of Nationalism.* 1983. Revised edition, London: Verso Press, 1991.

Anderson, Douglas. "Plotting William Byrd." *William and Mary Quarterly* 56, no. 4 (October 1999): 701–22.

Andrews, Charles M. *The Colonial Period of American History: The Settlements.* Vol. 3. New Haven: Yale University Press, 1934–38.

Anzilotti, Cara. "Autonomy and the Female Planter in Colonial South Carolina." *Journal of Southern History* 63, no. 2 (1997): 239–68.

Ashe, Samuel A' Court. *History of North Carolina.* Greensboro, N.C.: C. L. Van Noppen, 1908–25.

Ashe, W. W. *The Forests, Forest Lands, and Forest Products of Eastern North Carolina.* Raleigh, N.C.: J. Daniels, 1894.

Ayers, Edward, Patricia N. Limerick, Stephen Nissenbaum, and Peter S. Onuf. *All over the Map: Rethinking American Regions.* Baltimore: Johns Hopkins University Press, 1996.

Bailyn, Bernard. *The Peopling of British North America: An Introduction.* New York: Vintage, 1986.

———. *Voyagers to the West: A Passage in the Peopling of America on the Eve of the Revolution.* New York: Knopf, 1986.

Bassett, John Spencer. "Landholding in Colonial North Carolina." *Law Quarterly Review* 11, no. 2 (1895): 154–66.

———. *Slavery and Servitude in the Colony of North Carolina.* Baltimore: Johns Hopkins University Press, 1896.

Baxter, W. T. "Accounting in Colonial America." In A. C. Littleton and B. S. Yamey, *Studies in the History of Accounting,* 272–87. Homewood, Ill.: Richard D. Irwin, 1956.

Beaman, Thomas, Jr. "'Some Fragments of Blue Dutch Tiling' at Brunswick Town: Decorative Delftware Tiles from Russellborough, Prospect Hall and the Public House." *North Carolina Archaeology* 46 (1997): 16–34.

Beeman, Richard R. *The Evolution of the Southern Backcountry: A Case Study of Lunenburg County, Virginia 1746–1832.* Philadelphia: University of Pennsylvania Press, 1984.

———. "The New Social History and the Search for 'Community' in Colonial America." *American Quarterly* 29, no. 4 (1977): 422–43.

Berlin, Ira. *Many Thousands Gone: The First Two Centuries of Slavery in North America.* Cambridge: Harvard University Press, 1998.

Berlin, Ira, and Philip D. Morgan. "Labor and the Shaping of Slave Life in the Americas." In *Cultivation and Culture: Labor and the Shaping of Slave Life in the Americas,* edited by Ira Berlin and Philip D. Morgan, 1–45. Charlottesville: University Press of Virginia, 1993.

Bishir, Catherine. *North Carolina Architecture.* Chapel Hill: University of North Carolina Press, 1990.

Bishir, Catherine, and Michael T. Southern. *A Guide to the Historic Architecture of Eastern North Carolina.* Chapel Hill: University of North Carolina Press, 1996.

Bolen, Eric G. "The Bartrams in North Carolina." *Wildlife in North Carolina* 60 (May 1996): 16–21.

Boles, John B., and Evelyn Thomas Nolan, eds. *Interpreting Southern History: Historiographical Essays in Honor of Sanford W. Higginbotham.* Baton Rouge: Louisiana State University Press, 1987.

Bolland, O. Nigel. *The Formation of a Colonial Society: Belize from Conquest to Crown Colony.* Baltimore: Johns Hopkins University Press, 1977.

Bolster, W. Jeffrey. *Black Jacks: African American Seamen in the Age of Sail.* Cambridge: Harvard University Press, 1997.

———. "An Inner Diaspora: Black Sailors Making Selves." In *Through a Glass Darkly: Reflections on Personal Identity in Early America,* edited by Ronald Hoffman et al., 422–28. Chapel Hill: University of North Carolina Press, 1997.

Bolton, S. Charles. *Southern Anglicanism: The Church of England in Colonial South Carolina.* Westport, Conn.: Greenwood Press, 1982.

Bonomi, Patricia. *Under the Cope of Heaven: Religion, Society, and Politics in Colonial America.* New York: Oxford University Press, 1986.

Brewer, Holly. "Entailing Aristocracy in Colonial Virginia: 'Ancient Feudal Restraints' and Revolutionary Reform." *William and Mary Quarterly* 54, no. 2 (1997): 307–46.

Brewer, John, and John Styles, eds. *An Ungovernable People: The English and Their Law in the Seventeenth and Eighteenth Centuries.* New Brunswick, N.J.: Rutgers University Press, 1980.

Bridenbaugh, Carl. *Myths and Realities: Societies of the Colonial South.* Baton Rouge: Louisiana State University Press, 1952.

Brown, Kathleen. "Brave New Worlds: Women's and Gender History." *William and Mary Quarterly* 50, no. 2 (April 1993): 311–28.

Bruchey, Stuart W. "Success and Failure Factors: American Merchants in Foreign Trade in the Eighteenth and Early Nineteenth Century." *Business History Review* 32, no. 3 (1958): 272–92.

Burton, Orville Vernon. *In My Father's House Are Many Mansions: Family and Community in Edgefield, South Carolina.* Chapel Hill: University of North Carolina Press, 1985.

Bush, Barbara. "White 'Ladies,' Coloured 'Favourites,' and Black 'Wenches': Some Considerations on Sex, Race, and Class Factors in Social Relations in White Creole Society in the British Caribbean." *Slavery and Abolition* 2 (1981): 245–62.

Bushman, Richard Lyman. "Farmers in Court: Orange County, North Carolina, 1750–1776." In *The Many Legalities of Early America,* edited by Christopher L. Tomlins and Bruce H. Mann, 388–411. Chapel Hill: University of North Carolina Press, 2001.

———. *The Refinement of America: Persons, Houses, Cities.* New York: Vintage, 1993.

Butler, Jon. *The Huguenots in America: A Refugee People in New World Society.* Cambridge: Harvard University Press, 1983.

Calhoon, Robert M. *The Loyalists in Revolutionary America, 1760–1781.* New York: Harcourt Brace Jovanovich, 1973.

Carr, Lois Green. "The Development of the Maryland Orphans' Court, 1654–1715." In *Law, Society, and Politics in Early Maryland,* edited by Aubrey C. Land et al., 41–62. Baltimore: Johns Hopkins University Press, 1977.

Carr, Lois Green, and Lorena S. Walsh. "The Planter's Wife: The Experience of White Women in Seventeenth-Century Maryland." *Maryland Historical Magazine* 34, no. 4 (1977): 542–71.

Carr, Lois Green, Russell R. Menard, and Lorena S. Walsh. *Robert Cole's World: Agriculture and Society in Early Maryland.* Chapel Hill: University of North Carolina Press, 1991.

Carson, Cary, Ronald Hoffman, and Peter J. Albert, eds. *Of Consuming Interests: The Style of Life in the Eighteenth Century.* Charlottesville: University Press of Virginia, 1994.

Cashin, Edward J. *William Bartram and the American Revolution on the Southern Frontier.* Columbia: University of South Carolina Press, 2000.

Cecelski, David. *The Waterman's Song: Slavery and Freedom in Maritime North Carolina.* Chapel Hill: University of North Carolina Press, 2001.

Chaplin, Joyce E. *"An Anxious Pursuit": Agricultural Innovation and Modernity in the Lower South, 1730–1815.* Chapel Hill: University of North Carolina Press, 1993.

Chesnutt, David R. *South Carolina's Expansion into Colonial Georgia, 1720–1765.* New York: Garland, 1989.

Clark, Victor S. *History of Manufactures in the United States.* New York: McGraw-Hill, 1929.

Cleary, Patricia. *Elizabeth Murray: A Woman's Pursuit of Independence in Eighteenth-Century America.* Amherst: University of Massachusetts Press, 2000.

Clifton, James M. "Golden Grains of White: Rice Planting on the Lower Cape Fear." *North Carolina Historical Review* 50, no. 4 (1973): 365–93.

———. "The Rice Industry in Colonial America." *Agricultural History* 55, no. 3 (1981): 266–83.

Clowse, Converse D. *Economic Beginnings in Colonial South Carolina.* Columbia: University of South Carolina Press, 1971.

Coclanis, Peter A. *The Shadow of a Dream: Economic Life and Death in the South Carolina Low Country, 1760–1920.* New York: Oxford University Press, 1989.

Combs, Edwin L. III. "Trading in Lubberland: Maritime Commerce in Colonial North Carolina." *North Carolina Historical Review* 80, no. 1 (2003): 1–27.

Connor, R. D. W. *History of North Carolina.* Vol. 1, *The Colonial and Revolutionary Periods, 1584–1783.* Chicago: Lewis Publishing, 1919.

———. "The Settlement of the Cape Fear." *South Atlantic Quarterly* 5, no. 1 (July 1907): 272–87.

Cook, Edward M., Jr. "Local Leadership and the Typology of New England Towns, 1700–1785." *Political Science Quarterly* 86, no. 4 (1971): 586–608.

Corbitt, David Leroy. *Formation of the North Carolina Counties, 1663–1943.* Raleigh: State of North Carolina, 1950.

Crane, Elaine Forman. "The Socioeconomics of a Female Majority in Eighteenth-Century Bermuda." *Signs* 15, no. 2 (1990): 231–58.

Crane, Verner W. *The Southern Frontier, 1670–1732.* Ann Arbor: University of Michigan Press, 1929.

Crittenden, Christopher C. *The Commerce of North Carolina, 1763–1789.* New Haven: Yale University Press, 1936.

———. "Inland Navigation in North Carolina, 1763–1789." *North Carolina Historical Review* 8, no. 2 (1931): 145–54.

———. "Overland Travel and Transportation in North Carolina, 1763–1789." *North Carolina Historical Review* 8, no. 3 (1931): 239–57.

Cronin, William. *Changes in the Land: Indians, Colonists, and the Ecology of New England.* New York: Hill & Wang, 1983.

Crow, Jeffrey J. *The Black Experience in Revolutionary North Carolina.* Raleigh: State of North Carolina, 1977.

———. "Slave Rebelliousness and Social Conflict in North Carolina, 1775 to 1802." *William and Mary Quarterly* 37, no. 1 (1980): 79–102.

Crowley, John. "Family Relations and Inheritance in Early South Carolina." *Histoire Sociale/Social History* 17, no. 33 (1984): 35–57.

———. "The Importance of Kinship: Testamentary Evidence from South Carolina." *Journal of Interdisciplinary History* 16, no. 4 (1986): 559–77.

Cummings, William P. *The Southeast in Early Maps, with an Annotated Check List of Printed and Manuscript Regional and Local Maps of Southeastern North America during the Colonial Period.* Chapel Hill: University of North Carolina Press, 1962.

Curtin, Philip D. *The Rise and Fall of the Plantation Complex: Essays in Atlantic History.* Cambridge: Cambridge University Press, 1990.

Daniels, Christine. "Gresham's Laws: Labor Management on an Early Eighteenth Century Plantation." *Journal of Southern History* 62, no. 2 (1996): 205–38.

Davis, Richard Beale. *Intellectual Life in the Colonial South, 1585–1763.* Knoxville: University of Tennessee Press, 1978.

Dawdy, Shannon Lee. "The Meherrin's Secret History of the Dividing Line." *North Carolina Historical Review* 72, no. 4 (October 1995): 386–415.

Demond, Robert O. *The Loyalists in North Carolina during the Revolution.* Durham, N.C.: Duke University Press, 1940.

Dening, Greg. "Introduction: In Search of a Metaphor." In *Through a Glass Darkly: Reflections on Personal Identity in Early America,* edited by Ronald Hoffman et al., 1–6. Chapel Hill: University of North Carolina Press, 1997.

Dew, Charles. *Bond of Iron: Master and Slave at Buffalo Forge.* New York: W. W. Norton, 1994.

Ditz, Toby L. *Property and Kinship: Inheritance in Early Connecticut, 1750–1820.* Princeton, N.J.: Princeton University Press, 1986.

Dobson, David. *Scottish Emigration to Colonial America, 1607–1785.* Athens: University of Georgia Press, 1994.

Doerflinger, Thomas M. *A Vigorous Spirit of Enterprise: Merchants and Economic Development in Revolutionary Philadelphia.* Chapel Hill: University of North Carolina Press, 1986.

Duff, Meaghan N. "Creating a Plantation Province: Proprietary Land Policies and Early Settlement Patterns." In *Money, Trade, and Power: The Evolution of Colonial South Carolina's Plantation Society,* edited by Jack P. Greene, Rosemary Brana-Shute, and Randy J. Sparks, 1–25. Columbia: University of South Carolina Press, 2001.

Duffy, John. *Epidemics in Colonial America.* Baton Rouge: Louisiana State University Press, 1953.

Dunn, Richard S. "The English Sugar Islands and the Founding of South Carolina." *South Carolina Historical Magazine* 72, no. 2 (April 1971): 81–93.

Earle, Carville, and Ronald Hoffman. "Staple Crops and Urban Development in the Eighteenth-Century South." *Perspectives in American History* 10 (1976): 5–78.

Earnest, Ernest. *John and William Bartram: Botanists and Explorers.* Philadelphia: University of Pennsylvania Press, 1940.

Ekirch, A. Roger. *"Poor Carolina": Politics and Society in Colonial North Carolina, 1929–1776.* Chapel Hill: University of North Carolina Press, 1981.

Elias, Norbert. *The Court Society.* Translated by Edmund Jephcott. New York: Urizen Books, 1983.

———. *The History of Manners.* Translated by Edmund Jephcott. New York: Urizen Books, 1982.

Eltis, David, Stephen D. Behrendt, David Richardson, and Herbert S. Klein, eds. *The Transatlantic Slave Trade: A Database on CD-ROM.* Cambridge: Cambridge University Press, 1999.

Engerman, Stanley L., and Robert E. Gallman, eds. *The Cambridge Economic History of the United States.* Vol. 1, *The Colonial Era.* Cambridge: Cambridge University Press, 1996.

Ernst, Joseph Albert, and H. Roy Merrens. "'Camden's Turrets Pierce the Skies': The Urban Process in the Southern Colonies during the Eighteenth Century." *William and Mary Quarterly* 30, no. 4 (1973): 549–74.

Fischer, Kirsten. *Suspect Relations: Sex, Race, and Resistance in Colonial North Carolina.* Ithaca, N.Y.: Cornell University Press, 2002.

Fliegelman, Jay. *Prodigals and Pilgrims: The American Revolution Against Patriarchal Authority, 1750–1800.* Cambridge: Cambridge University Press, 1982.

Fogel, Robert W. *Without Consent or Contract: The Rise and Fall of American Slavery.* New York: W. W. Norton, 1989.

Fraser, Walter J., Jr. "The City Elite, 'Disorder,' and the Poor Children of Pre-Revolutionary Charleston." *South Carolina Historical Magazine* 84, no. 3 (1983): 167–79.

Frey, Sylvia R. *Water from the Rock: Black Resistance in a Revolutionary Age.* Princeton, N.J.: Princeton University Press, 1991.

Galenson, David. "Population Turnover in the English West Indies in the Late Seventeenth Century: A Comparative Perspective." *Journal of Economic History* 65, no. 2 (1985): 227–39.

———. *Traders, Planters, and Slaves: Market Behavior in Early English America.* Cambridge: Cambridge University Press, 1986.

Gallman, James M. "Determinants of Age of Marriage in Colonial Perquimans County, North Carolina." *William and Mary Quarterly* 39, no. 1 (1982): 176–91.

———. "Mortality among White Males: Colonial North Carolina." *Social Science History* 4, no. 3 (1980): 295–316.

Gallman, Robert E. "Influences on the Distribution of Landholdings in Early Colonial North Carolina." *Journal of Economic History* 62, no. 3 (1982): 549–75.

Gamble, Thomas, comp. *Naval Stores: History, Production, Distribution and Consumption.* Savannah, Ga.: Review Publishing, 1921.

Garland, John M. "The Nonecclesiastical Activities of an English and a North Carolina Parish: A Comparative Study." *North Carolina Historical Review* 50, no. 1 (January 1973): 32–51.

Genovese, Eugene D. *Roll, Jordan, Roll: The World the Slaves Made.* New York: Vintage, 1972.

———. *The World the Slaveholders Made: Two Essays in Interpretation.* New York: Pantheon Books, 1969.

Glover, Lorri. *All Our Relations: Blood Ties and Emotional Bonds among the Early South Carolina Gentry.* Baltimore: Johns Hopkins University Press, 2000.

Goodfriend, Joyce D. *Before the Melting Pot: Society and Culture in Colonial New York City, 1664–1730.* Princeton, N.J.: Princeton University Press, 1992.

Gray, Lewis C. *History of Agriculture in the Southern United States to 1860.* Clifton, N.J.: A. M. Kelley, 1933.

Greenberg, Douglas. "Crime, Law Enforcement, and Social Control in Colonial America." *American Journal of Legal History* 26, no. 4 (1982).

Greene, Evarts S., and Virginia D. Harrington. *American Population before the Federal Census of 1790.* New York: Columbia University Press, 1932.

Greene, Jack P. "Colonial South Carolina: An Introduction." In *Money, Trade, and Power: The Evolution of Colonial South Carolina's Plantation Society,* edited by Jack P. Greene, Rosemary Brana-Shute, and Randy Sparks, vii–xiii. Columbia: University of South Carolina Press, 2001.

———. "Colonial South Carolina and the Caribbean Connection." *South Carolina Historical Magazine* 88, no. 4 (1987): 192–210.

———. "The Constitution of 1787 and the Question of Southern Distinctiveness." In Jack P. Greene, *Imperatives, Behaviors, and Identities: Essays in Early American Cultural History,* 327–47. Charlottesville: University Press of Virginia, 1992.

———. "Courts and Society in Proprietary North Carolina: A Review Essay." *North Carolina Historical Review* 60, no. 1 (January 1983): 100–104.

———. "Independence, Improvement, and Authority: Toward a Framework for Understanding the Histories of the Southern Backcountry during the Era of the American Revolution." In *An Uncivil War: The Southern Backcountry during the American Revolution,* edited by Ronald Hoffman, Thad W. Tate, and Peter J. Albert, 3–46. Charlottesville: University Press of Virginia, 1985.

———. "Legislative Turnover in Colonial British America, 1695–1775: A Quantitative Analysis." In *Negotiated Authorities: Essays in Colonial Political and Constitutional History,* 215–37. Charlottesville: University Press of Virginia, 1994.

———. "Negotiated Authorities: The Problem of Governance in the Extended Polities of the Early Modern Atlantic World." In *Negotiated Authorities,* 1–24.

———. *Pursuits of Happiness: The Social Development of Early Modern British Colonies and the Formation of American Culture.* Chapel Hill: University of North Carolina Press, 1988.

———. "Search for Identity: An Interpretation of the Meaning of Selected Patterns of Social Response in Eighteenth Century America." *Journal of Social History* 3 (spring 1970): 189–220.

Greene, Jack P., and J. R. Pole. "Reconstructing British-American Colonial History: An Introduction." In *Colonial British America: Essays in the New History of the Modern Era,* edited by Jack P. Greene and J. R. Pole, 1–17. Baltimore: Johns Hopkins University Press, 1984.

Greven, Philip J. *Four Generations: Population, Land, and Family in Colonial Andover, Massachusetts.* Ithaca, N.Y.: Cornell University Press, 1970.

Hall, Gwendolyn Midlo. *Africans in Colonial Louisiana: The Development of Afro-Creole Culture in the Eighteenth Century.* Baton Rouge: Louisiana State University Press, 1992.

Hancock, David. *Citizens of the World: London Merchants and the Integration of the British Atlantic Community, 1735–1785.* Cambridge: Cambridge University Press, 1995.

Henretta, James A. "Wealth and Social Structure." In *Colonial British America: Essays in the New History of the Modern Era,* edited by Jack P. Greene and J. R. Pole, 262–89. Baltimore: Johns Hopkins University Press, 1984.

Herndon, Melvin. "Naval Stores in Colonial Georgia." *Georgia Historical Quarterly* 52, no. 4 (1968): 426–33.

Herrup, Cynthia B. *The Common Peace: Participation and the Criminal Law in Seventeenth-Century England.* Cambridge: Cambridge University Press, 1987.

Heyrman, Christine Leigh. *Commerce and Culture: The Maritime Communities of Colonial Massachusetts, 1690–1750.* New York: W. W. Norton, 1984.

Higman, B. W. *Slave Populations of the British Caribbean, 1807–1834.* Baltimore: Johns Hopkins University Press, 1984.

Hofstadter, Richard. *America at 1750: A Social Portrait.* New York: Knopf, 1971.

Horn, James P. "Adapting to a New World: A Comparative Study of Local Society in England and Maryland, 1650–1700." In *Colonial Chesapeake Society,* edited by Lois Green Carr et al.,165–74. Chapel Hill: University of North Carolina Press, 1988.

———. *Adapting to a New World: English Society in the Seventeenth-Century Chesapeake.* Chapel Hill: University of North Carolina Press, 1994.

———. "Moving On in the New World: Migration and Out-Migration in the Seventeenth-Century Chesapeake." In *Migration and Society in Early Modern England,* edited by Peter Clark and David Souden, 172–211. London: Hutchinson, 1988.

Innes, Stephen. "Fulfilling John Smith's Vision: Work and Labor in Early America." In *Work and Labor in Early America,* edited by Stephen Innes, 3–47. Chapel Hill: University of North Carolina Press, 1988.

Isaac, Rhys. *The Transformation of Virginia, 1740–1790.* New York: W. W. Norton, 1982.

Johnson, George Lloyd, Jr. *The Frontier in the Colonial South: South Carolina Backcountry, 1736–1800.* Westport, Conn.: Greenwood Press, 1997.

Johnson, Michael P., and James L. Roark. *Black Masters: A Free Family of Color in the Old South.* New York: W. W. Norton, 1984.

Jones, Alice H. *Wealth of a Nation to Be: The American Colonies on the Eve of the Revolution.* New York: Columbia University Press, 1980.

Jones, H. G. *North Carolina Illustrated, 1524–1984.* Chapel Hill: University of North Carolina Press, 1983.

Jordan, Winthrop D. *White over Black: American Attitudes toward the Negro, 1550–1812.* Chapel Hill: University of North Carolina Press, 1968.

Joyner, Charles. *Down by the Riverside: A South Carolina Slave Community.* Urbana: University of Illinois Press, 1984.

Kars, Marjoleine. *Breaking Loose Together: The Regulator Rebellion in Pre-Revolutionary North Carolina.* Chapel Hill: University of North Carolina Press, 2002.

Kay, Marvin Michael. "The North Carolina Regulation, 1766–1776: A Class Conflict." In *The American Revolution: Explorations in the History of American Radicalism,* edited by Alfred F. Young, 84–103. De Kalb: Northern Illinois University Press, 1976.

———. "Provincial Taxes in North Carolina during the Administrations of Dobbs and Tryon." *North Carolina Historical Review* 42, no. 4 (October 1965): 440–53.

Kay, Marvin Michael, and Lorin Lee Cary. "Class, Mobility, and Conflict in North Carolina on the Eve of the Revolution." In *The Southern Experience in the American Revolution,* edited by Jeffrey J. Crow and Larry E. Tise, 109–51. Chapel Hill: University of North Carolina Press, 1978).

———. *Slavery in North Carolina, 1748–1775.* Chapel Hill: University of North Carolina Press, 1995.

Kay, Marvin Michael, and William S. Price Jr. "'To Ride the Wood Mare': Road Building and Militia Service in Colonial North Carolina, 1740–1775." *North Carolina Historical Review* 57, no. 4 (October 1980): 361–409.

Klein, Rachel N. *Unification of a Slave State: The Rise of the Planter Class in the South Carolina Backcountry, 1760–1808.* Chapel Hill: University of North Carolina Press, 1990.

Kolp, John G. *Gentlemen and Freeholders: Electoral Politics in Colonial Virginia.* Baltimore: Johns Hopkins University Press, 1998.

Konig, David T. *Law and Society in Puritan Massachusetts: Essex County, 1629–1692.* Chapel Hill: University of North Carolina Press, 1979.

Laslett, Peter. *The World We Have Lost: England before the Industrial Age.* New York: Charles Scribner's Sons, 1965.

———, ed. *The Household and Family in Past Time; Comparative Studies in the Size and Structure of the Domestic Group in the Last Three Centuries in England, France, Serbia, Japan, and Colonial North America, with Further Materials from Western Europe.* Cambridge: Cambridge University Press, 1972.

Lee, Jean B. "The Problem of Slave Community in the Eighteenth-Century Chesapeake." *William and Mary Quarterly* 43, no. 3 (1986): 333–66.

Lee, Lawrence. *The Lower Cape Fear in Colonial Days.* Chapel Hill: University of North Carolina Press, 1965.

———. "Old Brunswick, the Story of a Colonial Town." *North Carolina Historical Review* 29, no. 2 (April 1952): 230–45.

Lee, Wayne E. *Crowds and Soldiers in Revolutionary North Carolina: The Culture of Violence in Riot and War.* Gainesville: University of Florida Press, 2001.

Lefler, Hugh T., and William S. Powell. *Colonial North Carolina: A History.* New York: Charles Scribner's Sons, 1973.

Lemon, James T. *The Best Poor Man's Country: A Geographical Study of Early Southeastern Pennsylvania.* Baltimore: Johns Hopkins University Press, 1972.

———. "Urbanization and the Development of Eighteenth-Century Southeastern Pennsylvania and Adjacent Delaware." *William and Mary Quarterly* 24, no. 4 (1967): 501–42.

———. "The Weakness of Place and Community in Early Pennsylvania." In *European Settlement and Development in North America: Essays on Geographic Change in Honour and Memory of Andrew Hill Clark,* edited by James R. Gibson, 190–207. Toronto: University of Toronto Press, 1978.

Lennon, Donald R. "Development of Town Government in Colonial North Carolina." *East Carolina Publications in History* 5 (1981): 1–25.

Lockhart, James, and Stuart Schwartz. *Early Latin America: A History of Colonial Spanish America and Brazil.* Cambridge: Cambridge University Press, 1983.

Lockridge, Kenneth. "Colonial Self-Fashioning: Paradoxes and Pathologies in the Construction of Genteel Identity in Eighteenth-Century America." In *Through a Glass Darkly: Reflections on Personal Identity in Early America,* edited by Ronald Hoffman et al., 274–339. Chapel Hill: University of North Carolina Press, 1997.

Loftfield, Thomas C., and Michael Stoner. "Brunswick Town Colonowares Re-examined." *North Carolina Archaeology* 47 (1997): 6–15.

MacPherson, C. B. *The Political Theory of Possessive Individualism.* Oxford, U.K.: Clarendon Press, 1962.

Malone, Joseph J. *Pine Tress and Politics: The Naval Stores and Forest Policy in Colonial New England, 1691–1775.* Seattle: University of Washington Press, 1964.

Mann, Bruce. *Neighbors and Strangers: Law and Community in Early Connecticut.* Chapel Hill: University of North Carolina Press, 1987.

Massey, Gregory De Van. "The British Expedition to Wilmington, January–November, 1781." *North Carolina Historical Review* 66, no. 4 (1989): 387–411.

McCain, Paul. *The County Court in North Carolina before 1750.* Durham, N.C.: Duke University Press, 1954.

———. "Magistrates Courts in Early North Carolina." *North Carolina Historical Review* 48 (1971): 23–30.

McCarron, William E., ed. *A Bicentennial Edition of Thomas Godfrey's* "The Prince of Parthia, A Tragedy." Colorado Springs: United States Air Force Academy, 1976.

McConville, Brendan J. *These Daring Disturbers of the Public Peace: The Struggle for Property and Power in Early New Jersey.* Ithaca, N.Y.: Cornell University Press, 1999.

McCurry, Stephanie. *Masters of Small Worlds: Yeoman Households, Gender Relations, and the Political Culture of the Antebellum South Carolina Lowcountry.* New York: Oxford University Press, 1995.

McCusker, John J., and Russell R. Menard. *The Economy of British America, 1607–1789.* Chapel Hill: University of North Carolina Press, 1985.

McDonald, Roderick A. "Independent Economic Production by Slaves on Antebellum Louisiana Sugar Plantations." In *Cultivation and Culture: Labor and the Shaping of Slave Life in the Americas,* edited by Ira Berlin and Philip D. Morgan, 275–99. Charlottesville: University Press of Virginia, 1993.

Meinig, D. W. *The Shaping of America: A Geographical Perspective on 500 Years of History.* Vol. 1, *Atlantic America, 1492–1800.* New Haven: Yale University Press, 1986.

Menard, Russell R. "Financing the Lowcountry Export Boom: Capital and Growth in Early South Carolina." *William and Mary Quarterly* 52, no. 4 (1995): 280–303.

Merrens, H. Roy. *Colonial North Carolina in the Eighteenth Century: A Study in Historical Geography.* Chapel Hill: University of North Carolina Press, 1964.

Merrens, H. Roy, and George D. Terry. "Dying in Paradise: Malaria, Mortality, and the Perceptual Environment on Colonial South Carolina." *Journal of Southern History* 50, no. 4 (1982): 533–50.

Merriweather, Robert L. *The Expansion of South Carolina, 1729–1765.* Kingsport, Tenn.: Southern Publishers, 1940.

Meyer, Duane. *The Highland Scots of North Carolina, 1732–1776.* Chapel Hill: University of North Carolina Press, 1957.

Miller, Perry. *The New England Mind: From Colony to Province.* Cambridge: Harvard University Press, 1953.

Minchinton, Walter E. "The Seaborne Slave Trade of North Carolina." *North Carolina Historical Review* 71, no. 1 (January 1994): 1–61.

Mintz, Sidney W., and Richard Price. *The Birth of African-American Culture: An Anthropological Perspective.* Boston: Beacon Press, 1992.

Mitchell, Robert D. *Commercialism and Frontier: Perspectives on the Early Shenandoah Valley.* Charlottesville: University Press of Virginia, 1972.

———. "The Formation of Early American Cultural Regions: An Interpretation." In *European Settlement and Development in North America: Essays on Geographical Change in Honour and Memory of Andrew Hill Clark,* edited by James R. Gibson, 66–90. Toronto: University of Toronto Press, 1978.

Moore, Alexander, ed. "Daniel Axtell's Account Book and the Economy of Early South Carolina." *South Carolina Historical Magazine* 95, no. 4 (1994): 280–301.

Moore, John Hebron. *Andrew Brown and Cypress Lumbering in the Old Southwest.* Baton Rouge: Louisiana State University Press, 1967.

Morgan, David T. "Cornelius Harnett: Revolutionary Leader and Delegate to the Continental Congress." *North Carolina Historical Review* 49, no. 3 (1972): 229–41.

Morgan, Philip D. "Black Life in Eighteenth-Century Charleston." *Perspectives in American History* 1 (1984): 187–232.

———. *Slave Counterpoint: Black Culture in the Eighteenth-Century Chesapeake and Lowcountry.* Chapel Hill: University of North Carolina Press, 1998.

———. "Task and Gang Systems: The Organization of Labor on New World Plantations." In *Work and Labor in Early America,* edited by Stephen Innes, 189–220. Chapel Hill: University of North Carolina Press, 1988.

———, ed. "Profile of a Mid-Eighteenth Century South Carolina Parish: The Tax Return of St. James' Goose Creek." *South Carolina Historical Magazine* 81, no. 1 (1980): 51–65.

Morris, Christopher. "The Articulation of Two Worlds: The Master-Slave Relationship Reconsidered." *Journal of American History* 85, no. 3 (1998): 982–1007.

———. *Becoming Southern: The Evolution of a Way of Life, Warren County and Vicksburg, Mississippi, 1770–1860.* New York: Oxford University Press, 1995.

Morris, Francis Grave, and Phyllis Mary Morris. "Economic Conditions in North Carolina about 1780; Part 1, Landholdings." *North Carolina Historical Review* 16, no. 2 (1939): 107–33.

———. "Economic Conditions in North Carolina about 1780: Part 2, Ownership of Town Lots, Slaves, and Cattle." *North Carolina Historical Review* 16, no. 3 (1939): 296–327.

Nash, Gary B. "Thomas Peters: Millwright and Deliverer." In *Struggle and Survival in Colonial America,* edited by David G. Sweet and Gary B. Nash, 69–85. Berkeley: University of California Press, 1981.

———. *The Urban Crucible: The Northern Seaports and the Origins of the American Revolution.* Cambridge: Harvard University Press, 1979.

Nash, R. C. "The Organization of Trade and Finance in the Atlantic Economy: Britain and South Carolina, 1670–1775." In *Money, Trade, and Power: The Evolution of South Carolina's Plantation Society,* edited by Jack P. Greene, Rosemary Brana-Shute, and Randy J. Sparks, 74–107. Columbia: University of South Carolina Press, 2001.

———. "South Carolina and the Atlantic Economy in the Late Seventeenth and Eighteenth Centuries." *Economic History Review* 45, no. 4 (1992): 677–702.

———. "Urbanization in the Colonial South: Charleston, South Carolina, as a Case Study." *Journal of Urban History* 19, no. 1 (1992): 3–29.

North, Douglas C. *Structure and Change in Economic History.* New York: W. W. Norton, 1981.

Offutt, William M., Jr. "The Limits of Authority: Courts, Ethnicity, and Gender in the Middle Colonies, 1670–1710." In *The Many Legalities of Early America,* edited by Christopher L. Tomlins and Bruce H. Mann, 356–87. Chapel Hill: University of North Carolina Press, 2001.

———. *Of "Good Laws" and "Good Men": Law and Society in the Delaware Valley, 1680–1710.* Urbana: University of Illinois Press, 1995.

Olwell, Robert. *Masters, Slaves, and Subjects: The Culture of Power in the South Carolina Low Country, 1740–1790.* Ithaca, N.Y.: Cornell University Press, 1988.

Onuf, Peter S. "Federalism, Republicanism, and the Origins of American Sectionalism." In Edward Ayers, Patricia N. Limerick, Stephen Nissenbaum, and Peter S. Onuf, *All over the Map: Rethinking American Regions.* Baltimore: Johns Hopkins University Press, 1996.

———. *The Origins of the Federal Republic: Jurisdictional Controversies in the United States, 1775–1787.* Philadelphia: University of Pennsylvania Press, 1983.

Otto, John Solomon. "Livestock-Raising in Early South Carolina, 1670–1700: Prelude to the Rice Plantation Economy." *Agricultural History* 61, no. 4 (1987): 13–24.

———. "The Origins of Cattle-Ranching in Colonial South Carolina, 1670–1715." *South Carolina Historical Magazine* 87, no. 2 (1986): 117–24.

Outland, Robert D. III. "Slavery, Work, and the Geography of North Carolina Naval Stores Industry, 1835–1860." *Journal of Southern History* 62, no. 1 (1996): 27–56.

Paden, John. "'Several & Many Grievances of Very Great Consequences': North Carolina's Political Factionalism in the 1720s." *North Carolina Historical Review* 71, no. 3 (July 1994): 285–305.

Paul, Charles L. "Factors in the Economy of Colonial Beaufort." *North Carolina Historical Review* 47, no. 4 (1967): 111–34.

Perry, James R. *The Formation of a Society on Virginia's Eastern Shore, 1615–1655.* Chapel Hill: University of North Carolina Press, 1990.

Perry, Percival. "The Naval Stores Industry in the Old South, 1790–1860." *Journal of Southern History* 34, no. 4 (1968): 509–26.

Powell, William S. *North Carolina through Four Centuries.* Chapel Hill: University of North Carolina Press, 1989.

———. *The North Carolina Gazetteer: A Dictionary of Tar Heel Places.* Chapel Hill: University of North Carolina Press, 1968.

Price, Jacob M. "Economic Function and the Growth of American Port Towns in the Eighteenth Century." *Perspectives in American History* 8 (1974): 121–86.

———. "The Transatlantic Economy." In *Colonial British America: Essays in the New History of the Modern Era,* edited by Jack P. Greene and J. R. Pole, 18–42. Baltimore: Johns Hopkins University Press, 1984.

Price, William S., Jr. "'Men of Good Estates': Wealth among North Carolina's Royal Councillors." *North Carolina Historical Review* 49, no. 1 (January 1972): 72–82.

———. "A Strange Incident in George Burrington's Royal Governorship." *North Carolina Historical Review* 51, no. 2 (1974): 149–58.

Quattlebaum, Paul. *The Land Called Chicora: The Carolinas under Spanish Rule with French Intrusions, 1520–1670.* Gainesville: University of Florida Press, 1956.

Rakove, Jack N. *The Beginnings of National Politics: An Interpretive History of the Continental Congress.* Baltimore: Johns Hopkins University Press, 1979.

Ramsey, Robert W. *Carolina Cradle: Settlement of the Northwest Carolina Frontier, 1747–1762.* Chapel Hill: University of North Carolina Press, 1964.

Rankin, Hugh F. "The Moore's Creek Bridge Campaign, 1776." *North Carolina Historical Review* 30, no. 1 (1953): 23–60.

Raper, Charles Lee. *North Carolina; A Study in English Colonial Government.* New York: Macmillan, 1904.

Reps, John W. *Town Planning in Frontier America.* Princeton, N.J.: Princeton University Press, 1969.

Robinson, Kenneth W. "Port Brunswick and the Colonial Naval Stores Industry: Historical and Archaeological Observations." *North Carolina Archaeology* 46 (1997): 51–67.

Rogers, George C., Jr. *The History of Georgetown County, South Carolina.* Columbia: University of South Carolina Press, 1970.

Rozbicki, Michael J. "The Curse of Provincialism: Negative Perceptions of Colonial American Plantation Gentry." *Journal of Southern History* 63, no. 4 (November 1997): 727–52.

Russo, Jean B. "Self-Sufficiency and Local Exchange: Free Craftsmen in the Rural Chesapeake Economy." In *Colonial Chesapeake Society,* edited by Lois Green Carr et al., 429–32. Chapel Hill: University of North Carolina Press, 1988.

Rutman, Darret B. "Community Study." *Historical Methods* 13, no. 1 (1980): 29–41.

———. "People in Process: The New Hampshire Towns of the Eighteenth Century." *Journal of Urban History* 1, no. 3 (1975): 268–92.

Rutman, Darret B., and Anita H. Rutman "'Of Agues and Fevers': Malaria in the Early Chesapeake." *William and Mary Quarterly* 33, no. 1 (1976): 31–60.

———. *A Place in Time.* Vol. 1, *Middlesex County, Virginia, 1650–1750.* Vol. 2, *Explicatus.* New York: W. W. Norton, 1984.

Rutman, Darret B., with Anita H. Rutman. *Small Worlds, Large Questions: Explorations in Early American Social History, 1600–1850.* Charlottesville: University Press of Virginia, 1994.

———. "The Village South." In Rutman, with Rutman, *Small Worlds, Large Questions,* 231–72.

Sacks, David Harris. *The Widening Gate: Bristol and the Atlantic Economy, 1450–1700.* Berkeley: University of California Press, 1991.

Sahlins, Peter. *Boundaries: The Making of France and Spain in the Pyrenees.* Berkeley: University of California Press, 1989.

Salmon, Marylynn. *Women and the Law of Property in Early America.* Chapel Hill: University of North Carolina Press, 1986.

Schulz, Ronald. "A Class Society? The Nature of Inequality in Early America." In *Inequality in Early America,* edited by Carla Gardina Pestana and Sharon V. Salinger, 203–21. Hanover, N.H.: University of New England Press, 1999.

Schwartz, Stuart B. *Sugar Plantations in the Formation of Brazilian Society: Bahia, 1550–1835.* New York: Cambridge University Press, 1985.

Seapker, Janet K., ed. *Time, Talent, Tradition: Five Essays on the Cultural History of the Lower Cape Fear Region, North Carolina.* Wilmington, N.C.: Cape Fear Museum, 1995.

Sellers, Charles G., Jr. "Private Profits and British Colonial Policy: The Speculations of Henry McCulloh." *William and Mary Quarterly* 8, no. 4 (1951): 535–57.

Shammas, Carole. "Anglo-American Household Government in Comparative Perspective." *William and Mary Quarterly* 52, no. 1 (1995): 104–66.

———. *The Preindustrial Consumer in England and America.* Oxford: Oxford University Press, 1992.

Shammas, Carole, Marylynn Salmon, and Michel Dahlin. *Inheritance in America from Colonial Times to the Present.* New Brunswick, N.J.: Rutgers University Press, 1987.

Sharrer, G. Terry. "Naval Stores, 1781–1881." In *Material Culture of the Wooden Age,* edited by Brooke Hindle, 241–70. Tarrytown, N.Y.: Sleepy Hollow Press, 1981.

Shepherd, James F. "Commodity Exports from the British North American Colonies to Overseas Areas, 1768–1772." *Explorations in Economic History* 8, no. 3 (fall 1970): 5–76.

Sheridan, Richard B. "The Domestic Economy." In *Colonial British America: Essays in the New History of the Modern Era,* edited by Jack P. Greene and J. R. Pole, 43–85. Baltimore: Johns Hopkins University Press, 1984.

———. *Sugar and Slavery: An Economic History of the British West Indies.* Baltimore: Johns Hopkins University Press, 1974.

Shields, David S. *Civil Tongues and Polite Letters in British America.* Chapel Hill: University of North Carolina Press, 1997.

Silver, Timothy. *A New Face on the Countryside: Indians, Colonists, and Slaves in South Atlantic Forests, 1500–1800.* New York: Cambridge University Press, 1990.

Skaggs, Marvin Lucian. "The First Boundary Survey between the Carolinas." *North Carolina Historial Review* 12, no. 3 (1935): 213–32.

———. "Progress in the North Carolina–South Carolina Boundary Dispute." *North Carolina Historical Review* 15, no. 4 (1938): 341–53.

Slaughter, Thomas P. *The Natures of John and William Bartram.* New York: Knopf, 1996.

Smith, Daniel Blake. *Inside the Great House: Planter Family Life in Eighteenth-Century Chesapeake Society.* Ithaca, N.Y.: Cornell University Press, 1980.

Sobel, Mechal. *The World They Made Together: Black and White Values in Eighteenth-Century Virginia.* Princeton, N.J.: Princeton University Press, 1987.

Spindel, Donna J. *Crime and Society in North Carolina, 1663–1776.* Baton Rouge: Louisiana State University Press, 1989.

———. "Law and Disorder: The North Carolina Stamp Act Crisis." *North Carolina Historical Review* 57, no. 1 (January 1980): 1–16.

Spruill, Julia Cherry. *Women's Life and Work in the Southern Colonies.* Chapel Hill: University of North Carolina Press, 1938.

Spufford, Margaret. *Contrasting Communities: English Villagers in the Sixteenth and Seventeenth Centuries.* Cambridge: Cambridge University Press, 1974.

Stahle, D. W., M. K. Cleaveland, and J. G. Hehr. "North Carolina Climate Changes Reconstructed from Tree Rings: A.D. 372 to 1985." *Science* 10, issue 240, no. 4858 (June 1988): 1517–19.

Steele, Ian K. *The English Atlantic 1675–1740: An Exploration of Communication and Community.* New York: Oxford University Press, 1986.

Stilgoe, John R. *The Common Landscape of America, 1580 to 1845.* New Haven: Yale University Press, 1982.

Taylor, Alan. *Liberty Men and Great Proprietors: The Revolutionary Settlement on the Maine Frontier, 1760–1820.* Chapel Hill: University of North Carolina Press, 1990.

Thompson, E. P. *Customs in Common: Studies in Traditional and Popular Culture.* New York: W. W. Norton, 1991.

Thornton, John. *Africa and the Africans in the Making of the Atlantic World, 1400–1680.* Cambridge: Cambridge University Press, 1992.

Thorp, Daniel B. "Doing Business in the Backcountry: Retail Trade in Colonial Rowan County, North Carolina." *William and Mary Quarterly* 48, no. 3 (1991): 387–408.

———. *The Moravian Community in Colonial North Carolina: Pluralism on the Southern Frontier.* Knoxville: University of Tennessee Press, 1989.

———. "Taverns and Tavern Culture on the Southern Colonial Frontier: Rowan County, North Carolina, 1753–1776." *Journal of Southern History* 62, no. 4 (1996): 661–88.

Tillson, Albert H. "The Localist Roots of Backcountry Loyalism: An Examination of Popular Political Culture in Virginia's New River Valley." *Journal of Southern History* 54, no. 3 (1988): 387–404.

Troxler, Carole Watterson. *The Loyalist Experience in North Carolina.* Raleigh: State of North Carolina, 1976.

Tully, Alan. *Forming American Politics: Ideals, Interests, and Institutions in Colonial New York and Pennsylvania.* Baltimore: Johns Hopkins University Press, 1994.

Ulrich, Laurel Thatcher. *"Good Wives": Image and Reality in the Lives of Women in Northern New England, 1650–1750.* New York: Knopf, 1982.

Usner, Daniel H., Jr. *Indians, Settlers, and Slaves in a Frontier Economy: The Lower Mississippi Valley before 1783.* Chapel Hill: University of North Carolina Press, 1992.

Van Deventer, David E. *The Emergence of Provincial New Hampshire.* Baltimore: Johns Hopkins University Press, 1976.

Van Young, Eric. *Hacienda and Market in Eighteenth-Century Mexico: The Rural Economy of the Guadalajara Region, 1675–1820.* Berkeley: University of California Press, 1981.

———, ed. *Mexico's Regions: Comparative History and Development.* San Diego: Center for U.S.-Mexican Studies, 1992.

Ver Steeg, Clarence. *Origins of a Southern Mosaic: Studies of Early Carolina and Georgia.* Athens: University of Georgia Press, 1975.

Vickers, Daniel. "Competency and Competition: Economic Culture in Early America." *William and Mary Quarterly* 47, no. 1 (1990): 3–29.

———. *Farmers and Fishermen: Two Centuries of Work in Essex County, Massachusetts, 1630–1850.* Chapel Hill: University of North Carolina Press, 1994.

Waddell, Alfred Moore. *A History of New Hanover County and the Lower Cape Fear Region, 1723–1800.* Wilmington, N.C.: Printed, not published, 1909.

Walsh, Lorena S. "Community Networks in the Early Chesapeake." In *Colonial Chesapeake Society,* edited by Lois Green Carr, Philip D. Morgan, and Jean B. Russo, 228–31. Chapel Hill: University of North Carolina Press, 1988.

———. "'Till Death Us Do Part': Marriage and Family in Seventeenth-Century Maryland." In *The Chesapeake in the Seventeenth-Century,* edited by Thad Tate and David Ammerman, 126–52. Chapel Hill: University of North Carolina Press, 1979.

Walton, Gary M., and James F. Shepherd. *The Economic Rise of Early America.* Cambridge: Cambridge University Press, 1979.

———. *Shipping, Maritime Trade, and the Economic Development of Colonial North America.* Cambridge: Cambridge University Press, 1972.

Waterhouse, Richard. "The Development of Elite Culture in the Colonial American South: A Study of Charles Town, 1670–1770." *Australian Journal of Politics and History* 28, no. 3 (1982): 391–404.

———. "Economic Growth and Changing Patterns of Wealth Distribution in Colonial Lowcountry South Carolina." *South Carolina Historical Magazine* 89, no. 4 (1988): 203–17.

———. "England, the Caribbean, and the Settlement of Carolina." *Journal of American Studies* 9, no. 3 (December 1975): 259–81.

———. *A New World Gentry: The Making of a Merchant and Planter Class in South Carolina, 1670–1770.* New York: Garland, 1989.

Watson, Alan D. "County Fiscal Policy in Colonial North Carolina." *North Carolina Historical Review* 55, no. 3 (July 1978): 284–305.

———. "The Ferry in Colonial North Carolina: Vital Link in Transportation." *North Carolina Historical Review* 51, no. 3 (July 1974): 247–60.

———. "Household Size and Composition in Pre-Revolutionary North Carolina." *Mississippi Quarterly* 31, no. 4 (1978): 551–69.

———. "Impulse toward Independence: Resistance and Rebellion among North Carolina Slaves, 1750–1775." *Journal of Negro History* 63, no. 4 (October 1978): 317–28.

———. *Money and Monetary Problems in Early North Carolina.* Raleigh: State of North Carolina, 1980.

———. "North Carolina Slave Courts, 1715–1785." *North Carolina Historical Review* 60, no. 1 (1983): 24–36.

———. "Ordinaries in Colonial Eastern North Carolina." *North Carolina Historical Review* 45, no. 1 (January 1968): 67–83.

———. "Orphanage in Colonial North Carolina: Edgecombe County as a Case Study." *North Carolina Historical Review* 52, no. 2 (1975): 105–19.

———. "Public Poor Relief in Colonial North Carolina." *North Carolina Historical Review* 54, no. 4 (1977): 347–66.

———. "Regulation and Administration of Roads and Bridges in Colonial Eastern North Carolina." *North Carolina Historical Review* 45, no. 4 (October 1968): 399–417.

———. *Society in North Carolina.* Raleigh: State of North Carolina, 1986.

———. *Wilmington: Port of North Carolina.* Columbia: University of South Carolina Press, 1992.

———. "Women in Colonial North Carolina: Overlooked and Underestimated." *North Carolina Historical Review* 58, no. 1 (1981): 1–22.

Watson, Alan D., et al. *Harnett, Hooper, and Howe: Revolutionary Leaders of the Lower Cape Fear.* Wilmington, N.C.: Lower Cape Fear Historical Society, 1979.

Webber, Mabel L., comp. "The First Governor Moore and His Children." *South Carolina Historical and Genealogical Magazine* 37, no. 1 (1936): 1–23.

Weir, Robert M. *Colonial South Carolina: A History.* Millwood, N.Y.: KTO Press, 1983.

———. "'The Harmony We Were Famous For': An Interpretation of Pre-Revolutionary South Carolina Politics." *William and Mary Quarterly* 26, no. 4 (October 1969): 473–501.

Whitman, T. Stephen. *The Price of Freedom: Slavery and Manumission in Baltimore and Early National Maryland.* Lexington: University Press of Kentucky, 1997.

Whittenburg, James P. "Planters, Merchants, and Lawyers: Social Change and the Origins of the North Carolina Regulation." *William and Mary Quarterly* 34, no. 2 (1977): 215–38.

Williams, Justin. "English Mercantilism and the Carolina Naval Stores Industry, 1705–1776." *Journal of Southern History* 1, no. 2 (1935): 169–85.

Williams, Michael. *Americans and Their Forests: A Historical Geography.* Cambridge: Cambridge University Press, 1989.

Wolf, Jacquelyn H. "Patents and Tithables in Proprietary North Carolina, 1663–1729." *North Carolina Historical Review* 56, no. 3 (1979): 263–77.

Wolf, Stephanie G. *Urban Village: Population, Community, and Family Structure in Germantown, Pennsylvania, 1683–1800.* Princeton, N.J.: Princeton University Press, 1976.

Wood, Joseph S. "Village and Community in Early Colonial New England." *Journal of Historical Geography* 8, no. 4 (1982): 333–46.

Wood, Peter H. *Black Majority: Negroes in Colonial South Carolina from 1670 through the Stono Rebellion.* New York: Knopf, 1974.

Woods, Michael. "The Culture of Credit in Colonial Charleston." *South Carolina Historical Magazine* 99, no. 4 (1998): 358–80.

Wrightson, Keith. *English Society, 1580–1680.* New Brunswick, N.J.: Rutgers University Press, 1982.

Zuckerman, Michael. "Penmenship Exercise for Saucy Sons: Some Thoughts on the Colonial Southern Family." *South Carolina Historical Magazine* 84, no. 3 (1983): 152–66.

———. "William Byrd's Family." *Perspectives in American History* 12 (1979): 255–311.

Unpublished Papers and Dissertations

Bontemps, Arna Alexander. "Social History of Black Culture in Colonial North Carolina." Doctoral dissertation, University of Illinois at Urbana-Champaign, 1989.

Boyd, Julian P. "The County Court in Colonial North Carolina." Master's thesis, Duke University, 1926.

Brewer, James H. "An Account of Negro Slavery in the Cape Fear Region prior to 1860." Doctoral dissertation, University of Pittsburgh, 1950.

Butler, Patrick Henry III. "Knowing the Uncertainties of This Life: Death and Society in Colonial Tidewater Virginia." Doctoral dissertation, Johns Hopkins University, 1998.

Deane, Glenn Donald. "Parents and Progeny: The Demography of Inequality in Colonial North Carolina, 1680–1759." Doctoral dissertation, University of North Carolina, 1993.

Edelson, S. Max. "Planting the Lowcountry: Agricultural Enterprise and Economic Experience in the Lower South, 1695–1785." Doctoral dissertation, Johns Hopkins University, 1998.

Fischer, Kirsten. "Dangerous Acts: The Politics of Illicit Sex in Colonial North Carolina, 1660–1760." Doctoral dissertation, Duke University, 1994.

Kay, Marvin M. "The Institutional Background to the Regulation in Colonial North Carolina." Doctoral dissertation, University of Minnesota, 1962.

Lowry, Charles B. "Class, Politics, Rebellion, and Regional Development in Proprietary North Carolina." Doctoral dissertation, University of Florida, 1975.

Perry, Percival. "The Naval Stores Industry in the Antebellum South, 1789–1861." Doctoral dissertation, Duke University, 1947.

Robinson, Kenneth W. "Archaeology and the North Carolina Naval Stores Industry: A Prospectus." Unpublished paper prepared for the Office of State Archaeology, North Carolina Division of Archives and History, Raleigh.

Stumpf, Stuart O. "The Merchants of Colonial Charleston, 1680–1756." Doctoral dissertation, Michigan State University, 1971.

Suttlemyre, Charles Greer, Jr. "Proprietary Policy and the Development of North Carolina, 1663–1729." Doctoral dissertation, Oxford University, 1991.

Terry, George D. "'Champaign Country': A Social History of an Eighteenth Century Lowcountry Parish in South Carolina, St. Johns Berkeley County." Doctoral dissertation, University of South Carolina, 1981.

Walsh, Lorena S. "Charles County, Maryland, 1658–1705: A Study of Chesapeake Social and Political Structure." Doctoral dissertation, Michigan State University, 1977.

Wolf, Jacquelyn. "The Proud and the Poor: The Social Organization of Leadership in Proprietary North Carolina, 1663–1729." Doctoral dissertation, University of Pittsburgh, 1977.

Wu, Yu. "Jamaican Trade, 1688–1769: A Quantitative Study." Doctoral dissertation, Johns Hopkins University, 1996.

INDEX